Michigan's Best Campgrounds

A Guide to the Best 150 Public Campgrounds in the Great Lakes State

Michigan's Best Campgrounds

A Guide to the Best 150 Public Campgrounds in the Great Lakes State

4TH EDITION

Jim DuFresne

MICHIGAN'S BEST PLACES TO CAMP, FISH, HIKE, CANOE, BIKE & BIRDWATCH

THUNDER BAY PRESS

West Branch, MI

Michigan's Best Campgrounds

Published by
Thunder Bay Press
West Branch, Michigan

First Edition 1992
Second Edition 2000
Third Edition 2005
Fourth Edition 2011

26 25 24 23 4 5 6

ISBN: 9781933272276

Library of Congress Control Number: 2011925939

All information in this book is accurate to the best of the author's knowledge at press time but is subject to change at any time. Author and publisher assume no liability for inaccuracies.

Images taken by the author except where credited.
Maps produced by MichiganTrailMaps.com.
Book cover and layout by Julie Taylor.

Printed in the United States of America

Contents

CENTRAL UPPER PENINSULA 250

Michigan's Best Campgrounds

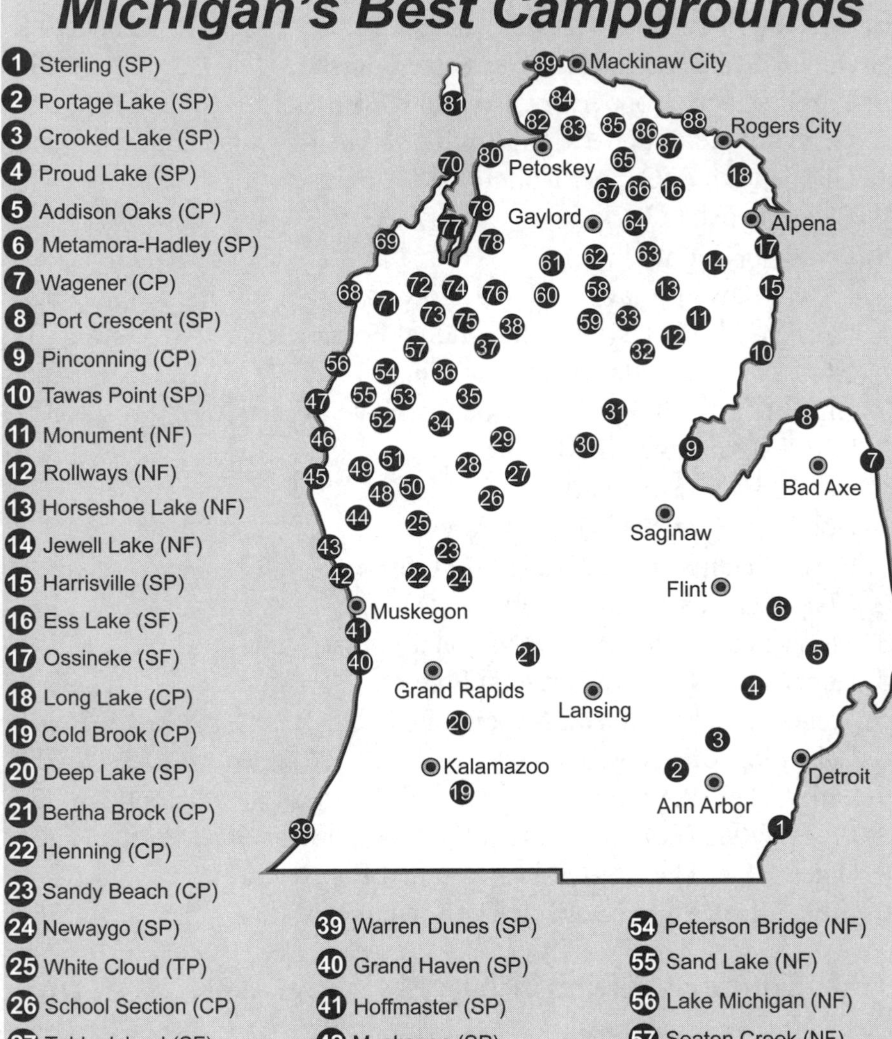

1 Sterling (SP)
2 Portage Lake (SP)
3 Crooked Lake (SP)
4 Proud Lake (SP)
5 Addison Oaks (CP)
6 Metamora-Hadley (SP)
7 Wagener (CP)
8 Port Crescent (SP)
9 Pinconning (CP)
10 Tawas Point (SP)
11 Monument (NF)
12 Rollways (NF)
13 Horseshoe Lake (NF)
14 Jewell Lake (NF)
15 Harrisville (SP)
16 Ess Lake (SF)
17 Ossineke (SF)
18 Long Lake (CP)
19 Cold Brook (CP)
20 Deep Lake (SP)
21 Bertha Brock (CP)
22 Henning (CP)
23 Sandy Beach (CP)
24 Newaygo (SP)
25 White Cloud (TP)
26 School Section (CP)
27 Tubbs Island (SF)
28 Paris (CP)
29 Merrill Lake (CP)
30 Herrick (CP)
31 Gladwin (CP)
32 Island Lake (NF)
33 Wagner Lake (NF)
34 Leverentz (SF)
35 Silver Creek (SF)
36 Hemlock (NF)
37 Goose Lake (SF)
38 Long Lake (SF)
39 Warren Dunes (SP)
40 Grand Haven (SP)
41 Hoffmaster (SP)
42 Muskegon (SP)
43 Pioneer (CP)
44 Pines Point (NF)
45 Mears (SP)
46 Buttersville (TP)
47 Ludington (SP)
48 Benton Lake (NF)
49 Nichols Lake (NF)
50 Shelley Lake (NF)
51 Highbank Lake (NF)
52 Bowman Bridge (NF)
53 Old Grade (NF)
54 Peterson Bridge (NF)
55 Sand Lake (NF)
56 Lake Michigan (NF)
57 Seaton Creek (NF)
58 Keystone Landing (SF)
59 Kneff Lake (NF)
60 Lake Margrethe (SF)
61 Upper Manistee (SF)
62 Hartwick Pines (SP)
63 Shupac Lake (SF)
64 Big Bear Lake (SF)
65 Pigeon River (SF)
66 Town Corner Lake (SF)
67 Pickerel Lake (SF)
68 Platte River (NP)

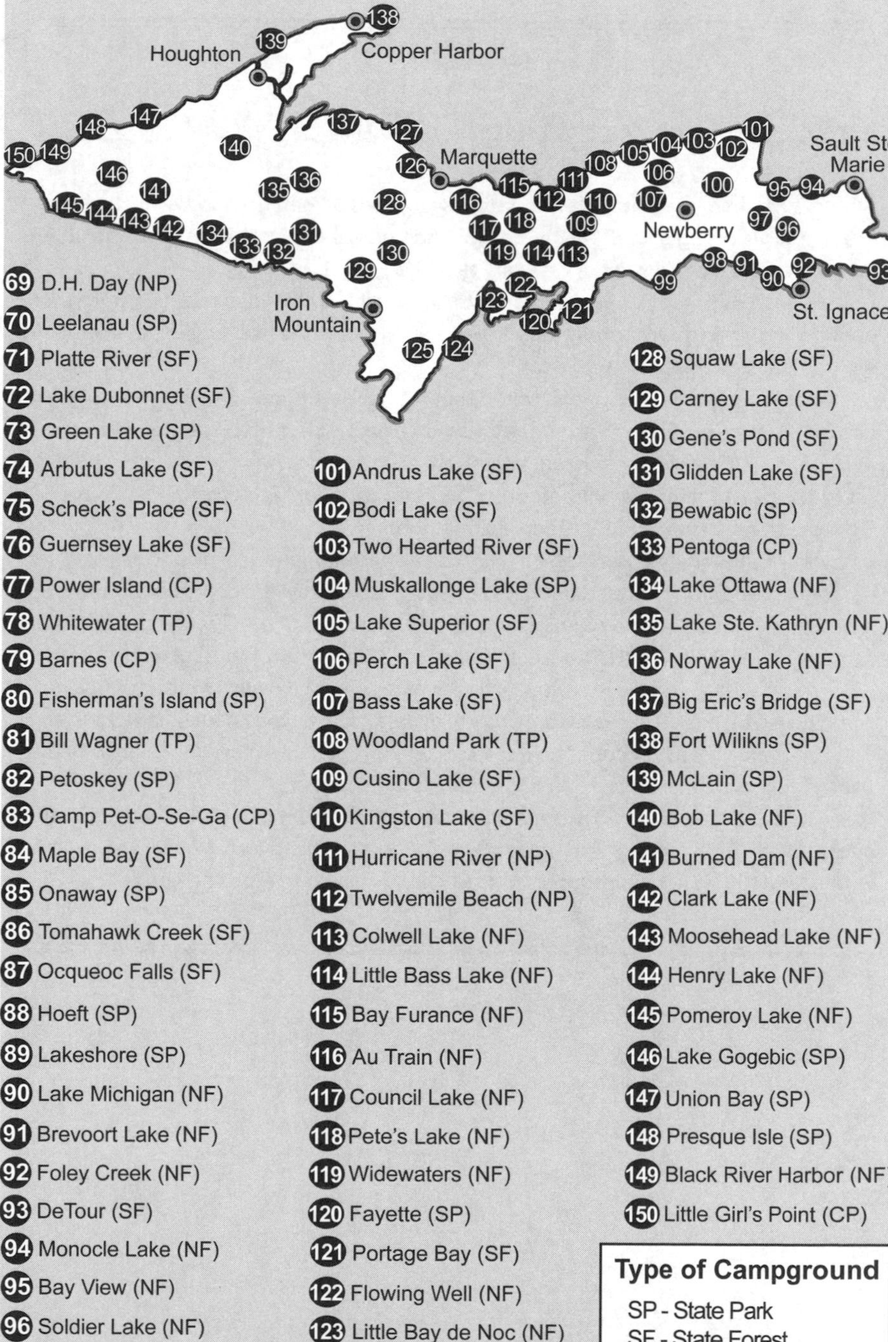

69 D.H. Day (NP)
70 Leelanau (SP)
71 Platte River (SF)
72 Lake Dubonnet (SF)
73 Green Lake (SP)
74 Arbutus Lake (SF)
75 Scheck's Place (SF)
76 Guernsey Lake (SF)
77 Power Island (CP)
78 Whitewater (TP)
79 Barnes (CP)
80 Fisherman's Island (SP)
81 Bill Wagner (TP)
82 Petoskey (SP)
83 Camp Pet-O-Se-Ga (CP)
84 Maple Bay (SF)
85 Onaway (SP)
86 Tomahawk Creek (SF)
87 Ocqueoc Falls (SF)
88 Hoeft (SP)
89 Lakeshore (SP)
90 Lake Michigan (NF)
91 Brevoort Lake (NF)
92 Foley Creek (NF)
93 DeTour (SF)
94 Monocle Lake (NF)
95 Bay View (NF)
96 Soldier Lake (NF)
97 Three Lakes (SF)
98 Hog Island Point (SF)
99 Big Knob (SF)
100 Tahquamenon Falls (SP)
101 Andrus Lake (SF)
102 Bodi Lake (SF)
103 Two Hearted River (SF)
104 Muskallonge Lake (SP)
105 Lake Superior (SF)
106 Perch Lake (SF)
107 Bass Lake (SF)
108 Woodland Park (TP)
109 Cusino Lake (SF)
110 Kingston Lake (SF)
111 Hurricane River (NP)
112 Twelvemile Beach (NP)
113 Colwell Lake (NF)
114 Little Bass Lake (NF)
115 Bay Furance (NF)
116 Au Train (NF)
117 Council Lake (NF)
118 Pete's Lake (NF)
119 Widewaters (NF)
120 Fayette (SP)
121 Portage Bay (SF)
122 Flowing Well (NF)
123 Little Bay de Noc (NF)
124 Fox Park (TP)
125 Big Cedar River (SF)
126 Tourist Park (TP)
127 Perkins Park (CP)
128 Squaw Lake (SF)
129 Carney Lake (SF)
130 Gene's Pond (SF)
131 Glidden Lake (SF)
132 Bewabic (SP)
133 Pentoga (CP)
134 Lake Ottawa (NF)
135 Lake Ste. Kathryn (NF)
136 Norway Lake (NF)
137 Big Eric's Bridge (SF)
138 Fort Wilikns (SP)
139 McLain (SP)
140 Bob Lake (NF)
141 Burned Dam (NF)
142 Clark Lake (NF)
143 Moosehead Lake (NF)
144 Henry Lake (NF)
145 Pomeroy Lake (NF)
146 Lake Gogebic (SP)
147 Union Bay (SP)
148 Presque Isle (SP)
149 Black River Harbor (NF)
150 Little Girl's Point (CP)

Type of Campground

SP - State Park
SF - State Forest
NF - National Forest
NP - National Park
CP - County Park
TP - Township or City Park

RESERVATIONS THROUGH THE INTERNET

It's hard to pass up site number 38 at Tawas Point State Park. The large, shady site is along one of the finest beaches on Lake Huron where you can pitch a tent or park a trailer in full view of Tawas Bay.

At site number 38 you can enjoy the sunrise with your morning coffee or cool off with an afternoon swim... if you can ensure it's still available when you arrive Friday evening. Now you can.

Site-specific reservations, choosing a site as opposed to being assigned one by a ranger, is available at almost all state parks that maintain campgrounds and a growing number of county parks. At state parks campers can book their favorite sites online for the summer season at Michigan State Park Central Reservations 🌐 www.midnrreservations.com.

After finding the park and filling dates, equipment (tent or trailer) and number of people, you can click the "Check Availability (Next)" button and see a list of all the sites in a campground along with a 20 to 40-word description for each one. The descriptions include everything from its size, whether its ADA accessible, if there is a view of the water, and the walking distance to the restroom. The park's campground map will show you its exact location. Once you have chosen a site and confirmed its availability, you use a credit card to finish the transaction and receive an immediate confirmation.

The advantages of site-specific reservations are that with advance planning you can finally snag that beachfront site at your favorite park. The disadvantage of site-specific reservations is that everybody else can too.

Why Camp?

Why camp? Why not?

It's affordable and nearby. It's lodging on the lake, great scenery from your front door, a nine-inch bluegill at the end of your line. It's fresh air, towering pines, a crackling fire on a starry night. It's an air mattress in a two-person tent or a waterbed in a recreational vehicle complete with a microwave oven, television, and an ice-maker in the freezer.

Camping is anything you want it to be. The purpose of this guide is not to tell you how to camp; there are many other books that will do that, but where to go. In Michigan there is no shortage of places to camp. Across the state there are approximately 1,280 campgrounds with 92,803 designated sites on public and private land. Within the Michigan State Park System alone there are 14,500 sites, the third highest of any state park system in the country. Add another 1,680 sites in the three national forests, 3,000 sites in the state forests and countless more in country parks and private campgrounds, and you can see the need for a guide.

To narrow it down, this guide book covers only public campgrounds and has chosen the best 150 facilities throughout the state. It's been my experience that the very nature of public land allows those campsites to be located more often along lakes, rivers or the Great Lakes and have the acreage to provide opportunities for hiking, swimming, boating and other traditional activities of the summer camping season.

For the purpose of easy reference, the state has been divided into eight regions: Southeast, Heartland, Lake Michigan, Lake Huron, Northwest, The Straits (covering both the tip of the Lower Peninsula and the east end of the U.P.), Central Upper Peninsula, and Western Upper Peninsula. The book has also been divided into three types of campsites:

Modern: Although modern campgrounds vary widely, all of these at least have electrical hook-ups at each site and a modern restroom with showers. When the facility also provides on-site spigots, sanitation stations for trailers, or other amenities, it has been clearly noted. Keep in mind that the high cost of equipping sites with electricity forces most parks to keep them relatively close together. For the want of an outlet, you sacrifice solitude.

Semi-modern: These sites either offer modern restrooms with showers but not hook-ups or the opposite, electrical hook-ups and vault toilets. Often state parks will close their modern restrooms during the off-season but make electricity available, turning modern sites into semi-modern and reducing the nightly rate to camp.

Rustic: These campgrounds lack hook-ups and, for the most part, modern restrooms and showers unless noted. Vault toilets (also known as pit toilets, outhouses, and the shack) are a way of life in rustic campgrounds. Also noted in each one is the terrain, forest, and ground cover. A rustic campground whose sites are well spread out in a thick forest with good underbrush is going to provide privacy between campers and a feeling that you're actually spending a night in the woods.

RESERVATIONS

Information on fees, reservations, amenities, and season of operation is given as well as a description of the campground and the area. Reservations allow you to secure a site in advance, so no matter how late you arrive you're guaranteed a spot for your trailer. Most modern campgrounds offer this service, but not all, and a growing number of rustic facilities are offering this as well.

Free-spirited campers and those who despise booking anything in advance need not despair. The 150 state forest campgrounds as well as sites in the Manistee-Huron National Forests and the Pictured Rocks National Lakeshore are still filled on a first-come-first-serve basis. If you need to be assured that come Friday evening you'll be sitting in the middle of a campground roasting marshmallows over a crackling fire, here's where you can reserve a site:

State Parks: You can reserve a site in 73 different state park campgrounds, and many campers do. The Michigan State Park Central Reservations ☎ 800-447-2757 🌐 www.midnrreservations.com handles 170,000 reservations a year, the overwhelming majority for a campsite in July and August. Central Reservations also books state park rustic cabins, mini-cabins, and yurts.

Sites are reserved in advance on a six-month rolling window, and a MasterCard, Visa, or Discover credit card is needed to instantly book and confirm a site. You cannot reserve a site through the individual park headquarters, and each reservation costs $8 plus the nightly charge of the site.

National Parks and Forests: Sites can also be reserved at Platte River Campground in Sleeping Bear Dunes and in select campgrounds in the Upper Peninsula national forests. In Manistee, you can book sites at Sand Lake and Bowman Bridge. In Hiawatha, sites can be reserved at a growing number of campgrounds. Reservations are booked through the National Recreation Reservation Service ☎ 877-444-6777 🌐 www.recreation.gov. Each reservation costs $9 plus the nightly charge of the site.

County Parks: You can reserve a site at many county park campgrounds by calling the park office in advance. Phone numbers and reservation fees are provided later in this guidebook with the descriptions of the campgrounds.

SEASONS & FEES

Seasons of operation are also listed with each campground description. Some campgrounds are literally locked during the off-season; others simple lack a host to collect fees. State forest campgrounds are technically open year-round though during the winter the roads may not be plowed and the handles may be removed from water pumps.

One last thing: in these deficit budget times, keep in mind that public facilities, policies, and fees can change quickly. Some are small such as a $1 increase in a camping fee; some are quite significant such as the state's decision to close a number of state forest campgrounds. It's best to always call the information number provided to double check. One thing will never change; however, a scenic little campground on a lake in the middle of the woods will always be a scenic little campground on a lake in the middle of the woods.

And that's the main reason why this guidebook should be in every camper's glovebox.

Southeast Michigan

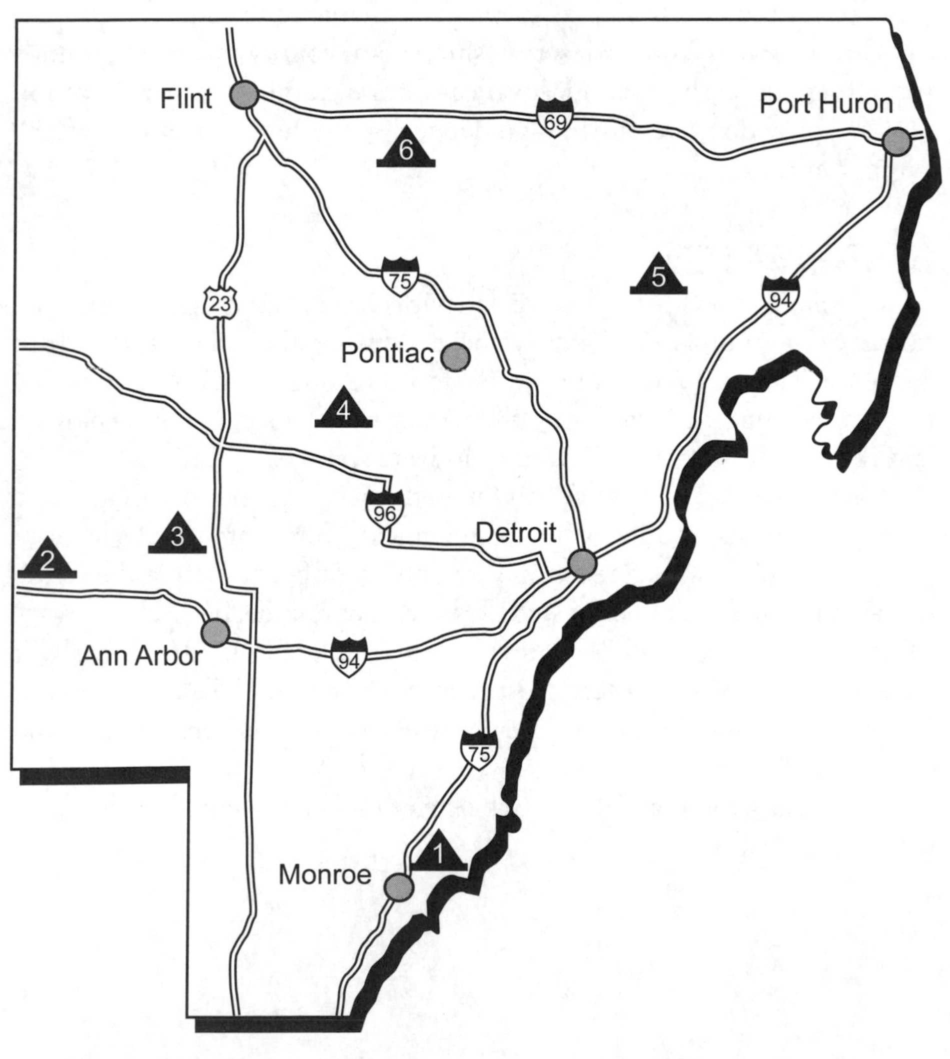

#	PARK	MODERN	SEMI-MODERN	RUSTIC	SITES	DAY-USE FACILITIES	FISHING	HIKING	BIRDING	INTERPRETIVE CENTER	BIKING	CANOEING/ KAYAKING	BOATING
1	William C. Sterling	•			256	•	•	•	•				
2	Portage Lake	•			136	•	•	•		•			
3	Crooked Lake			•	25	•	•	•			•		
4	Proud Lake	•			130	•	•	•				•	
5	Addison Oaks County Park	•			174	•	•	•			•		•
6	Metamora-Hadley	•			214	•	•	•					

1

William C. Sterling

State Park

Campground: Modern
County: Monroe
Nearest Community: Monroe
Sites: 256
Reservations: Yes
Fee: $22—$33 plus vehicle entry permit
Information: State park office
☎ (734) 289-2715

After closing in 2002 for renovation, this 1,000-acre park on the west end of Lake Erie reopened a year later to rave reviews by those who mattered the most, campers and visitors.

The $17 million project was the most the DNR has ever spent to revitalize a state park, but officials felt it was necessary because of Sterling's role as a gateway park. Like Warren Dunes near the Indiana border and Porcupine Mountains just east of Wisconsin, Sterling is often the first state park out-of-state visitors will stop at when entering Michigan.

Directions: Sterling State Park is 15 miles north of the Ohio border and reached from I-75 by departing at exit 15 and heading east on Dixie Highway for a mile.

Campground: The original campground was in a coastal wetland overlooking Sandy Creek Lagoon in the northwest corner of park. Campers were literally flooded out from time to time due to strong easterly winds that shifted shallow Lake Erie to the west.

The heart of the renovation and its single biggest cost was re-building the campground on higher ground at the south end of the park. The new campground has 256 sites in an open setting and overlooks the widest and nicest section of beach in the park.

Only two sites, numbers 25 and 26, are directly on the beach, but the rest have a good view of the lake and all of them have electrical service, paved pads, and a fire ring. There are also 39 pull-through sites for large

A family enjoys the beach at Sterling State Park, the only Michigan state park that is on Lake Erie.

recreation vehicles along with 77 sites with full hook-ups: water, sewer, and 50-amp electrical service.

Day-use Facilities: Sterling features more than a mile of beachfront along Lake Erie with a shallow swimming area. Bordering the beach is an open grassy picnic with tables and grills. The park renovation also included raising and repaving the park road along its causeway, consolidating the day-use parking lots into a single lot for 1,500 cars and adding new picnic shelters, bathrooms, and a unique children's playground.

Fishing: Other improvements include rebuilding Sterling's boat launch by increasing parking to 250 vehicles, upgrading the restrooms, and adding a fish-cleaning station.

Lake Erie is renown for its walleye fishing, and from April through mid-July, the prime season to catch a walleye, the boat launch is often filled. Anglers also fish the Great Lake for many other species including perch. There are bait and tackle shops along Dixie Highway for minnows and last-minute lures.

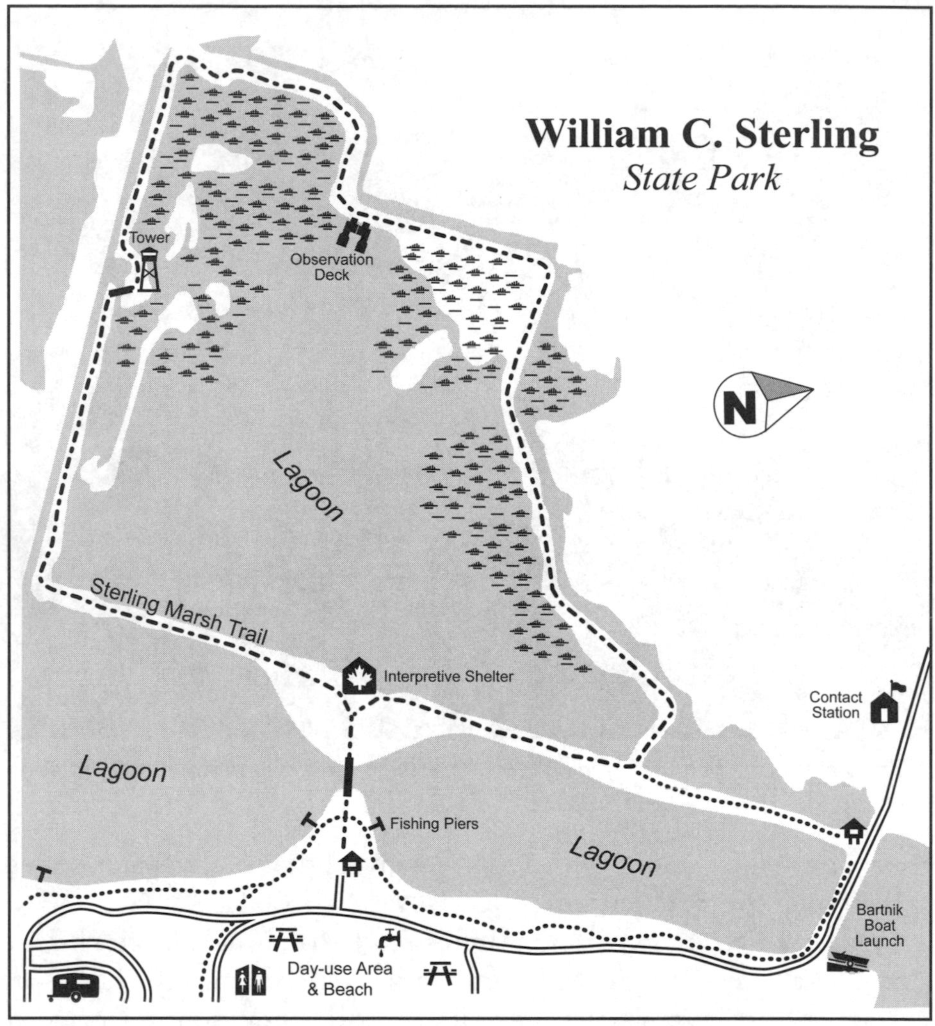

For boatless anglers, Sterling offers shore fishing opportunities on its two lagoons in the middle of the park. Most of the species caught are panfish, crappies, and bass, but occasionally a walleye will be hooked in the lagoons. Extending east from the park's pedestrian bridge is a paved trail that winds past three new fishing piers and then into the campground.

Hiking: One of the most popular additions to the park is the pedestrian bridge that now provides direct access from the campground and the day use area on the east side of a lagoon to Sterling Marsh Trail on the west side. Part of the park's 6-mile system of paved paths, Marsh Trail is a 3-mile loop around the park's largest lagoon, passing a tower, observation deck, and interpretive shelter all dedicated to viewing wildlife.

Birding: The park's improvements, particularly the addition of two spotting scopes at the interpretive shelter, and the lagoons now make Sterling something of a wild oasis in the middle of a heavily urbanized area. The park offers excellent opportunities for birders during the spring and fall migrations, as the lagoons attract a variety of birds and waterfowl including great blue herons, bluewing teals, mergansers, and large numbers of Canada geese along with smaller shorebirds.

Egrets are especially easy to spot here. The large, slender white birds that stand more than 30 inches high begin showing up at the park in late March and can be enjoyed until cold weather drives them south in mid-November. In late spring and early summer, it's possible to spot 30 to 40 egrets at a time.

Season: Being the only state park on Lake Erie, Sterling is often filled throughout the summer season, particularly on the weekends. To reserve a campsite contact Michigan State Park Central Reservations ☎ 800-447-2757 🌐 www.midnrreservations.com.

A young camper sorts through her tackle box at Sterling State Park looking for just the right fishing lure. The state park offers many opportunities for shore anglers to catch a variety of fish including walleye.

2

Portage Lake

Waterloo Recreation Area

Campground: Modern
County: Jackson
Nearest Community: Jackson
Sites: 136
Reservations: Yes
Fee: $22 to $24 plus vehicle entry permit
Information: State park office
☎ (734) 475-8307

At 20,367 acres Waterloo Recreation Area is the largest state park unit in southern Michigan and offers a wide range of activities in a rolling, lake-studded setting. That includes camping at five campgrounds, including two modern units bordering its largest lakes.

Of the park's campgrounds, Portage Lake is the most scenic facility. On a colorful October weekend, after the summer rush is long gone, there's no better place to set up camp in Southeast Michigan.

Directions: From I-94, six miles east of Jackson, depart at exit 147 and head north on Race Road and then east on Seymour Road. The campground entrance is off of Seymour Road.

Campground: Portage Lake Campground is on a rolling, semi-open bluff above Big Portage Lake and is part of a developed area on the west side of the park that also includes a swimming beach, boat launch, and foot trails. The 136 modern sites offer a bit of shade but little privacy when the campground is full, and none are directly on the water. Several overlook the lake while hardwoods and hills surround the area so it's easy to escape into the woods even on a busy weekend.

Campground amenities include several restroom buildings with showers, electric hook-ups, some with 50-amp service, a sanitation station for recreational vehicles, and firewood sales during the summer.

Day-use Facilities: A short walk from the campground is a designated swimming area with a sandy beach on Big Portage Lake, a bathhouse, and

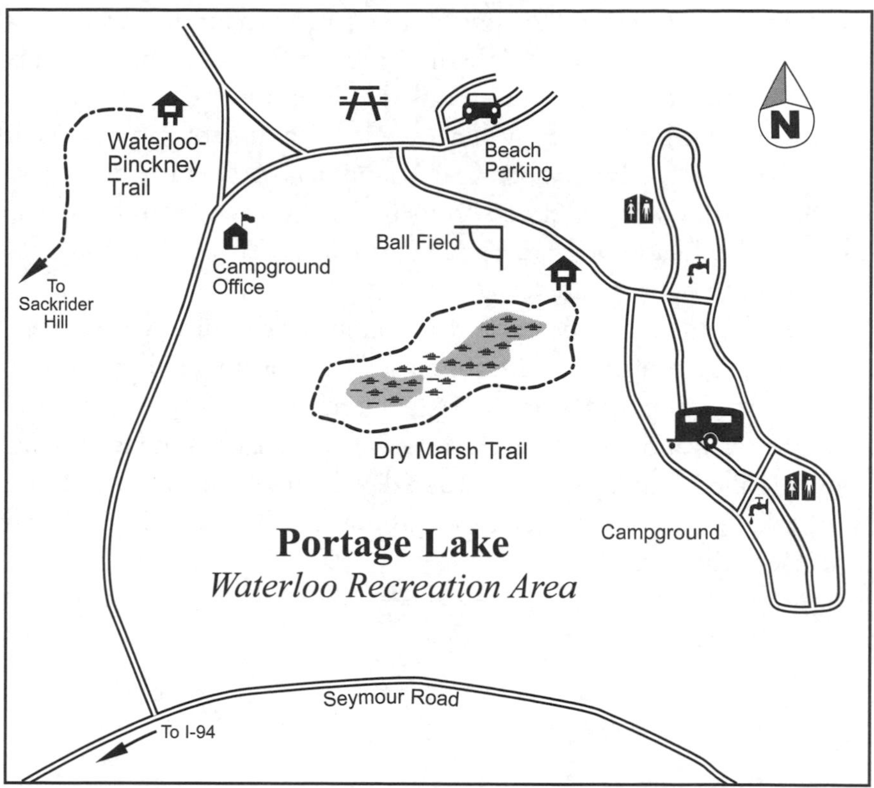

extensive picnic grounds. Nearby, families will find playground equipment and a baseball field.

Hiking: The half-mile long Dry Marsh Trail, an interpretive path that takes a close look at bogs and marshes, begins near the campground. Interpretive brochures are available at the contact station. In the day-use area is the trailhead for the Waterloo Pinckney Trail. This backpacking route is a 35-mile, three-day trek that ends at Silver Lake Day-use Area in Pinckney Recreation. Don't have three days to spare? The trek from Big Portage Lake to the scenic overlook and cross on top of Sackrider Hill makes for a one-way hike of 5.5 miles or a round trip of 11 miles.

Fishing: Waterloo provides access to 17 lakes with most of them featuring bass and panfish. There is a developed boat ramp and a fishing pier on Big Portage Lake, the largest in the park at 360 acres. Most anglers work the lake for largemouth bass with fish in the one-to-three-pound range common and occasionally one tipping the scales at four pounds or more. In the winter, it is a favorite spot for ice anglers in pursuit of panfish.

Interpretive Center: Within Waterloo Recreation Area is the Gerald Eddy Geology Center. The interpretive facility contains exhibits, displays, and video and slide programs that examine rocks, minerals, and oil resources in Michigan as well as its glacial and geologic history. The center ☎ 734-475-3170 is open year-round from 10 AM to 5 PM Tuesday through Saturday with extended hours in the summer. From I-94, depart at exit 157 and head north on Pierce Road and then west on Bush Road where the entrance is posted.

Season: Portage Lake is open year-round for camping with electrical service although the restrooms are closed in November. The off-season rate for a semi-modern site is $16 a night. From July through mid-August, the campground is full on most weekends and holidays and 50 to 90 percent filled Sunday through Thursday. To reserve a campsite contact Michigan State Park Central Reservations ☎ 800-447-2757 🌐 www.midnrreservations.com.

A happy angler holds up a 15-inch bass. Portage and the rest of the lakes in Waterloo Recreation Area support a productive fishery with catches including largemouth bass that occasionally tip the scales at four pounds or more.

3

Crooked Lake

Pinckney Recreation Area

Campground: Rustic
County: Washtenaw
Nearest Community: Pinckney
Sites: 25
Reservations: No
Fee: $12 plus vehicle entry permit
Information: Park headquarters
☎ (734) 426-4913

This may be southeast Michigan, but the drive to this campground is surprisingly scenic. It begins with North Territorial Road, and even though houses are popping up like mushrooms in the spring it's still a winding avenue past rolling farms and woodlots. Once in the park you follow a narrow dirt road through the hills of this rugged area north of Ann Arbor, reach a high point of 1,008 feet, and then descend to the lakeshore campground.

Crooked Lake not only combines a sense of being in the woods with a scenic site, but being in Pinckney Recreation Area, an 11,000-acre state park unit, it offers a variety of opportunities for hiking, mountain biking, fishing, and paddling in a chain of lakes.

Directions: From I-94 depart at exit 159 and head north on M-52 for 6 miles to North Territorial Road and then east. From US-23 north of Ann Arbor depart at exit 49 and turn west onto North Territorial Road for 12 miles. The campground is reached by turning north onto Dexter-Townhall Road from North Territorial and then left on Silver Creek Road to enter the park and drive past its headquarters. The dirt road ends at Crooked Lake.

Campground: This pleasant campground is situated on a hillside overlooking Crooked Lake. The sites are spread out in a semi-open area partially shaded by pines and large oaks. Only one site, No. 7, is directly on the shoreline, but most of them have at least a partial view of the water. The sites are well spread out and a few, No. 13 in particular, are

A site with a view of the water at Crooked Lake Campground in Pinckney Recreation Area, a state park north of Ann Arbor. Crooked Lake is one of the few rustic campgrounds in Southeast Michigan.

even off by themselves. Sites have fire rings and tables, while located in the loop are vault toilets and a hand pump for water.

Day-use Facilities: There is no swimming or beach on Crooked Lake. Just down the road, however, is the day-use beach on Silver Lake featuring an open grassy area, marked swimming area, tables, pedestal grills, a store, and a boat rental concession.

Fishing: Within the campground is an unimproved dirt boat launch while next to it is a handicapped access fishing pier. Children will enjoy the dock, but small panfish is all you can expect to catch in water this shallow. Crooked Lake has only a few homes along the shore opposite of the campground while its south end features a group of small islands. You can follow a channel into Pickerel Lake where at its east end flat bottom boats and canoes can even enter another small lake. Along with panfish, Crooked features bass, northern pike, and crappie. Pickerel, which has a fishing pier at its west end, is stocked every spring with rainbow trout.

Hiking: Crossing Silver Lake Road just uphill from the campground is Crooked Lake Trail, a 4-mile loop that begins in the Silver Lake Day-use Area. To avoid problems with mountain bikers, hikers are urged to follow the trail in a counter-clockwise direction and in 3 miles will cross a foot bridge over the channel between Crooked and Pickerel lakes.

Mountain Biking: The trail is also a popular route for mountain bikers who must follow it in a clockwise position. Traveling in this direction, bikers will reach Silver Lake Day Use area in a mile.

Season: The rustic campground is serviced May though October. Crooked Lake tends to fill up on the weekends from late June through early August but usually there are open sites mid-week. To reserve a campsite contact Michigan State Park Central Reservations ☎ 800-447-2757 🌐 www.midnrreservations.com.

Proud Lake

State Park

Campground: Modern
County: Oakland
Nearest Community: Wixom
Sites: 130
Reservations: Yes
Fee: $22 plus vehicle entry permit
Information: State park office ☎ (248) 685-2433

Wixom and the I-96 corridor in southwest Oakland County is a growing overload of shopping centers, strip malls, apartment complexes, and other signs of a metropolitan Detroit area bursting at the seams. You pass through all this and just before reaching Proud Lake skirt an incredibly large trailer park.

Not the kind of setting most people envision for a camping trip but be patient. Once in the park it's like entering a different world. Proud Lake is a 4,700-acre recreation area whose rolling forested hills, wetlands, and undeveloped stretch of the Huron River is the fortress against the uncontrolled growth of Oakland County. Next to Addison Oaks County

Park (see page 18), Proud Lake is probably the most pleasant modern campground in Southeast Michigan.

Hikers take a break on a boardwalk along the Proud Lake State Park trail system.

Directions: The state recreation area is just east of Milford or 12 miles southwest of Pontiac. From I-96, depart at exit 159 and head north on Wixom Road. The road passes through the town of Wixom and then makes a 90-degree turn left. You head right onto Glengary Road and the campground entrance is less than a mile to the east.

Campground: The campground is in the east half of the park and totally separated from the day-use beach and canoe livery. It's a large loop of 130 modern sites in an open, grassy area on a bluff that overlooks a chain of lakes formed by the Huron River. These are scenic lakes as the opposite bank is an undeveloped shoreline of cattails and marshes.

Sites are open and close together as is typical of most state park modern campgrounds, but the majority of them have a good view of the water below. Tables, fire rings, and hookups are provided in each site while along the loop are two restroom buildings with showers, vault toilets, and a sanitation station. There are also two mini-cabins available for rent. The only drawback at Proud Lake is the major power line that runs across the west end of the lake and skirts the campground.

Day-use Facilities: A staircase leads from the campground to an open grassy area along Proud Lake. No beach here, but the swimming area is shallow with a bottom of soft sand. Nearby is limited playground equipment. The main swimming area for Proud Lake is Powers Beach, located off Wixom Road in the west half of the park. The small sandy beach and pond was made by impounding the Huron River while nearby are two picnic areas.

Fishing: An improved boat launch with a cement slab is located next to the swimming area, but parking is back in the campground. Both Proud Lake and the Huron River are fished for panfish and smallmouth bass. The river within the park, from Moss Lake to Wixom Road, also has a special flies-only, catch-and-release trout season during April.

Hiking: A foot trail leads from the west end of the campground loop and connects with the main trailhead and parking area to the park's 11-mile trail system. This system winds along the Huron River and through the extensive wetlands that surround it and is by far the most interesting section of the park. Trail names can be a bit confusing here as you will see River Trail and Chief Pontiac Trail being used as well as a system of colors—blue, red, green and orange—marking the various paths. The River Trail/Blue Trail is the longest hike in the park, a 5.75-mile loop that will lead you from Wixom Road to Bass Lake Road and back again. It can be easily shortened in numerous ways. For young children, the best hike is Marsh Trail, a 1.25-mile loop around a wetland area.

Canoeing: A popular activity during the summer is paddling the Huron River, and within the park is a canoe rental concession located off Garden Road on the opposite side of the river from Powers Beach. The Heavner Canoe Center ☎ 248-685-2379 🌐 www.heavnercanoe.com is open 11 AM to 7 PM weekdays and from 9 AM to 8 PM weekends and holidays. You can either paddle up the river and then turn around or make arrangements with the concessionaire to be picked up down river.

Season: Because it's so close to metropolitan Detroit, the campground is heavily used on weekends from early May through mid-September. To reserve a campsite contact Michigan State Park Central Reservations ☎ 800-447-2757 🌐 www.midnrreservations.com.

Addison Oaks

Oakland County Park

Campground: Modern
County: Oakland
Nearest Community: Lake
Sites: 174
Reservations: Yes
Fee: $25–32
Information: Park office
☎ (248) 693-2432

A trip to Addison Oaks County Park is a drive through the country, passing apple orchards, strawberry farms, and fields where horse and cattle still graze. It's not the Northwoods, but this 794-acre park offers a remarkable escape from the urban sprawl of this region of the state as well as some of the best campsites to be found anywhere in Southeast Michigan.

You won't find that deep-in-the-woods serenity that many state forest campgrounds up north provide, but you will discover wooded sites and much to do here. Activities range from fishing and swimming to volleyball, renting a pedal boat, and even playing a round of disc golf.

Directions: From M-59 depart north on M-150 (Rochester Road) and follow it through downtown Rochester. The park is 9 miles north of Rochester and reached by turning west (left) on Romeo Road.

Campground: The Addison Oaks campground features 174 modern sites in four areas on the north side of Buhl Lake but not on the water itself. Lots can accommodate most trailers and RVs and are located in both an open grassy area and an area bordered by woods. Area B features 42 sites that are well separated from each other on a wooded hillside of towering white and red pine and hardwoods. Add a thick undergrowth and you have some of the most secluded sites in southern Michigan.

Day-use Facilities: Along the south side of Buhl Lake, less than half mile from the campgrounds, is a large, open day-use area that includes tables, pedestal grills, several shelters, horseshoe pits, volleyball courts, play equipment, and an 24-hole disc course that is played with Frisbees.

Along Adams Lake, a spring-fed pond, is the park's swimming area. The facilities include a large sandy beach surrounded by a grassy slope, lifeguards, bathhouse, and a concession building.

Boating: There is a unimproved launch on Buhl Lake next to the boat rental along with additional parking for vehicles and rigs. Boats are rented daily during the summer from 7 AM to sundown and include pedal boats, row boats, and kayaks.

Fishing: Buhl is heavily fished during the summer but attracts little attention after October. Prime species are bluegill, pumpkinseed sunfish, and black crappie. Anglers also catch an occasional largemouth bass, and every year a few three to four-pound northern pikes are landed. The boat rental shop also sells live bait.

Hiking: Addison Oaks offers hikers more than 12 miles of trails although half is shared with equestrians. The most popular path is the 2.5-mile paved Buhl Lake Trail that passes through the modern campground and features a number of rolling hills.

Mountain Biking: On the west side of park is a 6.8-mile loop of single track open to mountain bikers only. The trail is picked up from the main trailhead near the park office. The single track is packed dirt that includes slight to steep elevation changes as it passes through hilly, wooded areas and open fields. Mountain bikes can be rented at the park.

Season: Camping season is from mid-May to mid-October with the exact dates dependant on the weather. Modern sites are $32 a night on the weekends and holidays for non-Oakland County residents and $27 for county residents. From Sunday through Thursday sites are $25 a night for everybody.

This is a popular campground and fills daily June through Labor Day. Within the campground 48 sites can be reserved in advance by calling the park office ☎ 248-693-2432. Reservations must include a minimum Friday and Saturday nights, and reservations for Memorial Day, Fourth of July, or Labor Day weekends must include the entire holiday weekend. Full payment plus an $8 reservation fee must be made at the time of reservation.

Metamora-Hadley

Recreation Area

Campground: Modern
County: Lapeer
Nearest Community: Hadley
Sites: 214
Reservations: Yes
Fee: $23 plus a vehicle entry permit
Information: State park office
☎ (810) 797-4439

This would be a nice campground anywhere in the Lower Peninsula; for Southeast Michigan it's exceptional. Located in the southern half of Lapeer County, less than a half hour drive from Pontiac, Metamora-Hadley surrounds man-made Lake Minnawanna. The 683-acre state park unit features not only the lake and fishing opportunities but a nice beach, wooded trails, and even shoreline sites, yet the park draws only 220,000 visitors a year, most of them day users.

This campground can accommodate you even if your family doesn't want to sleep in a tent. Metamora-Hadley was one of the first state parks to offer mini-cabins. The small cabins are located within the campground and sleep four, but otherwise it's just like camping where you would spend most of your day outside.

Directions: From I-75 depart at exit 81 and head north on M-24 through Lake Orion and Oxford. At Pratt Road, 20 miles north of the interstate, turn west (left) for two miles and then south (left) on Hurd Road to the park entrance.

Campground: Metamora-Hadley has 214 sites on two loops along the west side of the lake. The first loop reached has sites 126-214 in an open, grassy area shaded by a handful of towering pines and hardwoods. Twenty of them are right on the water, directly across from the park's day-use area. The second loop is far more scenic with sites 1-125 situated in a hilly area lightly forested in oaks and maples. Nine sites are on the

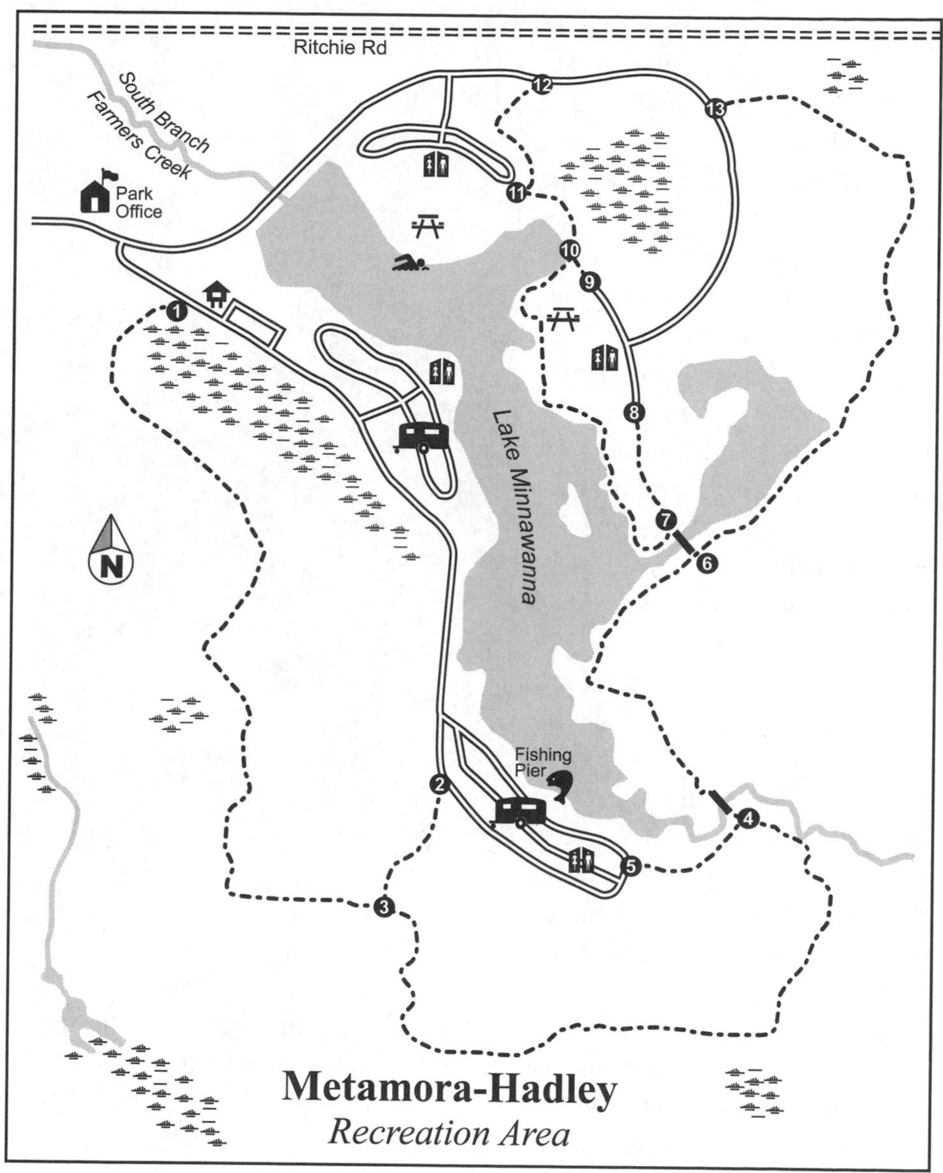

edge of a shoreline bluff with a scenic view of the entire lake. Posted trailheads and the two mini-cabins are located here, and both loops have sanitation stations, shower and restrooms, tables and fire rings at every site, and limited playground equipment.

Day-use Facilities: At the north end of the lake is a wide beach and open, grassy picnic grounds. Facilities include bathhouse, tables, pedestal grills, and a concession operator who rents rowboats, canoes, and pedal boats. Along the east side of the lake in a pleasant wooded setting is another picnic area with a shelter.

A hiker cuts through a grassy meadow during her hike around Lake Minnawanne in Metamora-Hadley Recreation Area.

Fishing: Lake Minnawanna, a 60-acre impoundment of the South Branch of Farmers Creek, features several species of fish but is best known by bass anglers. Anglers concentrate in the southern half of the lake and around a small island on the east side using standard bass baits and lures. Other species caught include bluegill, perch, and an occasional northern pike.

There is an unimproved boat launch and dock at the north end of the lake with additional parking for a handful of vehicles. There are also three fishing piers along the west shore of the lake: at the boat launch and one at each campground loop.

Hiking: The park has a 6-mile network of trails that basically forms a loop from the campgrounds around the lake to the beach area on the east side. On the west side you wander from a marsh area to woods to open fields. On the east side the path winds through a wooded area, and an especially nice walk is to begin near the mini-cabins, cross the South Branch of Farmers Creek, and then follow the loop around the picnic area, a round-trip hike of almost 2 miles.

Season: The campground is open April through October. Despite being so close to metropolitan Detroit, Metamora-Hadley receives only moderate use on weekdays during the summer and sites are often available on non-holiday weekends. To reserve a campsite contact Michigan State Park Central Reservations ☎ 800-447-2757 🌐 www.midnrreservations.com.

SCARY WEEKENDS IN STATE PARKS

The toughest weekend to secure a campground at many state parks isn't Memorial Day, Labor Day, or anytime during July.

It's when they celebrate Halloween during their Harvest Festivals from mid to late October, a time of year that can be cold, rainy, or even threatening to snow.

Ooooo! Now that's scary.

The wildly popular state park events date back to the early 1990s when a group of campers asked officials at Metamora-Hadley Recreation Area if they could stage a weekend of Halloween activities, including trick or treating.

It was so successful the park made it an official event the following fall and managed to fill its campground at a time of year when usually only a handful of sites are occupied. Soon campers were clamoring at other state parks to stage harvest festivals because the campground at Metamora-Hadley Recreation Area was filling up months in advance for their event.

Today more than 40 such weekends are staged at parks across the state with the first ones being held in early September in Upper Peninsula state parks. Metamora-Hadley, where it all started, now hosts three or four Halloween Harvest Weekends every fall.

Activities range from pumpkin carving contests and hay rides to picnic pavilions that have been turned into haunted houses. At Hayes State Park they offer pumpkin bowling. At Metamora-Hadley they erect a large outdoor screen and show Halloween movies. At Sleeper members of the Organization of Bat Conservation arrive with live bats.

The vast majority of campers also decorate their sites with jack-o'-lanterns, ghosts, headstones, and other ghoulish objects. The climax of almost every festival is the custom parade through the campground followed by an evening of trick-or-treating with children going from one site to the next.

The most popular time to camp at Metamora-Hadley Recreation Area and many other state parks is during their Harvest Festivals when campers participate in organized Halloween activities throughout the weekend.

Lake Huron

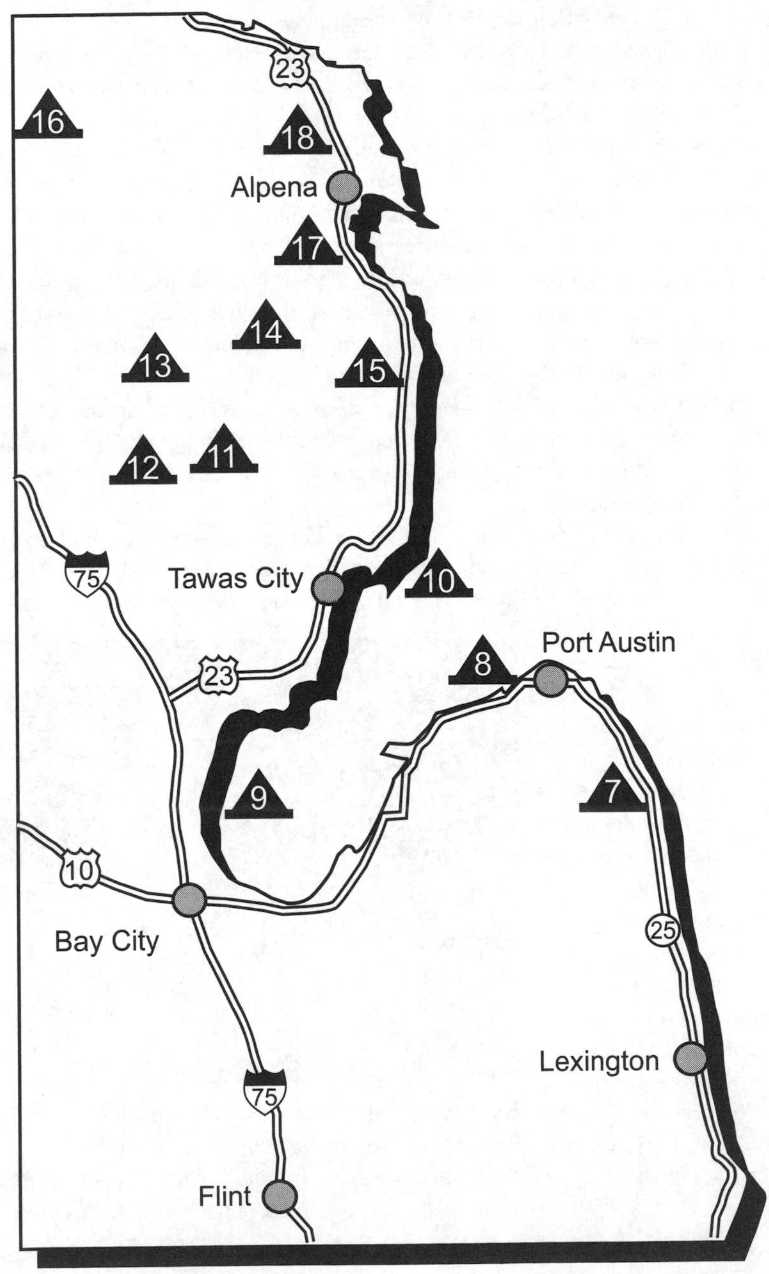

23
16
18
Alpena
17
14
13
15
12
11
75
Tawas City
10
Port Austin
8
23
7
9
10
Bay City
25
Lexington
75
Flint

#	PARK	MODERN	SEMI-MODERN	RUSTIC	SITES	DAY-USE FACILITIES	FISHING	HIKING	BIRDING	INTERPRETIVE CENTER	BIKING	CANOEING/ KAYAKING	BOATING
7	Wagener County Park	•			96	•	•	•					
8	Port Crescent	•			137	•	•	•					
9	Pinconning	•	•		42	•	•	•					
10	Tawas Point	•			193	•		•	•				
11	Monument			•	19	•		•				•	
12	Rollways			•	19	•	•					•	
13	Horseshoe Lake			•	9		•	•					
14	Jewell Lake			•	32	•	•	•					
15	Harrisville State Park	•			195	•	•	•					
16	Ess Lake			•	28	•	•						
17	Ossineke			•	42	•		•					
18	Long Lake	•	•		124	•	•						

7

Wagener

Huron County Park

Campground: Modern
County: Huron
Nearest Community: Harbor Beach
Sites: 96
Reservations: Yes
Fee: $15–$23
Information: Park office
☎ (989) 479-9131
www.huroncountyparks.com

At 132 acres, Wagener County Park is the largest unit in the Huron County Park system and includes a 96-site modern campground, rental cabins, a beach on Lake Huron, and more than 2 miles of hiking trails. Its best feature, however, might be its location in the Thumb. Michigan's most distinct appendage is only a two-hour drive from the northern Detroit suburbs and less from Flint and Saginaw, yet it is a world away from the cities.

Convention and visitor's bureaus promote the Lake Huron region as the Sunrise Side of the state, but many people think of Michigan's Thumb as the "Slowside." Not overrun by the tourist industry—or tourists—it's an area that can be refreshingly relaxing even on a holiday weekend. Wagener Park is an ideal place to pitch the tent or park the trailer while exploring the small towns and rural charm of this quiet corner of the Lower Peninsula.

Directions: Wagener County Park is on M-25, 5 miles south of Harbor Beach.

Campground: The 96 modern sites at Wagener are well spread out and divided into three different camping areas. Sites 1 through 38 are closest to the water in a semi-open grassy area and within view of Lake Huron. This area includes the Lakeview sites that are close to the shoreline and are $23 per night. Sites 39 through 68 are in a more wooded setting and

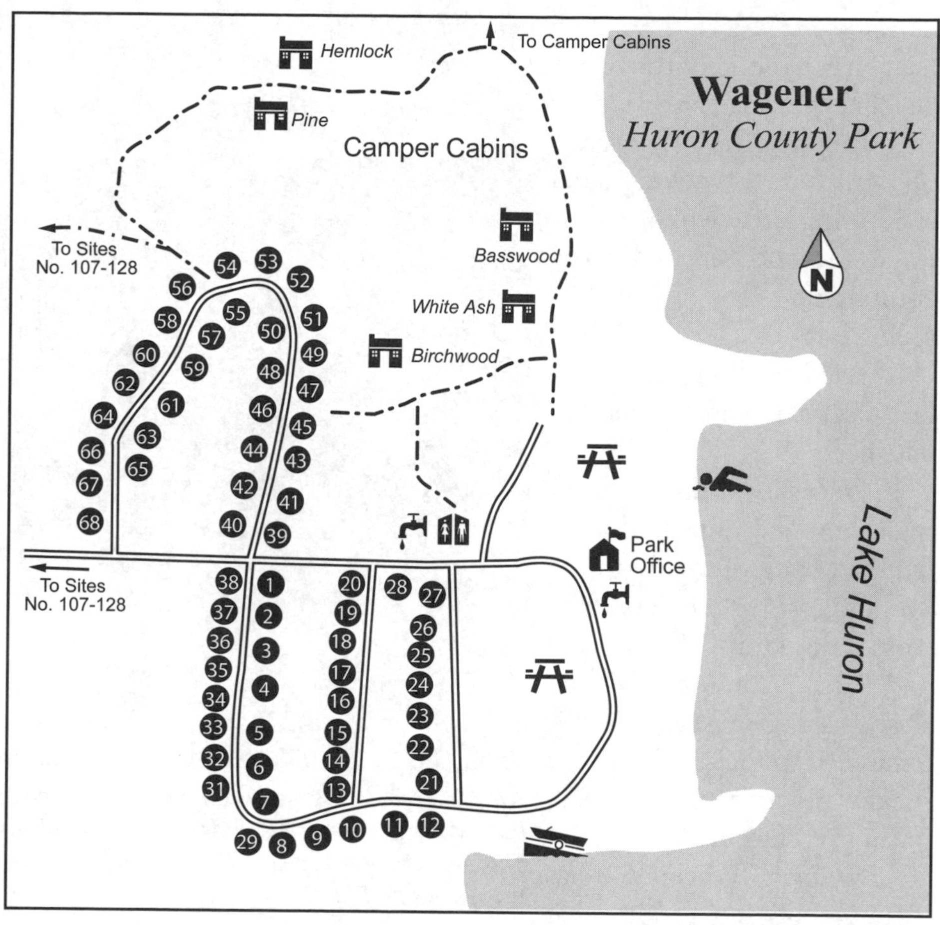

sites 101 through 128 are in a grassy field near the entrance of the park. Restrooms at the park include coin-operated showers.

The park also has eight camper cabins for rent. Located just inside the woods, the single-room structures sleep six in a pair of bunk beds and a double bed and include a table, electric lights and outlets, and a fire ring outside.

The daily rate for a site with a full hook-up is $22, for electric only $18, and for tent camping with no utilities $15. Camper cabins are $50 per night. There is an additional $5 per night charge for camping during the Memorial Day, Fourth of July, and Labor Day weekends and $5 per night discount for camping before Memorial Day weekend and after Labor Day.

Day-use Facilities: Wagener has one of the nicest beaches on the east side of the Thumb. The wide strip of sand borders a designated swimming area while nearby is a bathhouse and play equipment. The adjoining picnic area has grills, tables and two pavilions that can be reserved and rented in advance.

A family enjoys the Lake Huron surf at Wagener County Park. Wagener's beach is one of the best in Michigan's Thumb, a region that is only a two-hour drive from most of Metro Detroit.

Fishing: The park maintains an improved boat launch with additional parking for trailers for anglers who troll Lake Huron for salmon and lake trout. There is no shore fishing in Wagener, but fishing is popular along the breakwalls at the small boat harbor in Harbor Beach.

Hiking: Wagener has 2 miles of foot trails that basically form a mile-long loop with a handful of crossover spurs. The hiking is easy and begins by skirting Lake Huron for a quarter mile before heading into the wooded heart of the park. Keep an eye out for old-growth trees near the trail, including a giant white pine that somehow survived devastating forest fires in 1871 and 1881.

Season: The campground is open from May 1 to Oct. 15. The facility is busy on most weekends from mid-July to early August but is rarely filled. A two-night minimum and a $7 reservation fee are required to reserve a site in advance. Mail-in reservations are accepted beginning Jan. 2 with instructions and an application available online at 🌐 www.huroncountyparks.com. Phone-in reservations are accepted beginning in mid-January by calling the Parks Administrative Office at ☎ 877-404-7447.

8

Port Crescent

State Park

Campground: Modern
County: Huron
Nearest Community: Port Austin
Sites: 137
Reservations: Yes
Fee: $27 plus vehicle entry fee
Information: State park office
☎ (989) 738-8663

In the mid-1800s Port Crescent was a booming lumber town of almost 700 residents, known for its salt wells, fine sand, and good docks. Today it's one of the most scenic state parks along Lake Huron and known for having the biggest dunes on the east side of the state. The wind-blown, open dunes are located west of the park's day-use area and drop down to the shoreline. They are nowhere near the size of those along Lake Michigan, but they are still an interesting area to wander through, and to small children sand dunes are sand dunes regardless of their size.

The 565-acre unit also includes 3 miles of almost pure white beach along Saginaw Bay, a wooded interior of jack pine and oak, a scenic network of hiking trails, and a campground overlooking the bay that includes 25 beachfront sites.

Directions: The park is 5 miles southwest of Port Austin along M-25.

Campground: Port Crescent's campground is located in the eastern half of the park in a hilly section forested in oak and is bordered on one side by the Old Pinnebog River Channel and the other by M-25. Many sites have a partial view of Saginaw Bay, and 17 of them are right off the beach. These, understandably, are not only the most popular sites in the park but some of the most scenic on the east side of the state. They can be reserved six months in advance with a site-specific reservation through Michigan State Park Central Reservations ☎ 800-447-2757; 🌐 www.

A young hiker pauses at the base of a Port Crescent sand dune. The state park features the tallest dunes on the east side of Michigan.

midnrreservations.com. Facilities include tables, fire rings, two restrooms with showers, a sanitation station, a mini-cabin, and a camper cabin.

Day-use Facilities: The west half of the park is a day-use area and is separated from the campground and hiking trails by the Pinnebog River. The area includes two picnic grounds along the river, a shelter that can be rented near the beach, a fitness trail nearby, and limited play equipment. A boardwalk leads from the shelter to the beach, one of the finest along Lake Huron, passing along the way small decks with picnic tables perched on top of the low dunes.

Fishing: While Saginaw Bay is renowned for its walleye and, to a lesser degree, its perch fishery, the Pinnebog River is fished by shore anglers for bass, panfish, and northern pike during the summer. In September and October a few anglers will also be on hand to toss spoons and spawn for Chinook salmon. In the day-use area there is a launch for hand-carried boats and some barrier-free fishing piers over the river.

Hiking: Port Crescent has 3 miles of foot trails in an isolated area between the Pinnebog River and the Old Pinnebog River Channel. You can reach one trailhead by a beach access next to site 89 and then tiptoe through the channel where it empties into the bay. On the other side is a yellow trail marker. The entire loop is a 2.3-mile walk that passes several scenic viewing points of the shoreline and the Pinnebog River. By using the cut-off spur you can shorten it to a 1.3-mile walk.

Season: Port Crescent is open from April 15 to Oct. 15. The campground is filled most weekends during the summer and often daily from mid-July to early August. Best time to check in without a reservation is Sunday and Monday. To reserve a campsite contact Michigan State Park Central Reservations ☎ 800-447-2757 🌐 www.midnrreservations.com.

Pinconning

Bay County Park

Campground: Modern and semi-modern
County: Bay
Nearest Community: Pinconning
Sites: 42

Reservations: Yes
Fee: $12 to $19 plus vehicle entry fee
Information: Bay County Recreation
☎ (989) 879-5050

One of the most pleasant and, best of all, least crowded modern campgrounds along Lake Huron is Pinconning County Park on the Saginaw Bay. The park is only 3 miles from I-75, but most likely it's too far south for many campers to consider stopping for the night.

Too bad. This is a scenic park with an improved boat launch, some short but interesting hiking trails, and many sites that overlook a small bay and peninsula bordering Saginaw Bay.

Directions: From I-75 turn off at Pinconning (exit 181) 21 miles north of Bay City. Head east on Pinconning Road, through the town of Pinconning, and in 3 miles the road ends at the park entrance.

Campground: Pinconning is a single loop of 50 sites. Sites No. 1–42 are in a grassy area that is shaded by giant oak trees. Half the sites are

The modern campsites at Pinconning County Park located on Saginaw Bay in Bay County.

along the Bay, and some of them have a clear view of the water while the others are tucked behind a wall of cattails. The rest border the forest that surrounds the campground. Facilities include electric hook-ups, fire rings, tables, a restroom with showers, and a sanitation station. A number of the sites also have water faucets on-site.

Sites No. 43–50 are rustic sites while nearby are six rental cabins ($50 a night) equipped with electric lights and propane heaters.

The nightly fee for modern sites is $19 while rustic sites are $12. There is also a $2 vehicle entry fee into the park.

Day-use Facilities: One thing Pinconning does lack is a sandy beach. In recent years the water level had dropped so much in Saginaw Bay that the original beach has become a shoreline wetland, too muddy and unattractive for swimmers. There is a grassy picnic area with two shelters, tables, pedestal grills, play equipment, basketball court, horseshoe pit, and an open view of Saginaw Bay.

Fishing: There is a cement boat launch and dock in the day-use area. Saginaw Bay is renowned for its walleye and perch fisheries while in the small bay off the campground anglers target mostly large and smallmouth bass.

Hiking: The park has four posted trails, all short excursions into the surrounding woods and marshes. The most interesting by far is the Marsh

Trail, a round trip of 0.6 mile through the extensive cattail marshes that enclose the bay. The path passes views of the water and a small observation deck before turning around at a wooden bridge.

Season: The campground is open year-round although the hook-ups and restrooms may be closed during the off season. Reservations can be booked in advance by calling the park office at ☎ 989-879-5050 or online at 🌐 www.baycounty-mi.gov/PinconningPark but this is a lightly used facility that fills up only on an occasional weekend during the summer.

10

Tawas Point

State Park

Campground: Modern
County: Iosco
Nearest Community: Tawas City
Sites: 193
Reservations: Yes
Fee: $27 plus vehicle entry fee
Information: Park office
☎ (989) 362-5041

Tawas Point is a popular state park that combines a beautiful beach within walking distance of a large campground crowned by a classic lighthouse. The 200-acre park is the end of a sandy spit that separates Tawas Bay from Lake Huron and prompts a few people to call it "the Cape Code of the Midwest."

That's stretching it a bit, but Tawas Point is definitely a scenic area and even has a short trail to the end of the spit and back. The area also attracts birders from around the state as it is an important landfall for birds migrating across Saginaw Bay.

Directions: The park is 3.5 miles from East Tawas. Follow US-23 just northeast of the town and then turn east onto Tawas Point Road and follow signs to the park entrance.

Campground: Tawas Point is an open campground with little shade or privacy between parties. A handful of sites overlook a small beach

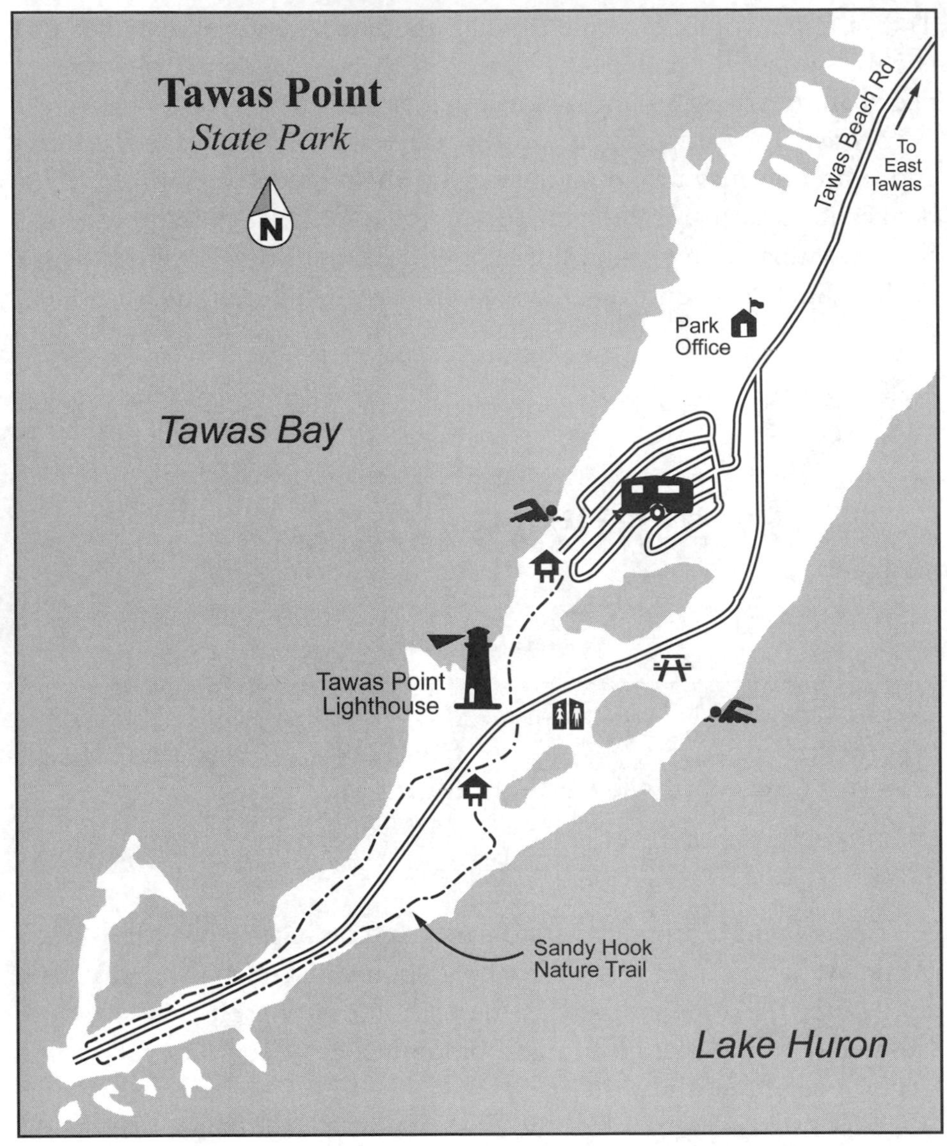

along Tawas Bay while a paved trail leads from the back of one loop to the day-use area beach along Lake Huron. Facilities include two restrooms with showers, play equipment, a sanitation station, two mini-cabins and a camper cabin within the campground, and fire rings and tables at each site.

Day-use Facilities: The most beloved structure at state park is the very photogenic Tawas Point Lighthouse. The first lighthouse was built in 1853 near the park headquarters and was replaced by the current one

The center piece of Tawas Point State Park is Tawas Point Lighthouse that was built in 1876 and today is open to the public.

in 1876. Fully restored and now open to the public, the Tawas Point Lighthouse also includes the original oil building, which serves as the Museum Store ☎ 989-362-5658, and a fog house. From Memorial Day to Labor Day, lighthouse tours are offered daily between noon and 6 PM. Admission is $2 per person.

The park's day-use beach is along Lake Huron where the sand is almost pure white and stretches more than 300 feet from where you park your car to where the waves are gently washing ashore. Located here is a bathhouse, picnic shelter, and more play equipment. The area is surrounded by several small ponds that occasionally attracts the interest of young anglers.

Hiking: Beginning at the day-use parking lot, near the lighthouse, is the Sandy Hook Nature Trail, a 1.5-mile loop to the end of the point. Its most scenic portion by far is along Lake Huron where you pass several small islets and skirt the tops of some small, very small, dunes.

Birding: During the spring and fall migrations, the point is said to be "alive with birds." Often spotted along beaches or the small inland ponds are terns and gulls, including Bonaparte's gulls and Caspian terns, along with shorebirds such as red knots, whimbrels, and even the rare piping plover. The ponds also attract loons, flocks of mergansers, and a variety of other waterfowl species. The end of the spit is practically treeless, but warblers, flycatchers, and hummingbirds feed among the willow thickets and shrubs such as sand cherry.

The contact station can provide a birding check list anytime, but the best time to arrive is in mid-May when for three days the park becomes the site of the Tawas Point Birding Festival 🌐 tawasbirdfest.com.

Season: The campground is open from mid-April to mid-October, and through most of the summer it's filled from Thursday until Sunday. In July, expect it to be filled any day of the week. Reservations are important if you want to plan a vacation around this campground. To reserve a campsite contact Michigan State Park Central Reservations ☎ 800-447-2757 🌐 www.midnrreservations.com.

11

Monument

Huron National Forest

Campground: Rustic
County: Iosco
Nearest Community: Tawas City
Sites: 19
Reservations: No
Fee: $15
Information: Huron Shores Ranger District
☎ (989) 739-0728

Monument Campground was established in 1909 as one of the first built in the newly created Huron National Forest. Monument is basically 20 sites in a red pine plantation and is not one of the most scenic campgrounds in the national forest, but the nearby interpretive center, museum, trails, and scenic overlooks make this facility an excellent and popular place to spend a weekend. There's much to do at the monument, and most of it is only a short walk from your site.

Directions: From Tawas City head west on M-55 for a mile and then north (right) onto Wilber Road for 1.5 miles to reach Monument Road. Head northwest on Monument Road until it ends at River Road. The entrance to the campground is east (right) on River Road.

Campground: Monument is a single loop in a red pine plantation. The sites are well spread out, but as is typical with pine plantations, there is little undergrowth to isolate one party from another. Sites have tables and fire rings with sliding grills while within the loop are vault toilets and spigots for water.

The entrance to the interpretive center is a quarter mile west of the campground, but the back of the loop borders the visitor center picnic area and from here a paved path winds past the museum and overlooks.

Lumbermen's Monument is the impressive bronze statue of three loggers that was erected in 1931 and today is the center piece of the Huron National Forest's most popular interpretive area.

Day-use Facility: Lumbermen's Monument is an impressive bronze statue of three loggers that was erected in 1931 and today is the centerpiece of the Huron National Forest's most popular attraction. The interpretive area includes a small museum and outdoor hands-on exhibits devoted to Michigan's logging era at the turn of the century and a stairway that leads down to a wanigan, a replica of a cook's raft that is tied up on the river. The overlooks of the Au Sable River valley are spectacular in the fall. The visitor center is open daily from 10 AM to 7 PM during the summer and until 5 PM to mid-October. There is no admission.

Just to the west on River Road is Iargo Springs, another interpretive area where a long stairway leads down the riverside bluff to the fresh water

IARGO: SPRINGS OF MANY WATERS

Traversing the steep river bluffs overlooking the Au Sable River—and passing through Monument Campground—is the Highbanks Trail. The linear footpath stretches 7 miles beginning in the west at Iargo Springs, where most people begin their walk with a 300-step descent to the Au Sable River.

At the bottom of the bluff you'll find a quarter mile of boardwalk that winds through towering cedars to eight observation decks; half of them perched above the gurgling springs, the rest overlooking the Au Sable.

Iargo is the Chippewa word for "many waters," and it's believed that Native Americans gathered here once for tribal pow-wows where they would drink the cold, clear water for medicinal powers.

Today Iargo is still a tonic. No matter how many leaf peepers are zipping along River Road, the springs are always a quiet and tranquil spot that soothes the soul.

From Monument Campground Iargo Springs is a one-way hike of 4 miles or a round trip of 8 miles that passes the overlook known as Canoer's Monument halfway there.

Iargo Springs, a popular stop along River Road, a National Forest Scenic Byway.

springs that were once a popular resting place for Chippewa Indians on the Saginaw-Mackinac Trail.

Hiking: Crossing the campground's entrance drive and marked in blue diamonds is the Highbanks Trail, a 7-mile point-to-point path that extends from Iargo Springs to Sidtown. The trail is named for the fact that it skirts the high bluffs above the AuSable River and along the way you pass many spectacular vistas of the river valley. To the west from the campground Iargo Springs is a 4-mile walk, and along the way you pass a viewing point known as Canoe Monument in 1.8 miles.

Canoeing: Au Sable River is a noted waterway for canoeists (see Keystone Campground), but Monument Campground is not a place to launch a boat due to the steep bluffs.

Season: The campground is managed Memorial Day to Labor Day but may be open earlier or later depending on weather and demand. Lumbermen's Monument is one of the most popular attractions in Huron National Forest, and thus the campground is a popular facility, often filled on weekends as early as Thursday evening.

12

Rollways

Huron National Forest

Campground: Rustic
County: Iosco
Nearest Community: Hale
Sites: 19
Reservations: No
Fee: $15
Information: Huron Shores Ranger District
☎ (989) 739-0728

Located on high bluffs above the Au Sable River is Rollways National Forest Campground, an alternative if Lumbermen's Monument is full. Rollways picks up its name from the turn of the century when lumbermen used to roll logs down the steep banks to the river below and then floated them to sawmills on Lake Huron.

You can spend an afternoon learning about Michigan's incredible lumber era at the Monument only 8 miles to the east. Then return to camp at Rollways that features the same spectacular panoramas of the Au Sable Valley as seen elsewhere along River Road.

Directions: Rollways is posted and located right off M-65 on Rollaway Road. From I-75 depart at exit 188 and take US-23 through Standish and Omer. Two miles out of Omer turn north on M-65, passing through the towns Whittemore and Hale. The campground is posted roughly 7 miles north of Hale.

Campground: Rollways is a single loop of 19 sites with paved spurs, tables, and fire rings with sliding grills. The campground, lightly forested in large oaks and red pines, is located near the edge of the river bluff. Most sites do not have a clear view of the valley below. The exception is site number 8 where from your picnic table there is incredible overlook of the river below and the ridges to the north. Although it is rustic, the pull-through sites make Rollways more accommodating to large motor homes and trailers. Vault toilets and hand pumps for water are in the middle of the loop.

Day-use Facilities: Rollways has a scenic day-use area featuring tables, pedestal grills, and a classic log picnic shelter with fieldstone fireplaces at each end. Many of the tables are within view of the Au Sable River and Loud Dam Pond to the east. Nearby a staircase leads down to the river though care should be used when descending. The picnic grounds are open from 6 AM to 10 PM

Fishing: Rollways is located where the Au Sable River flows into Loud Dam Pond. This is no Holy Waters. Upstream from the campground the river is 50 to 75 yards wide and so deep you can't wade it in most places, but Anglers say this is where the river yields some of its biggest brown and rainbow trout. Loud Dam Pond is known primarily for smallmouth bass but also yields walleye and pike.

Canoeing: For paddlers, across the road from the campground is Rollways Resort ☎ 989-728-3322 🌐 rollwayresort.com which runs a canoe livery during the summer. Most paddlers are taken upriver to either Alcona County Park, a 23-mile, 5-hour trip, or Stewart Creek, a 13-mile, 2-hour paddle from the campground.

Season: Rollways' managed season is from the end of May through mid-September. This is a lightly-used facility, and a site is easy to obtain here even on most weekends.

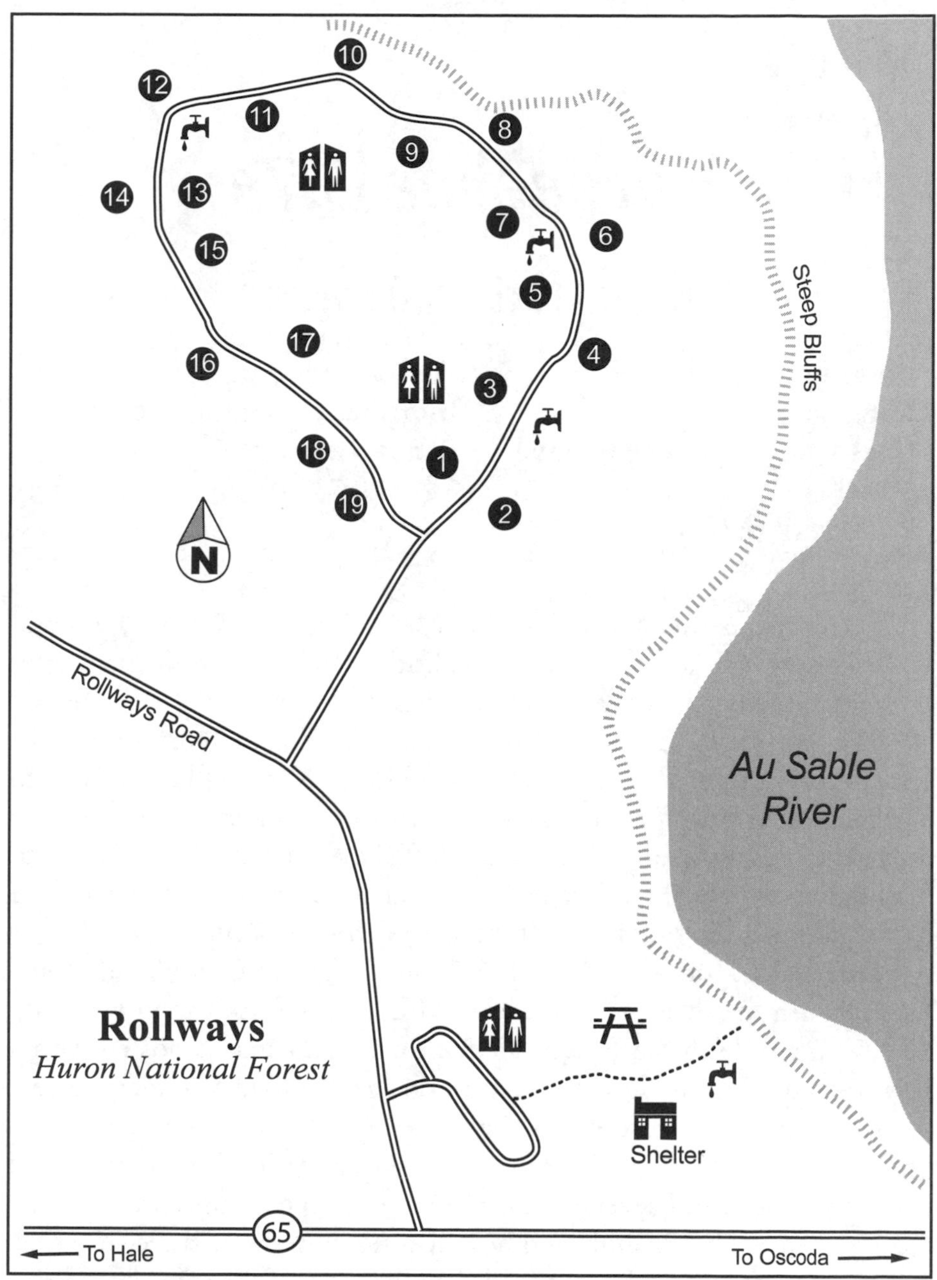

10
12
11
8
9
14
13
7
6
15
5
Steep Bluffs
4
17
16
3
18
1
19
2
N
Rollways Road
Au Sable
River
Rollways
Huron National Forest
Shelter
65
To Hale
To Oscoda

13

Horseshoe Lake

Huron National Forest

Campground: Rustic
County: Alcona
Nearest Community: Glennie
Sites: 9
Reservations: No
Fee: $15
Information: Huron Shores Ranger District
☎ (989) 739-0728

The brown national forest sign on M-65 simply says "Campground." It doesn't say if it is modern or rustic, if it's on a lake or how many sites there are. Go ahead, take a chance and follow the sign.

The best things in life are always unexpected, and Horseshoe Lake Campground, located in the heart of the Huron National Forest, is often an unexpected gem for most first-time visitors. It's a small facility with only nine sites, located on a wooded bluff above a undeveloped lake, and it's a lightly used facility. Often when you arrive in mid-July, the height of Michigan's camping season, only a few sites will be occupied.

Directions: Horseshoe Lake is 3.5 miles north of Glennie on M-65. From Harrisville head west on M-72 for 22 miles and then south on M-65 for a mile to the Forest Service Road 4124 that is posted with a "Campground" sign. Head a mile west on the dirt road to the entrance.

Campground: Horseshoe Lake is a single loop of nine sites with gravel spurs, tables, and fire rings with sliding grills. The campground is lightly shaded and several sites are in a semi-open grassy area, but the loop is enclosed by the hilly and heavily forested terrain. Three sites (No. 1, 3, and 4) are on the edge of the bluff with a view of the lake and a direct path down to the water. Other facilities include vault toilets and a hand pump for water.

Fishing: Within the campground is an unimproved launch that's strictly for carry-in boats, but you really don't need anything more for the

16-acre lake that is indeed shaped like a horseshoe. The west half of the lake is the best for fishing and is quite deep in the middle. At one time Horseshoe was stocked with rainbow trout, but that program has long since been discontinued. I've always found it a fun lake to catch bass, even though few are of legal size.

Hiking: Near the fee pipe is a marked trailhead for a 1.3-mile loop that winds around the lakeshore to a bench on the opposite shore and then circles back through the rolling hills.

Season: Horseshoe Lake's managed season is mid-April to the end of November. This is a small but lightly used facility where getting a site is usually not a problem.

14

Jewell Lake

Huron National Forest

Campground: Rustic
County: Alcona
Nearest Community: Barton City
Sites: 32
Reservations: No
Fee: $15
Information: Huron Shores Ranger District
☎ (989) 739-0728

One of the largest campgrounds in the Huron National Forest is Jewell Lake, offering not only numerous sites but several other attractive features. There's a pleasant beach and swimming area, a mile-long nature trail ideal for children, a separate picnic area, and fishing opportunities in the large lake.

Very little of Jewell Lake is on National Forest land, so expect a shoreline ringed by cottages and heavy traffic for boaters and anglers. Otherwise, this is a delightful place for a weekend camping trip.

Directions: From US-23 in Harrisville, head west on M-72 for 14.5 miles, then north on Sanborn Road for 1.7 miles, and left on Trask Road for 0.7 miles. Jewell Lake has a posted entrance on Trask Road.

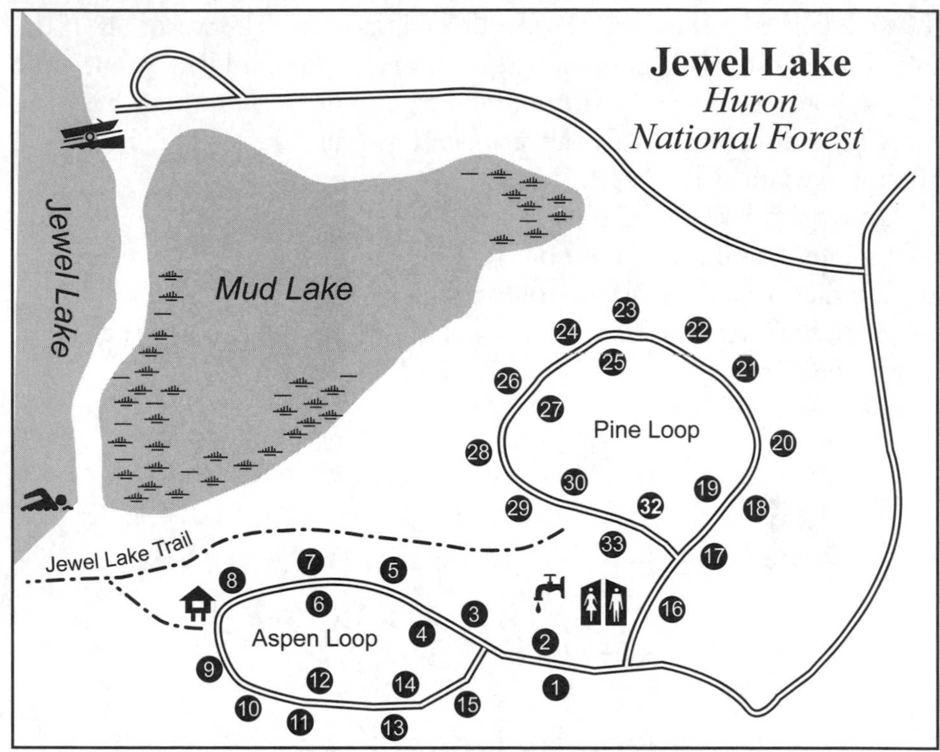

Campground: Jewell Lake has 32 graveled-spur sites with numbers 1–15 on Aspen Loop and 16–32 on Pine Loop. Both loops are lightly shaded, and although there are no sites directly on the lake, most of Aspen Loop is only a short walk from the beach and swimming area. Facilities include a handful of vault toilets, two hand pumps for water, tables, and fire rings with sliding grills.

Day-use Facilities: The campground has a small picnic area next to its boat launch, separated from the campground by a marsh. Next to Aspen Loop is a delightful beach and marked swimming area with shallow water and a sandy bottom.

Fishing: Jewel Lake has 193 surface acres and is exceptionally clear. Only the southeast corner of its shoreline is part of the National Forest; the rest of it is privately owned. A cement slab boat launch is located in the picnic area with parking for additional cars and trailers. The lake is best known for panfish, but anglers also work its waters for largemouth bass and northern pike.

Hiking: Departing from the beach area is a delightful mile-long loop that in its first half crosses a bridge over a beaver dam and then follows the shoreline of Jewell Lake. The second half winds through an enchanting paper birch forest.

Season: Jewell Lake's managed season is Memorial Day through Labor Day and fills only on the holidays and a rare weekend.

15

Harrisville

State Park

Campground: Modern
County: Alcona
Nearest Community: Harrisville
Sites: 195
Reservations: Yes
Fee: $23–25 plus vehicle entry fee
Information: State park office
☎ (989) 724-5126

Harrisville State Park is proof that Lake Michigan campgrounds do not have a monopoly on wide sandy beaches. The outstanding feature of this 107-acre park is its half-mile-long stretch of Lake Huron shoreline where its sugar-like sand is more than 30 yards wide in most places. Here you take a refreshing dip in the cooling waters of the Great Lake, lay out in the sun, or if you're lucky, set up camp at a beachfront campsite.

Although the park has a day-use area and even a nature trail, its relatively small size limits the facilities that other larger units offer, but there is a paved path that connects it with Harrisville. The quaint town is within easy walking distance of the state park and during the summer features bustling restaurants, ice cream parlors, gift shops, and the Harrisville Harbor where you can watch charter fishing boats return with their daily catch of salmon and trout.

Directions: The state park is on US-23, a half mile south of Harrisville.

Campground: The park has a single campground of several paved loops in a lightly forested area of pine and cedar. Sites feature hook-ups, tables, and fire pits and are within view of each other but not crammed together. Some sites have 50-amp service, and 15 of them are pull-through sites ideal for larger trailers and rigs. By far the most popular ones are located right along the lake where your tent or trailer would be in the shade of the trees but your beach blanket only a few yards away. These are some of the best places to camp along Lake Huron, and obtaining one during the summer camping season usually involves a site-specific reservation months in advance. Along with a pair of bathroom and shower buildings, the campground features two mini-cabins and the Sunrise Cabin that sleeps six.

Day-use Facilities: At the south end of the park is a day-use area with a bathhouse, shelter, picnic tables, playground equipment, and, of course, more of that wide, beautiful beach and Lake Huron surf. Here you can set up a lounge chair, take in the sun, or watch iron ore freighters pass by on the horizon. The bike/foot path begins near the entrance of the campground and is a paved trail that extends a half mile north to Harrisville, ending near First Street.

Fishing: Lake Huron is a noted deepwater fishery for salmon and lake trout and charters can be arranged at the Harrisville Harbor or bait shops in town. There is an unimproved launch for car-top and other hand-carried boats next to the park's day-use area but you need to go to town for anything bigger. Actually, the only fishing activity within the park is in the surf with anglers who work the beaches during the fall for salmon and brown trout feeding in the shallows.

Hiking: Departing and returning from the campground is the Cedar Run Nature Trail, a mile-long loop that takes 30 to 45 minutes to enjoy. There are 14 numbered posts on the trail, and an interpretive brochure, obtained from the contact station, points out different species of trees.

Season: Harrisville is open from mid-April to the end of October. The campground is often filled on the weekends by Friday afternoon and sometimes by Thursday afternoon. To reserve a campsite contact Michigan State Park Central Reservations ☎ 800-447-2757 🌐 www.midnrreservations.com.

16

Ess Lake

Mackinaw State Forest

Campground: Rustic	**Reservations:** No
County: Montmorency	**Fee:** $15
Nearest Community: Hillman	**Information:** Gaylord DNR office
Sites: 28	☎ (989) 732-3541

Almost since the earliest days of automobile travel, a small peninsula jutting out into Ess Lake has been a popular spot for campers to pull up and an official state campground since 1938. This mid-size lake, with its productive fishing, clear water, and fine beach still draws campers today.

The Forest Management Division enlarged the state forest campground in 1968 with a second loop of 13 sites, but the campground still fills weekends during the summer and sometimes by Thursday evening at the height of the camping season. Anglers are especially attracted to this lake because of its no-wake regulations during the prime fishing hours in the morning and evening.

Directions: The campground is 16 miles northeast of Atlanta in Montmorency County. From Atlanta head north on M-33 and then east on County Road 624, reached just after passing Jackson Lake State Forest Campground. The entrance to Ess Lake is 9.5 miles east on CR 624.

Campground: Ess has 28 sites divided on two loops situated almost across from each on the lake. The first loop is connected to the beach and day-use area by a foot path and features 13 sites secluded in a forest of mixed pine and hardwoods. Two sites overlook the water.

The second loop is farther from the beach but on a point that gives Ess its horseshoe shape. Almost all of these sites are on the water and 19–25 are on a low bluff with a scenic view of the lake. Both loops have tables, fire rings, hand pumps for water, and vault toilets.

Day-use Facilities: Accessed from the first loop is the day-use area with parking for additional vehicles. Ess features a beach and grassy area and a marked swimming area with a sandy bottom and a gentle slope. A few tables and vault toilets are also located here.

Fishing: The 114-acre lake is heavily developed with cottages, and boating traffic can be moderate to heavy on the weekends. For this reason a no-wake regulation is imposed on Ess from 7:30 PM to 11 AM

Near the second loop is an improved boat launch with a cement ramp, dock, and limited parking for a handful of vehicles and rigs. Ess has no outlet and ranges in depth up to 50 feet in the middle of the west bay. The lake has been planted with walleyes in the past while anglers also target smallmouth and largemouth bass, perch, and pike.

Season: From mid-July through late August, Ess Lake can be filled on any weekend and often is at least half filled by Thursday afternoon.

17

Ossineke

Mackinaw State Forest

Campground: Rustic
County: Alpena
Nearest Community: Ossineke
Sites: 42
Reservations: No
Fee: $15
Information: Gaylord DNR office
☎ (989) 732-3541

The only state forest campground on Lake Huron is a delightful facility that most travelers heading north on US-23 don't even realize is there. The tendency when passing through the hamlet of Ossineke is to overlook the small brown campground sign, and that's too bad.

The rustic campground is separated from the town, off by itself, and a place where you can wander undeveloped stretches of beaches for miles, right into Negwegon State Park if so desired. The facility offers a beautiful beach, sandy swimming area, and even a mile-long pathway where it's possible to spot deer in the early morning.

Directions: The campground is posted at the corner of US-23 and Ossineke Road, but the sign is easy to miss. Turn east onto Ossineke Road and follow it to another state forest sign at the corner of State Road. Turn right on State Road and drive to the entrance at the end.

Campground: Ossineke has 42 rustic sites on two loops winding along Lake Huron. The first loop has sites 1–26 of which 19 of them, including 18–26, are right off the water. Most sites have a thin line of trees or brush separating them from the sandy beach, but three are out in the open with a clear and beautiful view of the Great Lake. These sites for the most part are in a stand of white and red pine with little undergrowth and thus little privacy.

The second loop is situated in an oak/maple forest and sites 27–42 are more spread out and secluded from each other but not as close to the stretch of beach favored by swimmers. Fire rings, tables, hand pumps for water, and vault toilets are on each loop.

Day-use Facilities: A small picnic area with a handful of tables and pedestal grills is located within the west loop and closes at 10 PM. The beach here is beautiful. There is no marked swimming area, but most years the beach is a wide sandy strip with shallow water and a soft bottom that is ideal for young swimmers. On a clear summer day you can enjoy a view from the water towers of Alpena to Scarecrow Island of the Michigan Island National Wildlife Refuge to the south. The campground has no boat launch on the lake.

Hiking: Ossineke Pathway is a one-mile trail that begins next to site 14 and ends near site 42 of the second loop. You start off in an upland forest of a wide variety of trees ranging from white and red pine to oak, beech, paper birch, and maple. The trail winds across the entrance drive and then swings through a low lying forest, passing several grassy meadows and even crossing a boardwalk through a swamp.

You can also hike the beach south along one of the most undeveloped stretches of Lake Huron and within six miles reach South Point in Negwegon State Park. The shoreline switches from beautiful sandy bays and beaches to rocky shorelines. Two miles beyond South Point is the state park's parking area and water pump.

Season: Ossineke experiences moderate use on weekends in mid-July through mid-August, but getting a site anytime during the summer is usually possible.

18

Long Lake

Alpena County Park

Campground: Modern and semi-modern
County: Alpena
Nearest Community: Alpena
Sites: 124
Reservations: Yes
Fee: $15 to $24
Information: Park Office
☎ (989) 595-2401

Who says only the state or federal governments know how to run a campground? Long Lake County Park is an example of a pleasant modern campground that isn't filled every day of the summer like state parks and offers more amenities than national forest campgrounds.

An Alpena County park, Long Lake is a spot where you can spend a few days fishing, boating, and exploring the surrounding area, particularly the lighthouses of Presque Isle just to the north. To the south the city of Alpena is only 10 miles away and features museums, bike paths, and an interesting canoe trail.

Directions: From Alpena head north on US-23 for 10 miles and then west on Long Lake Park Road.

Campground: Long Lake has 124 sites located on East Bay in the northeast corner of this large lake. The campground is well shaded but not wooded, and the sites are close together with little privacy, even the rustic tent sites. Many of them are right on the water so close to the shoreline that campers pull their boats up to the edge of their sites.

Sites No. 1–80 are modern with water and electricity hook-ups with 12 of them right on the lake and commanding a higher nightly fee. Sites No. 81–124 are tent sites with 10 of those overlooking the shoreline.

The daily fees are $11 for a tent site, $16 for a modern site, and $19 for a modern site on the water.

Day-use Facilities: Long Lake has picnic areas, shelters, volleyball courts, and play equipment in two day-use areas, each with its own small beach for swimmers. There is also a small store in the park with limited supplies.

Fishing: The park has an improved boat launch and a large parking area for trailers, a testimony to Long Lake's popularity among anglers. There is a $3 fee to launch a boat. Long Lake covers 5,200 acres and generally is a long, shallow body of water, its deepest spot being only 25 feet. The lake has good smallmouth bass and perch fishing but anglers also target walleyes, northern pike and bluegills.

Season: Long Lake is open to camping from May 15 through Oct. 1 and is filled on many weekends in July and August. Reservation are accepted after Jan. 1 and be made by first calling the park office at ☎ 989-595-2401 and then sending in a deposit that includes one night paid in advance or two nights paid in advance for holiday weekends.

For more information on lighthouses or trails in the area contact the Alpena Convention and Visitors Bureau at ☎ 800-4-ALPENA or 🌐 www.alpenacvb.com.

At 113 feet, the New Presque Lighthouse is the tallest on the Great Lakes and only a short drive from Long Lake County Park. In the summer visitors can climb the tower for the spectacular view at the top.

The Heartland

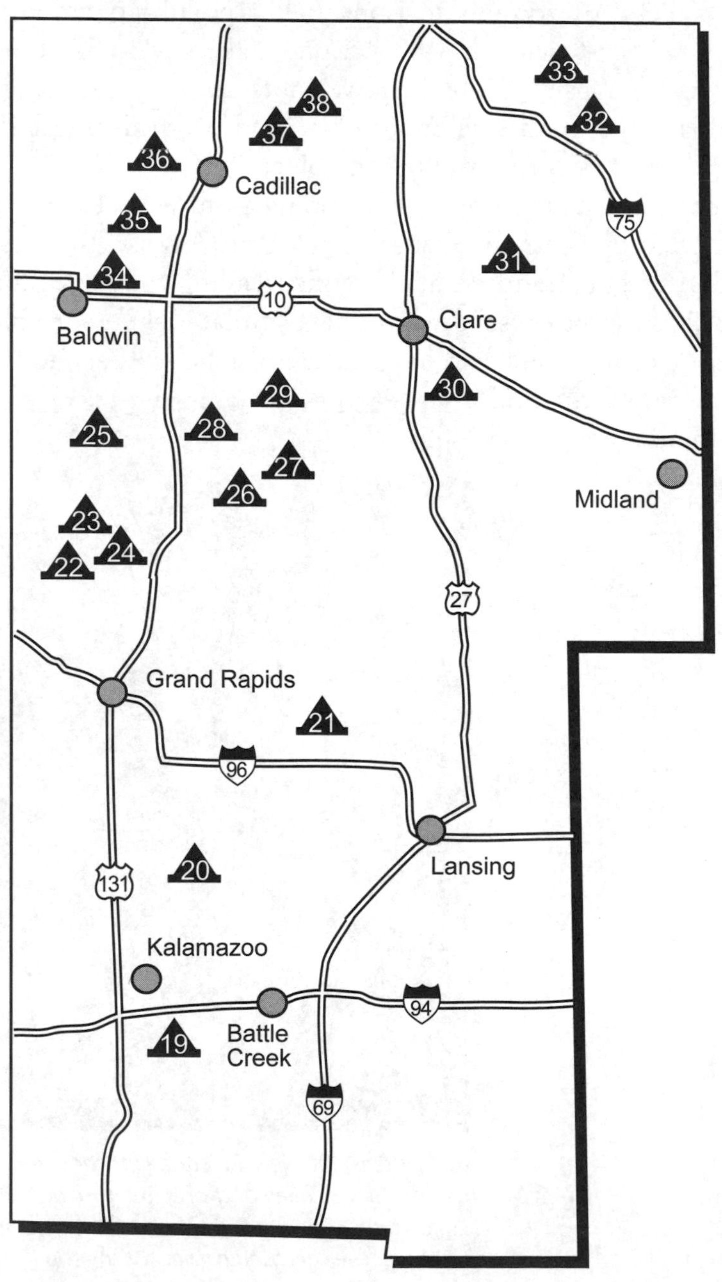

#	PARK	MODERN	SEMI-MODERN	RUSTIC	SITES	DAY-USE FACILITIES	FISHING	HIKING	BIRDING	INTERPRETIVE CENTER	BIKING	CANOEING/ KAYAKING	BOATING
19	Cold Brook	•	•		44	•	•	•					
20	Deep Lake			•	120	•	•	•			•		
21	Bertha Brock			•	23	•		•					
22	Henning	•	•		68	•	•	•				•	
23	Sandy Beach	•	•		200	•	•						
24	Newaygo			•	99		•						
25	White Cloud	•	•		103	•		•					
26	School Section Lake Veteran's Park	•			167	•	•						
27	Tubbs Island			•	12		•						
28	Paris	•			68	•	•	•				•	
29	Merrill Lake	•	•		146	•	•						
30	Herrick Recreation Area	•			73	•	•						
31	Gladwin City Park	•			61	•	•	•					
32	Island Lake			•	17	•	•	•					
33	Wagner Lake			•	12	•	•						
34	Leverentz Lakes			•	17		•	•					
35	Silver Creek			•	26		•	•				•	
36	Hemlock			•	19	•	•						
37	Goose Lake			•	54	•	•						
38	Long Lake			•	16		•						

19

Cold Brook

Kalamazoo County Park

Campground: Modern and semi-modern
County: Kalamazoo
Nearest Community: Climax
Sites: 44
Reservations: Yes
Fee: $15 to $20
Information: Kalamazoo County Parks
☎ (269) 383-877

At the headwaters of the Portage River are Portage and Blue Lakes, a sprawling body of water of many peninsulas, bays, channels, and the site of a modern campground that lies just a few miles off I-94 between Battle Creek and Kalamazoo. Cold Brook County Park is a 276-acre facility operated by Kalamazoo County with both rustic and modern sites.

The park is spread along the south and east shore of Portage Lake and totally encloses Blue Lake. Much of the west half of the lakes is a shallow marshy area, filled with lily pads and other aquatic plants that attract a variety of waterfowl during the spring and fall migrations.

Directions: Cold Brook is just south of I-94, 8 miles east of Kalamazoo along MN Avenue. From the east, depart at exit 92, Business I-94 for Battle Creek, but head south for the town of Climax. In 2 miles you'll merge onto MN Avenue and the entrance of the park is a mile west along the road.

Campground: Cold Brook has both modern sites and a rustic loop, each on a small peninsula of their own on the southwest corner of Portage Lake. The 29 modern sites are close together in an open grassy area with only a few small trees and little shade. There is a single restroom with showers along with grills, tables, a sanitation station, and limited play equipment. A bridge crosses the narrow channel into Blue Lake to the picnic area on the other side.

The rustic portion of the campground has 15 sites in a wooded area of small hardwoods with the sites well shaded but still close together. This loop has vault toilets, fire grills, tables, and a hand pump for water.

Day-use Facilities: A pleasant picnic area with a large shelter, play equipment, and tables and grills is located on a wooded hill overlooking both Blue and Portage Lake. Farther up the park road is another shelter, a ball field, and finally the beach area with its bathhouse, parking for additional vehicles, and more tables and grills. On the east side of Portage Lake, where the beach is located, the water is deep and clear. The beach contains very little sand but is bordered by a pleasant grassy area.

Fishing: An improved boat launch with cement ramp and dock is situated next to the beach and includes its own parking area. There is a no wake regulation between the narrow channels of the lakes, and no high-speed boating or water skiing is allowed from 7:30 PM to 11 AM The shorelines of these lakes are completely undeveloped, and anglers will work the east side of Portage as well as cast from a fishing pier in the day-use area for a variety of fish, including bass and panfish.

Hiking: A posted trail system that totals 2.5 miles departs from the beach area and skirts the park shoreline, passing through the picnic area and both campgrounds before crossing a dike at the rustic loop to a woods on the west side.

Season: Cold Brook is open from Memorial Day through October and is often filled on summer weekends. Nightly fees are $15 for a rustic site and $20 for a modern one. Campsites are available for reservation on Jan. 1 of the current year and require a non-refundable $5 reservation fee per site and full payment of nightly fees. You can reserve a site online at 🌐 www.kalcounty.com/parks/coldbrook or by calling Kalamazoo County Parks at ☎ 269-383-8778. To make reservations less than two weeks prior to your arrival date call Cold Brook park office at ☎ 269-746-427.

20

Deep Lake

Yankee Springs Recreation Area

Campground: Rustic	**Reservations:** Yes
County: Barry	**Fee:** $12 plus vehicle entry fee
Nearest Community: Middleville	**Information:** State park office
Sites: 120	☎ (269) 795-9081

Yankee Springs Recreation Area is a 5,017-acre state park between Kalamazoo and Grand Rapids, and its main campground is Gun Lake, a large, modern facility that is often filled during the summer. But even if it is, you don't have to leave the park.

Head east on Gun Lake Road and stake out a site at Deep Lake, the largest rustic campground in the Michigan State Park system. With 120 sites along this lake, you can usually count on an open spot in this campground throughout the summer, even on the weekends.

Directions: From US-131, depart at exit 61 and follow County Road A42 east for 7 miles to its junction with Gun Lake Road. Turn right on Gun Lake Road and follow it through the park and pass the entrance to Gun Lake Campground. Turn left on Yankee Springs Road and the entrance of Deep Lake Campground will be reached within a mile.

Campground: Deep Lake is a very scenic section of Yankee Springs. The campground has 120 sites with most of them well spread out in a wooded setting. None are directly on the lake, but a few are within view of the water and several sites have direct access to the park's mountain bike trail system.

Day-use Facilities: The swimming is poor in Deep Lake, but there are good beaches and a scenic picnic area on Murphy's Point Peninsula, which juts into Gun Lake near the modern campground. The peninsula features three beaches, picnic shelters, bathhouses, and a concessionaire that rents out rowboats and canoes.

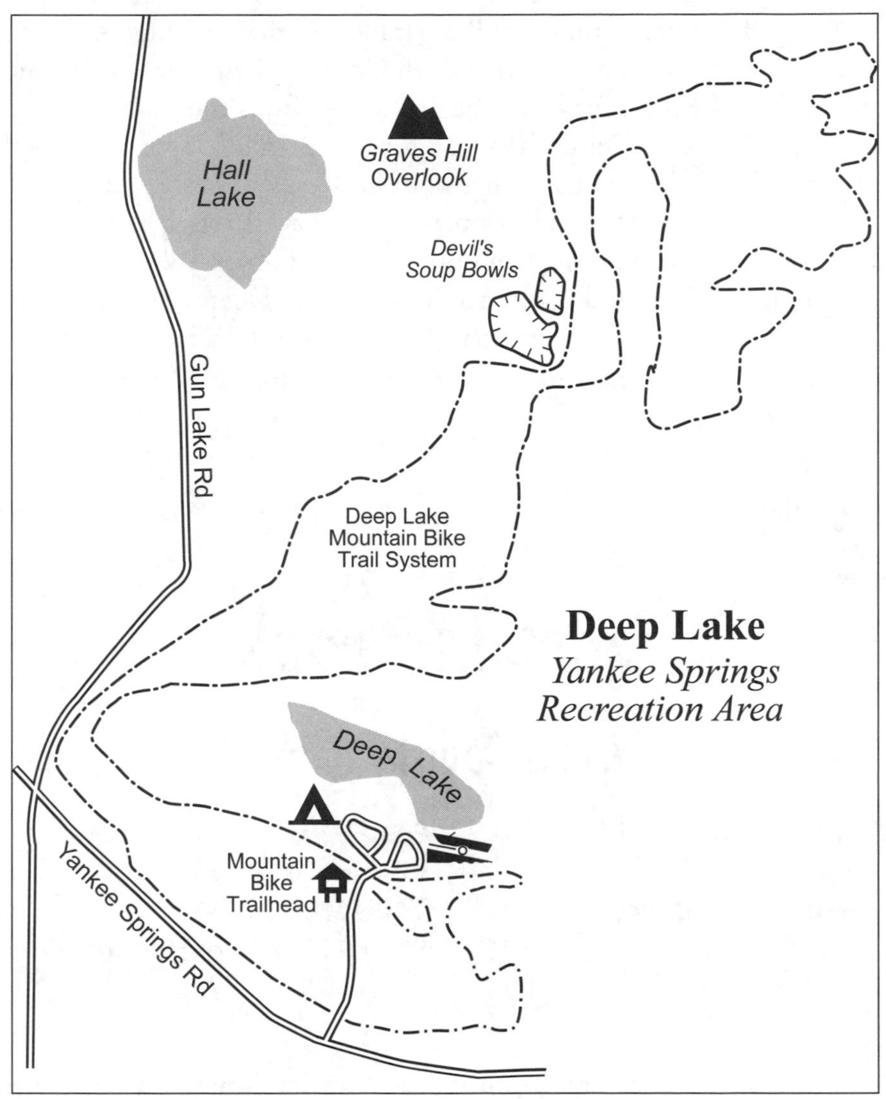

Fishing: Deep Lake is a shallow, 36-acre body of water with no-wake regulations and good fishing for bluegill and other panfish. The campground has a small boat launch and a fishing pier for shore anglers.

Mountain Biking: The campground is a popular destination for mountain bikers. Next to the campground is the trailhead for the Deep Lake Mountain Bike Trail, arguably one of the busiest off-road biking areas in western Michigan. The 13-mile trail system consists of two single-track segments: a 2-mile loop north of the campground for beginners and an 11-mile expert loop south of it.

Hiking: There are 17 miles of hiking trails in Yankee Springs Recreation Area, including a segment of the North Country Trail. One of the most scenic is Hall Lake Trail, which begins across from the entrance to the Long Lake Outdoor Center. The trail forms a 2-mile loop that skirts the shoreline of the lake and continues onto Graves Hill before returning.

Season: The campground is open from May through October and will fill on an occasional weekend during the summer. Like the modern campground on Gun Lake, you can book sites at Deep Lake six months in advance through Michigan State Park Central Reservations ☎ 800-447-2757 🌐 www.midnrreservations.com, but the reservations are not site specific.

21

Bertha Brock

Ionia County Park

Campground: Rustic	**Fee:** $15 plus vehicle entry fee
County: Ionia	**Information:** Park office
Nearest Community: Ionia	☎ (616) 522-7275
Sites: 23	🌐 www.berthabrockpark.info
Reservations: No	

Ionia County has three county parks but its crown jewel is Bertha Brock, a 208-acre tract of ridges and ravines, forested in towering pines and split in the middle by Bellamy Creek. You may not be that far from Lansing, but you feel like you're some place far up north. It's not just the pines and rugged terrain that make you feel like you're somewhere else; it's the architecture.

Named after a local historian, Bertha Brock was established in 1931, and many of its buildings were constructed during the Great Depression through the Works Progress Administration, a federal work program. That's why the pavilions, the caretaker's cottage, and the Ionia Fishing &

Hunting Club are classic log lodges while Bellamy Creek is crossed on stone bridges that arch high across the stream.

Scattered throughout the Bertha Brock are a variety of amenities—foot trails, tennis courts, baseball diamonds, and playgrounds to name a few—that make this park an excellent weekend destination that is still close to home for many Michigan campers.

Directions: Depart I-96 at exit 67 and head north on M-66 for 8 miles to Ionia and west on M-21. Within 4 miles you reach the posted park entrance.

Campground: Bertha Brock has a rustic campground of 23 sites scattered in the rolling wooded terrain in the east half of the park. A handful of sites over look Bellamy Creek and the rest are perched above. All of them are well separated and isolated from each other. Vault toilets are located within the campground, and a restroom with flush toilets are near historic Palmer Lodge. Winding through the campground is one of the park's hiking trails.

Bertha Brock also has a pair of camper cabins within its campground. The cabins feature a pair of bunks, a loft, and table and benches but no electricity or source of water. Outside are a picnic table, fire pit, and charcoal grill. The cabins are $35 per night on Friday and Saturday, and $25 per night Sunday through Thursday.

Day-use Facilities: The park has 17 unique picnic sites that are scattered throughout the woods for a high degree of privacy. Many overlook one of the three stone bridges that cross Bellamy Creek. Bertha Brock also has two picnic pavilions, tennis courts, softball field, horseshoe pits, and playground structures.

Hiking: Winding along the ridge on the south side of Bellamy Creek are three marked loops that total 4 miles of hiking trails. All three loops start at the Ionia Fishing & Hunting Club at the west end of the park and immediately begin by climbing the open slope that serves as the park's sledding hill in the winter.

From there they follow the contoured crest of the steep-sided ridge with the mile-long Bear Path descending the ridge first, then the 1.5-mile Deer Run Trail, and finally the 2-mile Turkey Trail which passes through the campground.

Season: Depending on the weather, the campground at Bertha Brock is usually open from May through October and sites are handed out on a first-come, first-served basis. Reservations are required for camper cabins and can be made by calling the park office ☎ 616-522-7275.

22

Henning

Newaygo County Park

Campground: Modern and semi-modern
County: Newaygo
Nearest Community: Newaygo
Sites: 68
Reservations: Yes
Fee: $15-$25 plus vehicle entry fee
Information: Park office
☎ (231) 652-1202
🌐 www.countyofnewaygo.com/parks

Ed H. Henning Park is an 82-acre Newaygo County park with a wide range of facilities that includes a modern campground, a special camping area for canoers, and a boat launch that is extremely popular with salmon and steelhead anglers who congregate on the Muskegon River in the fall in search of a 20-pound trophy.

All this and you're only a half mile from Newaygo and M-37 and just a 40-minute drive from Grand Rapids. For those who want to be up north camping without having to drive there, this well-managed facility is the perfect choice.

Directions: From downtown Newaygo, head north on M-37 and turn east on Croton Road just after crossing the Muskegon River. The park entrance is a half mile east on Croton Road.

Campground: Henning Park has 60 modern sites that are situated close together along three loops in an open grassy field that are surrounded by forests. Campground amenities include electric and water hook-ups, a large modern restroom, and a dump station for recreational vehicles. Nearby are eight rustic sites, set off by themselves in a more forested setting along a bluff above the Muskegon River. If you're packing a tent, these are a delight.

There is also an organization camping area near the boat launch on the river and designed for the large groups of canoers passing through

A camper relaxes in her site at Hennning Campground, a Newaygo County park on the Muskegon River near the city of Newaygo.

during an overnight paddle on the river. Modern sites are $25 a night, rustic sites $15.

Day-use Facilities: The park has an extensive day-use area that includes baseball and soccer fields and courts for basketball, tennis, beach volleyball, and horseshoes. There is a picnic area with tables and grills and a pond with one end developed as swimming beach. Due to strong currents, swimming is not recommended in the Muskegon River.

Fishing: The park also maintains an improved boat launch with parking for 75 vehicles and rigs. There is also a fish cleaning area because this portion of the Muskegon River is well known for its steelhead and salmon fishing after Labor Day as well as walleye fishing in Croton Pond and downstream from Croton Dam in spring and early summer.

Hiking: Henning Park has a mile-long nature trail that is posted in the parking lot across from the swimming area and dips into the woods north of the campground.

Canoeing: A popular canoe trip is to put in just below Croton Dam and pull out at Henning Park. This is a 16-mile float that most paddlers cover in three to five hours. Wisner Rents Canoes ☎ 231-652-6743 🌐 www.wisnercanoes.com is an Newaygo canoe livery that can arrange both rental canoes and transportation from the park. Shorter trips are also possible.

Season: Henning is open for camping from mid-April through fall colors in mid-October. The campground experiences moderate use but will fill up on weekends mid-June to mid-August and on Memorial Day and Labor Day weekends. Sites can be reserved during the off season by obtaining a reservation form online at 🌐 www.countyofnewaygo.com/parks and then mailing it to the Newaygo Parks Administration Office (4684 Evergreen Dr., Newaygo, MI 49337) with your full payment plus a $5 reservation fee. Once the camping season begins all reservations must be addressed to the park (500 Croton Road, Newaygo, MI 49337).

23

Sandy Beach

Newaygo County Park

Campground: Modern and semi-modern
County: Newaygo
Nearest Community: White Cloud
Sites: 200
Reservations: Yes
Fee: $15–$30 plus vehicle entry fee
Information: Park office
☎ (231) 689-1229
🌐 www.countyofnewaygo.com/parks

Hardy Dam Pond is hardly a pond. This reservoir, the result of a Consumers Energy dam across the Muskegon River, is 18 miles long, 100 feet deep, and spreads across 4,000 acres in Newaygo and Mescota Counties. Even more amazing, there isn't a single house or cottage on it.

Hardy Dam Pond could very well be the largest body of water in Michigan without any major development along its shoreline. This is

Sandy Beach County Park offers campers an opportunity to rent boat slips on Hardy Dam Pond.

the watery and woodsy setting for Sandy Beach County Campground, a 129-acre Newaygo County park overlooking the "pond" from a bluff along its west shore.

A popular destination with campers from the Grand Rapids area, Sandy Beach is well suited for a weekend away. The park features a mix of modern and rustic sites along with two camper cabins and a wide range of day-use facilities. Its biggest draw, however, is the large lake in front of it, attracting campers who arrive to rent a site for their trailer and a slip for their boat for a holiday of boating and camping.

Directions: From US-131, 35 miles north of Grand Rapids, depart at exit 124 and head west on Jefferson Road, which becomes 36th Street in 3.7 miles when you enter Newaygo County. Follow 36th Street as it winds across Hardy Pond Dam, and within 8 miles of US-131 turn north (right) on Elm Avenue. In less than a mile turn east (right) on 30th Street and follow it to the entrance of the park.

Campground: Sandy Beach has 200 sites on three loops as well as a group camping area. The 150 modern sites are in a lightly-shaded grassy area and include 22 that feature electric, water, and sewer hook-ups. None of the sites are directly on the water, but many have a view of the reservoir as the park's lakefront bluff serves as a common area with benches and a log fence along the edge. The park has two restrooms with showers and a dump station.

The 50 rustic sites are situated along the woods on the premiere of the campground while the two camper cabins are tucked in the trees and feature lights, heat, microwave, refrigerator, and sleeping accommodations for six. Modern sites with full hook-ups including sewer are $30, water and electric are $25, electric-only are $20, and rustic sites are $15. Cabins are $65 a night.

Day-use Facilities: Sandy Beach has a well-shaded day-use area that overlooks a long sandy beach and features tables, grills, and a new picnic pavilion. The park also has horseshoe pits, a playscape for children, and courts for volleyball and basketball.

Fishing: Hardy Dam Pond is known for its walleye fishery as the reservoir is stocked annually with the species, but it is also one of a handful of lakes where an experimental early bass season was held and attracts many anglers interested in trophy-size bluegills and other panfish. Sandy Beach has a boat launch and 26 slips that campers can rent on a nightly basis for a small fee.

Season: Sandy Beach is open for camping from early May through September and is often filled on weekends on Memorial Day, July and early August, and Labor Day. You can reserve sites in advance during the off season by obtaining a reservation form online at 🌐 www.countyofnewaygo.com/parks and then mailing it to the Newaygo Parks Administration Office (4684 Evergreen Dr., Newaygo, MI 49337) with your full payment plus a $5 reservation fee. Once the camping season begins all reservations must be addressed to the park (6926 30th Street, White Cloud, MI 49349).

24

Newaygo

State Park

Campground: Rustic
County: Newaygo
Nearest Community: Oxbow
Sites: 99
Reservations: Yes
Fee: $12 plus vehicle entry fee
Information: State park office
☎ (231) 856-4452

Newaygo is one of the few units of the state park system with a rustic campground and where there is actually a little space and privacy between sites. For these reasons the 257-acre park is also one of the few rustic facilities that can easily be filled on almost any weekend in the summer.

Situated on a 20-foot high bluff overlooking Hardy Dam Pond southwest of Big Rapids, the park features little beyond its campground and a boat launch, but the fishing is moderately good in the man-made lake, and the campground is a splendid place to park a trailer in October when the facility is empty and the surrounding hardwoods are at the peak of their autumn blaze of color.

Directions: The park is 43 miles north of Grand Rapids and can be reached from US-131. Depart west on Jefferson Road at the Morley exit for 7 miles and then head north on Beech Road to the park's entrance.

Campground: Newaygo has 99 sites well spread out on two loops. Oak Campground features sites No. 1–48 in a forest of young hardwoods and moderate undergrowth, providing privacy that is usually not associated with state parks. No sites are on the water, but a path from the back of the loop leads to a bluff where you view most of the reservoir. Depending on the water level, a small beach lies below the bluff here.

Sites No. 49–99 are located in Poplar Campground where campers set up in a forest of slightly older hardwoods. A couple of sites are a few feet from the edge of the bluff overlooking the lake, but the rest, like Oak Campground, are tucked into the trees and out of sight of the water. Both

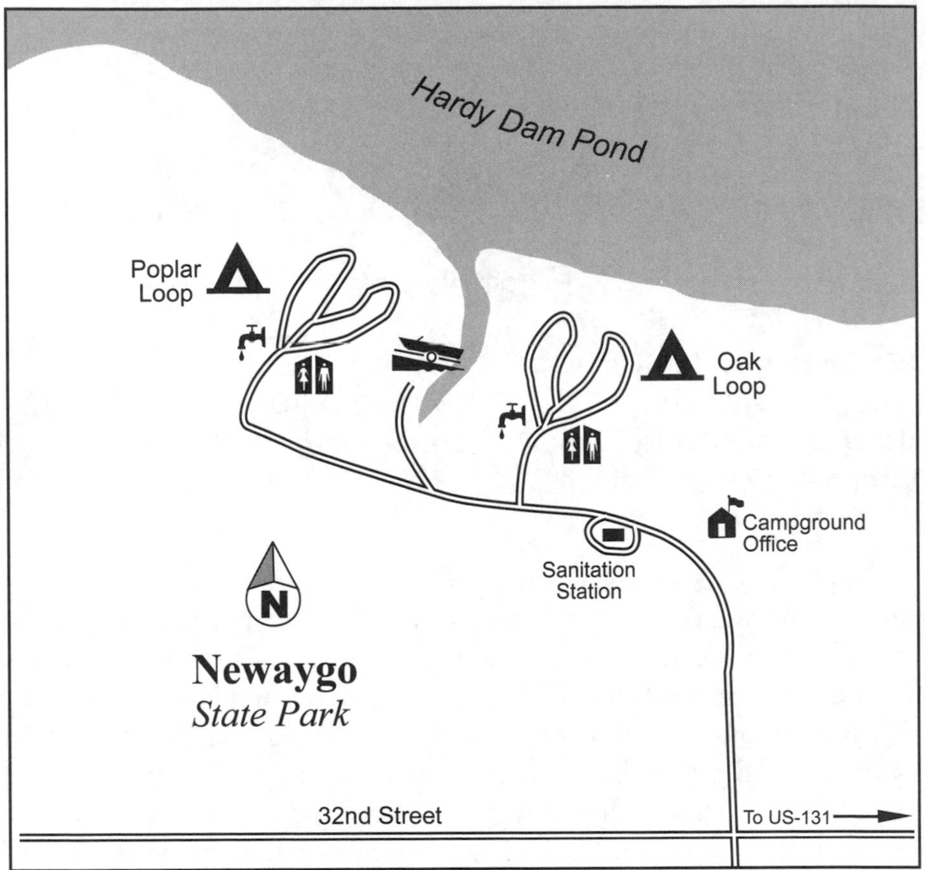

loops have limited playground equipment, vault toilets, hand pumps for water, tables, and fire rings.

Fishing: Newaygo features an improved boat launch along with a dock and parking for 50 additional vehicles and trailers on a small inlet of Hardy Dam Pond. The lake, often cited as "the third largest earthen-filled dam in the world," is 18 miles long and spread over 4,000 acres. It's stocked annually with walleyes and also was one of a handful of lakes where an experimental early bass season was held.

Season: Newaygo is open from May through October and, despite being a rustic facility, often fills up on weekends from mid-July to early August. During the week it's easy to obtain a site as well as before July 4 and after mid-August. You can book sites six months advance through Michigan State Park Central Reservations ☎ 800-447-2757 🌐 www.midnrreservations.com. After summer the campground contact station is closed and you must call ☎ 231-745-2888 for park information.

25

White Cloud

City Campground

Campground: Modern and semi-modern
County: Newaygo
Nearest Community: White Cloud
Sites: 103
Reservations: Yes
Fee: $20
Information: Park office
☎ (231) 689-2021

If White Cloud City Campground has the look of a state park to you, that's because it use to be a state park. The 99-acre park that borders the White River in Newaygo County was designated White Cloud State Park in 1920. In 1940 a small portion was given to the city of White Cloud and in the late 1950s the rest of the park was handed over.

The campground has always retained that "state park" appearance and today is a pleasant modern campground within easy walking distance of the shops and restaurants in this small town. White Cloud City Campground does have one feature that is unique to most state park campgrounds, however. You can usually get a site there during the summer, even on the weekends.

Directions: From M-37, turn west onto Wilcox Avenue to reach the campground entrance within a block.

Campground: White Cloud has 103 sites divided among modern sites with hook-ups, rustic sites, and group camping. The sites are close together and none of them are directly on the river, but the campground is well shaded by large hardwoods. Most of the modern sites have water and electric hook-ups with 20, 30, and 50 amp service, a few offer just electricity. The campground also has a bathhouse with showers and a dumping station.

Day-use Facilities: The campground has a picnic area, play equipment, horseshoe courts, and an enclosed pavilion with a fireplace and kitchen.

Hiking: River Walk is a nature trail that departs from the campground and follows the river west to Flowing Well Park, a city park with a natural mineral springs.

Tubing: Bring an inner tube! Upstream from the campground are Smith and Raceway Parks located off Walnut Avenue and right below Lake White Cloud, an impoundment of the White River. During the summer it's common for children and families to tube from these parks back to the campground.

Season: The campground is open from April 15 until the first weekend of October. It only fills on holidays and an occasional weekend during July or early August. All sites, rustic or modern, are $20 a night and can be reserved by calling the campground office at ☎ 231-689-2021. During the off season call the city of White Cloud ☎ 231-689-1194 for additional information.

26

School Section Lake Veteran's Park

Mecosta County Park

Campground: Modern	**Fee:** $20 plus vehicle entry fee
County: Mecosta	**Information:** Park office
Nearest Community: Mecosta	☎ (231) 972-7450
Sites: 167	🌐 www.mecostacountyparks.com
Reservations: Yes	

At School Section Lake Park in Mecosta County you have a lake, a campground, and a lot of history. Some of the earliest settlers in Mecosta and Isabella County were African American farmers and woodsmen who arrived in 1860 from southern Michigan and Ohio. Their pioneering spirit eventually led to the Old Settlers Reunions that began in 1890 at the homestead of one of the early families. That farm was on School Section Lake and today is the 86-acre county park and a Michigan Historic Site.

This interesting park also contains Little River School, a classic one-room schoolhouse from the early 1900s, and a giant oak tree in the picnic area that is probably 200 years old as well as an excellent day-use area and a large campground.

Directions: From Mecosta head south on M-20 and then west on 9 Mile Road which reaches the park in 2 miles.

Campground: School Section Lake has 167 modern sites that are situated close together in a semi-open area away from the lake. Each site has water and electricity and there is a dump station in the middle of the campground.

The park also has six rental cabins that are off by themselves and overlook the lake from a gently sloping hill. The 12-by-12-foot cabins sleep six each in a pair of bunks and a loft and contain a table and benches inside. Outside there are picnic tables, fire rings, and wooden "easy chairs" that allow you to relax with a view of School Section Lake.

The campsites are $20 per night, the cabins $40 per night. A vehicle entry fee is also required which is $25 for an annual pass, $15 for the weekend and $6 a day.

Day-use Facilities: School Section has a large, shaded picnic area with tables, grills, and five shelters that overlook the beach. Also within the park is a baseball field and courts for basketball, beach volleyball, and horseshoes. There is a long sandy beach on the lake that borders a designated swimming area.

Fishing: The park has a boat launch, a fish cleaning station, and a 10-horsepower limit on outboard motors. Many campers arrive with hand-carried boats and canoes and fish School Section Lake primarily for bass and bluegill.

Season: The park campground is open from May 1 to October and during the summer is often filled during holidays and the weekends. You can reserve a site or a cabin by calling the park office ☎ 231-972-7450 after May 1. For information from October to May call Mecosta County Park System at ☎ 231-832-3246.

27

Tubbs Island

Pere Marquette State Forest

Campground: Rustic
County: Mecosta
Nearest Community: Barryton
Sites: 12
Reservations: No
Fee: $15

Information: Mecosta County Parks
☎ (231) 832-3246
www.mecostacountyparks.com

There are two state forest campgrounds on Tubbs Lake in Mecosta County. The first is located on the east shore and is called, simply enough, Tubbs Lake Campground. It has 21 sites, many of them right on the water, and all of them secluded in a well forested area that is typical of most state forest facilities. It's a nice place to spend a weekend but the second is nicer. It's an island.

What was originally a hill overlooking the west side of the lake is now Tubbs Island when the surrounded areas were flooded to create a waterfowl habitat known as Martiny Flooding, but you don't need a boat to reach it.

Tubbs Island is reached by driving across a narrow dike, and once on the island you'll discover a delightful state forest campground where there is a view of water or marshes from every site. The state forest facility is managed by Mecosta County Park Commission, no doubt the reason it's so well maintained. While there are only 12 sites, two are walk-in and often are available for tent campers when the rest of the loop is filled.

The only drawback is the lack of swimming in the campground and the large number of cottages along the south shore of Tubbs Lake.

Directions: From US-10, head south on M-66, pass through the town of Barryton, and in 12 miles turn west on 17 Mile Road for 1.5 miles. Turn south on 45th Avenue and then west on Madison Road, and in a little over a mile you'll pass the posted entrance to Tubbs Lake State Forest Campground. The posted drive to Tubbs Island State Forest Campground is another 2 miles west.

An angler with his first bluegill from Tubbs Lake. Tubbs Island Campground provides an excellent opportunity for children and families to fish from shore for bluegill and other species of panfish.

Campground: It's easy to understand the popularity of Tubbs Island; every site overlooks the water. There is a single loop of 10 drive-in sites located in a lightly forested area of hardwoods with views of either Tubbs Lake or marshy Lost Lake to the west. The last two sites are designated as walk-in and are located at the top of the island in a semi-open area that has a great view of the lakes as well as all your neighbors below. Campers park their vehicles along the loop and walk 30 yards to where they can pitch their tent. All sites have tables and fire rings while vault toilets and hand pumps for water are along the loop.

Fishing: The 116-acre lake is an excellent fishery that includes northern pike, perch, largemouth bass, and black crappies, but it's best known as a panfish lake with bluegills and pumpkinseed sunfish. Tubbs Lake isn't stocked and hasn't been since 1941.

There is a fish cleaning station and an improved boat ramp on the island along with parking for a few vehicles and trailers. Bluegills and sunfish can also be caught from shore with simple bobber rigs, making the lake an ideal fishery for children. In all, there are six public boat ramps accessing the Martiny Flooding which is composed of six lakes, though many are little more than a small opening in a cattail marsh.

Season: The campground is generally open from early April through mid-November, closing when it's too hazardous to drive across the dike. It is often filled weekends from late June through August.

28

Paris

Mecosta County Park

Campground: Modern
County: Mecosta
Nearest Community: Paris
Sites: 68
Reservations: Yes

Fee: $15-$20 plus vehicle entry fee
Information: Park office
☎ (231) 796-3420
🌐 www.mecostacountyparks.com

In 1881, Michigan opened its second fish rearing facility near the town of Paris because of its excellent railroad connections with the rest of the state and abundant water source of the nearby Muskegon River. Biologists raised salmon and brown trout fingerlings which were then placed in milk cans (painted red so as not to confuse them with real milk cans) and shipped all over Michigan on railroad baggage cars.

The Paris Fish Hatchery went on to become the state's major supplier of salmon and trout and was even renovated and expanded in the mid-1930s before the Department of Natural Resources shut it down in 1964 as an outdated facility. The impressive white building, ponds, and raceways are still there and today are what make the Mecosta County park so unique.

Where else can you camp at a fish hatchery, look at huge trout, even feed a trout? The 15-acre park, which opened in 1976, also features a large picnic area, a canoe launch area, one of the state's newest rails-to-trails passing through, even a replica of the Eiffel Tower.

This is Paris, after all, isn't it?

Directions: Paris Park is 6 miles north of Big Rapids on Old US-131 (also labeled Northland Drive). From US-131 depart at exit 142 and head east on 19 Mile Road and then north on Northland Drive.

Children feed waterfowl in the old hatchery ponds and raceways at Paris County Park in Mecosta County.

Campground: The modern facility has electric and water hook-ups along with heated restrooms and showers. The 68-sites are located in a semi-open grassy area with scattered hardwoods. It's well shaded but offers little privacy, and none of the sites are near the Muskegon River or have a view of the water. Sites are $15 per night for water and electric hook-ups; $20 a night for electric, water and sewer. There are also three camper cabins in the campground for $35 a night.

Day-use Facilities: Across from the campground is a large day-use area with a shelter, tables, pedestal grills, swings and other playground equipment. Park here and stroll through the old hatchery ponds and raceways which have been converted into an interesting wildlife area where you see a variety of semi-domesticated ducks, Canada geese, and swans or some very impressive rainbow trout, some up to 10 pounds in weight. Both bird feed (dry corn) and fish feed (pellets) are available from dispensers for a handful while sidewalks, bridges, and stone fences wind through the area and past a small replica of the Eiffel Tower.

The historic Paris Fish Hatchery was opened in 1881 and today the building and the ponds and raceways are now part of Paris County Park in Mecosta County.

Fishing: The Muskegon river is a renowned fishery and this far upstream anglers target trout in spring and fall and smallmouth bass during the summer.

Canoeing: The park includes a canoe launch on the Muskegon River and parking for a limited number of vehicles for a trip down the Muskegon River. The paddle from Paris to Highbanks Park in Big Rapids is a 13-mile, four-hour trip through a mostly wide and easy river. Canoes can be rented in Big Rapids at Sawmill Canoe Livery ☎ 231-796-6408 🌐 www.sawmillmi.com.

Hiking: The newest linear state park, the White Pine Trail State Park, is the longest rail-trail in the Lower Peninsula and passes through the middle of Paris Park on its way from Cadillac to Big Rapids (see A Park Within A Park on the following page).

WHITE PINE TRAIL STATE PARK: A PARK WITHIN A PARK

Passing through Paris Park is White Pine Trail State Park, one of Michigan's four linear state parks. The White Pine stretches 92 miles from Cadillac south to Comstock Park near Grand Rapids, making it the longest rail-trail in the Lower Peninsula.

It was dedicated in July 1995, and within two years Friends of the White Pine Trail were formed to work towards paving its surface. More than 50 miles of the trail have been paved so far including a 13-mile segment from Big Rapids, through Paris Park to Reed City.

The converted abandoned railroad corridor makes for a relatively straight trail with very gentle grades. There are no heart-pounding hills here to confront cyclists or in-line skaters, and it's extremely scenic.

The main staging area in Big Rapids is a train depot on the corner of Maple Street and M-20 that was built a month after the Grand Rapids & Indiana Railroad arrived in 1870. From the depot you head north and within a mile cross the Muskegon River on the 319-foot-long Whites Bridge. The railroad trestle is the longest of the 14 bridges the trail utilizes and provides an excellent vantage point to gaze up and down the river.

Paris is another scenic stretch. A half mile south of the small town, the trail sidles a bluff to put you right above the swirling currents of the Muskegon River and along side wooded hillsides that come alive in the spring with skunk cabbage and wildflowers. Beyond the park, the White Pine winds another 6.5 miles through a rural landscape, woodlots, and Reed City to US-10, the end of the paved portion.

The White Pine is so popular that Paris County Park now rents bicycles at the campground office for $5 an hour or $15 for four hours. For a trail map or more information, contact the Friends of the White Pine Trail 🌐 www.whitepinetrail.com.

Season: The campground is open from May to October or sometimes later depending on the weather. On the weekends it is busy but rarely filled, and there is no problem obtaining a site Sunday through Wednesday. You can reserve a site or a cabin by calling the park office ☎ 231-796-3420 after May 1. For information from October to May call Mecosta County Park System at ☎ 231-832-3246.

29

Merrill Lake

Mecosta County Park

Campground: Modern and semi-modern
County: Mecosta
Nearest Community: Barryton
Sites: 146
Reservations: Yes
Fee: $14-$18 plus vehicle entry fee
Information: Park office
☎ (989) 382-7158
www.mecostacountyparks.com

Situated between two lakes in the heart of the Lower Peninsula, Merrill Lake Park is an excellent campground in a natural setting. Best of all, there always seems to be a site available. The park has a wide range of facilities including modern sites, rustic sites and even rental cabins. The two lakes, Gorrel and Merrill, double the opportunities for anglers while children can explore the surrounding woods and swamps that give this 90-acre Mecosta County park a Northwoods appearance.

Directions: Merrill Lake is located in the northeast corner of Mecosta County with an entrance off M-66 just a mile south of the Osceola County Line.

Campground: Merrill has a total of 146 sites. There are 122 modern sites with both water and electric hook-ups and located close together in an open setting. The modern sites are split between two loops, one overlooking each lake but not directly on the water. The 24 rustic sites are off by themselves in a stand of woods that is almost entirely surround by a marsh. This can be a beautiful spot to pitch the tent in the fall and a little buggy in late May and June.

The park also has four rental cabins with a pair located side-by-side near the modern sites on Gorrel Lake and the other two along the rustic loop. The cabins sleep six with two sets of bunk beds and a loft. Other amenities include a table, benches, and a cooking counter inside.

A modern site is $18 per night, a rustic site $14 per night, and the cabins are $35 per night. A vehicle entry fee is also required and is $25 for the season, $15 for three-days or a weekend, or $6 per day.

Day-use Facilities: The park has a pair of beaches with one on each lake along with a picnic area, playground equipment, and a shelter on Merrill Lake. Near the modern sites is also a baseball field and horseshoe courts.

Fishing: There is a boat launch with additional parking for trailers on each lake along with a fishing pier for shore anglers on Gorrel Lake and a fish cleaning station in the modern campground. Merrill Lake is the larger of the two and is fished for bass, perch, crappies, and even northern pike. Gorrel Lake is smaller, totally undeveloped, and restricts the size of motors to 10 horsepower. It's a very scenic place to cast for bass and panfish.

Season: The park is open for camping from May 1 to October. Other than an occasional holiday weekend, this campground is rarely filled. You can reserve sites or cabins in advance by calling the park office ☎ 989-382-7158 and then sending in the full payment at least three days before your arrival.

30

Herrick Recreation Area

Isabella County Park

Campground: Modern
County: Isabella
Nearest Community: Clare
Sites: 73
Reservations: Yes

Fee: $20 to $25
Information: Park office
☎ (989) 386-2010
🌐 www.isabellacounty.org/parks

Herrick County Park is a 113-acre unit of Isabella County, protecting four spring-fed ponds. After a major renovation in the early 1990s, Herrick went from rustic to modern with vastly improved day-use facilities, making the park a much more pleasant weekend getaway for campers. Its location just south of Clare also means it is an easy-to-reach destination for people in Lansing, Flint, Saginaw, and Midland.

Directions: Herrick is 2.5 miles southeast of Clare. From US-27, turn east on Herrick Road to the park entrance.

Campground: Herrick has 73 modern sites offering 20/30 amp service and central water hook-ups at every site along with a dump station and heated restrooms. A portion of the sites is in a stand of red pine, the rest in a semi-open setting. On a hill overlooking South Pond are five rental cabins that sleep four persons in two rooms. Each cabin has electric outlets, an outside faucet for water, and a covered porch overlooking the pond.

A campsite is $20 per night for Isabella county residents, $25 for non-county residents. Cabins are $40 for county residents and $45 for non-county residents. No vehicle entry permit is required when camping.

Day-use Facilities: Herrick features an elaborate railroad-theme play area for children along with additional play equipment within the campground. The Swimming Pond includes a beach and a modern bathhouse, and two pavilions in the large picnic area can be reserved in advance.

Fishing: All four ponds within the park can be fished and have access sites on them for anglers. The South Pond is the largest and has a place to launch small boats. Anglers target primarily bluegill and other panfish, and park officials have worked with DNR biologists in recent years in an attempt to eliminate the problem of stunted fish. Because of the numerous but small panfish, the ponds are excellent places to introduce young children to fishing.

Season: Campsites and cabins can be reserved by contacting Herrick Recreation ☎ 989-386-2010 or emailing parks@isabellacounty.org.

31

Gladwin

City Park

Campground: Modern	**Reservations:** Yes
County: Gladwin	**Fee:** $21
Nearest Community: Gladwin	**Information:** Park office
Sites: 61	☎ (989) 426-8126

Entering Gladwin City Park can be a little discomforting. From M-61 you turn into the entrance drive where on one side is the Gladwin County Courthouse and on the other the Gladwin County Jail, complete with coils of razor wire on its roof. Once past the jail, you enter one of the most delightful campgrounds in mid-Michigan. This is a place where anybody not on a 10 Most Wanted List can relax.

Originally a state park, the city acquired the 25-acre facility in 1983 and turned it into a modern campground that is a short walk from downtown Gladwin. The fact that it's right behind the county jail, a place swarming with police cars, is a good thing. "We never have any problems down there," said one city official.

Directions: From I-75 depart at exit 190 and head west on M-61 to reach Gladwin in 23 miles. The entrance drive for the park is on the south side of M-61 between the Gladwin County Courthouse and the County Jail.

Campground: You may be in downtown Gladwin—only a five-minute walk from a steamed latte at the Northern Espresso Shop—but you would never know it from your campsite. The park is set in the bottomlands of the Cedar River and is well shaded by a scattering of mature maple, ash, and beech trees. The grassy sites are bordered on one side by the river, on the other by a forested bluff. What you hear from your campsite is the gurgle of the Cedar, not the traffic on M-61.

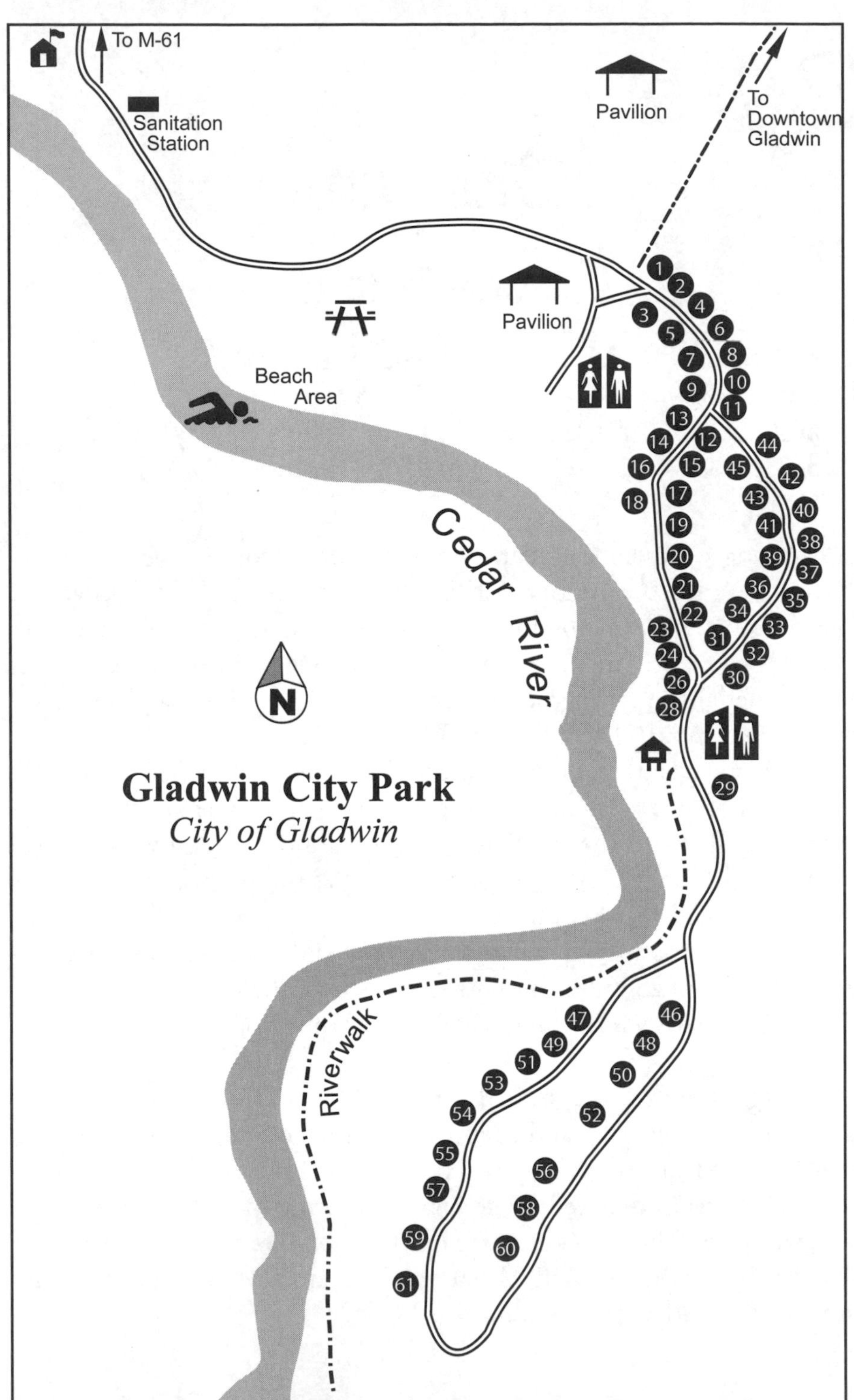
To M-61
Sanitation Station
Pavilion
To Downtown Gladwin
Pavilion
Beach Area
Cedar River
Riverwalk
N
Gladwin City Park
City of Gladwin
1
2
3
4
5
6
7
8
9
10
11
12
13
14
15
16
17
18
19
20
21
22
23
24
26
28
29
30
31
32
33
34
35
36
37
38
39
40
41
42
43
44
45
46
47
48
49
50
51
52
53
54
55
56
57
58
59
60
61

The campground has 61 sites, all of them with electric hook-ups and 16 sites with water hook-ups. A few of them in the Lower Campground (No. 23 through No. 26) are right on the river. The 16 sites in the Upper Campground are on a bluff above the river. Other amenities include a restroom and dump station for recreational vehicles.

Day-use Facilities: The park also has courts for tennis, basketball, volleyball, and horseshoes along with play equipment and a special Tot Lot. One spot of the Cedar has been developed into a small beach and swimming area. Within the picnic area are two pavilions that can be reserved in advance.

Fishing: Anglers fish the Cedar River for trout and often follow Riverwalk to holes and runs downstream from the campground.

Hiking: Departing from site No. 28 is Riverwalk, a footpath that skirts the Cedar River for more than a mile. There is also a short path that leads from the park to downtown Gladwin.

Tubing: The most popular activity in the park during the summer is tubing. Young floaters will drop their inner tubes into the Red Cedar near the park office, drift past the picnic area and campground and then continue on for another half mile or so, using the Riverwalk to return to their campsites.

More adventurous floaters will load their gear into the car and drive six blocks north of the campground on Bowery Road and then west on First Street to the city's North Park. By beginning here you can enjoy a three-mile float and only know you're in Gladwin when you drift underneath M-61.

Season: The campground is open from May to December, remaining open for the entire firearm deer season. There are discounted rates after Labor Day weekend. You can reserve sites online at 🌐 www.gladwin.org and then clicking on "City Park and Campground."

32

Island Lake

Huron National Forest

Campground: Rustic
County: Oscoda
Nearest Community: Rose City
Sites: 17
Reservations: No
Fee: $15
Information: Mio Ranger District
☎ (989) 826-3252

First impressions can be misleading. Take Island Lake Campground for example. The first thing many people notice driving through the Huron National Forest campground are the cottages bordering the loop.

And then maybe the cottages across from the small beach, cottages all along the shoreline of the 65-acre lake, cottages everywhere.

Ugh! How do you escape?

You pitch your tent in one of the lightly shaded sites that overlook the water, throw swim suits and towels in a small pack, and lose yourself along the Island Lake Nature Trail on your way to Loon Lake Recreation Area. Within minutes you're trudging up a ridge, deep in a stand of impressive oaks and an occasional towering white pine and seemingly miles from anywhere, not a cottage in sight.

The campground and nearby day-use area are linked by foot trails and together make for an excellent place to camp, providing opportunities for limited hiking, fishing, boating, or just wiggling your toes in two different beaches.

Directions: From I-75 depart onto M-33 (exit 202) and head north through Rose City. Six miles north of the town turn west on County Road 486. The campground is a half mile past the entrance of Loon Lake along CR 486.

Campground: The campground is a single loop located on a gently sloping hillside leading down to Island Lake. The 17 sites feature paved parking spurs, fire rings with sliding grills, and tables while nearby are four vault toilets and two hand pumps for water. The sites are lightly

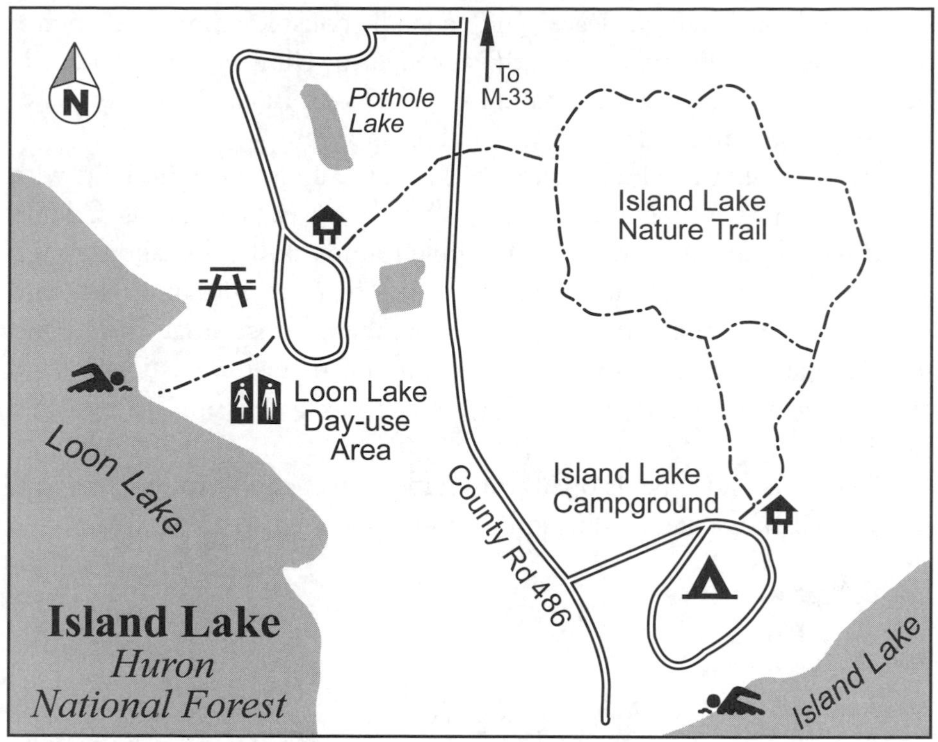

shaded with little privacy between them. Cottages border each side of the campground, but one rents out canoes, rowboats, and pedalboats to campers and the other sells firewood.

Day-use Facilities: There is a small day-use area within Island Lake composed of a parking area, grassy area with tables and pedestal grills, and a thin strip of beach overlooking a marked swimming area. Hours are 6 AM to 10 PM.

Even better is Loon Lake Recreation Area and well worth the two-minute drive or the 0.8-mile hike. The 90-acre lake has few visible cottages on it as most of the north and west shore is national forest, and the beach is wider than at Island Lake. There is also a bathhouse with flush toilets, tables, pedestal grills, and drinking fountains. A Huron National Forest vehicle pass is required to enter Loon Lake ($5 daily, $25 annual).

Fishing: There are no boat ramps at either facility although hand-carried boats could be easily launched. Island Lake is 65 acres large with fair fishing for perch, rock bass, bluegill, and largemouth bass, though it's rare to see any bass larger than 12 inches here. There is a ban on boat motors in the lake.

Loon Lake is larger, clearer, and generally considered to have a better fishery, particularly for largemouth bass but also yellow perch and bluegill. Although there is no public boat ramp here, Loon Lake Campground ☎ 989-685-2407 off M-33 has bait and boats for rent.

Hiking: Island Lake Nature Trail is basically a one-mile loop with a spur near post number 14 leading off to Loon Lake, crossing County Road 486 along the way. It is a 1.4-mile round trip to the lake through an area laden with glacial evidence in the form of morainal hills and potholes. Along the way you pass 20 numbered posts that correspond to a pamphlet available from the campground manager. Posts point out everything from where a lightning bolt struck a red pine to an 1890 logging trail.

Season: Island Lake is open from mid-May to mid-September and is often filled on weekends during July and early August.

33

Wagner Lake

Huron National Forest

Campground: Rustic	**Reservations:** No
County: Oscoda	**Fee:** $15
Nearest Community: Mio	**Information:** Mio Ranger District
Sites: 12	☎ (989) 826-3252

Wagner Lake is a small body of water 7 miles south of Mio and completely surrounded by National Forest land. Bordering its east side is a small campground. One compliments the other extremely well, and a stay here is usually a quiet, relaxing night on the shore of a scenic lake. The key is getting a site.

With only 12 sites, Wagner Lake tends to be full most weekends from late June through mid-August. The facility is rustic, but its paved interior road and spurs make it especially popular with RV campers. Site availability is on a first-come-first-serve basis, and to ensure getting a spot, plan on arriving Wednesday evening or Thursday morning.

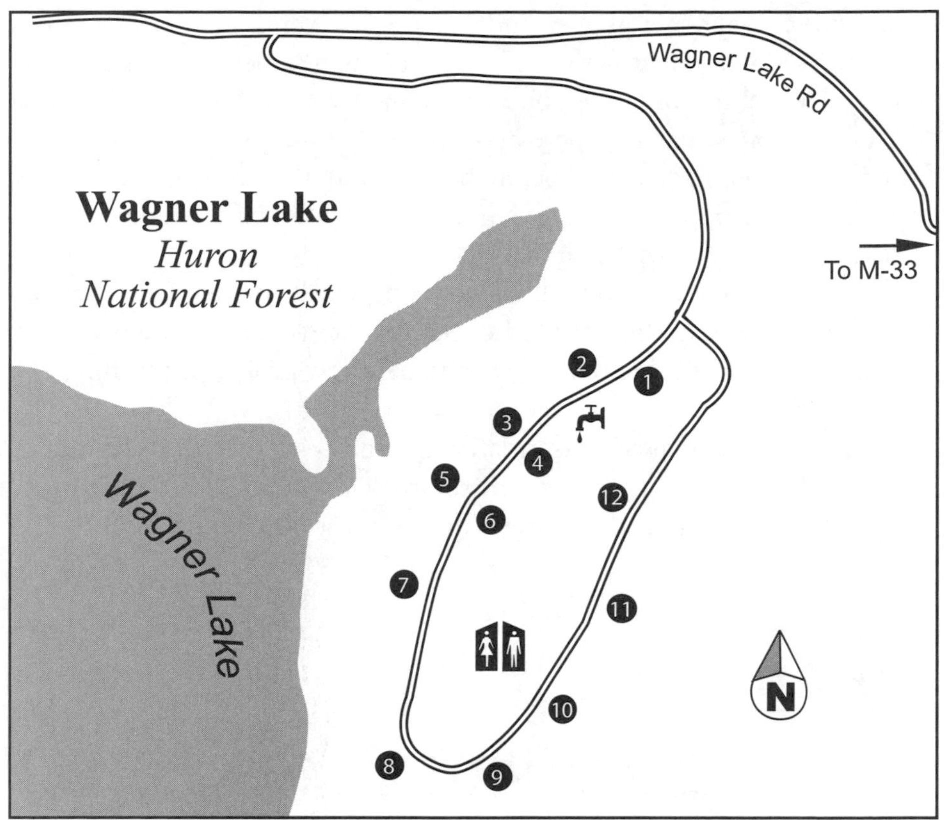

There are no hiking trails nearby and the beach is limited, but there is good bluegill fishing in a lake small enough for canoes or cartop rowboats.

Directions: From Rose City head north on M-33 for 9 miles then turn west (left) on Wagner Lake Road, a dirt road that passes the paved entrance of the campground in 1.2 miles. Wagner Lake Road is 7 miles south from M-72 in Mio.

Campground: The campground is a single loop of 12 paved sites in an area wooded in both pines and towering hardwoods. Both the loop and sites can be easily handled by the largest motor homes while in the middle of the loop is a pair of vault toilets and a hand pump for water. Half of the sites are just up from the shoreline with a full view of the lake. The other half is located on a gently sloping hillside and still provide partial views of the water.

Day-use Facilities: The campground features a small sandy beach with a marked swimming area that is shallow. Though there is a visitor's parking lot near it, the beach is limited to campers only.

Fishing: Wagner Lake extends across 26 acres and is free from cottages or docks to provide a pleasant angling experience in a scenic setting. The fishing must be good at times, as a few locals often stash a small boat along the shore here and there. Forest Service rangers report fisheries of bluegill, bass, and perch, but without a doubt this is primarily panfish waters. Bluegill fishing is good while most bass landed tend to measure less than 10 inches in length.

There is no boat launch within the campground, making hand-carried boats ideal here. Children and other boatless anglers can follow a sandy path along the north side of the lake and have few problems reaching any stretch of the shore.

Season: The managed season is from Memorial Day through Labor Day, but if spring weather is warm the park hosts begin collecting fees earlier. This campground is often filled on the weekends in July and August.

34

Leverentz Lakes

Pere Marquette State Forest

Campground: Rustic
County: Lake
Nearest Community: Baldwin
Sites: 17
Reservations: No
Fee: $15
Information: DNR Cadillac Service Center
☎ (231) 775-9727

Is this one or two campgrounds? There are two separate loops, each with its own entrance, each its own lake, with its own vault toilets and other facilities. Yet the numbering system that begins on the sites along Big Leverentz Lake finish on Little Leverentz Lake.

Does it matter? Either way this is a delightful place to camp with lake-view sites, good fishing opportunities, and a trail system that wanders into the woods. Best of all, despite its close proximity to Baldwin, it does not receive an overload of campers and other users.

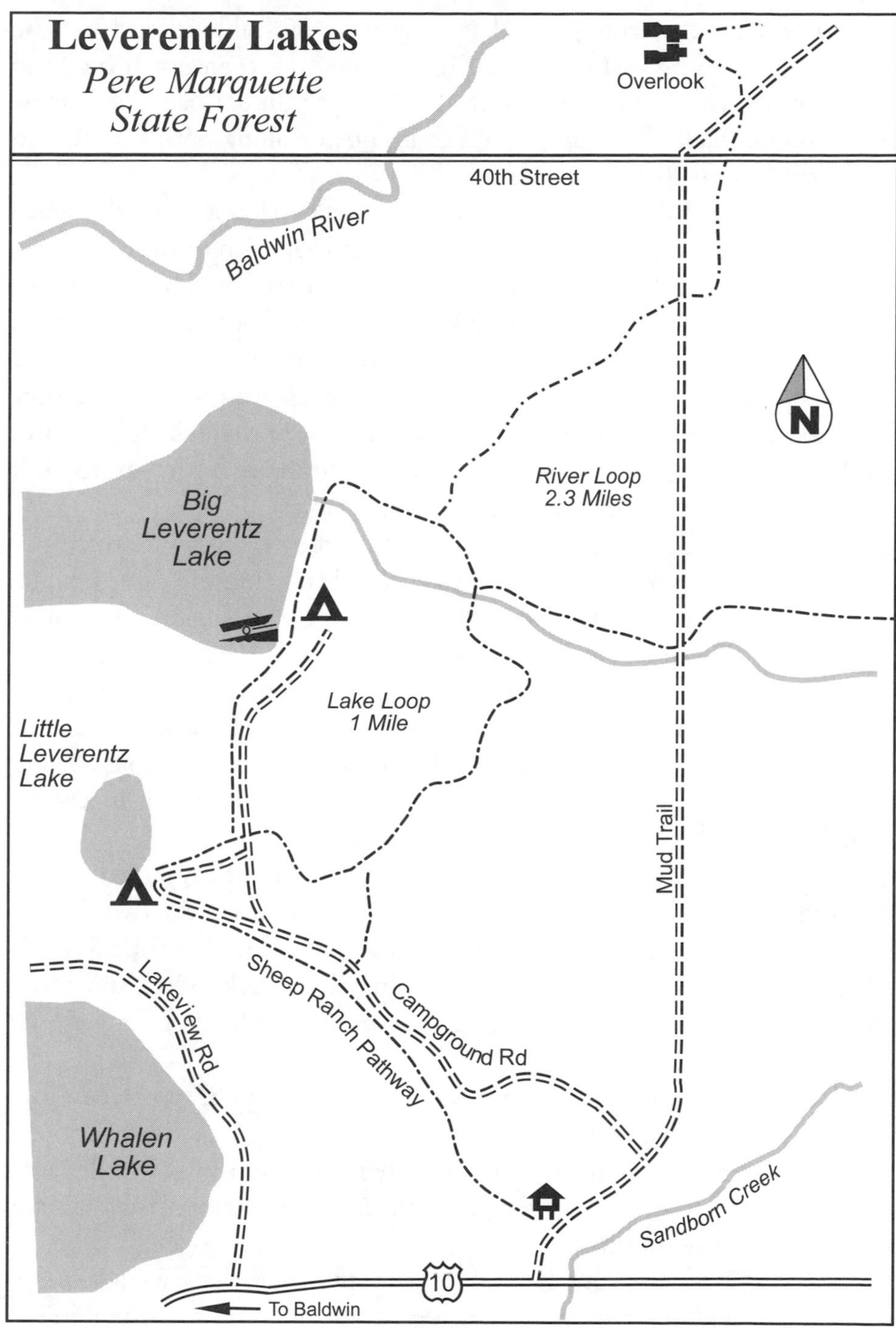
Leverentz Lakes
Pere Marquette
State Forest
Overlook
40th Street
Baldwin River
River Loop
2.3 Miles
Big
Leverentz
Lake
Lake Loop
1 Mile
Little
Leverentz
Lake
Mud Trail
Lakeview Rd
Sheep Ranch Pathway
Campground Rd
Whalen
Lake
Sandborn Creek
10
To Baldwin
N

Directions: The campground is northeast of Baldwin and can be reached by heading east on US-10 for 2 miles and then north on Mud Trail. Immediately turn west (left) on Campground Road and follow signs to either lake. The campgrounds are posted along both US-10 and on Campground Road.

Campground: Big Leverentz has 10 sites on two loops along the south side of the lake. Eight sites are situated on one loop with most of them on a low rise for a nice view of the water. The other two are off by themselves near the boat launch, and all of them are well spread out in a mixed stand of pines and hardwoods with moderate undergrowth.

Little Leverentz is to the south and has seven sites on a single loop. The area is a little more forested in pine, but only one site is on the water while within view are the backsides of several cottages. Both feature vault toilets, hand pumps for water, fire rings, and tables.

Fishing: On Big Leverentz there is an unimproved dirt boat launch and additional parking for two, maybe three, vehicles within the campground. Floating on Big Leverentz next to the launch is a 50-foot-long, T-shaped fishing pier and, in a lake this small, you can reach a lot of water with a good cast from it. The lake is completely undeveloped, and its west side is heavy weeded with aquatic plants and lily pads but the rest is clear. For the most part, Big Leverentz is panfish waters with an occasional bluegill reaching nine to ten inches but most of them small. Every once in a while somebody will also pull out a largemouth bass.

There is no launch on Little Leverentz, but a pathway next to site number 14 leads to the shoreline. The lake is the better of the two though it is slightly smaller at 5.6 acres. It has a weedy shoreline, but the middle is 30 feet deep. Little Leverentz contains bluegill, pumpkinseed, and perch along with largemouth bass and northern pike and attracts moderate pressure in the summer.

Hiking: The trailhead for Sheep Ranch Pathway is posted in Big Leverentz. It's composed of several loops including the River Loop, a 2.3-mile trek to an overlook on the Baldwin River to the north. Because of clearcuts, this pathway is a far better ski trail in the winter than it is for hikers during the summer.

Season: Big Leverentz is the more popular of the two lakes and occasionally will fill up on a July or August weekend but not often due to the large number of state and national campgrounds in the Baldwin area.

35

Silver Creek

Pere Marquette State Forest

Campground: Rustic
County: Lake
Nearest Community: Luther
Sites: 26
Reservations: No
Fee: $15
Information: DNR Cadillac Service Center
☎ (231) 775-9727

No matter how you arrive at Silver Creek State Forest Campground, whether it's in the bow of a canoe or the backseat of a car, this is a delightful spot to spend a night or even a few days.

The Pine River is one of the state's blue ribbon trout streams as well as one of the most popular canoe routes during the summer. You can paddle downstream, hike along its banks upstream, or just sit in your riverbend campsite dabbling a worm in hopes of landing a trout.

The rustic facility features many sites along the water along with a handful of walk-in sites and is not nearly as busy as the national forest campgrounds downstream.

Directions: Silver Creek is located north of Baldwin and west of Cadillac. From US-131 the campground is reached by exiting onto Luther Highway and heading west for Luther, a town on the banks of the Little Manistee River. At Luther head north on State Road for 6 miles to the posted entrance of the facility.

Campground: Situated along a single loop are 26 sites in a forest of young beech and other hardwoods with a thick undergrowth. The sites are well spread out and secluded from each other while a handful are right on the river, some so close people set up lawn chairs in front of their trailer and fish for trout. All sites feature the usual fire rings, tables, hand pumps, and vault toilets.

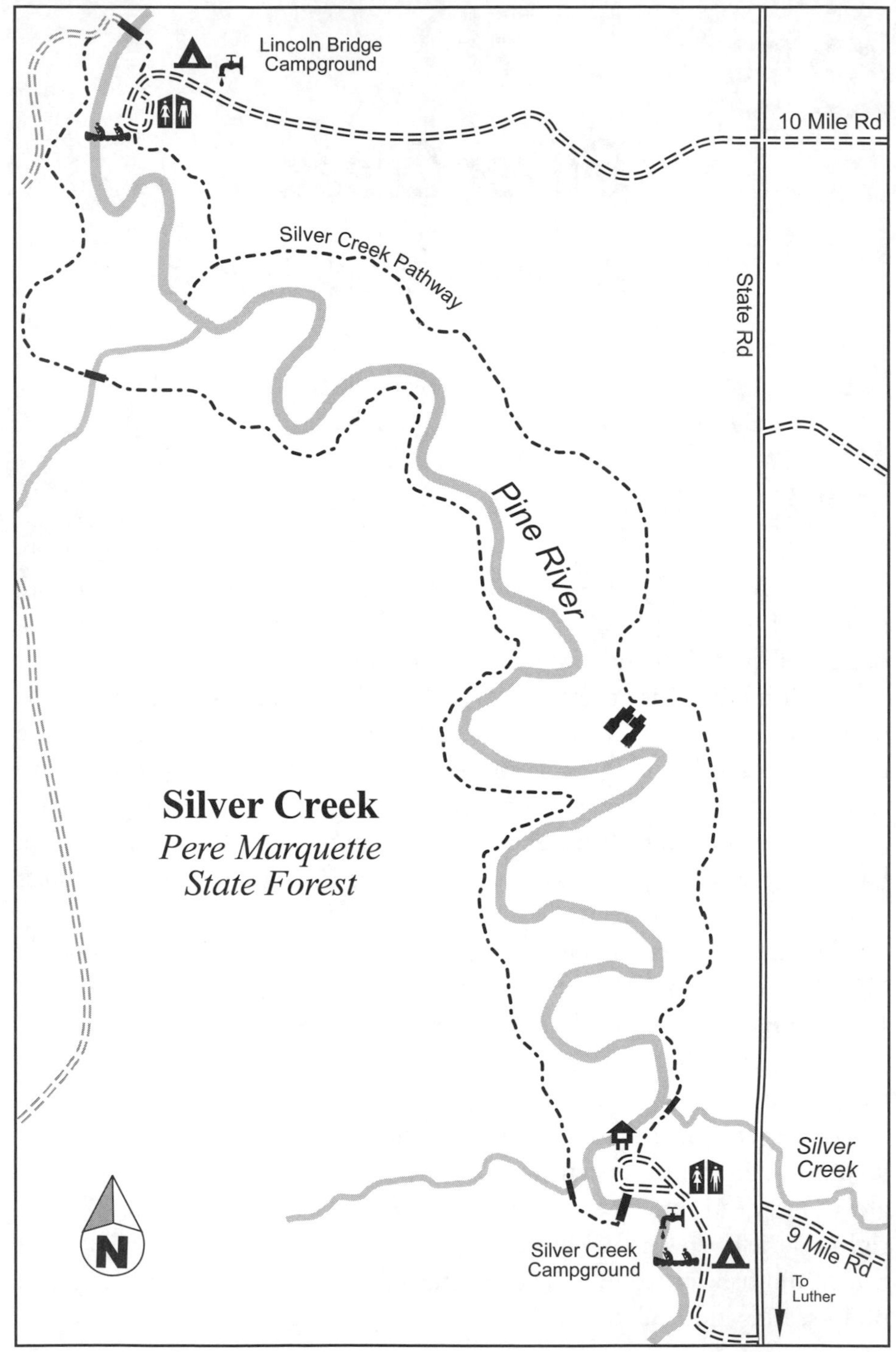
Lincoln Bridge
Campground
10 Mile Rd
Silver Creek Pathway
State Rd
Pine River
Silver Creek
Pere Marquette
State Forest
Silver
Creek
9 Mile Rd
Silver Creek
Campground
To
Luther
N

A canoer prepares dinner at his Silver Creek campsite after a day of paddling the Pine River.

Another nine sites are walk-in or canoe sites located on a point formed by a big horseshoe curve in the Pine River. Most overlook this gentle river and No. 23 is one of the best riverbank sites in the Lower Peninsula as it's shaded by several tall cedar and spruce trees and lies above a small stretch of rapids. The parking lot is less than 25 yards from the walk-in sites.

Fishing: The Pine is regarded as a good-to-excellent trout stream with anglers focusing on rainbow and brookies. This far upstream the Pine is 10–15 yards wide and wadable in most places while fishing pressure is moderate. Most anglers toss worms or small spinners into deep pools, under log jams, and past undercut banks for primarily brown trout. Brook trout tend to dominate the river upstream near Skookum Bridge. Use the foot bridge and the Silver Creek Pathway along the west side of the river for the best access to the river downstream.

Hiking: Silver Creek Pathway was rerouted in the late 1990s and is now a 4-mile loop that extends between Silver Creek and Lincoln Bridge State Forest Campgrounds along both sides of the scenic Pine River. The key to the trail's development was the installation of a pair of bridges, one in each campground, that allow hikers and mountain bikers to cross the river and return to the trailhead.

The pathway begins near site No. 10 and quickly crosses the creek near its confluence with the Pine, a popular swimming spot—especially its rope swing—for children staying in the campground. One of the most scenic stretches of the trail is along the west bank, just beyond the Silver Creek Bridge. At one point you are within view of the Pine for almost a mile, making this leg of the pathway one of the finest river trails in Michigan.

Canoeing: The Pine originates near LeRoy in Osceola County and flows 60 miles before merging with the Manistee River. Almost 40 miles of it is floatable in a canoe, making the entire river an ideal three-day float. The first put-in is Edgett's Bridge on Raymond Road, and from here it's a five-hour paddle to Silver Creek. The last take-out point is Low Bridge on M-55, a nine-hour paddle.

A permit for each canoe is required for paddling the Pine in the Manistee National Forest between May 1 and September 30. With less than 700 permits available per day for both private and livery canoes, reservations are mandatory for any weekend from mid-June through August. For more information or to reserve a permit for the Pine River, call the Baldwin USFS Ranger Station ☎ 231- 745-4631.

Canoe liveries that service the river include Pine River Paddlesport Center ☎ 231-862-3471 🌐 www.thepineriver.com and Shomler Canoe & Kayak Rental ☎ 231-862-3475 🌐 www.shomlercanoes.com. Pine River Paddlesport Center also operates the Walker Bridge Canoe Livery located just south of the campground off of State Road.

Season: The only time this campground is filled on the weekends is when a large group of canoeists pass through, but that is rare this far upstream.

36

Hemlock

Manistee National Forest

Campground: Rustic
County: Wexford
Nearest Community: Cadillac
Sites: 19
Reservations: No
Fee: $14
Information: Manistee Ranger District
☎ (231) 723-2211

A rustic and much more quiet alternative to the William Mitchell State Park is Hemlock on a back bay of Lake Mitchell just 5 miles east of Cadillac. Unlike the large and compact campground at the state park that borders M-119, an extremely busy road during the summer, Hemlock is a considerably smaller facility with a wooded appearance while still providing access to fisheries of Lake Mitchell and Lake Cadillac.

The drawback is the national forest campground does not have a swimming area of any kind and it tends to fill up as often as the state park, where at least you can reserve a site in advance.

Directions: From US-131, head north on M-115 and then just before reaching Mitchell State Park, turn west on M-55. Within a mile turn right on Pole Road and the campground entrance is reached in another mile.

Campground: Hemlock is a managed campground of 19 rustic sites. The loop is paved and so are the spurs with many of them pull-throughs, ideal for large RVs. The sites are well separated and secluded in an area that includes both a pine plantation and a stand of spruce and hardwoods.

Six sites (5, 7, 9, 11, 13, and 14) are labeled lakefront but only a few of them actually overlook the water and provide direct access to the lake. The others, most notably site 14, overlook the heavy growth of cattails along the shore, not the water.

Day-use Facilities: Near the boat launch are a few tables and fire rings including two on each side of the ramp that overlook the entire back bay. Otherwise there is no swimming area nor any hiking trails.

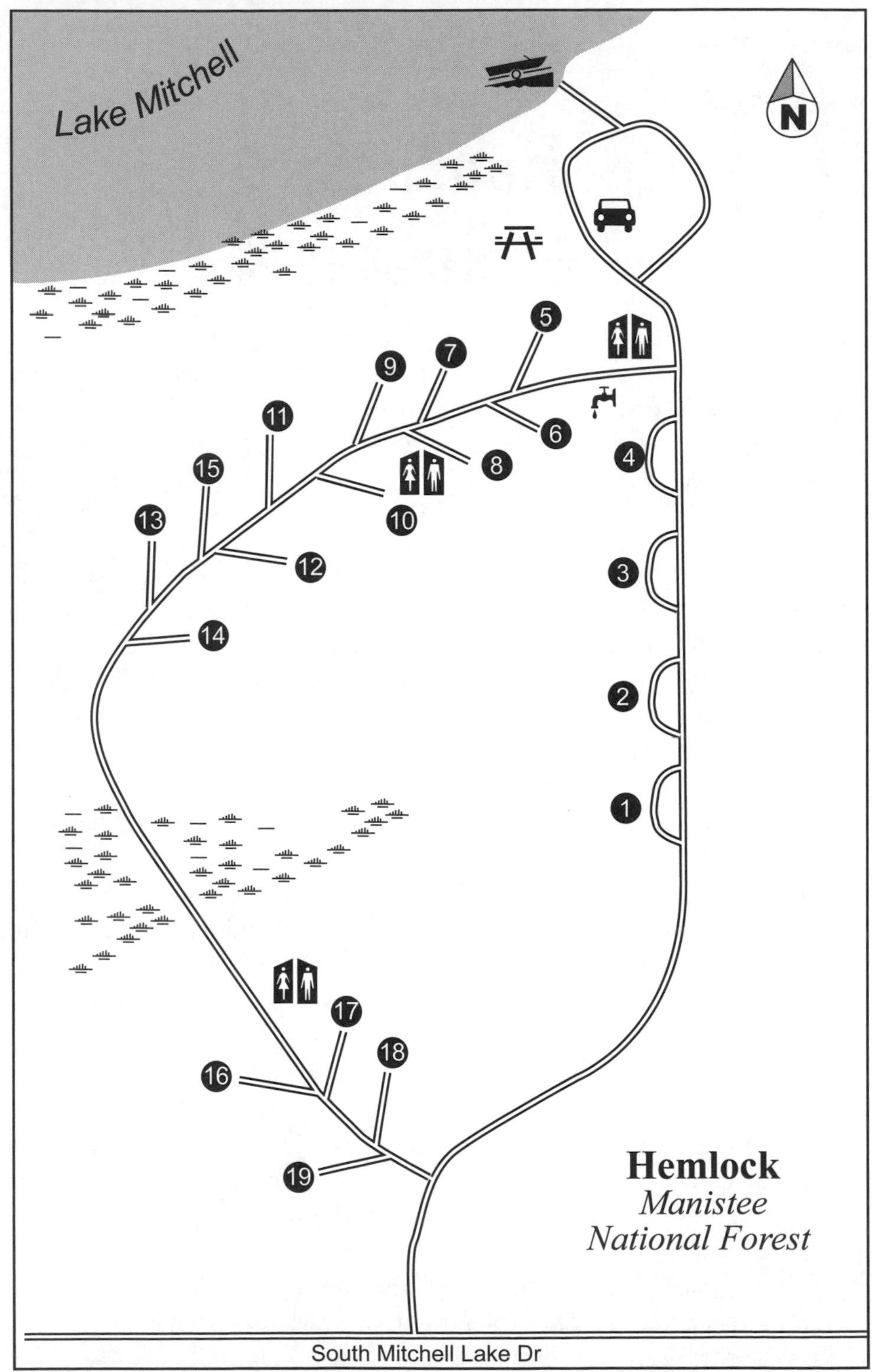
Lake Mitchell
N
1
2
3
4
5
6
7
8
9
10
11
12
13
14
15
16
17
18
19
Hemlock
Manistee
National Forest
South Mitchell Lake Dr

Fishing: An improved ramp with a metal grate bottom is situated on the lake along with parking for a handful of vehicles. The back bay is for the most part undeveloped except for cottages and docks near its entrance. Most of the shore supports a heavy growth of cattails, reeds, and other aquatic plant life—the reason, no doubt, you always see a good number of anglers.

Both Mitchell and Cadillac are known as fine walleye fisheries and are heavily fished during the summer. The 1,150-acre Lake Cadillac is an extremely busy body of water as it lies totally within the city limits of Cadillac, and its shoreline is totally developed. For that reason many anglers prefer the 2,580-acre Mitchell which also supports walleyes as well as perch, various panfish, and bass. You can put in at Hemlock and reach Cadillac by a quarter-mile canal that runs along the state park and connects the two lakes.

Season: Hemlock is open from mid-May through September. Because of its close proximity to Cadillac, the facility fills up most weekends July through August and often during the middle of the week.

37

Goose Lake

Pere Marquette State Forest

Campground: Rustic
County: Missaukee
Nearest Community: Lake City
Sites: 54
Reservations: No

Fee: $15
Information: DNR Cadillac Service Center
☎ (231) 775-9727

Goose Lake is the largest state forest campground in the Lower Peninsula and when combined with Long Lake provides almost 70 sites on the neighboring lakes. That's a lot of campsites, yet on many summer weekends these facilities are nearly filled. Located just northwest of Lake

City in a hilly and scenic section of the Pere Marquette State Forest, Goose Lake offers everything most campers seek in a rustic facility. There is good swimming and fishing opportunities and a choice of sites with many overlooking the sandy shoreline of this horseshoe-shaped lake. If this facility has too many campers for you, then just continue along the forest road to Long Lake, a much smaller campground.

Directions: From Lake City head north on M-66 and then west (left) on Sanborn Road to Al Moses Road. Here state forest signs direct you west along Goose Lake Road, a well-graded dirt road that leads a mile to Goose Lake.

Campground: Strung out along the northern shore, Goose Lake has 54 sites with most of them gathered in a half dozen small loops. Many sites are located right on the water or within view of the lake, and a few are even situated on a high shoreline bank, an especially scenic spot from your tent.

Most of the sites along the lake are close together and lack privacy, but those on the other side of the road, away from the water, are well separated and secluded in a young hardwood forest. Vault toilets and hand pumps for water are scattered throughout the campground, but many tables and fire rings are missing.

Day-Use Facilities: There isn't a marked beach area, but much of the lake's shoreline is sandy and shallow, making it pleasant for swimming.

Fishing: An improved boat ramp with a cement slab is located within the campground, but small boats can be launched from many shoreline sites. Goose Lake is a horseshoe-shaped body of water with a point in the middle and an island on its west side. Its eastern arm is narrow and very weedy, but the west arm is free of heavy aquatic growth in the middle and holds the deepest sections. Panfish are plentiful though a bluegill over 10 inches seems to be a rare catch. Anglers also target smallmouth bass and occasionally catch small northern pike.

Season: Goose Lake is managed by a campground host and on July and August weekends can be more than three-quarters filled by Saturday afternoon. The first sites to go, naturally, are those along the lake's sandy shoreline.

38

Long Lake

Pere Marquette State Forest

Campground: Rustic
County: Missaukee
Nearest Community: Lake City
Sites: 16
Reservations: No
Fee: $15
Information: DNR Cadillac Service Center
☎ (231) 775-9727

Long Lake is reached by first driving through Goose Lake campground and then following a one-way loop past several ponds before arriving at the small lake. On the way back you skirt a bluff with an overlook of Goose Lake, all part of this very hilly and scenic area just northwest of Lake City.

If you want a large campground with lakeview sites and lots of sandy shoreline for swimming, stop at Goose Lake. If you want a small, somewhat remote and quieter facility on a lake of its own, continue on to Long Lake. Many people do, the reason Long Lake is occasionally full on a summer weekend while Goose Lake has open sites.

Directions: From Lake City head north on M-66 and then west (left) on Sanborn Road to Al Moses Road. Here state forest signs direct you west along Goose Lake Road that in a mile arrives at the entrance of Goose Lake State Forest Campground. You have to drive through the campground and continue on the forest road to reach Long Lake.

Campground: Located on the northeast corner of the lake are 16 sites. Half of them are right on the shoreline with a scenic view of the length of this long and narrow body of water. The forest here is hardwoods with little undergrowth and sites tend to be close together. There is no marked swimming area or beach, but the edges of Long Lake are sandy and shallow, making it possible for children to enjoy some swimming activity.

Fishing: There is an unimproved boat launch near the end of the campground. The middle of Long Lake is free of heavy aquatic plants, but lily pads are thick at the north end. The lake supports smallmouth bass, bluegill, and some pike. Overall there is less fishing pressure here than Goose Lake because of the size of the campground. Most anglers arrive with canoes or small rowboats, and the lake is so narrow it could even be tackled in a belly boat.

Season: Long Lake usually has its own campground host and because of its limited number of sites will occasionally fill up on a July or early August weekend.

Long Lake in Pere Marquette State Forest near Lake City.

Lake Michigan

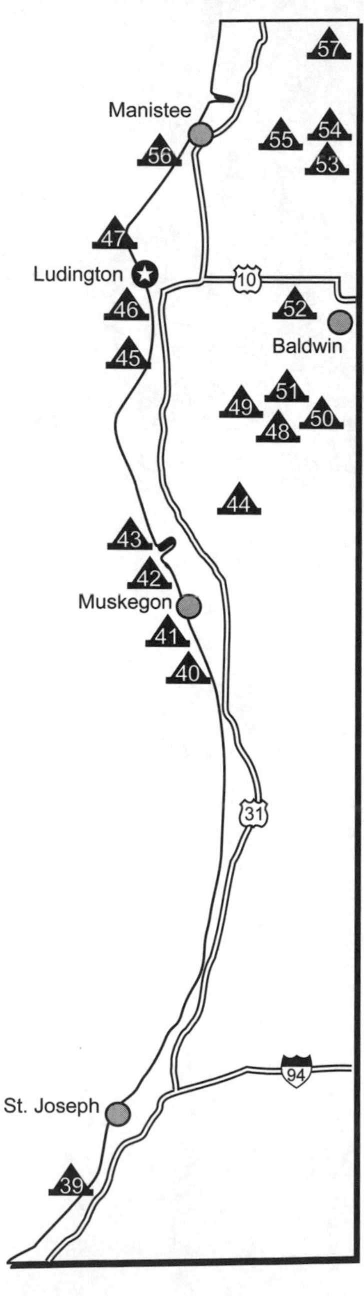

#	PARK	MODERN	SEMI-MODERN	RUSTIC	SITES	DAY-USE FACILITIES	FISHING	HIKING	BIRDING	INTERPRETIVE CENTER	BIKING	CANOEING/ KAYAKING	BOATING
39	Warren Dunes	•	•		221	•		•					
40	Grand Haven	•			174	•	•						
41	P.J. Hoffmaster	•			293	•		•					
42	Muskegon	•			106	•	•	•					
43	Pioneer	•			235	•							
44	Pines Point			•	33	•	•	•				•	
45	Charles Mears	•			175	•	•	•					
46	Buttersville	•			44	•							
47	Ludington	•	•		355	•	•	•					
48	Benton Lake			•	24	•	•	•					
49	Nichols Lake			•	28	•	•	•					
50	Shelley Lake			•	8		•						
51	Highbank Lake			•	9	•	•	•					
52	Bowman Bridge			•	20		•	•				•	
53	Old Grade			•	20		•	•					
54	Peterson Bridge			•	30	•	•					•	
55	Sand Lake			•	45	•	•	•					
56	Lake Michigan Recreation Area			•	99	•		•					
57	Seaton Creek			•	17	•	•	•				•	

39

Warren Dunes

State Park

Campground: Modern and semi-modern
County: Berrien
Nearest Community: Bridgman
Sites: 221
Reservations: Yes
Fee: $16–$27 plus vehicle entry fee
Information: State park office
☎ (269) 426-4013

Warren Dunes may be a Michigan state park, but every summer it's invaded by Hoosiers and Chicagoans. The 1,952-acre unit is the first preserve along Lake Michigan and only 12 miles north of the state border. Thus, of the 1.3 million visitors Warren Dunes draws every year, more than 80 percent of them are from outside Michigan. For this reason Warren Dunes was the first state park to charge a higher entry fee for non-residents.

Still, they pack this beautiful stretch of dunes and shoreline, and the reason is clear. The park has 2.5-miles of undeveloped lakeshore, 200-foot high sand dunes that lure an occasional hang glider, and a modern campground that still provides a little space between parties. The trick here is getting a site and sometimes during the summer just getting inside the park.

Directions: Warren Dunes is reached from I-94 by departing at exit 16 and following Red Arrow Highway south to the park entrance.

Campground: Warren Dunes has 185 sites located well away from the beach. This facility is two loops in a wooded area on the backside of the dunes, offering shade and, surprisingly, for the number of sites in it, a small degree of privacy between campers. On the southern loop are three Mini-cabins and a foot trail that leads around Mt. Randal to the day-use area on Lake Michigan. Along with tables and fire rings, each loop has a restroom with showers and play equipment for children. Some sites have

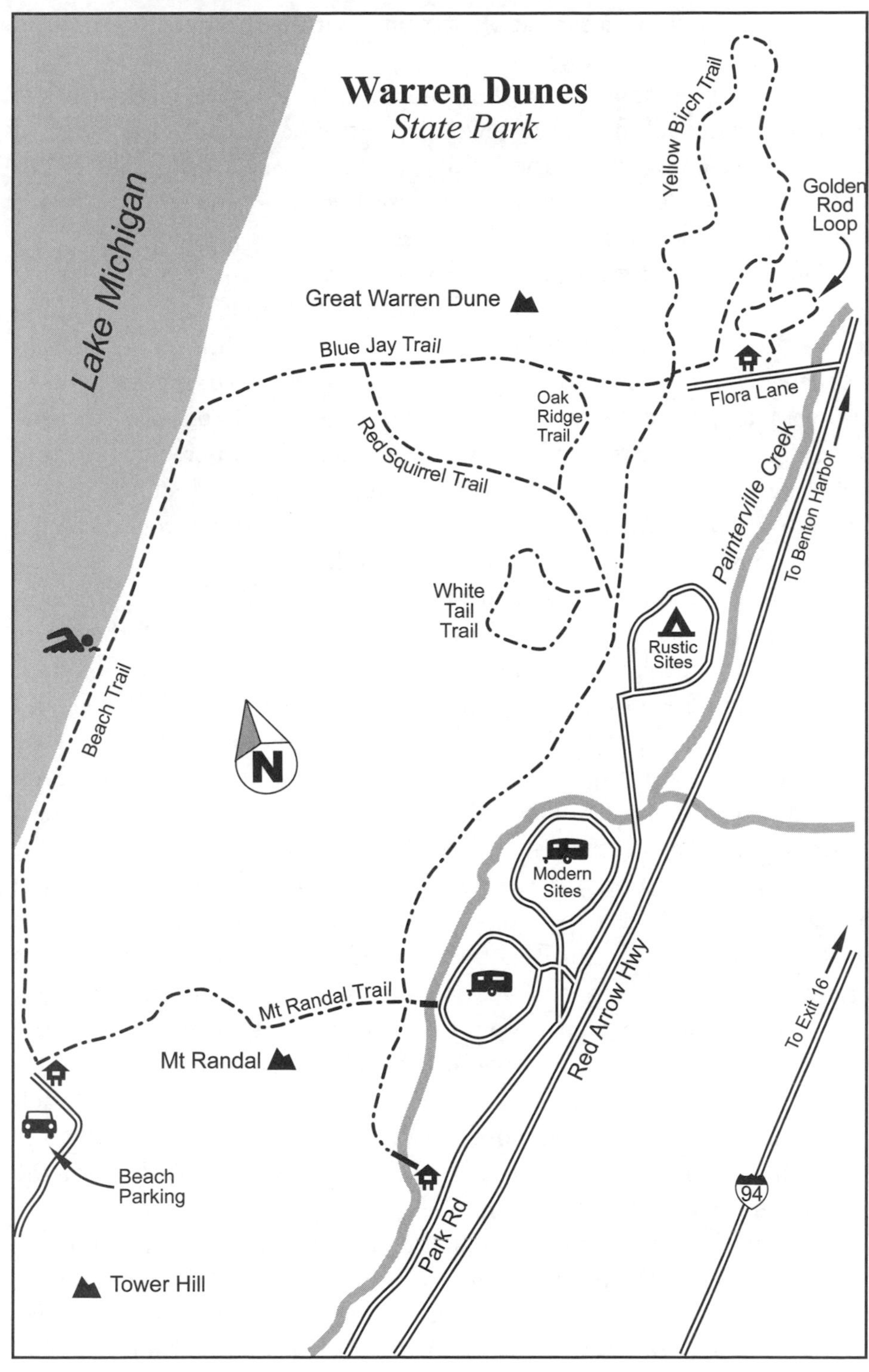
Warren Dunes
State Park
Lake Michigan
Yellow Birch Trail
Golden Rod Loop
Great Warren Dune
Blue Jay Trail
Oak Ridge Trail
Flora Lane
Red Squirrel Trail
Painterville Creek
To Benton Harbor
White Tail Trail
Rustic Sites
Beach Trail
N
Modern Sites
Mt Randal Trail
Red Arrow Hwy
To Exit 16
Mt Randal
Beach Parking
94
Park Rd
Tower Hill

50 amp service while a sanitation station is located near the registration station.

What was once an organizational camp is now the park's 36-site rustic campground located in a wooded setting a quarter mile north of the modern campground. The facility has vault toilets, but campers can walk to the modern campgrounds to use the restrooms and showers if they wish. A modern site is $25-$27 per night; a rustic site is $16.

Day-use Facilities: Separated from the rest of the park by several towering dunes is the day-use beach area of the park. There is parking for 1,500 cars along Lake Michigan, but the area still fills up on summer weekends and occasionally the staff sets up overflow parking for another 600 vehicles before they start turning people away. The popularity of the beach is easy to understand. The wide sandy beach is bordered by towering dunes on one side and the light blue waters of Lake Michigan on the other. In between are three bathhouses. The park also has a wooded picnic area bordered on one side by a wind-blown dune.

Hiking: There are more than 5 miles of maintained hiking trails in Warren Dunes with most of it forming a 4-mile loop through the dunes in the park's interior, along Lake Michigan, and back to the modern campground. The loop is a combination of the Mt. Randal, Beach, and Blue Jay trails and passes through both wooded terrain and open dunes. You enter the loop from the northern parking lot of the day-use beach area, the rustic campground, and a small trailhead near the modern campground. Plan on three hours for the entire hike.

Yellow Birch Loop is located at the end of Flora Lane, north of the park entrance on Red Arrow Highway, where there is a small parking area, trash cans, and a trail sign. This trail is a mile loop to the north that was originally built as part of the cross country ski system, but after the park constructed a 400-foot boardwalk over a marsh, hikers began using the loop, especially in the spring when it is possible to sight a variety of birds.

Finally, a popular hike in early spring is to simply walk the beach from the park's day-use area north to Weko Beach, a City of Bridgman park that adjoins the state park. Round-trip to Weko Beach from the day-use area would be a 5-mile hike.

Season: The campground is filled 90 percent of time during the summer and every weekend from the beginning of May through October. Best bet is to make reservations far in advance of your trip. To reserve a campsite contact Michigan State Park Central Reservations ☎ 800-447-2757 🌐 www.midnrreservations.com.

Grand Haven

State Park

Campground: Modern
County: Ottawa
Nearest Community: Grand Haven
Sites: 174
Reservations: Yes
Fee: $27–$29 plus vehicle entry fee
Information: State park office
☎ (616) 847-1309

Sites at Grand Haven State Park are little more than a cement slab with no trees, no vegetation to keep the blowing sand at bay, and little privacy from your neighbor who is but four feet away. There are no maintained trails at this 48-acre park, no boat launch, and it's located in one of the most popular tourist towns along Lake Michigan. But what a beach! Many consider Grand Haven's 2,500-foot strip of Lake Michigan the finest beach in the state, and it is one reason why this park draws more than 1.3 million visitors annually.

The other reason is Grand Haven, the town. The park is connected to the restaurants and shops of downtown Grand Haven by Lighthouse Connector Park, a delightful boardwalk along the Grand River that ends with a popular fishing pier and picturesque Grand Haven Lighthouse.

If an urban campground is what you like, Grand Haven is a gem.

Directions: The park is a mile southwest of US-31 in Grand Haven along Harbor Drive. From US-31 follow directional signs to "Downtown."

Campground: Grand Haven has 174 modern sites in a setting that is open with no shade and little space between campers. A few sites actually border the beach with an open view of Lake Michigan, and all of them are a short walk away from the surf. Each site has a table and hook-up but no fire rings or grills of any kind. Some sites are equipped with 50-amp service. Showers, modern restrooms, and a sanitation station round out the facilities.

Grand Haven State Park feature open sites that overlook one of the best Lake Michigan beaches in the heart of Grand Haven.

Day-use Facilities: Grand Haven's beach possesses some of the finest sand along Lake Michigan and during the summer is a colorful scene with wind surfers, swimmers, sunbathers, and kite flyers. There is day parking for 800 vehicles, but often on weekends in July and August the lot fills and additional cars are turned away. People are then encouraged to park downtown and hop the city trolley bus to the beach for a small fee. Also located within the day-use area are picnic facilities, play equipment, bathhouse, and a concession store.

Fishing: Adjacent to the park is Grand Haven Lighthouse and a pier connecting it to the boardwalk along Grand River. This is a popular Great Lakes fishing pier with anglers jigging for perch during the summer and casting spoons and plugs for brown trout, steelhead, and salmon during the fall and spring.

The park maintains a fishermen's parking lot with a posted entrance off Harbor Drive, and it opens at 5 AM as often the best fishing is in the early morning. Lake Michigan is a noted deepwater fishery for salmon and steelhead although in recent years the catch has been down. There is no ramp facility in the park, but there are public boat ramps and marinas in the city. A number of charter boat captains work out of Chinook Pier.

Season: Grand Haven's campground is open from April to November with electricity and water available, but restrooms are closed by mid-October. The facility is full daily from mid-June to the end of August and on weekends throughout June and most of September. Due to the park's overwhelming popularity, there is little chance of getting a site during the summer without a reservation. To reserve a campsite contact Michigan State Park Central Reservations ☎ 800-447-2757 🌐 www.midnrreservations.com.

41

P.J. Hoffmaster

State Park

Campground: Modern
County: Muskegon
Nearest Community: Muskegon
Sites: 293

Reservations: Yes
Fee: $27–$29 plus vehicle entry fee
Information: State park office ☎ (231) 798-3711

Like many Lake Michigan state parks, P.J. Hoffmaster features a wide and sandy beach and a rolling terrain of both wooded and open dunes. Unlike most units along Michigan's Gold Coast, P.J. Hoffmaster is large enough to be more than a campground and a beach.

The 1,100-acre park includes 2.5-miles of shoreline, a 10-mile network of trails, even a "quiet area" where often it's possible to escape the summer crush of tourists found elsewhere along this side of the state. P.J. Hoffmaster also has a huge campground of several hundred modern sites that, despite the large number, still maintains something of a rustic wooded appearance.

What P.J. Hoffmaster does share with the other Lake Michigan state parks is the difficulty of booking a site. Don't expect to show up on a Thursday in mid-July and obtain a site. Advance reservations are strongly recommended during the summer season, but they are far easier to book here than at Grand Haven State Park just down the shore. And P.J. Hoffmaster is definitely worth a little pre-vacation planning.

Directions: The park is located just south of Muskegon. From I-96 depart at exit 4 and head south on 148th Avenue and then immediately turn west (right) onto Pontaluna Road, which ends in 6 miles at the park entrance.

Campground: The P.J. Hoffmaster's modern campground is 293 sites on four loops located at the north end of the park in a wooded valley. The loops are well forested in hardwoods and pines, and being dune country, the sites are in a sandy area covered with needles but little undergrowth.

The largest loop, the only one on the south side of Little Black Creek, is especially nice as many of the sites back up to a steep wooded dune while others overlook the clear, gently flowing stream. The trees here are older pines and hardwoods for a more natural setting than the red pine plantation that two other loops are located in. A quarter-mile trail leads from the back of this loop to a camper's beach on Lake Michigan.

Sites have tables, fire rings, and electric hook-ups, some with 50-amp service, while three shower/restrooms service the campground. A sanitation station for trailers is located just beyond the contact station.

Day-use Facilities: P.J. Hoffmaster maintains a day-use area on Lake Michigan with parking for 550 cars. The facility includes a bathhouse, concession store, and picnic areas near a golden stretch of Lake Michigan beach. Farther south along the park road are additional picnic areas in a wooded setting and Gillette Nature Center. Built in 1976 as Michigan's sand dune interpretive center, the two-story building is in fact overshadowed by a huge, wind-blown dune. The center features an exhibit hall, 82-seat theater, and a hands-on display area, all related to dunes and the biological zones that surround them. Gillette ☎ 231-798-3573 is open year-round Tuesday through Sunday. In the summer, the hours are 10 AM to 5 PM Monday through Saturday and noon to 5 PM Sunday.

Hiking: The park is large enough to be laced by a 10-mile network of foot trails that loop through the wooded dunes and along the Lake Michigan shoreline. The most popular walk is Dune Climb Stairway that

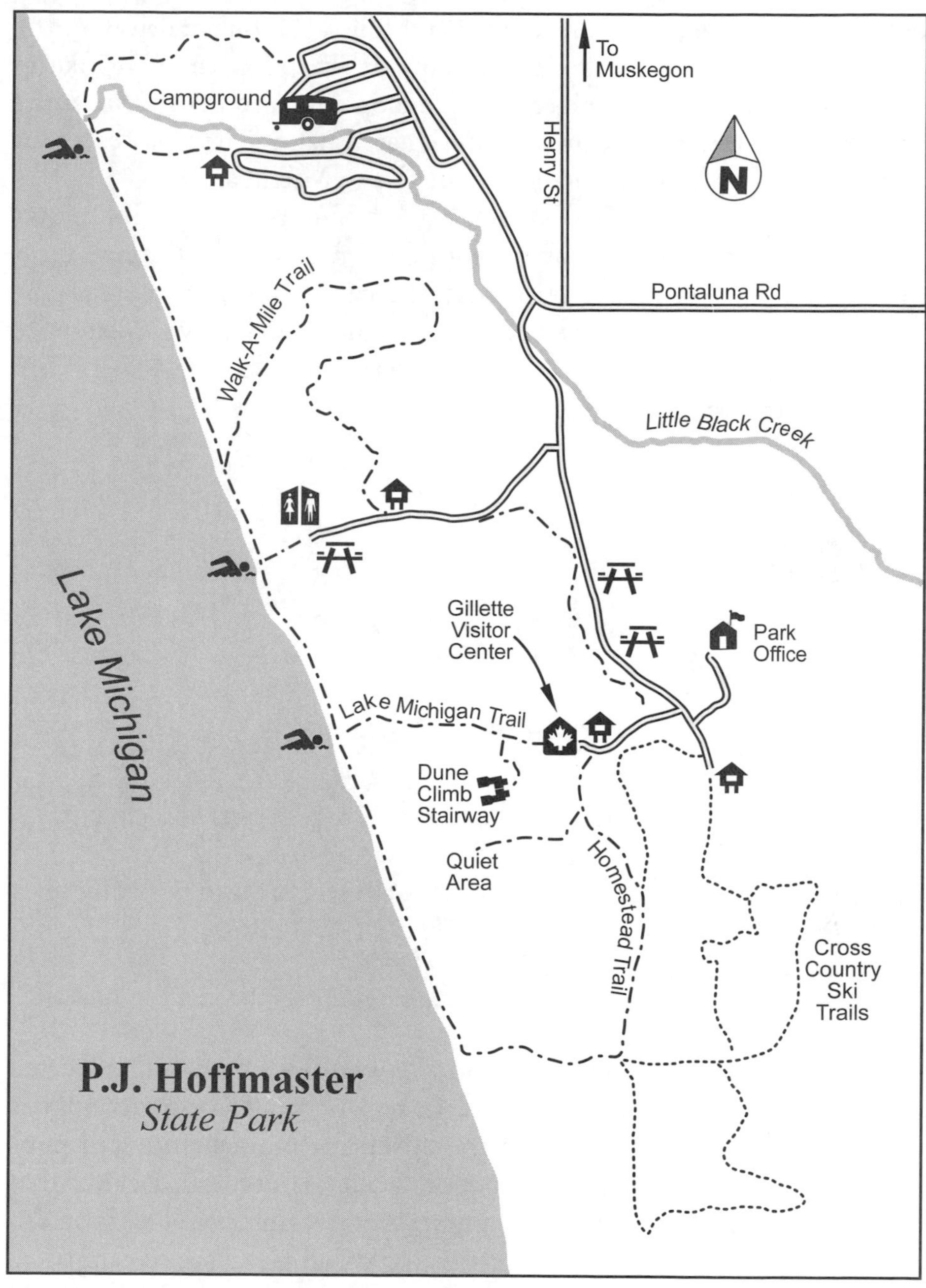
To
Muskegon
Campground
Henry St
N
Walk-A-Mile Trail
Pontaluna Rd
Little Black Creek
Lake Michigan
Gillette
Visitor
Center
Park
Office
Lake Michigan Trail
Dune
Climb
Stairway
Quiet
Area
Homestead Trail
Cross
Country
Ski
Trails
P.J. Hoffmaster
State Park

departs from Gillette Nature Center and follows a long stairway to the top of a high sand dune for a panorama of the park. The best hike in the park is Homestead Trail, a 3.5-mile loop that also departs from the nature center and winds through a designated natural area, passes a spur to the park's Quiet Area, and ends up on Lake Michigan.

Season: Like most other Lake Michigan state parks, P.J. Hoffmaster fills up daily from Wednesday through Sunday mid-June through most of August. On Monday and Tuesday the campground is generally 75 percent full throughout most of the summer. To reserve a campsite contact Michigan State Park Central Reservations ☎ 800-447-2757 🌐 www.midnrreservations.com.

42

Muskegon

State Park

Campground: Modern
County: Muskegon
Nearest Community: Muskegon
Sites: 106
Reservations: Yes
Fee: $26–$28 plus vehicle entry fee
Information: State park office ☎ (231) 744-3480

One of the oldest campgrounds on the west side of the state is located in Muskegon State Park. The park's Lake Michigan Campground was constructed in the 1930s, before the advent of motorhomes and pop-up trailers. Subsequently this modern facility is atypical, lacking that plowed-out, paved-over look of many state park campgrounds. If you can maneuver your trailer into the site, this is a delightful place to camp.

The 1,233-acre park is a peninsula surrounded by Lake Michigan on one side and Muskegon Lake on the other and is best known as the home of the only luge run in the Lower Peninsula. Of more interest to summer campers is the trail network that winds through the dunes and the three miles of wide sandy beach.

The Lake Michigan Campground in Muskegon State Park.

Directions: The park is 5 miles west of North Muskegon. From US-31 depart at M-120 and head southwest, following park signs to Memorial Drive, which terminates at the park's south entrance. Lake Michigan Campground is closer to the north entrance reached by Scenic Drive from Whitehall.

Campground: The Lake Michigan campground has 106 sites on a loop of several lanes. The pre-motorhome era facility is neither level nor is it easy to pull trailers into many of the sites, and large RVs are sent down to Muskegon Lake campground at the south end of the park. The gently rolling area at Lake Michigan campground is well wooded in deciduous trees and bordered to the west by wind-blown sand dunes. Within the campground is a pair of mini-cabins. There are no sites directly on the water, but the beautiful Great Lake shoreline is only a short walk away. The facility has two restrooms with showers, sites with 50-amp service, and a sanitation station.

Day-use Facilities: The park has two day-use areas. The most popular one is on Lake Michigan where there is parking for 600 vehicles, a bathhouse-store, and a wide sandy beach that is typical for this side of the state. The second is on Snug Harbor on Muskegon Lake near the south entrance of the park. Snug Harbor has tables, pedestal grills, a shelter, and a small sandy beach though the water here is not nearly as desirable as Lake Michigan.

The Blockhouse along Scenic Drive provides a view of Muskegon State Park's rugged interior and serves as a trailhead.

Fishing: There are two improved boat launches with docks and cement ramps within the park. Both are on Muskegon Lake, onc in the Snug Harbor day-use area and the other in the nearby modern campground. Boaters then use Ship Canal to gain quick access into Lake Michigan. Fishing opportunities abound in this park. The 4,150-acre Muskegon Lake is noted for its perch and bass as well as being stocked annually with walleye. Shore anglers can use piers in Snug Harbor or along Ship Canal or follow the beach south to reach a rocky breakwall where the catch is perch during the summer and steelhead and salmon in the spring and late fall.

Hiking: The park maintains 12 miles of foot trails through a terrain of mostly well forested lowlands and dunes. Most of the network is a series of loops and side trails spread between Muskegon Lake Campground and the East Campground, but you can also enter the system at the Blockhouse on Scenic Drive south of Lake Michigan Campground and from Snug Harbor day-use area. Often the trails involve steep climbs to the crest of dunes where there are scenic views, particularly in the southern half of the park, or past such interesting spots as Devil's Kitchen, the village site of Old Bay Mills, or Lost Lake, a small, isolated inland lake in the northern half. There is no mountain biking on the trails.

Season: Lake Michigan Campground is not quite as popular as the one on Muskegon Lake, but both campgrounds fill on the weekends from July through Labor Day and are usually near capacity during the week. To reserve a campsite contact Michigan State Park Central Reservations ☎ 800-447-2757 ⊕ www.midnrreservations.com.

43

Pioneer

Muskegon County Park

Campground: Modern
County: Muskegon
Nearest Community: Muskegon
Sites: 235
Reservations: No
Fee: $24 plus vehicle entry fee
Information: Park office
☎ (231) 744-3580
⊕ www.co.muskegon.mi.us/parks

Located north of Muskegon State Park on Lake Michigan, Pioneer County Park is the most popular unit in the Muskegon County park system. Unlike the state park, reservations are not accepted at Pioneer, so you are more likely to find an open site on a Thursday or Friday afternoon.

Directions: Pioneer is three miles north of Muskegon State Park on Scenic Drive. From US-31, depart at M-120 and head north to Giles Road. Turn west on Giles Road and follow it to Scenic Drive. The park entrance is a quarter mile north on Scenic Drive.

Campground: Pioneer has 235 modern sites equipped with both electric and water hook-ups. The sites are close together, but most of them are well shaded by red pines. Three restrooms service the campground, and a sanitary station for recreational vehicles is located in the middle. None of the sites have a view of Lake Michigan, but all are a short stroll from the beach. Along with a nightly camping fee, a $5 daily or $20 annual motor vehicle permit is also required to camp.

Day-use Facilities: A boardwalk with a series of observation decks skirts the bluff above the Lake Michigan shoreline, providing a pleasant view and access to the park's 2,200 feet of surf and sand. Like Muskegon State Park to the south, the beach here is wide and beautiful. The park also has a picnic area with tables, grills, play equipment, and a log lodge that can be rented out in advance. Near the picnic area are basketball, tennis, and volleyball courts as well as a softball field. There are no hiking trails in Pioneer.

Season: Although the campground is full most weekends during the summer, sites are often still available on Thursday afternoon and even Friday morning and generally on Sunday and Monday. When the campground is full, new arrivals are given a number by the park staff beginning at 8 AM and a drawing is held at 10 AM to fill any sites being vacated that day.

Pines Point

Manistee National Forest

Campground: Rustic
County: Newaygo
Nearest Community: Hesperia
Sites: 33
Reservations: Yes
Fee: $14
Information: Baldwin Ranger District
☎ (231) 745-4631

In many ways, Pines Point is your typical national forest campground. It's rustic with vault toilets, hand pumps for water, and well spread and wooded sites. It is your typical national forest campground with one exception. Pines Point has a tuber's loop where people can float the South Branch of the White River in an inner tube, ending where they began, in the campground.

There are opportunities to go fishing, hiking, even backpacking, but what most campers enjoy best about this Manistee National Forest facility is spending a hot afternoon cooling off in the gin-clear waters of the White River and never worrying about special transportation or arranging a drop-off that tubers do in other rivers.

Directions: From White Cloud head west on M-20 to Hesperia where you turn south on Maple Island Road. In a mile turn west on Garfield Road for five miles and then south on 168th Avenue where the campground is posted. Follow the blacktop for 2.5 miles to the campground.

Campground: Pines Point has 33 sites along a paved loop on a high bluff above the South Branch of the White River. The area is heavily forested, and the sites are well spread out and secluded from each other. Ten sites are on the edge of the bluff with a view of the river and log stairways nearby that lead down the to the water. The gravelled parking spurs makes this facility ideal for large RVs while other amenities include fire rings with sliding grills, tables, drinking fountains, and a flush toilet along with vault toilets.

Day-use Facilities: A picnic area is situated in a grove of red pine on the bluff above the water and includes a separate entrance, tables, pedestal grills, and a large parking lot. Both the trailhead for the White River Foot Trail and the departure point for tubers are located here.

Fishing: The White River is the southernmost major trout stream draining into Lake Michigan. At Pines Point you'll find fall and spring steelhead fishing as well as fall salmon, which is extremely popular among anglers. White River Trail can also be used to access more remote sections of the river. Other species caught during the summer include smallmouth bass and northern pike.

Tubing: The South Branch of the White River forms an oxbow at Pines Point Campground where tubers can put in at the canoe launch and then get out at the picnic area for a 30 to 40-minute float. This far upstream the South Branch is 20 to 30 yards wide and so shallow in many stretches even children can stand up.

Canoeing: Pines Point has a canoe landing along the South Branch with boat racks and a pull-through drive for vehicles. Designated a Country Scenic River by the state, the White River flows through primarily wooded and agriculture land. Most paddlers begin in the

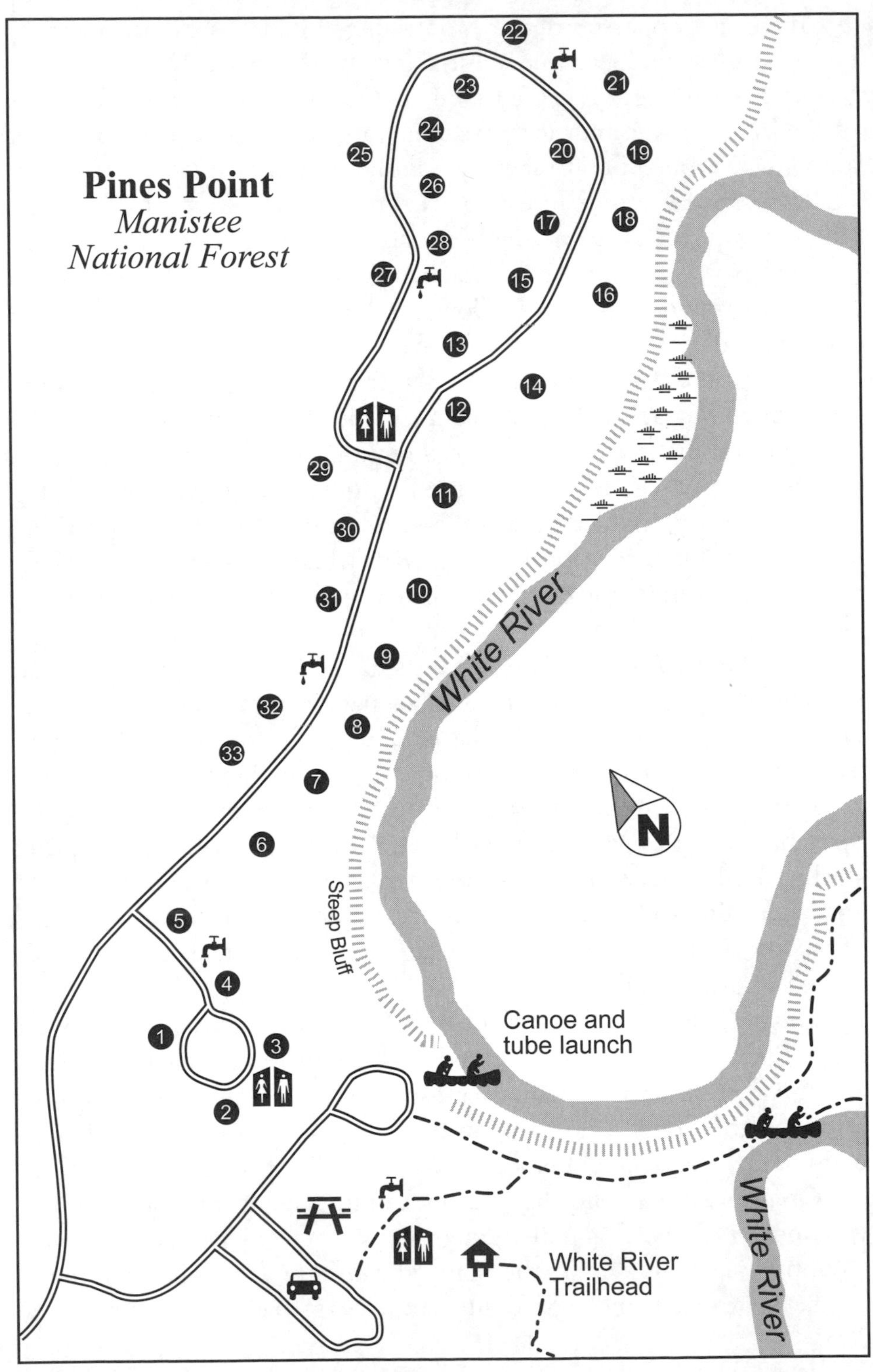
Pines Point
Manistee
National Forest
White River
Steep Bluff
Canoe and
tube launch
White River
Trailhead
White River
N

town of Hesperia, and from there it's a 6-mile, two-hour paddle to the campground. The next take-out is Sischo Bayou, a 7-mile, three-hour journey. Canoes and transportation can be arranged through Happy Mohawk Canoe Livery ☎231-894-4209, 🌐 www.happymohawk.com.

Hiking: Departing from the day-use area is White River Trail, a trail system that is being developed by the U.S. Forest Service. Currently there are 12 miles of paths marked by blue blazes. The first 2 miles of the trail follows the high banks overlooking the river much of the way.

Season: Pines Point has a campground manager from Memorial Day through Labor Day and possibly earlier if there is a demand. It's rarely filled in mid-week and only full on holidays and an occasional weekend. Some sites can be booked six months in advance through National Recreation Reservation Service ☎ 877-444-6777 🌐 www.recreation.gov.

Charles Mears

State Park

Campground: Modern
County: Oceana
Nearest Community: Pentwater
Sites: 175
Reservations: Yes
Fee: $27 plus vehicle entry fee
Information: State park office
☎ (231) 869-2051

It might be small at only 50 acres in size, but Charles Mears State Park is still one of the most popular campgrounds in the entire state. As an urban campground, it's hard to match. It's tucked away on a beach of its own, away from the traffic of Business US-31, but within a short walk are the shops, stores, and restaurants of downtown Pentwater, a popular resort town.

Mears is a "destination campground" as opposed to a stopover on the way up north. People work so hard or wait so long to get a site they end up staying here four to five days on the average. Plan ahead if you want to make this park a part of your summer vacation.

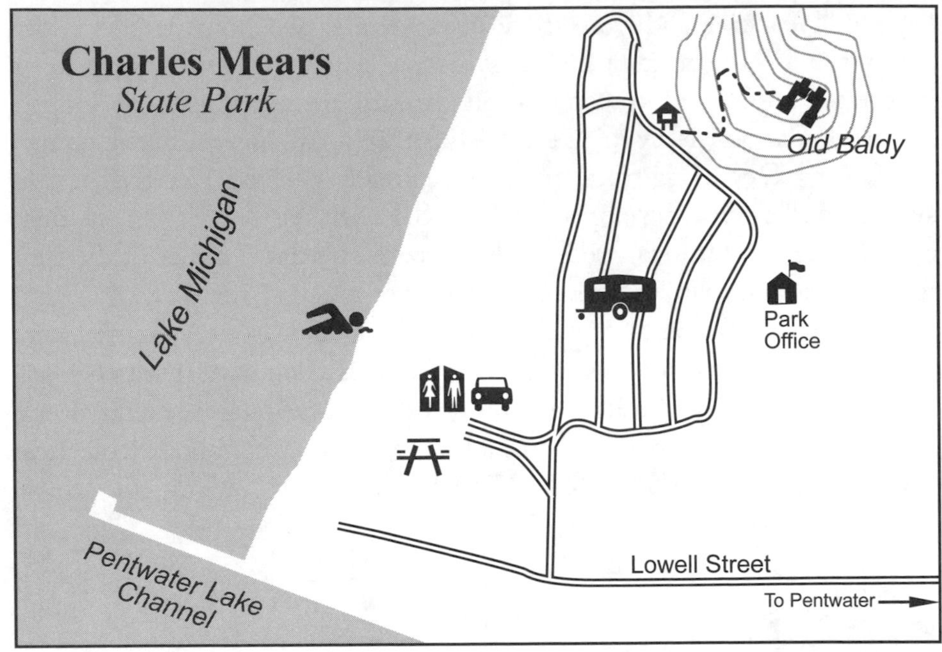

Directions: From US-31, follow Business US-31 through Pentwater and look for state park signs. Mears is four blocks from the downtown area.

Campground: Mears has 175 sites that feature not only electric hookups but also paved pads for recreational vehicles because the campground is little more than an open sandy area. There is little to no shade, nor do any of the sites overlook Lake Michigan like at Grand Haven as a string of dunes separate them from the beach. Within the campground are two modern restrooms with showers, a sanitation station, and a fish cleaning hut.

Day-use Facilities: Mears has a beautiful beach while the small dunes that border it are a great place to catch a Great Lakes sunset. The day-use area has a shelter, bathhouse, beach volleyball courts and play equipment, concession store, and picnic area. Often on summer weekends the parking lot will fill and all other visitors must park elsewhere in town and walk in.

Fishing: Adjacent to the park is Pentwater Pier, where anglers cast for perch and smallmouth bass during the summer. There is no boat ramp in the park, but public facilities are located downtown, and Pentwater is a popular port for deepwater fishing for salmon and steelhead in Lake Michigan. If you don't have a boat, several charter captains work out of Pentwater.

Hiking: There is a half mile of trail that winds around to the top of Old Baldy, a wooded and partially wind-blown sand dune that provides an excellent view of the Lake Michigan shoreline, the town of Pentwater, and its extensive boat harbor.

Season: The campground is filled every day from mid-June to late August. Sites can be obtained without a reservations on weekends in April and May and usually in September and October... just don't plan to do too much swimming in Lake Michigan at that time of year. Otherwise, a reservation is necessary to camp here and should be booked four to six months in advance through Michigan State Park Central Reservations ☎ 800-447-2757 🌐 www.midnrreservations.com.

46

Buttersville

Pere Marquette Township

Campground: Modern
County: Mason
Nearest Community: Ludington
Sites: 44
Reservations: No
Fee: $22 to $25
Information: Campground office
☎ (231) 843-2114
🌐 www.peremarquettetwp.org

Once the site of lumber mills operated by businessman Marshall Butters in the mid-to-late 1800s, today Buttersville Park is a lakeshore bluff campground located south of Ludington. Because it is a township facility and a small park of only 18.5 acres, you're more likely to find an open site here than other better known Lake Michigan campgrounds such as Ludington or Mears State Parks.

Directions: From US-31 south of Ludington, exit north onto Pere Marquette Highway and then head west on Iris Road for 1.4 miles. Turn north on Lakeshore Drive and follow it past White Pine Historic Village to the park.

Campground: Buttersville was originally a rustic campground that featured restrooms and showers before the township upgraded the facility with electricity in 2002. If you need a hook-up for your trailer, it's $25 per night; if you pass on it, it's only $22. The sites are well shaded and not jammed together like those at Ludington State Park. Seven sites have a view of Lake Michigan from the edge of the bluff, and from any of them you can enjoy the breeze off the Great Lake that will keep you comfortable even on the hottest summer night.

Day-use Facilities: A stairway leads down to the beach where you can relax with a view of the Ludington North Breakwall Lighthouse. In the evening you can watch the ferry, S.S. Badger, return from Wisconsin and then stick around for the sunset. Within the campground is a shelter and play equipment, and at the north end of the park is a small day-use area with a few picnic tables and a separate parking area. There are no hiking trails in the park, but you can stroll the beach along Big Sand Bay for more than 3 miles.

Season: The park is open for camping from Memorial Day to Labor Day. Although it tends to be full on most weekends from early July to mid-August, sites are often still available on Thursday afternoon. It is not possible to reserve a site in advance.

Ludington

State Park

Campground: Modern and semi-modern
County: Mason
Nearest Community: Ludington
Sites: 355
Reservations: Yes
Fee: $23–$25 plus vehicle entry fee
Information: State park office
☎ (231) 843-8671

Like many state parks along Lake Michigan, Ludington State Park is a popular unit and a tough place to get a site without a reservation or waiting a day or two. Unlike most other parks, however, once you have set up camp, it's easy to escape the crowds in this wonderful stretch of shoreline, dunes, and forest.

At 5,202 acres, Ludington is the largest state park on Lake Michigan and second largest in the Lower Peninsula. It includes 5.5 miles of Great Lake shoreline, another four miles along popular Hamlin Lake, and a 1,699-acre Wilderness Natural Area that is undeveloped and forms a border with Nordhouse Dunes Wilderness to the north.

The popularity of this park is easy to understand. There are paved bike paths, the Great Lakes Interpretive Center to visit, an 18-mile network of hiking trails, and Big Point Sable Lighthouse, a photographer's delight with its distinctive black and white tower. All this accounts for the more than 750,000 visitors annually with the vast majority arriving from May through September. If the crowds turn you off, then just start hiking the Lake Michigan shoreline north and eventually the beach towels, the bikes, the bustle, and even the foot prints in the sand disappear.

Directions: The state park is 8.5 miles north Ludington at the end of M-116.

Campground: The park has three separate modern campgrounds that stretch from Lake Michigan to Hamlin Lake on the north side of the Big Sable River. All three are well wooded, offering shady sites, and are connected to the day-use areas by the paved bike paths. There is little privacy between sites, but there is just enough space and trees to avoid a campground that looks like a used RV lot.

Pines Campground has 97 sites and is closest to Lake Michigan, separated by the golden beach by only a sand dune, thus the popularity for the west side of the loop. In the middle is Cedar Campground with a pair of loops that feature 105 modern sites and eight tent sites with no hook-ups. Just north of the Hamlin Lake day-use area is Beachwood Campground, which has 147 sites.

Beachwood is my personal choice when setting up camp. Composed of three loop, Beachwood's sites surround forested knolls and low dunes in the middle. On the east side, the sites border a low dune that can be climbed for a pleasant view of Hamlin Lake and its many islands and lagoons as well as provide direct access to the Beachwood Trail. In the northeast corner of the campground, 18 sites actually look out onto Lost Lake, the only place in the park where a waterfront view is possible. Sites include tables and fire rings while six restroom/shower buildings service the campgrounds. There are also mini-cabins in every campground.

Day-use Facilities: There are two beaches in the park, one on Lake Michigan just north of where the Big Sable River empties into the Great Lake and the second on Hamlin Lake. Both have parking and a bathhouse, but early in the summer the Hamlin beach is more popular because its water warms up quicker. M-116 follows Lake Michigan for almost 3 miles after entering the park, and it's common for visitors to just pull over along the road to enjoy a stretch of beach.

Fishing: Hamlin Lake, with its many coves, inlets, and bayous, is a renowned warmwater fishery. There is heavy spawning of northern pike and tiger muskellunge in the shallow coves, and anglers frequently have landed muskies over 15 pounds. The 4,490-acre lake, which is nearly 10 miles long, is also noted for bass and bluegill as well. The lake has been stocked with tiger muskies since the early 1980s, and in 1987 a walleye stocking program began. The park maintains an improved boat ramp on the inland lake near the day-use area with parking for 75 trailers and vehicles and a fish cleaning station near the Lake Michigan beach house. Other fishing activity in the park includes surf fishing in the early spring and October for salmon and trout off the Lake Michigan shoreline.

Hiking: The park boasts a well-posted trail network featuring a number of stone shelters that make for an ideal place to enjoy lunch. There are 11 named and color-coded trails within the 18-mile network with the shortest and most spectacular located south of the Big Sable River. The Skyline Interpretive Trail is less than half mile long but involves a steep winding stairway to the top of a dune where a boardwalk has been constructed along the crest. How steep is the dune? Helicopters were needed to carry the lumber to the top. The view from the boardwalk is spectacular, and along the way there are numbered interpretive posts that correspond to a brochure available at each of the three stairways.

The rest of the trail system is north of the river with posted trailheads located in the campgrounds or the Hamlin Lake Day-use Area. Several trails can be combined for day-long loops through the unique terrain of the park's Wilderness Natural Area. The Ridge and Island Trails make a 5.2-mile loop that features viewing the perched dunes above Hamlin Lake and winding around the inlets and bays along the lake. Plan on three to four hours for the trek. Equally scenic is the Logging and Lighthouse Trails out to Big Point Sable Lighthouse with a return along the beach. The 4.8-mile hike would include an extended break to climb the stairs to the top of the historic lighthouse.

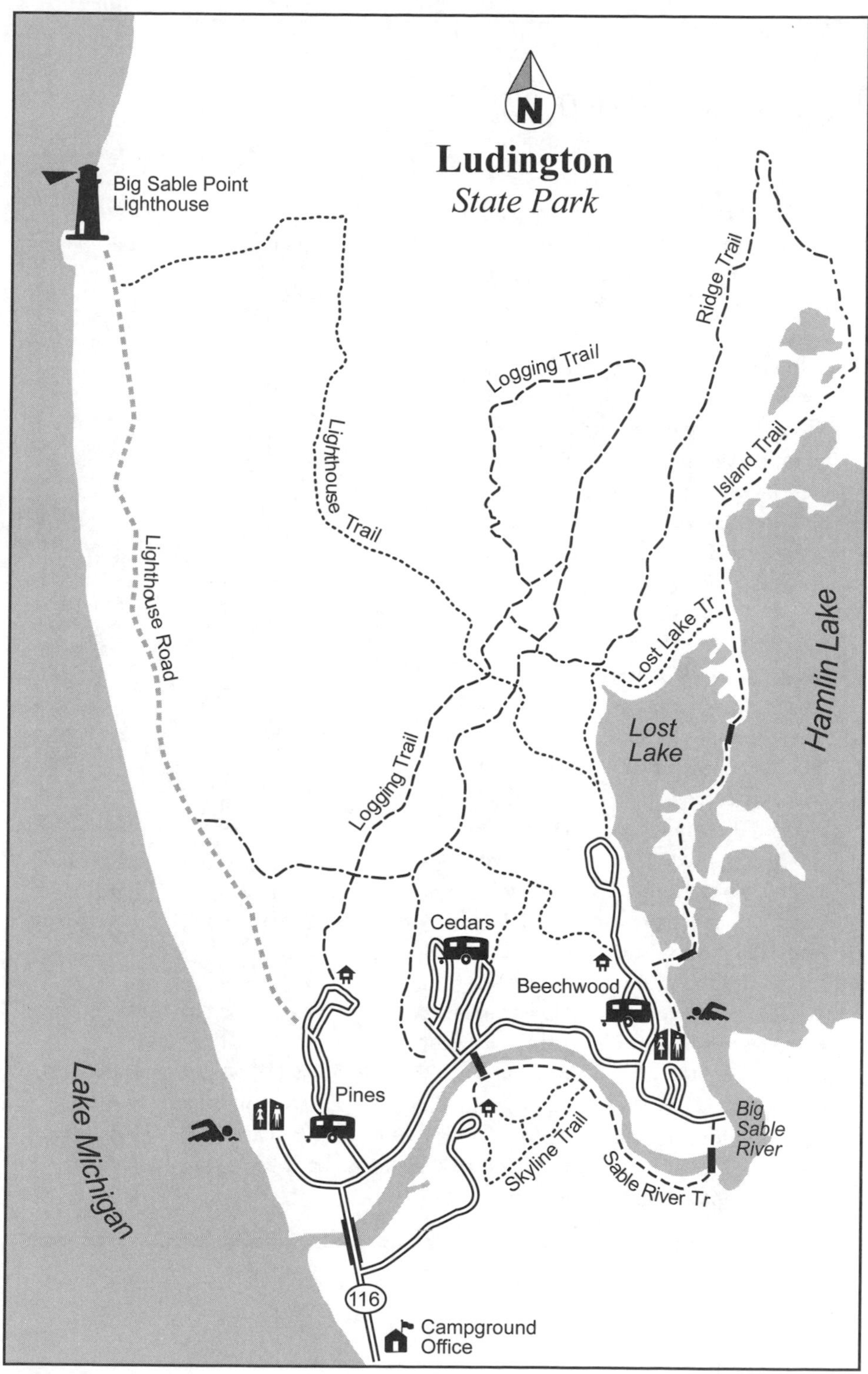
Ludington
State Park
N
Big Sable Point Lighthouse
Lighthouse Road
Lighthouse Trail
Logging Trail
Ridge Trail
Island Trail
Lost Lake Tr
Logging Trail
Lost Lake
Hamlin Lake
Cedars
Beechwood
Pines
Skyline Trail
Sable River Tr
Big Sable River
Lake Michigan
116
Campground Office

A HIKE TO A LIGHTHOUSE

At the tip of Big Sable Point is Big Sable Point Lighthouse, whose black-and-white tower is Ludington State Park's distinctive trademark. The classic structure was authorized by President James Buchanan in 1858 after the barge, Neptune, sank off the point and 37 people drowned. Actual construction began in 1866, and a year later its light was illuminated by Burr Caswell, Mason County's first resident and the first caretaker of the lighthouse.

Big Sable Point Lighthouse's black-and-white tower is Ludington State Park's distinctive trademark and a popular hike at the park.

The light was placed on the National Register of Historic Places in 1983 and today is an interesting maritime museum that can only be reached on foot. The shortest route is to follow the service road, a hike of almost a mile. The attached lightkeeper's residence contains furnished rooms, historic displays, and a gift shop. You can then climb a circular, iron stairway of 130 steps to the top of the tower and step outside. The view is worth every step as Ludington State Park lies to the east and the blue horizon of Lake Michigan to the west.

Big Sable Point Lighthouse ☎ 231-845-7343 🌐 www.splka.org is open from 10 AM to 5 PM daily from May through October. Admission is a $2 donation for adults and $1 for children. Outside there are picnic tables while nearby is the marked Lighthouse Trail that heads east to the heart of the park and the rest of the trail system.

Season: Ludington's campgrounds are booked daily July through Labor Day and are full on weekends beginning in Memorial Day. Late April is a particularly pleasant time to camp as reservations (☎ 800-447-2757 🌐 www.midnrreservations.com) are unnecessary and the park is practically empty at that time of year. The campground is open year round, but the modern restrooms are available only from April 15 to Nov. 1.

48

Benton Lake

Manistee National Forest

Campground: Rustic
County: Newaygo
Nearest Community: Brohman
Sites: 24
Reservations: No
Fee: $14
Information: Baldwin Ranger District
☎ (231) 745-4631

What was a turkey farm in the 1940s is now a lightly used campground in the Baldwin District of the Huron-Manistee National Forests. Benton Lake is a mid-size facility of 24 sites located on the south shore of this 33-acre lake. Half of the sites are in the wooded area, but the other half are in an open, grassy area, remnants of the poultry farm here.

The farm also had a profound effect on the lake itself. Until the 1950s, Benton Lake was private water that was rarely fished and that, say some locals, is the reason for the Benton Lake's excellent bluegill fishery.

Directions: The campground is an hour drive north of Grand Rapids. From M-37 in Brohman turn west on Pierce Drive (also labeled Forest Road 5308) and drive 4.5 miles to the posted entrance of the campground.

Campground: There are 24 sites on two loops with sites 1-12 located in an area forested in young hardwoods with moderate undergrowth. Much of the second loop is open, however, and the grassy sites are closer

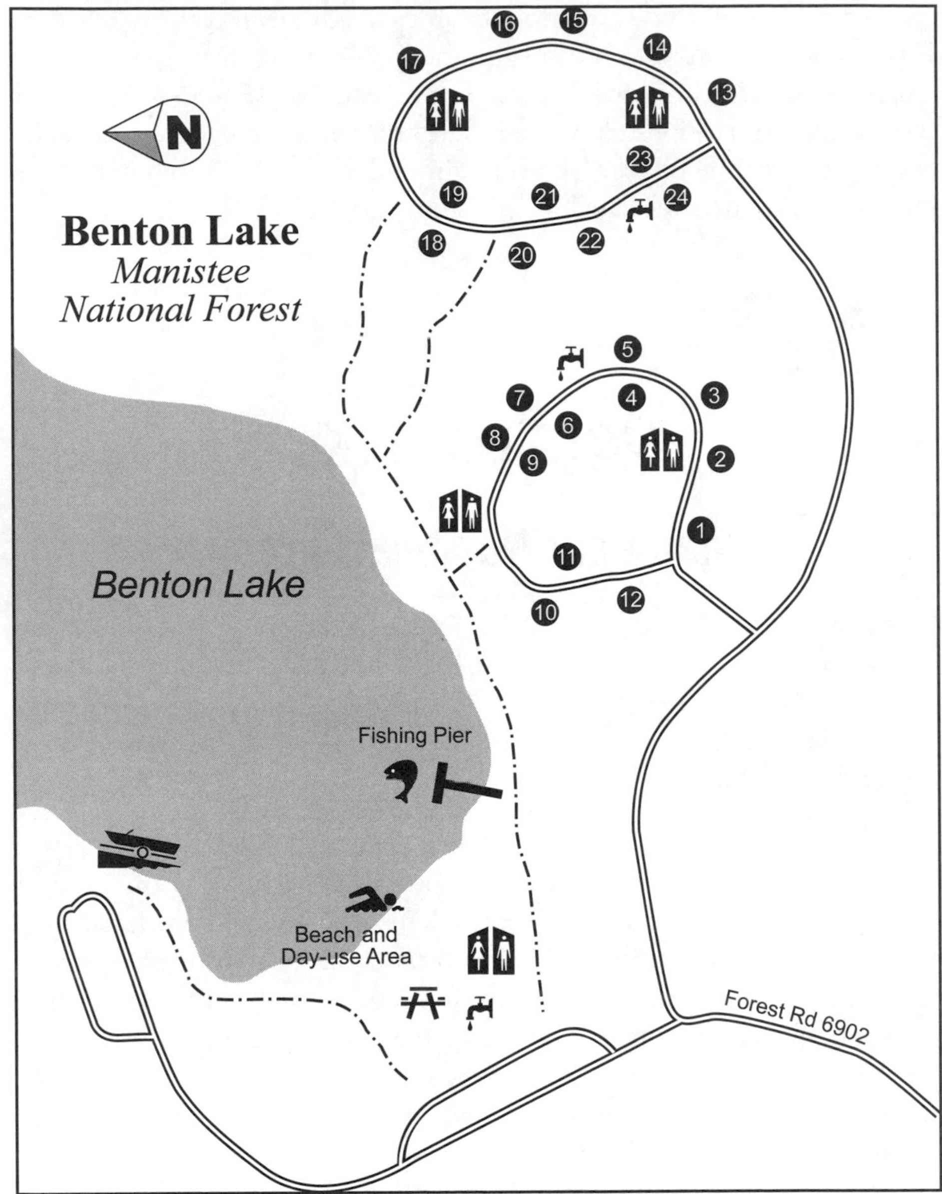

to the lakes. There are none directly on the water but several are only a few steps away. Sites feature a table, fire ring with sliding grill, lantern post, and paved spurs, making them ideal for RVs. Both loops have vault toilets and hand pumps for water.

Day-use Facilities: The campground has a pleasant picnic area with some of the tables and grills on a grassy hillside overlooking the

Campers enjoy breakfast at Benton Lake Campground in the Manistee National Forest.

lake. Although a beach and swimming area is marked on handouts, it's little more than a small clearing in the aquatic vegetation, just enough for young children. There is additional parking and a vault toilet at the picnic area.

Fishing: Benton is a 33-acre lake that lies completely in national forest land thus free of any cottages or other development. It's not large and attracts only light fishing pressure throughout most of the summer. There is a drop-off 15 to 20 yards off shore, and during the summer anglers who fish the edge of it with wax and leaf worms can often entice a variety of panfish. Some bluegills that have come out of the lake have easily exceeded a pound. Near the picnic area there is a fishing pier and on the northwest corner of the lake is an unimproved boat launch with parking for 31 vehicles.

Hiking: There is a trailhead for the North Country Trail located off Pierce Drive, 2 miles east of the campground entrance. To the north along the NCT, it's approximately a 4 to 5-mile trek to Nichols Lake Campground, to the south a 3 to 4-mile hike to Loda Lake Wildflower Sanctuary.

Season: The campground is managed by a concessionaire from Memorial Day to Labor Day. Sites are occupied on a first-come-first-serve basis and have a capacity of eight people and two vehicles.

49

Nichols Lake

Manistee National Forest

Campground: Rustic
County: Newaygo
Nearest Community: Brohman
Sites: 28
Reservations: No
Fee: $15
Information: Baldwin Ranger District
☎ (231) 745-4631

Of the eight National Forest campgrounds located between White Cloud and Baldwin, Nichols Lake is one of the most poplar because it's one of the nicest. Overlooking a scenic lake, the facility is wooded with well spread out sites and paved spurs. You can sneak into the woods on the North Country Trail, fish for bluegill in Nichols Lake, or trailer your boat to dozens of other lakes in the area.

Little wonder then that this facility is often filled on a summer weekend. No reservations are accepted, but Nichols Lake is well worth arriving a day early to beat the Friday night crowd.

Directions: From White Cloud, head north on M-37 for 13 miles and then turn west on 11 Mile Road. The posted entrance of the campground is reached in 4.5 miles or 3 miles beyond the community of Woodland.

Campground: Nichols Lake is a single loop of 28 sites with paved spurs situated on a bluff wooded predominantly by oaks. Sites are well spread out but within sight of each other due to thin undergrowth. One side of the bluff borders the lake, and a few sites have a partial view of the water. On the other side several sites overlook a grassy marsh, an excellent area to watch for deer in the early evening.

Sites include not only fire rings with sliding grills and tables but also lantern posts. Sites No. 16 and 17 are large two-family sites. Within the loop are both vault and flush toilets and three spigots for water. The other nice aspect about Nichols Lake is the bluff catches any breeze at all on the lake, making the campground a little less bug infested during the summer.

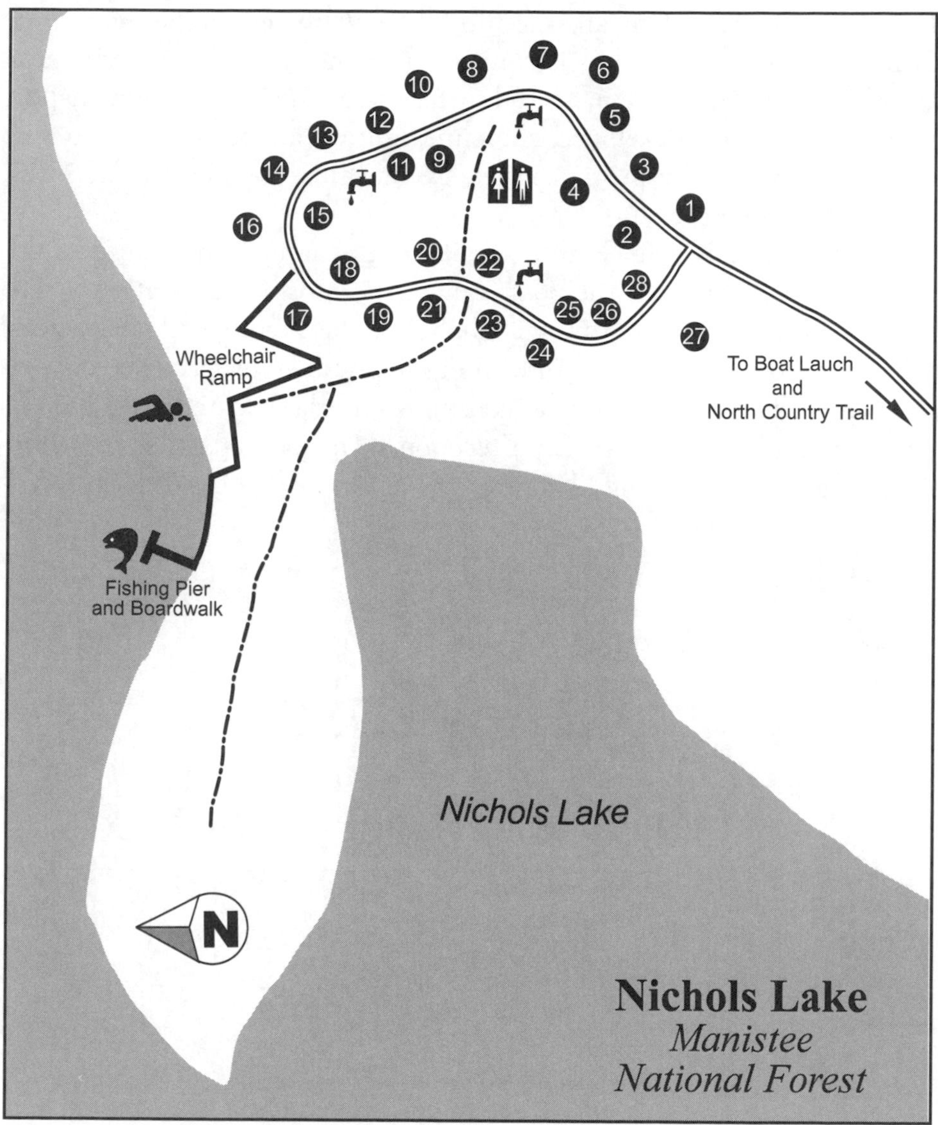

Day-use Facilities: A wheelchair ramp next to site No. 17 leads to the narrow peninsula that gives Nichols Lake its horseshoe shape. At the base of the point is small strip of sand with a posted swimming area. From here the path climbs to the end of the point for nice overview of the entire lake and who's fishing wherc. On the northwest corner of the lake is a separate picnic area that is reached from Cleveland Road via Bitely.

Fishing: Before entering the campground you pass a separate spur that leads to the trailhead for the North Country Trail and an improved boat launch. There are parking areas for both here. Also next to the swimming beach is a fishing pier that is connected to the wheelchair ramp via a boardwalk. Nichols Lake has a 160 surface acres and is horseshoe-shaped with cottages and developed shoreline limited almost entirely to the northeast corner. The prime species are bluegills, and the lake receives moderate fishing pressure.

Hiking: The North Country Trail passes through the campground and has a trailhead near the boat launch. The most scenic section by far is to head north to pass through Nichols Lake Picnic Area and across Cleveland Road. In the next three miles the trail winds past five lakes.

Season: The managed season is from Memorial Day to Labor Day. If arriving on a Friday or Saturday afternoon, be prepared for the possibility of this campground being filled.

Shelley Lake

Manistee National Forest

Campground: Rustic
County: Newaygo
Nearest Community: Brohman
Sites: 8
Reservations: No
Fee: $10
Information: Baldwin Ranger District
☎ (231) 745-4631

Spending a night at Shelley Lake in Manistee National Forest is something that falls between hiking in and pulling up to your site with a car full of coolers, lawn chairs and a deluxe, three-burner Coleman stove. The U.S. Forest Service calls it a "dispersed recreation area" which means it is non-developed: no toilets, no fire rings, no facilities whatso-ever. It means you're out in the woods and off on by yourself, all by careful design.

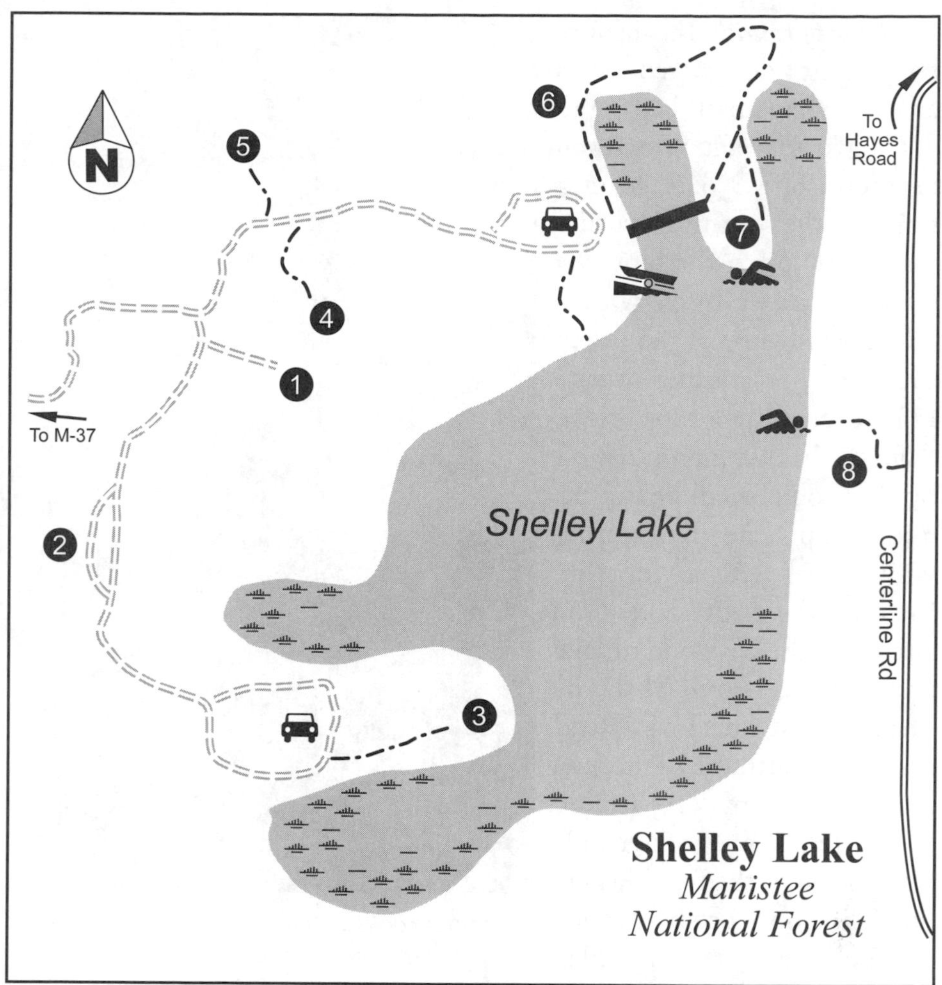

The recreation area was set up after unrestricted use of the scenic area began causing irreversible damage to the small, 15-acre lake. So barriers were built across the old logging roads leading up to the shoreline and nine campsites were designated. You can pull right up to a couple of the campsites away from the lake. But the best ones are along the shoreline overlooking the water, and those you have park and walk to. Not far, just enough to make you cringe at the thought of carrying in a cooler full of ice and cans of soda.

Directions: From White Cloud head north on M-37 and then look for a gravel parking area to the east. From the parking lot, a very rough forest road (not recommended for large recreation vehicles) heads east to the lake.

Campground: The facility has eight designated sites around the small lake, and you have to walk into seven of them. Site No. 3 is on a point in the southwest corner where you pitch the tent in a stand of paper birch with a 180-degree view of the water. Site No. 7 is another a gem. It is reached by a foot bridge from the boat launch and is off by itself on a small peninsula. You camp beneath towering white pines with a view that includes the entire lake. One site is on the east side of lake and reached from M-37 by heading east on Hayes Road and then south on Centerline Road. From a parking area on Centerline, it's a quarter mile walk through the forest where you break out at a small sandy beach. There are no tables, fire rings, vault toilets, or safe water source within the campground.

A camper cooks dinner on the shores of Shelley Lake, a dispersed campground in the Manistee National Forest north of Baldwin.

Fishing: At the north end of the lake there is an unimproved boat launch onto the lake and parking for two, maybe three, vehicles. The 15-acre lake is completely surrounded by national forest land and can be fished for both bluegill and other species of panfish as well as bass. The fishing pressure on Shelley Lake is moderate to light.

Season: Camping is allowed year-round, but keep in mind this campground is hard to reach during spring and late fall or after any extended period of rain.

51

Highbank Lake

Manistee National Forest

Campground: Rustic
County: Newaygo
Nearest Community: Baldwin
Sites: 9
Reservations: No
Fee: $12
Information: Baldwin Ranger District
☎ (231) 745-4631

Highbank Lake is well named. It is indeed encircled by bluffs, forested in hardwoods, and towering above the water. Add the fact that the entire lake lies in the Manistee National Forest, and you have the reasons why this small campground is a somewhat remote, secluded but charming place to spend a night or even longer.

There are a couple of cottages along the southeast corner of the lake, but they're tucked away up on the shoreline bluff and not obtrusive at all. Nor does the lake buzz with motor boats or water skiers. Small at 20 acres, Highbank Lake has only an unimproved boat launch at the campground. Anything bigger than a hand-carried rowboat and you're going to have problems launching it.

Fishing opportunities abound in the area, and the North Country Trail swings nearby and can be reached by a spur from the campground. Be forewarned; with only nine sites this facility is filled most weekends from mid-June through Labor Day and often during the middle of the week.

Directions: To reach the campground from US-10 in Baldwin, head south on M-37 for 9 miles to the junction of 16 Mile Road in Lilley. Turn west on 16 Mile Road for a half mile then north (right) on Roosevelt Drive where the campground is posted. The lake is reached 1.5 miles up Roosevelt Drive. From the south, 16 Mile Road is 17 miles from White Cloud.

Campground: Highbank Lake campground is a single loop of nine sites. There are hard gravelled parking spurs on seven of them, of which four allow you to park the recreational vehicle within a few yards of the water. Two other sites are labeled "walk-in," and the sites are actually located up a short staircase from where you park the car. Vault toilets and a hand pump for water round out the facilities while sites have tables and fire rings with sliding grills.

Day-Use Facilities: Forest service handouts show a beach near site No. 3, but in reality it's a grassy bank leading down to the lake's sandy bottom where children can spend a hot afternoon splashing away. Two benches are located here and angled in such a way that you can catch the sun dipping behind the shoreline bluff in the evening or watch fishermen enticing bluegills.

Fishing: Near the beach you can launch a hand-carried boat. Canoes are perfect for this 20-acre lake; haul one along. Panfish, most notably bluegill, and bass are the species most anglers are targeting here. Shore fishermen can follow a foot path along the shore at the east end of the lake where a small inlet can be especially productive when bluegills are spawning in May.

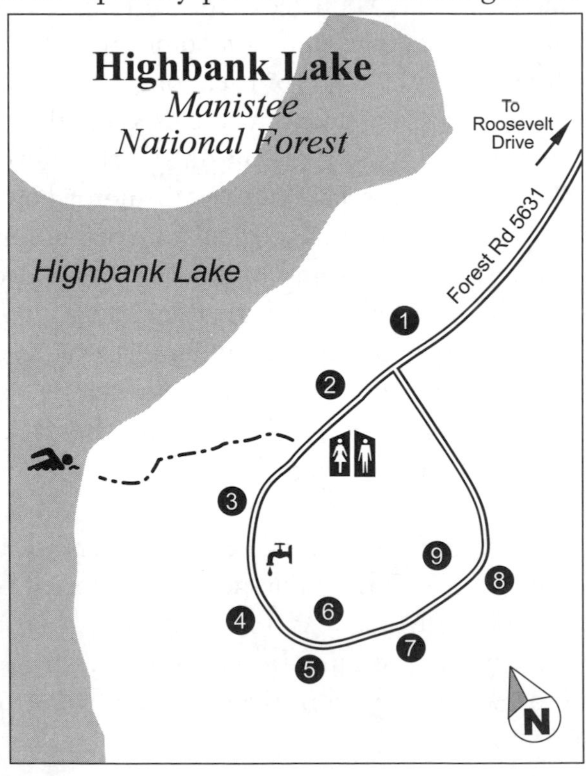

For a little angling adventure try fishing Amaung Lake. The lake lies due east of Highbank, but there is no ramp on it or even a road to it. Follow Roosevelt Drive (also Forest Road 5396) past the entrance of the campground for another quarter mile and then just head into the woods. The lake is only a few hundred yards away, and it's hard to miss as it is considerably larger than Highbank. Amaung offers less fishing pressure and seems to have a better population of largemouth bass as well as panfish. Haul a canoe or belly boat in, and it could be a rewarding afternoon for the extra effort.

Hiking: From the campground a half-mile spur follows the east side of the lake and then climbs to the top of the west shore bluff to a junction with the North Country Trail (NCT). This is one of the most scenic stretches of the Baldwin Segment of the NCT. North of Highbank is a small lake that can be reached only on foot while to the south the trail winds around Condon and Leaf Lakes before reaching a trailhead on Cleveland Road. From the junction with the NCT to Cleveland Road is a trek of 3.5 miles.

Season: The managed season is from Memorial Day through Labor Day, but if spring weather is warm the concessionaire will begin collecting fees earlier. The campground often fills on weekends. If you want a site here, plan on arriving early in the day and have an alternative campground picked out just in case.

52

Bowman Bridge

Manistee National Forest

Campground: Rustic
County: Lake
Nearest Community: Baldwin
Sites: 20
Reservations: Yes

Fee: $15
Information: Baldwin Ranger District
☎ (231) 745-4631

Location and quick access is the nicest aspect of this national forest campground just west of Baldwin. Bowman Bridge lies on the banks of the Pere Marquette, a National Scenic River and a very popular destination with canoers during the summer, as evident by the number of group campsites found here.

Also within the campground is a foot path that connects it to the North Country Trail and the Bowman Lake Foot Travel Area, both excellent areas for hiking. The rustic facility lacks the solitude and privacy of many others in the national forest, especially when it's filled, but at this campground it's easy to wander off into the woods or paddle up the river to escape the crowds.

Directions: From the junction of US-10 and M-37, head south through downtown Baldwin and in less than a half mile, right before you pass the US Forest Service office, turn west (right) on Seventh Street. In 0.4 miles swing south (left) on Cherry Street and then immediately west (right) on 52nd Street. This road merges into 56th Street and 4.3 miles from Baldwin you cross the Pere Marquette River and pass the posted entrance to the campground.

Campground: Bowman Bridge has 16 sites with paved spurs, four group sites designed primarily for the canoers, and four walk-in sites for tent campers. All are located on two loops along a bluff above the river in an area lightly forested in maples and oaks with thin undergrowth. Facilities include hand pumps, tables, fire rings with grills, and vault toilets.

Canoeing: A large canoe launch is featured below the campground with a paved pull-through, racks, and parking lot. There is even additional parking on the other side of 56th Street, that's how popular Bowman Bridge is for paddlers.

The Pere Marquette is the only free-flowing river in the Lower Peninsula without any impoundments, and for most canoeists it's an exhilarating paddle. Permits are required for all watercraft on the river from May 15 to Sept. 10 and are free. If you rent a canoe, the livery will provide a permit; if you use your own, pick one up from the Forest Service office in Baldwin.

Canoers can paddle 66 miles of the river. From M-37 in Baldwin, it's a 12-mile, four-hour paddle to Bowman Bridge. The next take out is Rainbow Rapids, two hours downstream. You can obtain rentals in Baldwin from either Ivan's Canoe Rental ☎ 231-745-3361 or Baldwin Canoe Rentals ☎ 231-745-4669.

Fishing: Bowman Bridge is the start of the "flies only" stretch of the Pere Marquette which extends 8.7 miles downstream to Rainbow Rapids. Heaviest use of the river by anglers is at the peak of the salmon spawning run in September and October and the height of the steelhead run in

March through mid-April. The river also supports brown trout, though many feel this fishery has diminished at the expense of the salmon.

Hiking: Along the group loop is a trailhead for a half mile spur, marked in blue diamonds, that leads to the North Country Trail. On the NCT you can head north and in a mile reach the Bowman Lake Foot Travel Area. Bowman Lake is a 1,000-acre non-motorized preserve with a 2.2-mile pathway that circles the scenic lake. You can spend an hour hiking this area or carry in a fishing rod and some bait and spend an afternoon catching bluegills from the shore.

Season: The campground is managed from April 15 through Labor Day but may be open earlier or later depending on demand. Due mostly to canoers, Bowman is a popular campground and will often be filled on the weekends and even mid-week at the height of the camping season. Sites can be reserved through the National Recreation Reservation Service ☎ 877-444-6777 🌐 www.recreation.gov six months in advance. There is a reservation fee of $9 for booking sites in advance.

Old Grade

Manistee National Forest

Campground: Rustic
County: Lake
Nearest Community: Wolf Lake
Sites: 20
Reservations: No
Fee: $14
Information: Baldwin Ranger District
☎ (231) 745-4631

Old Grade Campground is named for a railroad grade that dates back to the logging era of the late 1800s and still can be seen today. The campground is a lightly used facility in the Manistee National Forest that will appeal to anglers, berry pickers, and campers who want to avoid crowds and reservations. There is also an interpretive path that departs

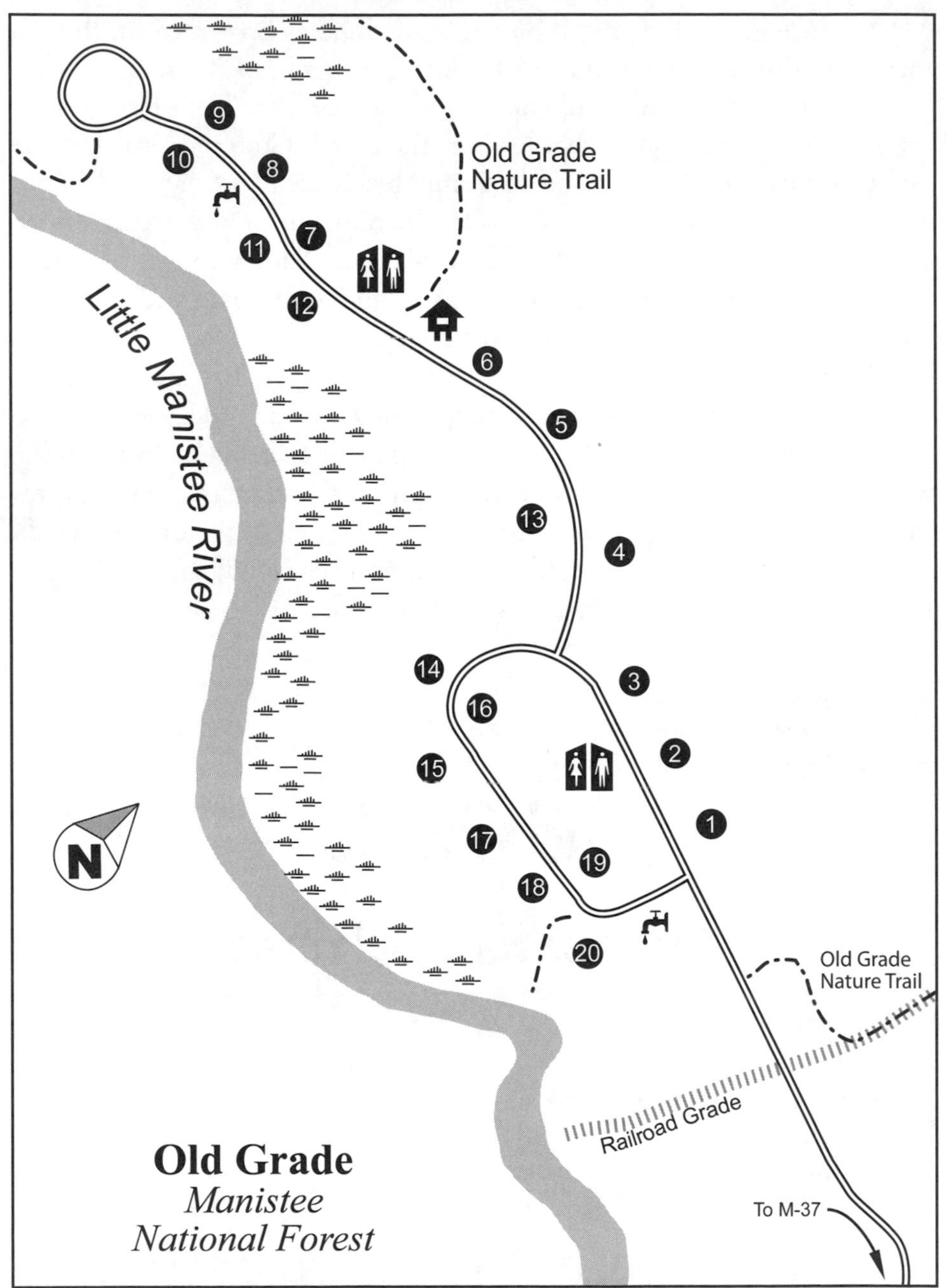

Old Grade
Manistee National Forest

from the campground and provides an opportunity to spot wildlife, including whitetail deer, beavers, and a variety of songbirds.

Be forewarned; there is considerable low-lying forest and marshy areas nearby, and the insects can be thick at times. Avoid this campground through much of June and early July. On the other hand, the fishing for trout is good in late May in the Little Manistee River, and the fall colors are spectacular in early October. Both are excellent times to pitch a tent here.

Directions: From Baldwin, head north on M-37 for 11 miles. The campground entrance is reached just after crossing the Little Manistee River.

Campground: Old Grade has 20 rustic sites including several overlooking the Little Manistee River. The sites are well spread out in a wooded area, offering a good deal of privacy. Campground amenities include fire rings, tables, four vault toilets, and hand pumps for water.

Fishing: The Little Manistee is best known as a steelhead stream (see Driftwood Valley Campground), but this far upstream it is often fished for brown trout and rainbows. Below the campground the river is 25 yards wide with a mix of gravel and sand. The river is lightly fished through much of the summer and can be easily accessed from angler's paths that depart from the Old Grade Nature Trail. Fly fishermen will find inviting pools and good hatches of caddis, Sulphurs, brown brakes and Hexagenia here. Best of all, the river this far upstream is too shallow for canoers. You should have it to yourself.

Hiking: The Old Grade Nature Trail is a 1.5-mile loop with eight interpretive displays and a trailhead near site No. 6. You begin in low-lying woods and quickly cross a stream but within a quarter of a mile are on the banks of the Little Manistee River, one of the most beautiful trout streams on the west side of the state. Within a half mile, the trail merges into the old railroad grade and leads you past patches of wild strawberries and raspberries on the way back to the campground.

Season: Old Grade is open from Memorial Day to Labor Day. It is rare for this campground to be filled on a weekend much less in the middle of the week.

54

Peterson Bridge

Manistee National Forest

Campground: Rustic
County: Wexford
Nearest Community: Wellston
Sites: 30
Reservations: No
Fee: $5–$14
Information: Manistee Ranger District
☎ (231) 723-2211

In 1925, Gideon Gerhardt stepped into the Pine River to do a little trout fishing, but when he waded downstream to his favorite hole, he discovered the river had been fenced off and posted with "No Trespassing" signs. The Ne-Bo-Shone Association, a private club of wealthy sportsman that owned the land surrounding the Pine River, had erected the barrier across the stream to prevent access by anglers wading or canoeing.

The incident triggered the case *Collins vs. Gerhardt*, which eventually made its way to the Michigan Supreme Court. In 1926, the state's highest court ruled in a landmark decision that the club may own the land but not the water, and the public had a common right of fishing in any part of a navigable stream.

It was a historical decision for all outdoor enthusiasts, and today it is remembered with a historical marker overlooking the Pine River in Peterson Bridge Campground. The facility occupies both sides of the blue-ribbon trout stream, with a campground on the south side and a day-use and canoe landing on the north bank. It's a scenic and popular facility, especially with canoers who can be seen paddling the river from June through August. Thanks, in no small part, to Gideon Gerhardt.

Directions: The campground is right on M-37, 1.5 miles south of M-55 or 21.5 miles north of Baldwin.

Campground: Peterson Bridge has a loop of 20 paved sites, well separated and secluded from each other in a mixed forest of hardwoods.

Six sites along the back of the loop are enclosed by a towering wooded bluff while others are on the edge of a steep bank that leads down to the river. Site No. 20 is the only one with a view of the water as it overlooks where the river sweeps past the canoe landing.

An additional 10 walk-in group sites are located at the base of the bank along the river and can be reached by a stairway near the fee station though they are used mostly by canoeists. Within the campground are both vault toilets and one flush toilet, water spigots, tables, and fire rings with sliding grills. A drive-in site is $14 a night; a walk-in site is $5.

Day-use Facilities: The picnic area and canoe landing is situated across the river from the campground and is a very pleasant, though often busy, place during the summer. Along with the canoe launch, there are tables and pedestal grills, some overlooking the river, vault toilets, a small shelter, canoe racks, and additional parking for the large number of paddlers that depart from here. Next to a historical marker dedicated to the famous Michigan Supreme Court case, there is a group of benches in a stand of red pine where undoubtedly more than one tired paddler has sat down, glad that the day on the river is finally over.

Fishing: The Pine is a blue ribbon trout stream, holding good populations of brown trout. The stretch upstream between Walker Bridge and Dobson Bridge was once considered the best stretch of water for trout in the Lower Peninsula. To avoid canoers, fish before noon below Peterson Bridge.

Canoeing: The Pine flows 60 miles from near Leroy until it merges into the Manistee River in Manistee County. To paddle the river in national forest land, you need a free permit between May and October, and they can be reserved in advance (see Paddling The Pine on page 142) One popular put-in is Elm Flats, and it's a 12-mile, four-hour paddle from there to the campground passing Dobson Bridge along the way. Beyond the campground the final take-out is Low Bridge on M-55, an 8-mile, three-hour journey. Canoes and transportation can be arranged with Pine River Paddlesport Center ☎ 231-862-3471 🌐 www.thepineriver.com and Horina's Canoe and Kayak ☎ 231-862-3470 🌐 www.horinacanoe.com. River hours for paddlers are 9 AM to 6 PM.

Season: Thc managed season for Peterson Bridge is May through September, and the campground can be filled on any weekend from mid-June through mid-August.

PADDLING THE PINE

Already considered fast water, the Pine River is more exciting than ever for canoers and kayakers thanks to a draw down. In 1997 Consumers Energy and the U.S. Forest Service began removing the Stronach Dam downstream from Peterson Bridge in a gradual process called a "staged draw down." Every three months eight inches of the dam was removed, a little more of the backwater disappeared, and farther upstream the river became a little faster.

The process was completed by 2004, and today the Pine has a river gradient of 7 percent and offers the fastest average flow of any river in the Lower Peninsula. At times in the spring and during periods of heavy rain, the light Class I riffles above Peterson Bridge are legitimate Class II whitewater with two-foot standing waves, long chutes, and numerous obstacles.

Not that the Pine needed anything else to make it more appealing. The scenic, largely unspoiled river is already one of the most popular in the state. The river was attracting 6,000 to 7,000 paddlers on a summer weekend when in 1978 the U.S. Forest Service instituted a watercraft permit system, the first of its kind in Michigan, to eliminate the overcrowding.

A permit for each canoe is now required for paddling the Pine in the Manistee National Forest between May 15 and September 10. With only 658 permits available per day for both private and livery canoes, reservations are mandatory for any weekend from mid-June through August.

The Pine originates near LeRoy in Osceola County and flows 60 miles before merging with the Manistee River. Almost 40 miles of it is floatable in a canoe, making the entire river an ideal three-day float with the final day for many being a three-hour paddle from Peterson Bridge Campground to Low Bridge, the last access point just before the Pine flows underneath M-55 and into backwaters of Tippy Dam.

For more information or to reserve a permit for the Pine River, call the Baldwin Ranger Station ☎ 231-745-4631 or the Pine River Paddlesport Center ☎ 231-862-3471 🌐 www.thepineriver.com.

55

Sand Lake

Manistee National Forest

Campground: Rustic
County: Manistee
Nearest Community: Wellston
Sites: 45
Reservations: Yes
Fee: $18
Information: Manistee Ranger District
☎ (231) 723-2211

Vault toilets get you down? So do modern campgrounds with their crowded sites? Sand Lake in the Manistee National Forest is an excellent compromise. Sites here are well spread out in a heavily forested area. Some are even off by themselves.

Yet at this national forest facility you can reserve a site in advance, though it is usually not necessary, not even on most weekends. Best of all for some people, Sand Lake has flush toilets as well as old fashion vault toilets. Sometimes that's all you need to get mom to go camping.

Directions: From M-55 head to Wellston and then turn south on Seaman Road. Follow the road 4.5 miles as it passes through the village of Dublin. A mile south of Dublin, turn west on Forest Service Road 5728 where the campground is posted.

Campground: Sand Lake has three loops of 45 sites with tables, fire rings with sliding grills, and paved spurs. The loops with sites 1 through 30 on them are in a hilly area forested in a variety of hardwoods. The sites here are well separated, some without a neighbor in view. There are none directly on Sand Lake but a handful (sites 16-19) are conveniently located next to a stairway that leads directly to campground's beach. Other facilities on the loops include flush toilets, vault toilets, and spigots for water.

Day-use Facilities: The campground has a beautiful and very wide beach with a marked swimming area, bathhouse, and separate parking

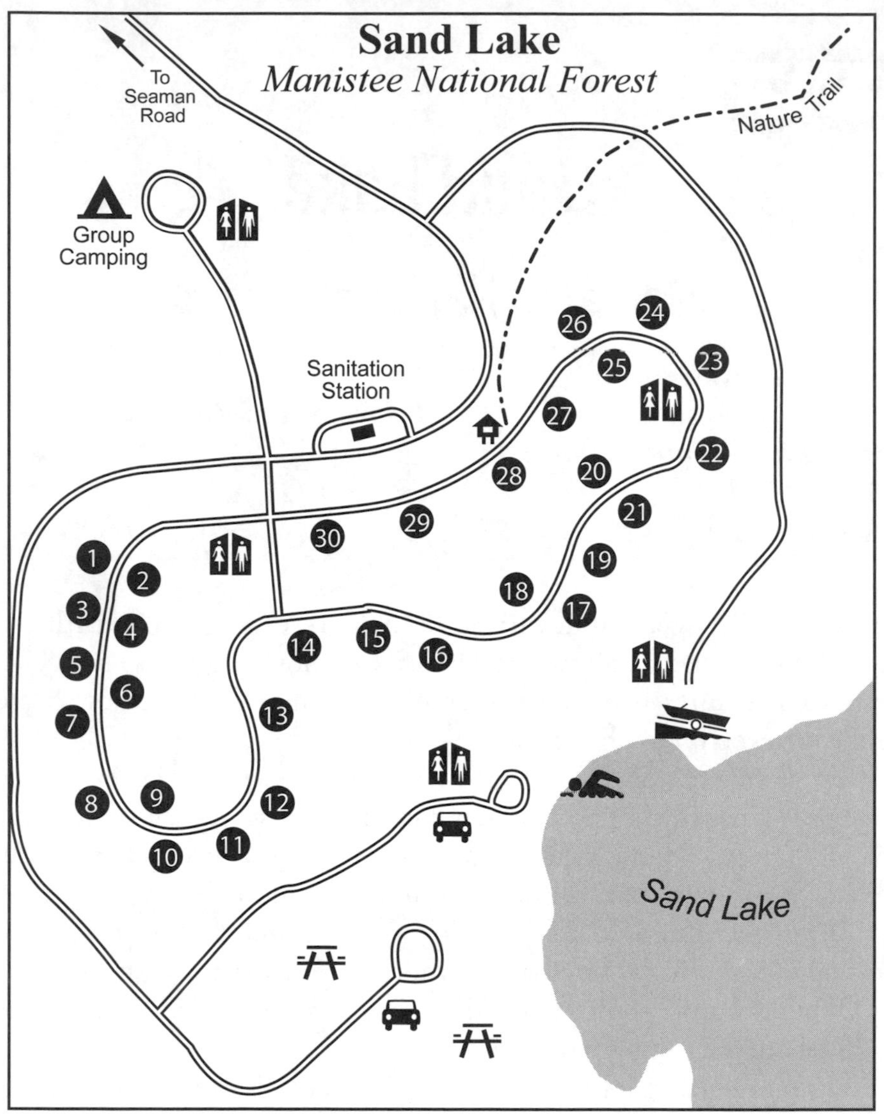

lot. During the summer a lifeguard arrives at 11 AM. Located on a bluff overlooking the beach is a small picnic area with tables and grills.

Fishing: The campground has a ramp area for carry-in boats only, with additional parking for anglers. Canoes and rowboats are available for rent during the summer.

Sand Lake has 50 surface acres and a shoreline that, except for the small portion in the campground, is privately owned. There are many cottages, yet the lake doesn't appear to be as developed as many farther south. Sand Lake's fishery is a mixed bag. It's stocked with rainbow trout, but many anglers target it for bass while others are just happy to catch a few perch or bluegill.

Hiking: There's a short nature trail here that is less than a mile long and begins across from site No. 28. It has 12 interpretive posts, but you might be hard pressed to find the corresponding guide.

Season: The campground is managed from Memorial Day through Labor Day. Sand Lake is rarely full in the middle of the week, and open sites exist even on many weekends. Sites can be reserved through the National Recreation Reservation Service ☎ 877-444-6777 🌐 www.recreation.gov six months in advance. There is a reservation fee of $9 for booking sites in advance.

56

Lake Michigan Recreation Area

Manistee National Forest

Campground: Rustic
County: Mason
Nearest Community: Manistee
Sites: 99
Reservations: Yes
Fee: $18
Information: Manistee Ranger District
☎ (231) 723-2211

Even though it's a rustic facility, the Lake Michigan Recreation Area is the most popular unit in the national forest and probably one of the most popular campgrounds anywhere in the state regardless who administers it. Located 13 miles south of Manistee on the edge of the Nordhouse Dunes Wilderness, the U.S. Forest facility was once called by Family Circle magazine, "one of the 20 best campgrounds in America."

It's easy to understand why.

The beach is beautiful, the dunes provide spectacular vistas, there are great hiking opportunities into the Nordhouse Dunes, and just getting to the campground provides a sense of adventure. The recreation area is at

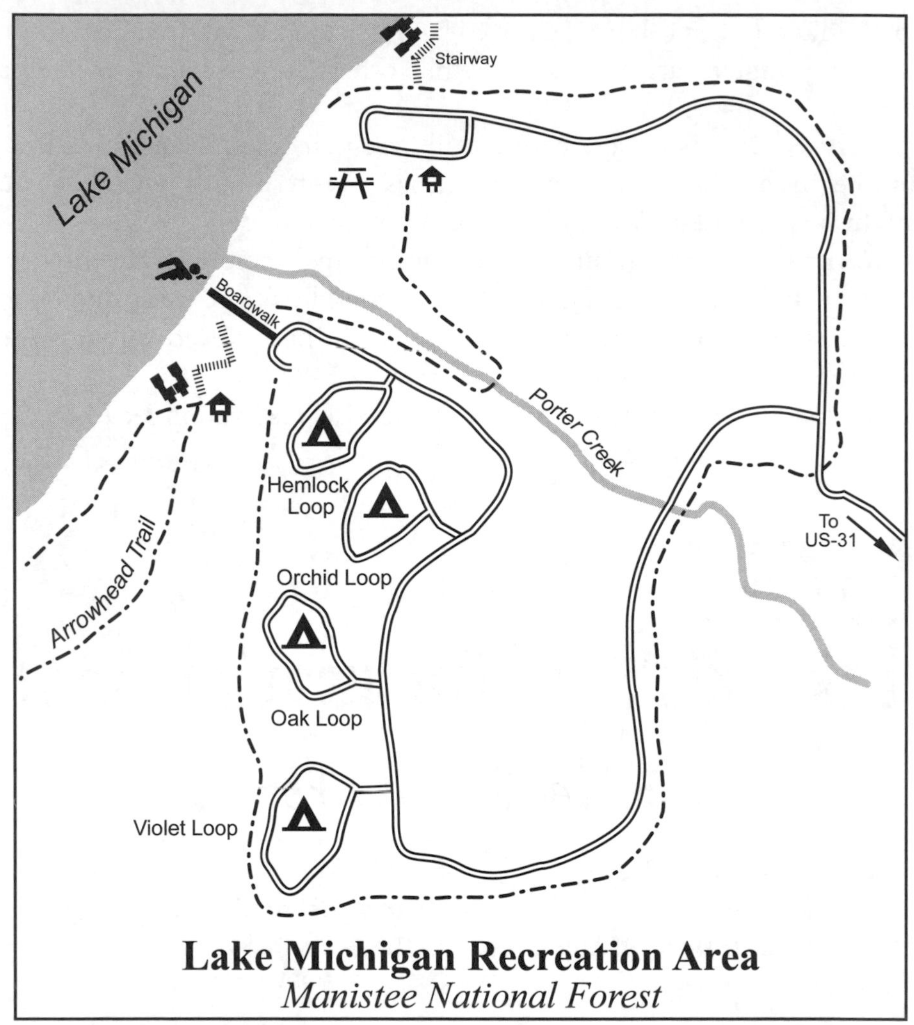

Lake Michigan Recreation Area
Manistee National Forest

the end of Lake Michigan Road (FR 5629), an 8-mile drive from US-31 through nothing but woods. Arrive at dawn or dusk and chances are you'll spot a handful of deer if not a dozen or two along the way.

About the only thing this campground lacks is good fishing opportunities, but there are so many other things to do, you won't miss the rod and reel for a few days.

Directions: To reach the campground from Manistee, head south on US-31 for 10 miles and then right at Lake Michigan Road. The recreation area is reached in eight miles at the end of the road. If coming from Ludington, Lake Michigan Road is 11.5 miles north of the junction of US-31 and US-10 in Scottville.

Campers at Lake Michigan Recreation Area in the Manistee National Forest enjoy the view from one of the campground's two overlooks of Lake Michigan.

Campground: The 99 sites are located on four loops of 25 each with Hemlock and Orchid loops the most popular due to their close proximity to the beach access point and the fact they have flush toilets. The others have vault toilets. The campsites are spacious and well spread out in an area forested in pines and hardwoods, especially oak trees. There is a fire ring, table, and a lantern post at each site.

There are no showers, but what a beach!

A forested dune separates the sites from Lake Michigan, and access to the beach is where Porter Creek empties into the Great Lake. Stone and wood chip paths lead from all the loops to a wooden walkway that serves as entry to a beautiful stretch of golden sand and turquoise surf. If the night is clear, you can sit on a bench or the small foredunes and watch a dying sun melt into the dark blue horizon of Lake Michigan.

Day-use Facilities: North of Porter Creek is a day-use area with playground equipment, tables, pedestal grills, and two small shelters as well as vault toilets and its own beach access. Paths and a foot bridge allow campers to cross over and climb the observation deck in the day-use area, one of the two found here. It's 167 steps up to the top of a towering dune

A young camper heads out to the beach at the Lake Michigan Recreation Area during a camping trip in April.

but well worth it. From the viewing platform on a clear day you can see miles of beach, acres of dunes, and to the south the distinctive black and white tower of the Big Point Sable Lighthouse in Ludington State Park.

Hiking: The second observation deck is reached via a long staircase from the beach walkway near the campground. The view is not nearly as good, but located next to the platform is the trailhead for the Nordhouse Dunes Wilderness, the only federally-designated wilderness in the Lower Peninsula.

There's a 10-mile network of foot paths in the 3,450-acre preserve, including Arrowhead Trail, a 0.8-mile loop that is idea for families with young children. If a child can climb the 122 steps to the observation deck, he or she can handle this short trail. Even better is the route that parallels the shoreline along the crest of a dune. At one time referred to as the Michigan Trail, this hike is an enchanting walk where you walk while viewing the white sandy beach below or the endless blue of Lake Michigan on the horizon. Return on the first spur back from this trail and it makes for a 2.4-mile loop. Those up for an easy but all-day adventure can hike the beach all the way to the Big Point Sable Lighthouse, a round-trip of eight miles to the historic tower.

Season: The managed season is mid-May to mid-September, but the campground is open year-round unless the access road is closed by snowfall. Sites in the off season are $10 a night. The facility is often filled from Thursday through Sunday from July 4 through early August. The 25 sites along the Oak Loop can be reserved six months in advance through the National Recreation Reservation Service ☎ 877-444-6777 🌐 www.recreation.gov, which charges a $9 reservation fee.

57

Seaton Creek

Manistee National Forest

Campground: Rustic
County: Wexford
Nearest Community: Mesick
Sites: 17
Reservations: No

Fee: $14
Information: Manistee Ranger District
☎ (231) 723-2211

Located in a remote area on the backwaters of Hodenpyl Dam Pond, Seaton Creek Campground is hard to find but a very enjoyable spot to spend a weekend once you do. The rustic campground is situated on a bluff above where its namesake creek flows into west end of this impoundment of the Manistee River.

This is a section of the Manistee National Forest with lots to do, including excellent opportunities for fishing, canoeing, and morel hunting in the spring. Hikers have it even better. Located within the campground is the trailhead for the Manistee River Trail, an 11.5-mile route along the river, while nearby a footbridge leads across the Manistee River to a segment of the North Country Trail.

Directions: From Mesick head south six miles on M-37 and then turn right on 26-Mile Road near Yuma. Follow it for 1.7 miles then turn right on Fork Road (also labeled O'Rourke Drive on some maps) for 1.3 miles and right again on Forest Road 5993. The campground is 0.4 miles at the end of FR 5993.

Campground: Seaton Creek has 17 sites on a single loop in a wooded area that offers good privacy between campers. The sites are gravel spurs, and 13 of them are pull-through making it easier for those who arrive in trailers and pop-ups.

Other amenities include four vault toilets, fire rings, tables, and a hand pump for water.

Day-use Facilities: There is a small picnic area closer to the edge of the bluff overlooking Seaton Creek. From here, trails and steps lead to the water below and then upstream along the creek, providing shore anglers with places to cast.

Hiking: Within the picnic area is the trailhead for the Manistee River Trail, which extends 11.5 miles along the east side of the river to Red Bridge on Coates Highway. Built in 1990, this scenic trail passes numerous views the river. It is also relatively level with few major hills or ridges to climb, unlike the North Country Trail on the west of the river.

A popular dayhike is to a small waterfall along the trail, a round-trip trek of 6 miles from the campground. In the middle of the summer, the falls are not overly impressive but in the spring or after a hard rainfall the cascade can be an eight-foot leap towards the river.

Within 1.25 miles of the campground, you pass an impressive suspension bridge that spans 245 feet across the Manistee River just below the Hodenpyl Dam. On the other side of the foot bridge is the Manistee Segment of the North Country Trail which winds 9 miles south to Red Bridge. Unlike the Manistee River Trail, this section of the NCT is a rugged trek with considerable climbing. When the two trails are combined, they form a 23-mile loop for backpackers, a two- to three-day trek from Seaton Creek Campground.

Canoeing: A trail and stairway lead from the picnic area to a small dock where paddlers can drop a canoe into Seaton Creek. The creek here is a sluggish body of water and easy to paddle. You can also dip into Hodenpyl Dam Pond, but paddlers need to remember to stay well away from the nearby dam.

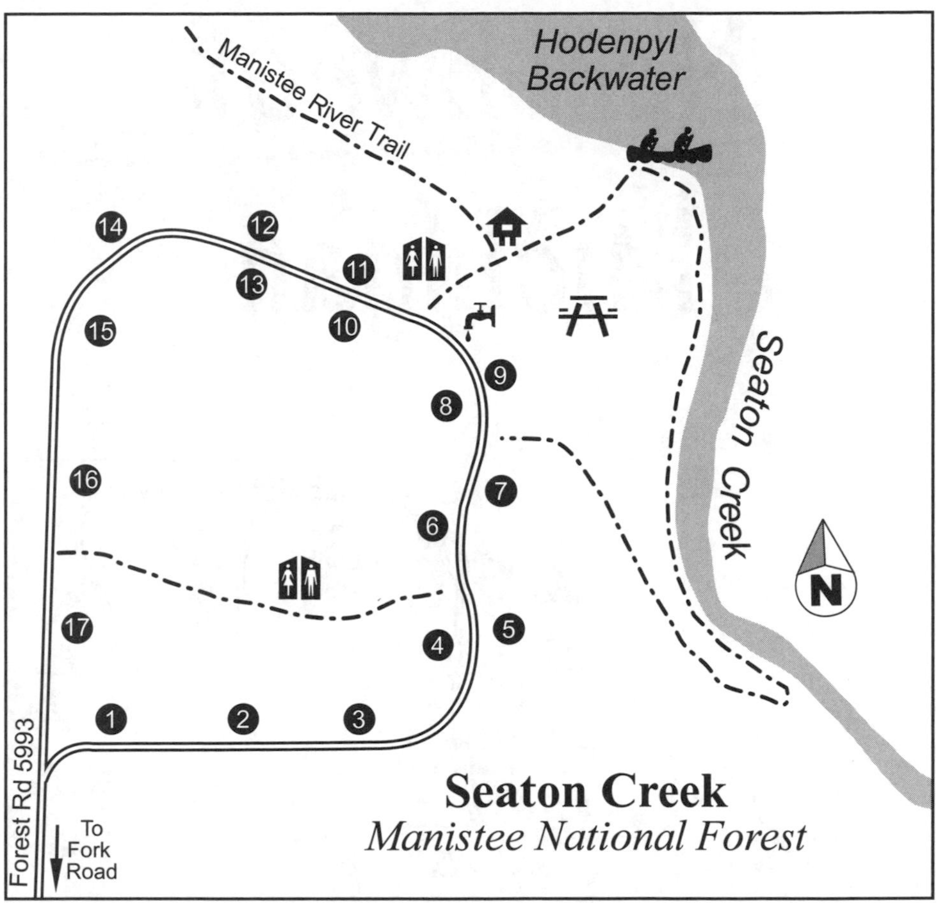

Fishing: Hodenpyl Dam Pond is a 1,798-acre, 5-mile long impoundment of the Manistee River that was created in 1925. It reaches depths of up to 30 feet and is usually fished for walleye, smallmouth bass, and northern pike. Seaton Creek near the campground and at its mouth into the impoundment also offers fishing opportunities, particularly for bluegills and black crappies.

Season: Seaton Creek is open from mid-May through September. The campground can get filled during weekends in July and August, but otherwise sites are usually available.

Northwest Michigan

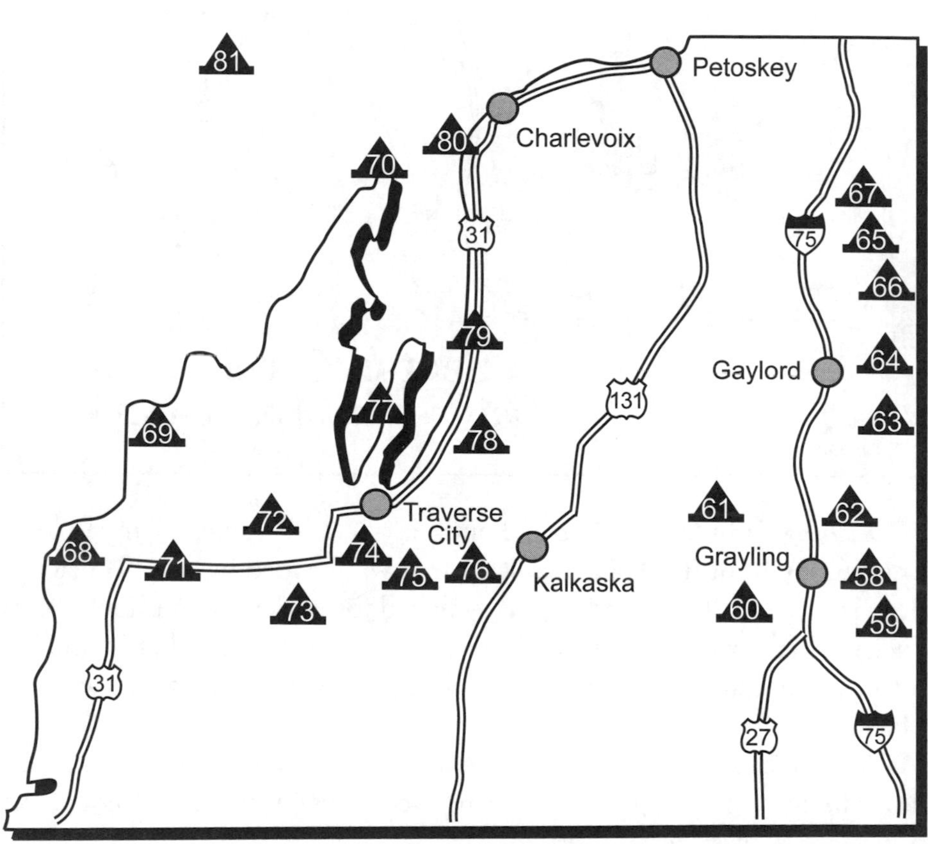

#	PARK	MODERN	SEMI-MODERN	RUSTIC	SITES	DAY-USE FACILITIES	FISHING	HIKING	BIRDING	INTERPRETIVE CENTER	BIKING	CANOEING/ KAYAKING	BOATING
58	Keystone Landing			•	18		•					•	
59	Kneff Lake			•	26	•	•	•					
60	Lake Margrethe			•	40	•	•						
61	Upper Manistee River			•	40		•					•	
62	Hartwick Pines	•			100	•	•	•		•	•		
63	Shupac Lake			•	30	•	•						
64	Big Bear Lake			•	44	•	•	•					
65	Pigeon River			•	19	•	•	•					
66	Town Corner Lake			•	12		•	•					
67	Pickerel Lake			•	39	•	•	•					
68	Platte River (Sleeping Bear)	•	•		174	•	•	•				•	
69	D.H. Day			•	88	•		•					
70	Leelanau			•	51	•		•		•			
71	Platte River (Pere Marquette)			•	26		•	•				•	
72	Lake Dubonnet			•	50		•	•					
73	Green Lake			•	60	•	•	•					
74	Arbutus Lake			•	40	•	•						•
75	Scheck's Place			•	30		•	•				•	
76	Guernsey Lake			•	30	•	•	•					
77	Power Island			•	5	•		•					
78	Whitewater	•	•		55	•	•	•					
79	Barnes	•	•		86	•		•					
80	Fisherman's Island			•	81	•	•	•					
81	Bill Wagner			•	22	•		•					

58

Keystone Landing

Au Sable State Forest

Campground: Rustic
County: Crawford
Nearest Community: Grayling
Sites: 18
Reservations: No
Fee: $15
Information: Grayling DNR office
☎ (989) 348-6371

A fly fisher's haven, Keystone Landing is one of several state forest facilities along the Au Sable River. It is a scenic facility overlooking Au Sable's legendary Holy Waters and utilized by both anglers and canoeists. The campground is not big, and at only 18 sites it's easy for Keystone Landing to fill up.

Directions: From the junction of Business Loop I-75 in Grayling, head east on M-72 and then in 6 miles turn north (left) on Keystone Landing Road.

Campground: Keystone Landing is a single loop of 18 sites located on a bluff along the south bank of the Au Sable. The area is heavily forested with the sites well spread out and secluded from each other. You can wander to the edge of the bluff and spend a quiet evening watching fly fishermen work their magic. Tables, fire rings, hand pump for water, and vault toilets are provided.

Fishing: This stretch of the Au Sable is part of the Holy Waters, a flies-only, no-kill quality fishing area open year-round. The river is 30 yards wide here, ranging from two to four feet in depth and for the most part can be waded. In May and June, this is one of the most popular sections of the Au Sable for fly fishermen to catch both brown and brook trout.

A pair of stairs in the campground provide easy access down to the river for wader-attired anglers. You can also drive past the entrance of the campground and park at the end of Keystone Landing Road where there is a public access site.

A fly angler fishes for trout in the Au Sable River near Keystone Landing State Forest Campground.

Canoeing: The Au Sable is almost as famous a canoe route as it is a trout stream. The river makes for a 135-mile journey to Oscoda on Lake Huron, and the most popular stretch is from Grayling to Mio. There are seven state forest campgrounds posted in the river for canoeists between Grayling and Mio. A number of canoe liveries work the Au Sable, including Borchers Canoeing ☎ 989-348-4921 🌐 www.canoeborchers.com, Penrod's Au Sable River Resort ☎ 989-348-2910 🌐 www.penrodscanoe.com and Carlisle Canoes ☎ 989-348-2301 🌐 www.carlislecanoes.com.

Season: From early May through June this campground can be filled any weekend with fly fishermen. In July and August, it can be canoeists who take up all the sites. Getting a site midweek is rarely a problem.

59

Kneff Lake

Huron National Forest

Campground: Rustic
County: Crawford
Nearest Community: Grayling
Sites: 26
Reservations: No
Fee: $15
Information: Mio Ranger District
☎ (989) 826-3252

In an area of Michigan blessed with numerous campgrounds, Kneff Lake is a delightful little facility that is worth searching for. Although the national forest campground could be filled on a mid-summer weekend, it doesn't seem to draw the heavy pressure of Hartwick Pines State Park to the north or some of the state forest facilities west of Grayling along M-72.

Kneff Lake features an excellent beach and picnic area and a hilly terrain that allows sites to be well separated and secluded from each other. Kneff is also a designated trout lake, but many anglers are dismayed once they arrive to discover that it lacks a boat ramp or any other kind of launch facility.

Directions: From the Business Loop I-75 in the heart of Grayling head east on M-72 for 6.5 miles and then south (right) on Stephan Bridge Road. In 1.4 miles turn east (left) on Forest Road 4003, and the entrance of the campground is reached in a half mile.

Campground: Sites 1–19 are located on Jack Pine Loop and 20–26 on Oak Loop. Both loops are on a bluff that surrounds the lake. Sites 10 and 12 actually have a partial view of the water, but the rest are in a forest of predominantly oak with moderate undergrowth, and while you can't see the lake, you can't see your neighbor either. A posted trail from each loop leads down to the beach, and all sites have a table, fire ring with sliding grill, lantern post, and graveled parking spurs. The campground also has vault toilets and spigots for water.

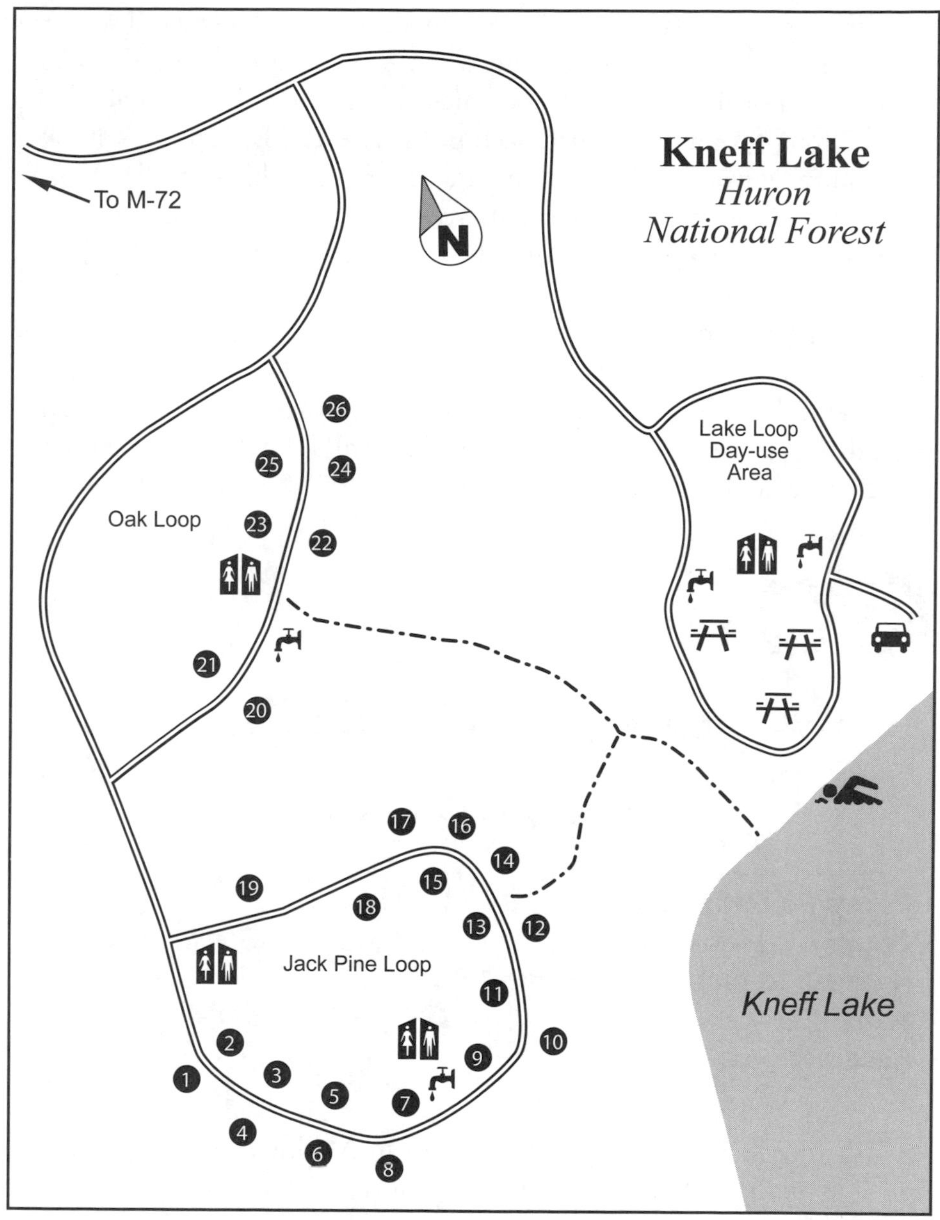

Day-use Facilities: Kneff Lake has a picnic area separate from the campground loops with tables and pedestal grills that are well spread out. The best part is the beach. The sand here is 15 to 20 yards wide and enclosed by extensive log terraces. A swimming area is marked off, but beware—the water is cold and the bottom slopes off quickly.

Fishing: The 14-acre lake lies mostly in national forest land with the exception of a few cottages on the south end. It's a cold and deep lake, with depths of 40 to 50 feet and once was stocked with grayling in a failed attempt to bring the fish back in the late 1980s. Today it's stocked with rainbow trout with most anglers using slip bobbers to fish worms right off the bottom of the lake. There is no boat launch, but it's easy to carry a canoe down to the water through the picnic area. A belly boat would be perfect here.

Hiking: A network of foot trails spans from site to site, down to the beach, and through the surrounding hills.

Season: Kneff has a campground host and is managed from mid-May to mid-September. Occasionally the facility will fill up on a weekend, but usually you can count on getting a site.

Lake Margrethe

Au Sable State Forest

Campground: Rustic
County: Crawford
Nearest Community: Grayling
Sites: 40
Reservations: No
Fee: $15
Information: Grayling DNR Office
☎ (989) 348-6371

This might be the only campground in Michigan with signs along one side that say "Military Boundary," but don't worry about tanks from neighboring Camp Grayling rolling through the sites or missiles streaking overhead.

Lake Margrethe is a large but peaceful facility situated in the hilly terrain along the west shore of this popular lake. There is a variety of sites available, including some secluded walk-ins, others on the lakeshore, and even a handicapped-accessible site. The only drawback of Lake

Margrethe is its popularity, often filled on the weekends, and the lack of a boat launch.

Directions: The campground is 5 miles west of Grayling. From M-72 turn south onto McIntyre Landing Road.

Campground: Lake Margrethe has 40 sites spread out along many loops on the west side of the lake. The hilly shoreline makes this a beautiful campground with most of it forested in pine and hardwoods. More than half of the sites are situated right on the water with a fine view of this huge lake while others are merely across the park road.

A dozen of the sites, including seven of the first eight, are walk-in; you park your car and haul the tent to the site. Sites No. 1–3 are at the south end of the campground, off by themselves and right on the lake for a somewhat secluded setting. Sites No. 35–38 and a few others are up on a small hill from where you park the car and provide a unique overview of the lake.

Overall the sites are close together and lack the privacy of most state forest campgrounds. Site No. 32 is reserved for handicapped campers. It's located next to a barrier-free vault toilet and near a special wood ramp and deck onto the lake. Facilities include vault toilets, hand pumps for water, fire rings, and tables.

Day-use Facilities: A beach and picnic area is located just north of the campground and consists of a separate parking lot and a handful of tables in an open grassy area. There is no real beach here, but the swimming is excellent with shallow water and a sandy bottom in a lake that is gin clear.

Fishing: Unfortunately, there is no boat launch within the campground and the nearest public facility is at the south end of the lake in Camp Grayling. Hand-carried boats can easily be launched from most sites.

The mile-wide Lake Margrethe is 1,920-acres large and well developed. An all-sports lake, there is considerable use by motor boaters, water skiers, and jet skiers. The lake is a warm-water fishery best known for smallmouth bass and muskies though the bulk of its catch by anglers is bluegill and other panfish.

Season: The heavy recreational use of Lake Margrethe and the campground's location just off M-72 and makes it a popular facility. Expect it to be filled any weekend from July through August and occasionally in the middle of the week.

61

Upper Manistee River

Au Sable State Forest

Campground: Rustic
County: Crawford
Nearest Community: Grayling
Sites: 40
Reservations: No
Fee: $15
Information: Grayling DNR office
☎ (989) 348-6371

There are eight state forest campgrounds on the Manistee River, and the most popular facility is 8 miles west of Grayling where M-72 crosses the famous trout stream. If you camp to get away and value a little solitude in the woods, you don't want to stay at Manistee River Bridge. If nothing else, thc fact that it is located across from a canoe livery should tell you everything.

Instead, find your way to Upper Manistee River because this far upstream there is less development along the river and far less traffic on it. The campground is more of the wooded setting you expect up north, and there's no M-72, a virtual interstate with travelers during the summer, 50 yards from your trailer.

Directions: From M-72, turn north on Manistee River Road, a dirt road that is reached from Graying right before you cross the river. Follow it 6 miles to County Road 612, turn west, cross the river, and then turn south (left) on Goose Creek Road where the campground is posted. The entrance is a mile south of CR 612.

The quickest way to reach the campground from I-75 is to skip Grayling all together and depart at Frederic (exit 264) and head west on CR 612.

Campground: Upper Manistee River has 30 vehicle sites on two loops situated in a pine forest with an undergrowth of ferns. The sites are well spread out, and a few are along the bank above the river but not

A fly angler casts during a hatch on the Manistee River at the Upper Manistee River State Forest Campground.

within view of the water. There are also 10 more walk-in sites in an area lightly forested with little undergrowth. This is a very pleasant section, well-worth the short walk in if you have a tent. Many sites are along the edge of the bank with a nice view of the Manistee gently flowing through a grassy area. Facilities include vault toilets, hand pumps for water, tables, and fire rings.

Fishing: The Upper Manistee is a popular fly fishing area for rainbow and brown trout. The river has been stabilized in many areas while log railings have been constructed along the banks in the campground. This far upstream the Manistee is 15 to 20 yards wide, more than enough to cast a fly rod at the raising rings. Most of the stream is less than four feet deep and can be easily waded though you might encounter a few deep holes in this area.

Canoeing: Upper Manistee has a canoe landing within its group sites along with canoe racks. Another canoe landing is situated just upriver at the CR 612 bridge. From the county road it is an 18-mile paddle, or four-hour trip, to Manistee River Bridge Campground. The next state forest campground is CCC Campground, another 30 miles down stream. Canoes can be rented from Long's Canoes ☎ 989-348-7224 and Shel-Haven ☎ 989-348-2158 🌐 www.shelhaven.com on M-72.

Season: Normally you can obtain a vehicle site and surely a walk-in at this campground even on the weekends. Just keep in mind that can change quickly if a large group of paddlers have chosen to stay overnight here.

62

Hartwick Pines

State Park

Campground: Modern
County: Wexford
Nearest Community: Grayling
Sites: 100
Reservations: Yes
Fee: $25–$33 plus vehicle entry fee
Information: State park office ☎ (989) 348-7068

Loggers, lumber barons, and towering white pines made Michigan the greatest lumber-producing state in the country between 1869 and 1900. Only a few parcels of virgin pine escaped the cutting, and by far the most popular one is a 49-acre tract north of Grayling, the heart of Hartwick Pines State Park. Within this stand of 300-year-old trees are big wheels, a reconstructed logging camp, and a logging museum that recounts Michigan's White Pine Era.

The interpretive area is fascinating, but there is more to this Crawford County state park than big trees. At 9,672 acres, Hartwick is the largest unit in the Lower Peninsula and features four small lakes, the Au Sable River's East Branch, miles of hiking trails, and one of the newest campgrounds in the Michigan state park system.

Directions: From 1-75 north of Grayling, depart at exit 259 and head north on M-93 for 3 miles to the park entrance.

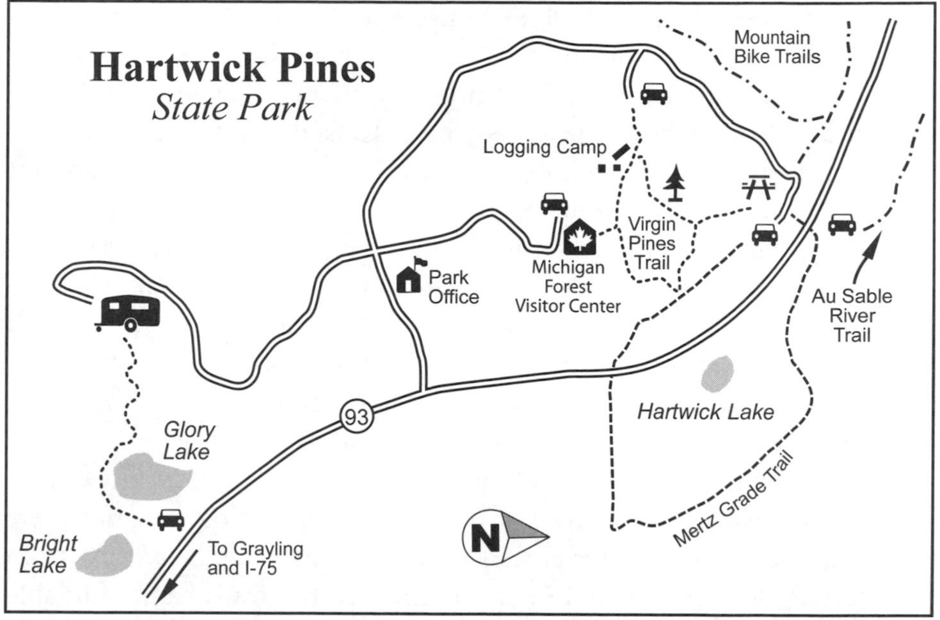

A MONARCH NO MORE

A camper at Hartwick Pines State Park admires a towering pine along the Au Sable Trail.

The Monarch has died. The star attraction of the Hartwick Pines State Park and easily the most recognized and beloved tree in Michigan was a 350-year white pine that somehow escaped the swinging axes of the lumberjacks who marched through Crawford County in the late 19th century. By the late 1990s, however, park naturalists noticed that what little green the tree had produced the year before had not returned. Basically, the 155-foot-tall white pine, the largest tree most people ever saw in Michigan, died of old age but not until overwhelming millions by its size and grandeur, especially children who would stand there and gaze at that massive trunk and unknowingly gain a sense, and maybe even an appreciation, for old growth forests. You can still see the tree's massive trunk, and there are plans to someday crown a new Monarch, a 130-foot tall white pine with a diameter of almost 44 inches, and then re-route the trail toward the tree and erect a fence around it.

Campground: Hartwick Pines' campground was moved and rebuilt in the mid-1990s and is now located in a much more isolated corner of the park. The modern campground is now considerably larger at 100 sites, with most of them in an open grassy area. Tucked into the wooded edge of the campground are a number of sites that offer a surprising amount of privacy for a modern campground.

Along with a sanitation station for RVers and modern restroom/shower buildings, the campground also has paved sites, many of them drive-through for larger recreational vehicles, and full hook-ups with water and electricity at 36 sites. Hartwick Pines also has a rustic cabin near Glory and Bright lakes with a foot trail that connects it to the rest of the park. The stone and log cabin sleeps six and is just off M-93.

Nightly fees are $33 for a full hook-up and $25 for electricity only.

Day-use Facilities: Hartwick Pines has no swimming area, but there is a picnic area with shelters at the end of the park road. Departing from the parking lot are the trailheads for the Mertz Grade Trail, AuSable River Trail, and the mountain biking trail system.

Interpretive Center: The park's stand of virgin pine is best enjoyed by first visiting the Michigan Forest Visitors Center. The history and growth of the Michigan forest is traced through a number of hands-on, computer generated exhibits, displays, and photos of the men who cut the trees and the camps they-lived in. During the summer the center is open 10 AM to 6 PM daily. After Labor Day, the center switches to winter hours: 9 AM to 4 PM ☎ 989-348-2537.

From the interpretive center you then follow Virgin Pines Trail, a paved path that winds through this rare stand of white pine. Along the way you pass a "big wheel," the device used to haul the massive logs out of the forest, the Monarch, and a logging camp of several buildings that was constructed by the CCC. Within the camp there is a bunkhouse and mess hall you can walk through, the camp boss' quarters, blacksmith's shop, and a steam-powered sawmill.

Fishing: The East Branch of the Au Sable River, which flows 16 miles from its source southwest into the main stream, is especially scenic in Hartwick Pines. Here the river is a crystal-clear stream that gurgles over gravel banks and undercuts the banks around deadheads and trees. Too narrow to be a good canoeing waterway, the East Branch is an excellent brook trout stream. Most anglers are spin or bait fishermen using worms to entice brookies or brown trout that have been known to exceed 20 inches at times. Access to the river is along the Scenic Drive, a dirt road within the park that crosses it twice, or the Au Sable River Trail.

The state park also has four inland lakes of which two are stocked annually. Bright and Glory lakes lie side by side off M-93, south of the park entrance, and possess a good population of smallmouth bass and panfish but are also stocked with trout. There is an unimproved boat launch to each lake and a fishing pier on Bright Lake.

A family pauses on the Virgin Pines Trail at Hartwick Pines State Park.

Hiking: Hartwick has six miles of designated foot trails with the longest walk being the Au Sable River Trail. The 3-mile loop has a trailhead at the day-use parking area and begins by immediately crossing M-93 and then Scenic Drive. The trail passes through a hardwood and conifer forest, twice crosses the East Branch of the AuSable River, and at one point reaches the height of 1,240 feet.

The Mertz Grade Trail shares the same trailhead with the AuSable River Trail but swings south after crossing M-93. This 2-mile trail loops around Hartwick Lake before recrossing M-93. The other designated foot trail is the popular Virgin Pines Trail, a mile loop through the tract of old growth white pines. All three paths are marked with numbered stops and corresponding trail brochures.

Mountain Biking: The ski trails at Hartwick Pines are open to mountain bikers spring through fall and make for a 10-mile system that basically forms a 7.5-mile loop with two crossover spurs. The route is a wide path through a rolling forested terrain and is rated for beginner and intermediate bikers. The bike trailhead is in the day-use area parking lot at the end of the park road.

Season: The campground is open from April to mid-November. During April and again from mid-October to mid-November, there are electric hook-ups at the sites and vault toilets. The off-season rate then is $16 a night.

Hartwick Pines is filled every weekend from late June through early October when the fall colors are peaking and 70 to 80 percent filled midweek throughout most of the summer. To reserve a campsite contact Michigan State Park Central Reservations ☎ 800-447-2757 🌐 www.midnrreservations.com.

Shupac Lake

Au Sable State Forest

Campground: Rustic
County: Crawford
Nearest Community: Lovells
Sites: 30
Reservations: No
Fee: $15
Information: Grayling DNR Office
☎ (989) 348-6371

Shupac Lake is a scenic body of water and a quiet one by law. Special regulations prevent high-speed boating while the limited number of cottages, mostly restricted to the southeast shoreline, allow the campers on the northwest corner to enjoy a little solitude in the woods.

The state forest campground is a long-time haven of trout fishermen who either take to the nearby North Branch of the Au Sable or fish Shupac Lake itself, which is stocked annually with rainbow trout.

You don't have to be a fly fisher to enjoy this rustic facility. Practically all of the sites have a view of the water, the beach is sandy, the swimming excellent, and there is even a perch fishery to entertain those anglers not interested in tossing around feathers on a hook.

Directions: From I-75, depart at exit 264 and head east. In 8 miles you pass the posted side road to Jones Lake State Forest Campground at which point County Road 612 begins curving its way to the village of Lovells. Just before crossing the North Branch into town, you turn north onto Twin Bridge Road and in 2 miles reach the posted entrance to the campground.

Campground: Shupac has 30 sites located on a long loop with almost every one of them on the edge of a bluff overlooking the lake. Situated in a forest of predominantly oak with moderate undergrowth, the sites are well spread out and secluded from each other, and many feature their own log staircase leading down to the water. The northern half of the loop is especially scenic as you look out over a small, undeveloped bay at the north end of the lake. Tables, fire grills, a hand pump for water, and vault toilets are found along the loop.

Day-use Facilities: A small picnic area with a few tables is located at the south end of the campground and features a narrow beach of sorts next to the boat launch. There is no marked swimming area, but the water is extremely clear and the sandy bottom gently slopes into the lake.

Fishing: There is a cement ramp in the day-use area with a large parking area, attesting to the popularity of the lake to anglers. Boating regulations include a ban on water skiing and "no high speed boating" which most locals interpret as no wake. The deep lake is stocked with rainbow trout but also supports perch and panfish. During the summer anglers usually fish for trout with corn, live minnows, or night crawlers about 20 feet down and rigged to a slip bobber.

Just before entering the campground, you cross Twin Bridge, an access point for fly fishermen entering the North Branch of the Au Sable. This is a Quality Fishing Area, meaning artificial flies only. The daily limit is six trout of which brook trout have to be a minimum eight inches, all others 10 inches. The North Branch is one of Michigan's blue ribbon trout streams and attracts steady pressure. Fly shops in Lovells will be able to assist interested anglers with fly patterns and other access points.

Season: Occasionally this campground can fill on a mid-summer weekend, but usually a site can be obtained throughout the summer.

64

Big Bear Lake

Mackinaw State Forest

Campground: Rustic
County: Otsego
Nearest Community: Vienna Corners
Sites: 44
Reservations: No
Fee: $15
Information: Gaylord DNR Office
☎ (989) 732-3541

The main campground on Big Bear Lake lacks a boat ramp as well as the privacy usually associated with state forest campgrounds. However, it does have one feature most other units would be hard pressed to match, a beautiful beach only a few steps from your site.

The clear water of the lake combined with the sandy strip at its north shore is no doubt the reason for its popularity. This is one of the few state forest units that can easily be filled on any summer weekend. Big Bear also features a foot trail, an opportunity to watch beavers, and moderately good fishing for several species including walleye and pike.

Directions: From I-75 depart at exit 282 and head east through downtown Gaylord on M-32. The hamlet of Vienna Corners is reached in 19 miles where you turn south on County Road F-01 for 1.2 miles and then west on Little Bear Road to the posted entrance of the campground.

Campground: There are two loops on the lake, each with their own entrance off Little Bear Lake Road. The main loop is called Big Bear Lake and has 30 sites on the northeast corner of the lake with 15 of them overlooking the beach and 11 of them large enough to accommodate 40-foot trailers. The area is lightly forested in hardwoods with little undergrowth thus the lack of isolation from your neighbors.

The smaller loop, called Big Bear Point, is on the northwest corner of the lake and has 14 sites in a thicker forest and heavier brush. Not only do these sites offer more privacy, but four of them are situated on a low bluff with a scenic view of the entire lake.

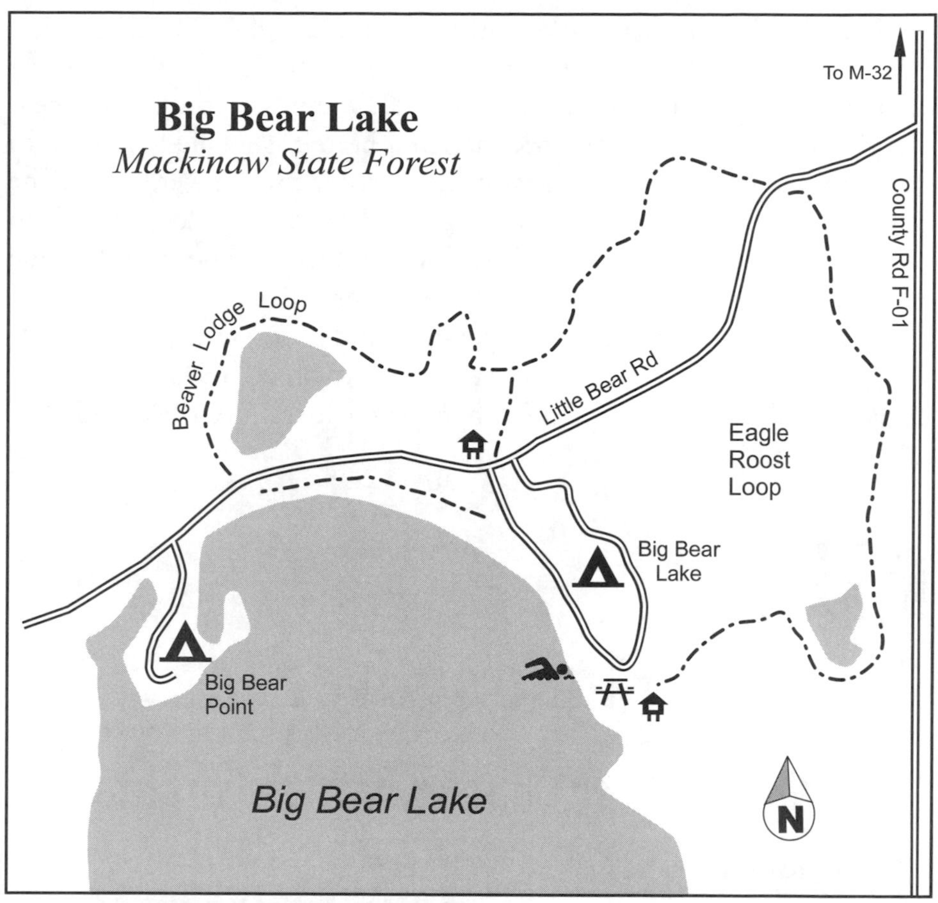

Day-use Facilities: A small picnic area is situated along the beach in the main campground and has tables, pedestal grills, and limited parking. The beach is nice, the reason this loop fills up first, and there is a large marked swimming area with a sandy bottom that gently slopes towards the deeper sections of the lake.

Fishing: The campground lacks a cement ramp, but hand-carried boats are easy to launch from either loop and a few campers even use their trailers along the shore to put in something larger. Big Bear is primarily known as a walleye fishery with most anglers working the drop-offs with jigs and crawlers to entice the popular gamefish. There is also northern pike as the small loop borders a pike spawning marsh and, of course, bluegill, pumpkinseed, and other panfish. One of the best places for children to fish for bluegills from shore is the sandy spit that extends out from the small loop.

Hiking: The Big Bear Lake Pathway is a 2.2-mile trail divided into two loops. Some sections are difficult to follow, but it's hard to get lost because you are never very far from a road. One posted trailhead is near the picnic area in the large loop, and from here it is a half-mile walk to reach a pond where there is usually one or two active beaver lodges. The trail also departs west from the opposite end of the large loop, and from here you skirt the lake, cross Little Bear Lake Road, and on the other side come to a much bigger pond with more beaver activity.

Season: This campground is popular, and from mid-July to mid-August you might have difficulty getting a site on a Saturday afternoon or even Friday evening. I've been here when it has even been filled in mid-week, but that is rare.

Pigeon River

Pigeon River Country State Forest

Campground: Rustic
County: Otsego
Nearest Community: Vanderbilt
Sites: 19
Reservations: No
Fee: $15
Information: State forest headquarters
☎ (989) 983-4101

Within the Pigeon River County State Forest, a tract of more than 100,000 acres east of Vanderbilt, are six rustic campgrounds. With the exception of Pickerel Lake, all are small, out-of-the-way campgrounds in this rugged corner of the Lower Peninsula, home of the largest elk herd east of the Mississippi.

This includes Pigeon River where it's easy to get turned around trying to find the rustic campground... or trying to find your way back to the highway. But that is also the nicest feature. If you camp to escape into the woods, Pigeon River is a good destination, a miles-from-anywhere campground with little more than fire rings, tables, and vault toilets.

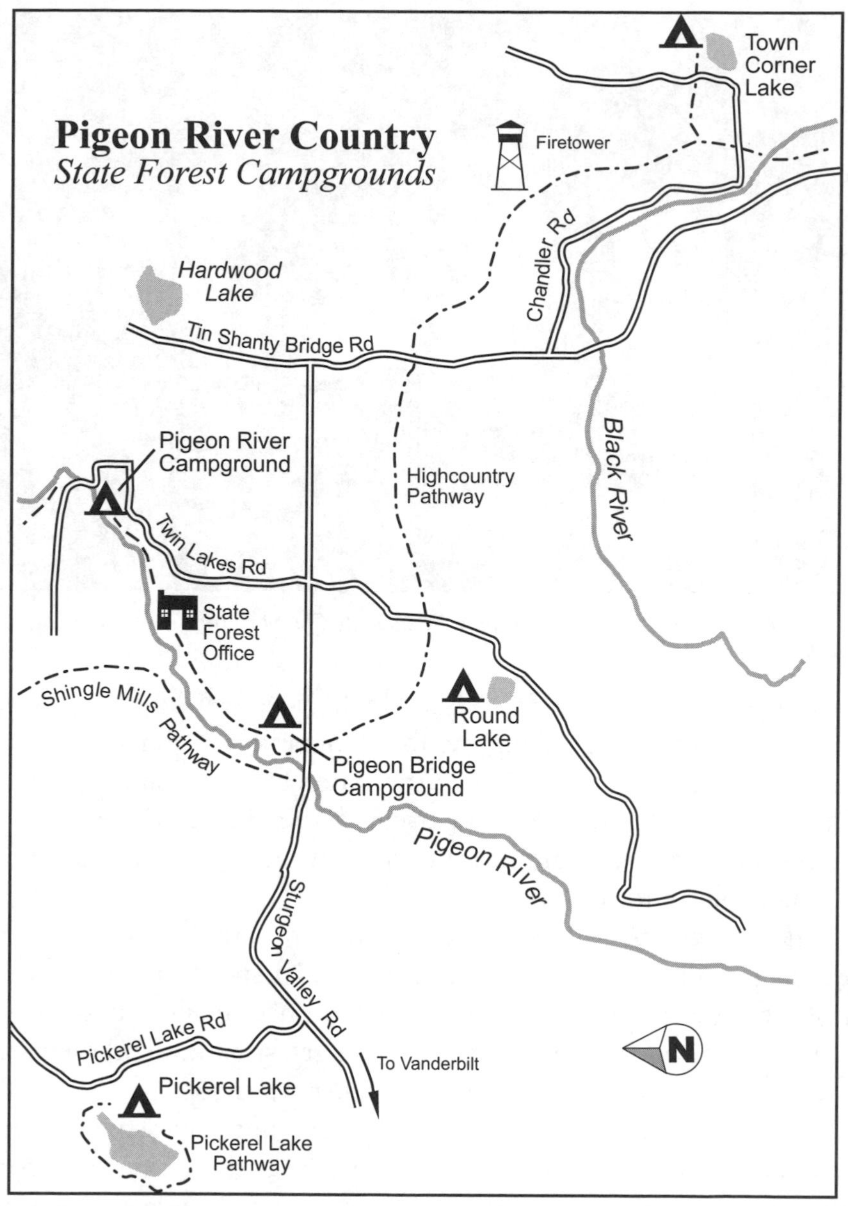

Directions: The campground is 13 miles east of Vanderbilt and reached by departing I-75 at exit 290. In downtown Vanderbilt turn east (left) on Sturgeon Valley Road and in 10 miles you will enter the state forest. After crossing the Pigeon River, turn north (left) on Osmond Road to arrive at the forest headquarters, an impressive log lodge. Stop and get a map and then continue north on Osmond Road as it curves and winds its way past the posted entrance to the campground.

A fly fisherman relaxes at a site in Pigeon River State Forest Campground while waiting for the afternoon hatch to begin.

Campground: Pigeon River is a single, one-way loop of 19 well-secluded sites spread out along the forested banks of its namesake river. Most of the sites are out of view of the water, but a few are right on the bank, including site No. 19, off by itself overlooking a bridge across the river. Facilities include tables and fire rings at most sites and vault toilets and a hand pump for water.

Day-use Facilities: A small, overgrown picnic area is at the south end of the loop with a table and a grill. The popular spot to picnic, however, is at the bridge. Here the river has been dammed up slightly to create a pool for wading and cooling off while open grassy banks lend themselves well to laying out in the sun on a hot August afternoon.

Fishing: Although many say the Pigeon is not supporting the trout populations it did a decade ago, the river still attracts a fair number of anglers. In June, half the sites here will have a pair of waders drying from a branch in mid-afternoon. In the campground the river is 30 to 40 feet wide and rarely more than 4 feet deep, making it easy wading with the exception of a few deep holes. Both brown and brook trout inhabit the Pigeon though you're most likely to catch a brown.

Hiking: The Shingle Mill Pathway passes through the campground and crosses the bridge over the Pigeon River here. The pathway is a series of loops that begins at Pigeon Bridge Campground on Sturgeon

Valley Road and follows the river much of the way. The hike from the campground to Sturgeon Valley Road and back would be a 6-mile trek.

Season: This campground is not nearly as poplar as the smaller Pigeon Bridge Campground or Pickerel Lake. On an average July weekend it will be less than half filled. A campground host manages the facility during the summer.

66

Town Corner Lake

Pigeon River Country State Forest

Campground: Rustic
County: Otsego
Nearest Community: Vanderbilt
Sites: 12
Reservations: No
Fee: $15
Information: State forest headquarters
☎ (989) 983-4101

You'll never have a problem finding an open site in Pigeon River Country State Forest even when arriving on a Friday evening. That's because spread across the 105,000-acre state forest are walk-in sites for backpackers, two trail camps for equestrians, and six campgrounds for people with a trailer on a hitch or a tent in the trunk. This makes Pigeon River Country an ideal destination when on Friday afternoon you suddenly decide to take the family camping.

If the first campground you pull into is full, just head to the next one. Eventually you'll find an open site. Or an entire campground. This is particularly true about Town Corner Lake, one of the more remote campgrounds in the state forest. Like the others, Town Corner has sites overlooking a lake, fishing opportunities, and a foot path passing through it.

But unlike the others, Town Corner is harder to find. It's best to begin any trip by stopping at the forest headquarters on Twin Lakes Road to pick up a map because there are few road signs in this area.

Directions: Town Corner Lake is tucked away in the southeast corner of the state forest. From the town of Vanderbilt follow Sturgeon Valley Road east to enter the state forest. Drive pass Pigeon Bridge Campground and stay on Sturgeon Valley Road until it ends at a stop sign. Head south on Tin Shanty Bridge Road (not posted) and in 2 miles veer southeast on Chandler Road, marked by a blue-tipped post at the intersection. The campground is reached in 2.5 miles on Chandler Road.

Campground: Town Corner is located on a low bluff along the south side of the lake. Seven of the 12 sites have a view of the water and all of them are located a short walk from the shoreline in a forested area with good privacy between sites.

Hiking: A spur connects Town Corner Lake to the High Country Pathway, the 70-mile backpacking trail that winds through four counties in the northeast corner of the Lower Peninsula. An excellent day hike from the campground is to head north on the pathway to reach the Pigeon River Lookout Tower in 2 miles. The 55-foot tower is located on the top of a ridge and a round-trip outing to it is a 4-mile trek with a bit of climbing.

Fishing: There is a boat ramp in the campground for anglers who want to fish the lake for bass and bluegill. Others, particularly fly fishermen, will fish nearby Black River in the effort to entice a brook trout.

Season: This campground is rarely filled, even on the weekends.

Pickerel Lake

Pigeon River Country State Forest

Campground: Rustic
County: Otsego
Nearest Community: Vanderbilt
Sites: 39
Reservations: No
Fee: $15
Information: State forest headquarters
☎ (989) 983-4101

How rugged is Pigeon River State Forest? On Pickerel Lake Road is a scenic pull-off with a view of nothing but forested ridges and hills for

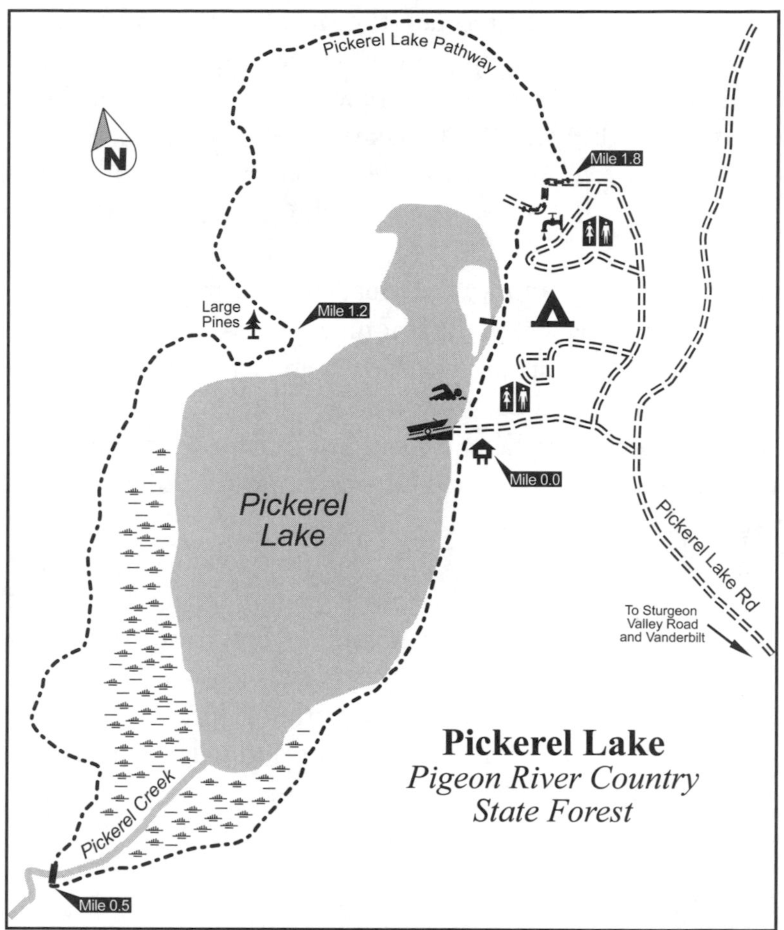

miles. From there it's a straight drop down to the campground that will have your children gripping the back of your seat and you worried about the trailer. That's how rugged.

The state forest comprises almost 105,000 contiguous acres and includes 60 miles of foot trails, 27 miles of horse trail, and the largest elk herd east of the Mississippi River. Of the campgrounds, Pickerel is on the largest, most popular, and, from an angler's point of view, nicest lake.

Directions: From I-75 depart at exit 290 and in the town of Vanderbilt head east on Sturgeon Valley Road. Ten miles from Vanderbilt turn north (left) on Pickerel Lake Road to reach the posted campground entrance in two miles.

Campground: The north shore of Pickerel Lake was a camp for the Civilian Conservation Corps during the 1930s. There are enough trees for shade but not enough to isolate the sites for the kind of privacy you find in most state forest campgrounds. Three loops contain 39 sites, but tables and fire rings are lacking on many of them. None of the sites are on the water or within view of the lake.

Day-use Facilities: There is no beach on the lake, but a grassy area serves as one while the water here is shallow for 30 or 40 yards with a sandy bottom.

Fishing: There is an unimproved boat launch with limited parking for a handful of vehicles. Pickerel Lake is completely undeveloped and has a ban on boat motors other than electric. Most anglers target bass and bluegill.

Hiking: Passing the boat launch area is Pickerel Lake Pathway, a 2-mile hike that circles the lake. It's marked by blue blazes and most of it stays within sight of the water. Halfway along the loop you pass some impressive white and red pines.

Elk Watching: Just east of Pickerel Lake Road on Sturgeon Valley Road is an elk viewing area. The bugle season, when the bulls emerge from the forests to call in their harem, is best from mid-September through October.

Season: With the exception of Fourth of July, it is rare for this campground to fill up during the summer, and even if it did, there are several more nearby.

Platte River

Sleeping Bear Dunes National Lakeshore

Campground: Modern and semi-modern
County: Benzie
Nearest Community: Honor
Sites: 174
Reservations: Yes
Fee: $12–$24
Information: Park headquarters
☎ (231) 326-5134
🌐 www.nps.gov/slbe

One of the newest campgrounds in Michigan is also one of the oldest campgrounds. Platte River Campground was originally Benzie State Park until the state deeded it over to the National Park Service in 1975 as part of Sleeping Bear Dunes National Lakeshore.

In the early 1990s, the NPS spent almost $4 million in renovation and then opened what was then Michigan's newest modern facility. And what a facility! It's a state-of-the-art campground, providing modern, rustic, and walk-in sites in one of the most beloved areas of the Lower Peninsula.

Directions: From the Sleeping Bear Dunes park headquarters on the corner of M-72 and M-22 in Empire, head south on M-22 and in 9.5 miles you'll reach the campground before crossing Platte River. From US-31, north of Beulah, head west on County Road 706 around the south side of Platte Lake and then north on M-22.

Campground: Platte River is a large facility of four paved loops in an area lightly forested predominantly in pines. Of the 174 sites, 96 of them have electric hook-ups and 53 others are rustic. None of the sites are near the water as Lake Michigan Road lies between the campground and the river. At the back of the campground, there are 25 walk-in sites where you camp in a much more secluded, wooded area 50 yards from where you park your car. There are also group sites. Facilities include paved spurs, tables, fire rings, a sanitation station, and modern restrooms with pay-to-use showers. The sites are $21 a night for modern facilities, $16 for rustic, $12 for walk-in, and $3 a night more when reserved in advance.

Day-use Facilities: The major change in the campground was re-routing Lake Michigan Road and rebuilding the picnic area on the shores of the Platte River. The picnic area now lies across the road from the campground and includes tables and grills within view of the water.

There is no swimming area within the campground, but one of the most scenic beaches in the state lies less than two miles away at the west end of Lake Michigan Road. Here the Platte River empties into Lake Michigan, forming a delightful sandy spit that is reached by wading through the shallow current. To the north is a view of undeveloped Platte Bay and Sleeping Bear Dune. One of the favorite activities at the beach is to float down the Platte River along the spit into Lake Michigan in an inner tube.

Fishing: The campground has a fish cleaning station because Platte Bay is renowned for its salmon and brown trout fishery during the spring and fall as the fish gather to spawn up the river. The deepwater fishery

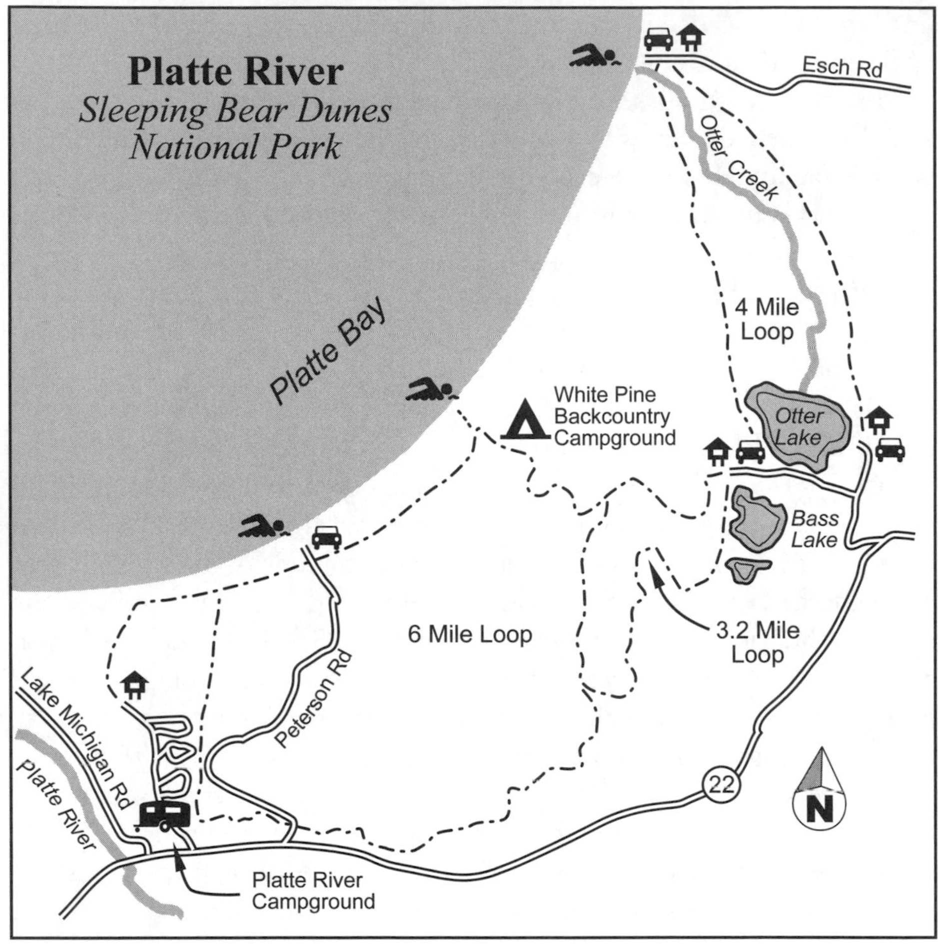

here is also very productive during the summer but the nearest Great Lakes boat launch is in Frankfort.

Hiking: Platte Plains Trail is a 15-mile network of trails with two trailheads in the campground. The one at the back near the walk-in sites provides the quickest route to the beaches of Lake Michigan, a walk of little over a half mile. There is also a six-mile loop that begins and ends at Platte River and within 2.4 miles passes the backcountry campsites of White Pine Campground.

Canoeing: The lower Platte River from the campground makes for an easy, 2-hour canoe trip while an equal number of people float it during the summer in an inner tube. The river averages only 3 feet in depth and along the way passes through a small lake before emptying into Lake

For a day in the sun, visitors hike out to the beach that surrounds the mouth of the Platte River near Platte River Campground in Sleeping Bear Dunes National Lakeshore.

Michigan. Riverside Canoes ☎ 231-325-5622 🌐 www.canoemichigan.com can provide either canoes or inner tubes and are located across the river from the campground. During the height of summer, you may want to reserve a boat in advance.

Season: Platte River is open year round, but facilities such as restrooms and showers are seasonal. Since being renovated, the campground fills up almost daily from mid-June to late August. Campsites can be reserved six months in advance from Memorial Day weekend to Oct. 1 through the National Recreation Reservation Service ☎ 877-444-6777 🌐 www.recreation.gov. In 2010, the NPS increased from 25 to 66 percent the number of sites that can reserved in advance. The rest are handed out on a first-come-first-serve basis.

69

D.H. Day

Sleeping Bear Dunes National Lakeshore

Campground: Rustic
County: Leelanau
Nearest Community: Glen Arbor
Sites: 88
Reservations: No
Fee: $12
Information: Park headquarters
☎ (231) 326-5134
🌐 www.nps.gov/slbe

D.H. Day was the first chairmen of the State Park Commission that, in the wake of a growing number of motorized campers in the 1920s, had the task of setting up Michigan's present system. Ironically, Day's name is attached to one of the most popular National Park Service facilities in Michigan, not a state park.

The conservationist would hardly mind. D.H. Day Campground in Sleeping Bear Dunes National Lakeshore is an excellent facility, featuring somewhat secluded sites despite its size, nightly ranger programs during the summer, and one of the finest beaches in a state known for great beaches.

All of this plus the popularity of the dunes themselves makes D.H. Day Campground one of the busiest public facilities in Michigan. To put it simply, it's filled nightly from June through Labor Day. Either show up early in the morning or keep heading north. There's rarely an open site for afternoon arrivals here.

Directions: From the park headquarters on the corner of M-72 and M-22 in Empire, head north on M-22 and veer left onto M-119. Within five miles you'll pass the Dune Climb and in another mile curve right towards the town of Glen Arbor. Before reaching the town you'll pass the posted entrance to the campground.

Campground: D.H. Day has 88 sites along one large loop and two smaller ones. Located right off Sleeping Bear Bay, the campground

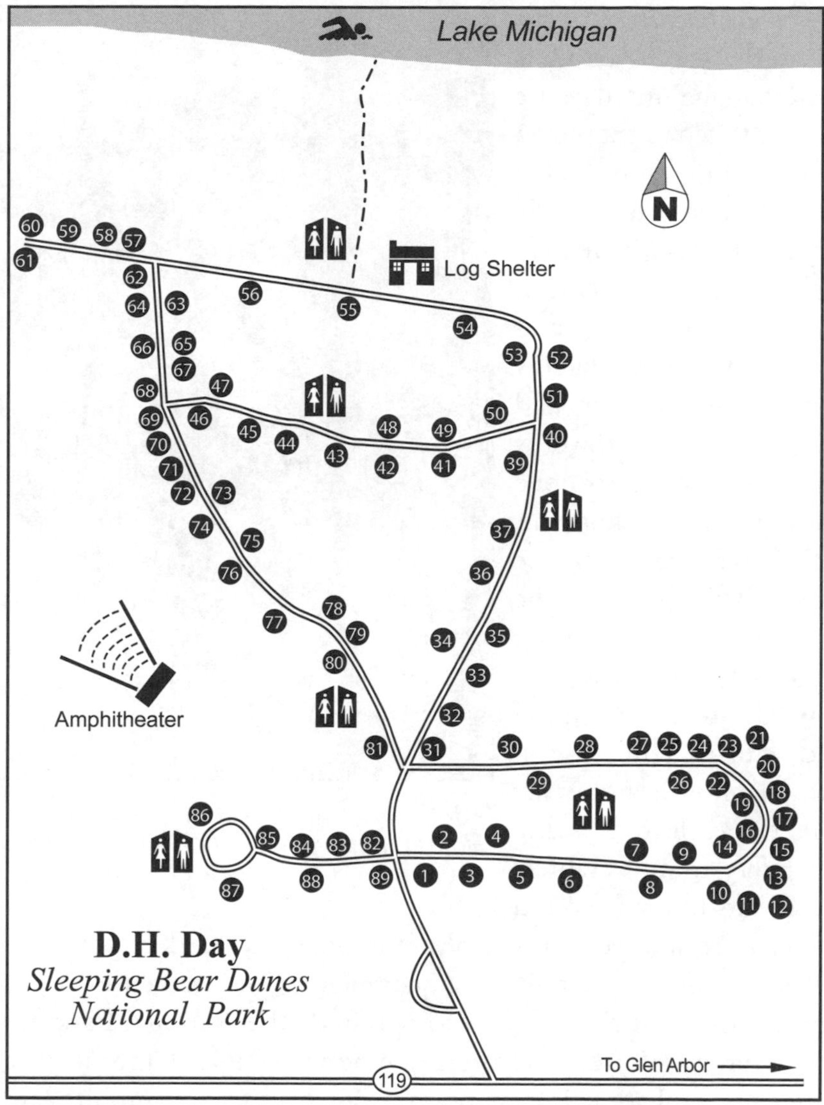

features a rolling terrain well forested in pine and hardwoods giving most sites a bit of seclusion despite the number of tents and trailers they pack in here. None of them are within sight of Lake Michigan but four sites, No. 58–61, are off by themselves.

Amenities include fire rings, tables, vault toilets, and hand pumps for water. Although this is a rustic facility, there is also a sanitation station for recreational vehicles along with pay phones and a firewood concession. Site No. 86 is a handicap-accessible site and located next to a barrier-free vault toilet.

Day-use Facilities: In the back of the campground is limited parking for day-use visitors located next to a warming cabin. From here a path leads north to quickly emerge at an incredible stretch of Lake Michigan beach. The sand is as finc as sugar, the water is shallow and turquoise in color, and the view from your towel is a panorama second to none on any Michigan shoreline. To the west you can see Sleeping Bear Dune, to the east Pyramid Point rising straight out of the lake, and due north are the Manitou Islands with the lighthouse on South Manitou Island easily visible on a clear day. The boat traffic, from freighters and sailboats to the Manitou Islands ferries, adds yet another pleasant dimension to this spot.

D.H. Day Campground is near the famous Dune Climb in Sleeping Bear Dunes National Lakeshore.

There is also an amphitheater, complete with a screen in a wooded hollow on the west side of the campground. The National Park Service offers a variety of free interpretive programs nightly throughout the summer and a schedule is posted at the entrance to the amphitheater.

Hiking: Although there are no trails that depart from the campground, the northern portion of the Sleeping Bears Dunes abounds with hiking opportunities. The closest and one of the most popular in the park is the Dunes Trail located a mile south on M-119. It begins with the steep Dune Climb and then continues another 1.5 miles out to Lake Michigan. Round trip is a good 4 miles and of moderate difficulty. West beyond the Maritime Museum on County Road 209 is Dunes Trail-Sleeping Bear Point, a 2.8-mile loop with much of it through loose sand of moderately rolling dunes. A short spur at the beginning leads to Lake Michigan.

Alligator Hill Trail is located south of the campground on Stocking Road and consists of three loops of 2.5 miles each. Although more popular with Nordic skiers in the winter, hikers will enjoy the Island Lookout, a 1.4-mile trek from the trailhead along the Easy Loop. Equally scenic is Pyramid Point Trail, located 3.7 miles north of Glen Arbor via Port Oneida Road north then Basch Road east. The 2.6-mile loop includes a spur to a high point on Pyramid Point with a spectacular view of Lake Michigan.

Nearby Attractions: Along with the renowned Dune Climb, other attractions in this end of the park include the Maritime Museum along County Road 209. The renovated Lifesaving Station features displays and exhibits on the U.S. Lifesaving Service, which predated the U.S. Coast Guard, and a fascinating interpretive program on how they used a breeches buoy and a cannon to save distressed sailors. Pierce Stocking Drive is an 8-mile, one-way loop that you cover in your car or on a bicycle. Along the way there is a covered bridge, interpretive posts, and several scenic overlooks.

Season: The campground is open April through November and managed by a host from June through Labor Day. No reservations are accepted as all sites are handed out on a first-come-first-serve basis. D.H. Day is filled daily during the summer, usually by 1 PM. Plan on camping nearby the night before and arriving between 8–9 AM to stake out sites that are vacated. Pitch your tent and fill out a form; then you can continue your tour of Sleeping Bear Dunes.

70

Leelanau

State Park

Campground: Rustic
County: Leelanau
Nearest Community: Northport
Sites: 51
Reservations: Yes
Fee: $15 plus vehicle entry fee
Information: State park office
☎ (231) 386-5422

The campground at Leelanau State Park may be rustic, but it's popular. Despite the lack of modern restrooms, showers, or electrical hook-ups, the facility fills up daily throughout most of the summer due to both its location and scenery.

The campground is situated at the very top of the Leelanau Peninsula, providing splendid views of where the waters of Grand Traverse Bay merge with those of Lake Michigan. Lakeside sites are plentiful while a short walk away is Grand Traverse Lighthouse that has been converted into an interesting museum. There is no beach at the tip but an enjoyable afternoon can be spent hiking into the park's separate Cathead Bay area for sand and surf.

Directions: The state park is split between two sections with the campground at the tip, 8 miles north of Northport on County Road 629. Access to Cathead Bay is 4 miles north of the town and reached by turning off CR 629 onto Densmore Road and heading west to the trailhead at the end.

Campground: There are 51 sites along several loops at the tip of the peninsula. Most are situated in an area forested in pines and are not grouped together as tight as the average state park. Almost half of them have a view of the water and 11 sites are right on the shore, combining a little shade and easy access to Lake Michigan. These sites are very sandy but the beach is rocky, poor for swimming but great for Petoskey stone hunters.

The sites have tables and fire rings while nearby are vault toilets and hand pumps for water. Also located within the campground are the remnants of the first lighthouse on the point (1853-1857) in a fenced-in area next to site No. 47.

Day-use Facilities: Away from the shore is an open grassy area with play equipment, shelter, picnic tables, and pedestal grills.

Interpretive Center: Within the state park is Grand Traverse Lighthouse Museum 🌐 www.grandtraverselighthouse.com. Built in 1916, Grand Traverse Lighthouse is the most recent in a series of lighthouses that have been guiding ships around the peninsula since 1852. Several rooms on the first floor contain maritime displays while a staircase winds to the top of the tower for an immense view.

Grand Traverse Lighthouse is open 10 AM to 6 PM daily from June through Labor Day. In May the lighthouse is open daily from noon to 4 PM, and in November it is open noon to 4 PM on Saturday and Sunday. There is a small admission fee for the museum.

Hiking: Most of the 1,350-acre park is an area of wooded dunes and six miles of trails around Cathead Bay. To reach the bay's beautiful sandy

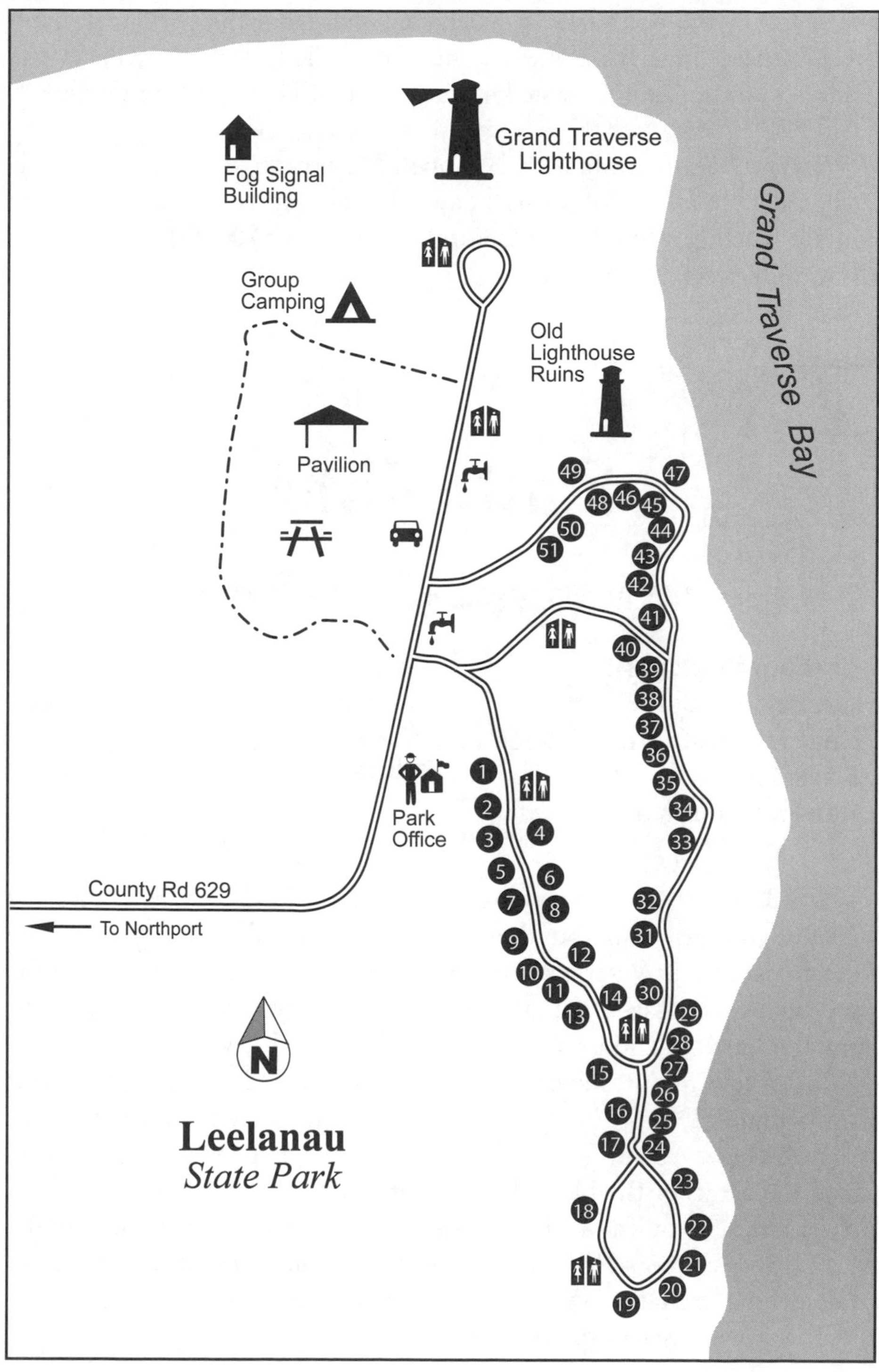
Grand Traverse
Lighthouse
Fog Signal
Building
Grand Traverse Bay
Group
Camping
Old
Lighthouse
Ruins
Pavilion
Park
Office
County Rd 629
To Northport
N
Leelanau
State Park

beach follow the posted Lake Michigan Trail from the parking lot and then Cathead Spur. It's a one-way hike of a mile to Lake Michigan. The Cathead Bay trailhead is posted 4 miles north of Northport on Densmore Road.

Season: Leelanau State Park is open May through October and fills every day from Fourth of July holiday to Labor Day. To reserve a campsite contact Michigan State Park Central Reservations ☎ 800-447-2757 🌐 www.midnrreservations.com.

71

Platte River

Pere Marquette State Forest

Campground: Rustic
County: Benzie
Nearest Community: Honor
Sites: 26
Reservations: No
Fee: $15
Information: Traverse City DNR office
☎ (231) 922-5280

US-31 can be a busy avenue in Northwest Michigan during the summer, and the campgrounds along it reflect that. Pere Marquette State Forest near Honor Veterans Memorial Campground is located where the state highway crosses the Platte River, and in July and August its canoe launch is bustling and its sites are often filled on the weekends.

Just a few minutes away, but lying south of US-31, is Platte River Campground. Despite being so close and on the same river, Platte River is a world away from Veterans Memorial. It's a quiet wooded setting along the banks of the blue ribbon trout stream that's rarely filled. For a little adventure you can kick off your boots and ford the river to hike the Platte River Springs Pathway on the other side. Then afterwards dash back across the Platte to warm the toes at a campfire in your site.

This is why we camp, isn't it?

Directions: From Honor head east on US-31 for a mile and then turn south on Goose Road. Within 1.5 miles is the posted entrance to Platte River State Forest Campground.

A hiker fords the Platte River to reach the Platte River Springs Pathway on the opposite bank from the state forest campground.

Campground: Platte River is a rustic facility with 26 sites along a single loop. The sites are spread out in a well forested area and can accommodate tents and small trailers. Although the campground borders the Platte River, none of the sites are directly on the water. Amenities include fire rings, vault toilets, and hand pumps for water.

Hiking: Platte River Springs Pathway is a short, 1.6-mile loop packed with adventure, starting with that ford across the trout stream. On the south side of the river the trail winds through 35 acres of rugged bluffs, from which a handful of springs emerge to keep the Platte cold and clear. Lining the trail is a handful of towering beech and maples, making this pathway an especially delightful place to hike in the fall. The pathway is marked on the south side of the campground loop, and within 100 yards of the trailhead you arrive at the Platte River where there is a bench to kick off your boots for the watery crossing.

Canoeing: Within the campground is a canoe launch and small parking lot near it. As far as paddlers are concerned, the river is divided between the Upper Platte, the section upstream from Platte Lake, and the Lower Platte, the section from M-22 to Lake Michigan which is covered in Platte River Campground in Sleeping Bear Dunes National Lakeshore (page 176).

HITTING THE TRAIL IN NORTHWEST MICHIGAN

In Northwest Michigan it's easy to spend all day hiking and mountain biking and then camp at night. This region is blessed with not only campgrounds but a wide variety of trails including state forest pathways, rail-trails, paved urban trails and even a section of the North Country Trail. Where to go? Here are a few web sites that will lead you to the trail of your choice:

🌐 www.michigantrailmaps.com: Maps, photos and descriptions for hiking and backpacking trails around the state with the ability to locate them by county.

🌐 www.traversetrails.org: Traverse City is home to Michigan's premier trail network, all managed by TART Trails and used by cyclists, inline skaters, Nordic skiers, hikers and mountain bikers.

🌐 www.michigantrails.org: Go to the Michigan Trails & Greenways Alliance and click on "Trail Finder" to locate information on rail-trails.

🌐 www.mmba.org/trail-guide: The Michigan Mountain Biking Association has information on more than 100 mountain bike trails across the state.

🌐 www.northcountrytrail.org: On the North Country Trail Association web site you'll find maps and descriptions for the NCT which winds through Northwest Michigan from the Mackinac Bridge south past Traverse City.

A rustic campsite at Platte River State Forest Campground just east of Honor.

The Upper Platte tends to be much faster and more shallow, demanding more attention from canoers and kayakers, but most paddlers believe it is much more scenic than the lower stretch and offers a greater chance of encountering wildlife. It is a three- to four-hour paddle to put in at Veteran's Memorial Campground and pull out at Indian Hill Road just past Honor. Canoe liveries servicing the river include The Honor Trading Post ☎ 231-325-2202 🌐 www.canoeplatteriver.com and Lake Michigan Riverside Canoes ☎ 231-325-5622 🌐 www.canoemichigan.com.

Fishing: Already known as a fine trout stream, the Platte became renown in the late 1960s as the site of the first successful planting of coho and chinook salmon in the Great Lakes. To learn more about the introduction of salmon visit the Platte River State Fish Hatchery ☎ 231-325-4611 on US-31 across from Veterans Memorial Campground. The hatchery features interpretive displays and is open to the public from 8 AM to 4 PM Monday through Friday.

Fishing on the Upper Platte River focuses on brown trout during the summer and then becomes intense in during the salmon runs in September and October. In March and April anglers fish the river for steelhead.

Season: This is a lightly used campground where getting a site is usually not a problem.

72

Lake Dubonnet

Pere Marquette State Forest

Campground: Rustic
County: Grand Traverse
Nearest Community: Interlochen
Sites: 50
Reservations: No
Fee: $15
Information: Traverse City DNR office
☎ (231) 922-5280

Lake Dubonnet is one of the largest state forest facilities in Michigan, but come evening it can still be an enchanting place. A pair of loons nest

The fishing pier on Lake Dubonnet at Lake Dubonnet State Forest Campground near Traverse City.

here, and after nightfall their eerie laugh can often be heard from every site. That wild call along with the fact that the lake, with the exception of one cottage, is totally undeveloped, gives the campground a Northwoods setting, a rarity for any facility this big and this close to Traverse City.

The lake was actually created in 1956 when a stream was dammed to improve fishing and waterfowl habitat. As a result the size of the lake nearly doubled as two lakes were merged into one by the rising water. Across the inlet on its north side is a rustic campground, built for equestrians following the Shore-To-Shore Trail that passes through the area. Lake Dubonnet also has a handicap-accessible site located near a fishing pier that is accessible to the physically impaired but enjoyed by all who like tossing a fishing line from shore.

Directions: From Traverse City head west on US-31 and in 14 miles, or a mile past M-137, turn north on Wildwood Road.

Campground: The facility has four loops of 50 sites, but don't despair at its size. The sites are well spread out in an area forested with a mix of maple, oak, aspen, and even some paper birch with a good growth of undercover. Sites have tables, fire rings, and angled spurs that make pulling an RV in and out easy. There are also hand pumps for water and vault toilets. None of the sites are directly on the lake, but a handful are on the edge of the bluff overlooking the lake while a few more are located along an inlet. A special handicap-accessible site is located in the second loop and includes a handicap-accessible vault toilet nearby.

Fishing: There is an improved boat launch with a cement ramp and parking for a handful of cars near the entrance of the campground. Lake Dubonnet has bass and northern pike populations but is best for bluegill and other panfish, especially from the fishing pier that extends out at the mouth of the inlet that borders the campground. This close to shore the fish tend to be stunted, but children still find them fun to catch.

Hiking: The Lost Lake Pathway begins from a trailhead on Wildwood Road and passes through the campground on its way to Lost Lake, a scenic bog. The pathway is basically a pair loops with the northern loop being a 4.5 mile hike or mountain bike ride from the state forest campground.

Season: Lake Dubonnet can become busy during the height of the summer camping season, but it is rare for this campground to fill-up, even on a weekend.

73

Green Lake

Interlochen State Park

Campground: Rustic
County: Grand Traverse
Nearest Community: Interlochen
Sites: 60
Reservations: Yes
Fee: $12 plus vehicle entry fee
Information: State park office
☎ (231) 276-9511

Bach, Beethoven, and a bass at the end of your line—only at Interlochen State Park. The 200-acre state park is Michigan's second oldest, preserved in 1917 after some of its virgin stand of white pine had somehow escaped

A lakefront campsite in the Green Lake rustic campground at Interlochen State Park.

the swinging axes of lumberjacks. Today it's best known as the park next to renowned Interlochen National Music Camp. This might be the only place in Michigan where you bed down to classical music as opposed to campfire songs from the site next door.

Interlochen is actually a thin strip of land between two lakes, Duck and Green, and features almost a mile of shoreline as well as its towering pines. Along Duck Lake is a modern campground and 421 of the park's 481 sites. My favorite, however, is the rustic campground along Green Lake where the sites are farther apart and more private than those across the road.

Directions: Interlochen is located 15 miles southwest of Traverse City and is reached from the resort town by heading south on US-31. The park's entrance is on M-137, 3 miles south of US-31.

Campground: Green Lake has two loops of 60 rustic sites with tables, fire rings, vault toilets, and hand pumps for water. Many of them are along the edge of a shoreline bluff with an excellent view of the water. All of them are spread out in a well forested area that is generally a little cooler at night than the other campground. You give up a shower but you get a lot more privacy in return.

A historical Big Wheel on display at Interlochen State Park. Loggers used the device in the late 1800s to move logs during the winter.

Day-use Facilities: The park's picnic and swimming areas are on Duck Lake where you'll find a wide sandy beach, a designated swimming area, tables, and a shelter that can be rented. There is also a boat rental concession that has rowboats on both Duck and Green Lake and is open daily in the summer.

Fishing: There is considerable fishing activity in the park as both lakes are considered excellent smallmouth bass waters with a number of tournaments staged here throughout the summer. Green Lake, however, has a wider variety of fish including perch, northern pike and brown trout as well as panfish. The park maintains three improved boat launches with cement slabs. Two are at the end of each loop in the modern campground and the third is in the rustic campground.

Hiking: The only path is Pines Nature Trail, a 0.6-mile loop that winds through the towering stand of white pine and begins in the modern campground.

Season: The campground is open from mid-April to mid-October. The modern campground is filled weekends and often by Thursday from late June through late August. The demand on Green Lake is not nearly as great but it also fills most summer weekends. Either arrive in mid-week or reserve a site in advance through Michigan State Park Central Reservations ☎ 800-447-2757 🌐 www.midnrreservations.com.

74

Arbutus Lake

Pere Marquette State Forest

Campground: Rustic
County: Grand Traverse
Nearest Community: Traverse City
Sites: 40
Reservations: No
Fee: $15
Information: Traverse City DNR ☎ (231) 922-5280

A mere 10 miles south of Traverse City is Arbutus Lake No. 4 State Forest Campground, overlooking the shores of this chain of five lakes. The facility is no more than a 15-minute drive from downtown but a world away as far as this bustling tourist town is concerned.

The campground is unique, built on the side of a hill with many of the sites terraced lots above the water, while the lakes themselves are a haven of boating and fishing activities during the summer. There is also a beach and even a pathway, and the only sign that Traverse City is on your doorstep is the lack of empty sites on the weekends.

Directions: From Traverse City head south on Garfield Road (M-611), then turn east (left) on Hobbs Highway. The road is a scenic and hilly drive around Arbutus Lake No. 5 before arriving at the junction with Arbutus Road. Head north (left) and in two miles a sign will direct you to turn west on a gravel road to the campground entrance.

Campground: This delightful campground is basically a loop around a prominent hill rising straight above the lake. Many of the sites can only be reached via a stairway from where you park your vehicle, while others are situated on the edge of the bluff above the water and have been terraced to make room for a tent. The view of waves lapping against the shore almost straight below makes these sites the first to be picked.

Most of the hill is forested in maples and other hardwoods, but a few sites on the back site are in a small clearing. All of them have a table and fire ring while nearby are vault toilets and hand pump for water. Needless to say, much of the campground and certainly the most scenic sites are not conducive to recreation vehicles of any size.

Day-use Facilities: The campground features a grassy area leading to a thin beach and a marked swimming area that is shallow with a sandy bottom. Also in the area are a few tables, vault toilets, and a hand pump.

Boating: The campground lies on the fourth lake of a chain of five lakes that is popular with boaters. To the north is Arbutus Lake No. 5 while to the south lie No. 1, 2, and 3. An East Bay Township ordinance limits high speed boating and water skiing on Lakes No. 2, 3, and 4 from 10 AM until 6:30 PM each day and bans it entirely on Lakes No. 1 and 5.

A new boat launch has been built on Arbutus Lake No. 4 next to the campground. The access site has a separate entrance along Arbutus Road and parking for 20 cars and trailers. A foot trail connects it to the campground.

Fishing: Lake No. 4 has a lily-pad covered bay next to the campground and shore anglers can toss worms and crickets along its edges for bluegill, sunfish, and other panfish. The chain as a whole has a mixed bag of a fishery including yellow perch, northern pike, and black crappie. It is best fished for bass, with some largemouth exceeding 20 inches in length, and bluegill.

Season: The campground is not managed during the summer and all sites are available on a first-come-first serve basis. Arbutus Lake's close proximity to Traverse City makes it a popular destination, and often the campground will be filled on the weekends in July and August.

75

Scheck's Place

Pere Marquette State Forest

Campground: Rustic
County: Grand Traverse
Nearest Community: Traverse City
Sites: 30
Reservations: No
Fee: $15
Information: Traverse City DNR
☎ (231) 922-5280

Only 5 miles from this state forest campground is the birthplace of one of the best known and most productive dry flies ever tied, the Adams. The famous fly was created by Leonard Halladay of Mayfield for his friend, Charles F. Adams, an Ohio attorney who could often be found fishing the Boardman River during the summer.

In 1922, Adams was casting when a hatch of insects caught his eye. He described the insect to Halladay who quickly came up with a dry fly to match it. Adams tried the fly for the first time that evening on the Boardman. The next morning he excitedly told Halladay it was "a knock out," and asked what the fly was called. For the lack of anything else the fly tier named it after his friend and today many anglers claim if their fly box could contain only one pattern it would be the Adams.

The famous fly is still a common sight at Scheck's Place because the state forest campground provides some of the best access along the Boardman River for anglers. It also lies at an important trail crossroads; heading north to the Mackinac Bridge is the North Country Trail while extending west to east from Lake Michigan to Lake Huron is the Michigan Shore-to-Shore Trail, an equestrian route.

Directions: From M-72, head south on Williamston Road which is also labeled County Road 605. Within 5.7 miles south you arrive at an intersection with Supply Road. Continue south (left) on Supply Road and in 1.3 miles, just after crossing the Boardman River, turn west (right) on Brown Bridge Road. Within 4 miles is the posted entrance to Scheck's Place. Don't confuse Scheck's Place Trail Camp, an equestrian

An angler fishes the Boardman River near Scheck's Place, a rustic campground in Pere Marquette State Forest.

campground that is also posted along Brown Bridge Road, with Scheck's Place State Forest Campground, another half-mile to the west.

Campground: Scheck's Place is actually a pair of campgrounds, one on each side of Brown Bridge Road where it crosses the Boardman River. To the south there are 10 sites with several close to the river bank. To the north the campground has 20 sites. Although on the north side none of the sites are directly on the water, there is an observation deck overlooking a scenic bend in the Boardman.

Most of the sites are in a semi-open area but are well spread out for a secluded setting. Facilities includes vault toilets, tables, fire rings, and hand pumps for water.

Fishing: Emerging as springs on the outskirts of Kalkaska and ending in downtown Traverse City, the Boardman is one of the best streams in Michigan for resident brown trout. The most popular area for anglers is the Upper Boardman, a 7-mile stretch from the former Forks Campground to Brown Bridge Pond downstream from Scheck's Place. This is ideal fly water with an excellent population of brown trout and a fair population of brookies.

On both sides of Brown Bridge Road there is parking and angler access to the river. The Boardman here is 40 to 50 feet wide and averages two feet deep at mid-channel, making it easy to wade at normal flows. State land extends from the bridge upstream about a half-mile and downstream about one-quarter mile.

Hiking: The NCT is posted just east of the campground on the north side of Brown Bridge Road. From there you climb a high ridge to break out at paved Ranch Rudolf Road. Across the road is the trailhead for the Muncie Lakes Pathway, reached less than a mile from Scheck's Place and featuring a large parking area, vault toilet, and a display board with maps.

Muncie Lakes Pathway is an 8.5-mile loop, with four cross-over spurs, that is used by both hikers and mountain bikers. The NCT follows the west half of the loop before departing the pathway for scenic Dollar Lake near post No. 8. The most interesting section of the pathway is the loop from posts No. 5 to No. 7 where the trail winds past the largest of the Muncie Lakes and then more ponds and marshes.

Canoeing: The Upper Boardman and the undeveloped valley it flows through makes it an attractive paddle for canoers. Most put in at the former Forks State Forest Campground where there is a canoe launch and pull out at Brown Bridge Dam, a 7-mile, three- to four-hour paddle. Halfway through this float you reach Scheck's Place. Located upstream from Scheck's Place is Ranch Rudolf Resort ☎ 231-947-9528 🌐 www.ranchrudolf.com which offers canoe rentals.

Season: Although the campground can occasionally fill, sites are generally available throughout the summer even on weekends.

76

Guernsey Lake

Pere Marquette State Forest

Campground: Rustic
County: Grand Traverse
Nearest Community: Kalkaska
Sites: 30
Reservations: No
Fee: $15
Information: Traverse City DNR
☎ (231) 922-5280

Located just 8 miles west of Kalkaska, Guernsey Lake is a state forest campground overlooking an undeveloped lake with lots of opportunities for fishing, hiking, mountain biking, even an overnight backpacking adventure if you wish.

Small lakes abound in this part of the Pere Marquette State Forest. Surrounding the entrance of the campground are Little Guernsey Lakes, three small bodies of water within view of Campground Road. The more adventurous can explore, fish, or even camp along Sand Lakes, five lakes in the middle of the Sand Lakes Quiet Area which has a trailhead in the state forest campground.

Directions: You can reach the campground from County Road 660 just south of Traverse City, but once on Scenic Drive you'll find it is a very rough ride. A smoother route is from Kalkaska where you turn west on Island Lake Road just north of the McDonalds on US-131. Within 5.5 miles you pass Island Lake then veer to the left on the dirt road and follow it 1.5 miles to Campground Road. Although Campground Road is not posted, there is a state forest campground symbol here. Turn south (left) and the campground entrance is reached in a mile.

Campground: Guernsey Lake has a pair of loops with 12 sites on one and 18 on the other. All sites are situated on a bluff above the lake with stairways and log fences leading down to the water in several places. Forested in oak, maple, and red pine, the sites are shaded and well spaced but not totally secluded from each other. A few on the large loop have a glimpse of the lake but none directly overlook the water. Facilities include tables and fire rings, though many are missing, as well as a hand pump for water and vault toilets.

Day-use Facilities: On a fenced-in bluff overlooking the lake near the boat launch is a pleasant, well shaded spot that, unfortunately, lacks most of its tables.

Fishing: The campground has an unimproved boat launch directly on Guernsey Lake with additional parking for a handful of vehicles and rigs. Guernsey is stocked annually with rainbow and brown trout, but during the summer most anglers end up catching bluegill and, to a much lesser degree, bass. There is a "No Wake" regulation on Guernsey and the lake can easily be fished from a canoe or rowboat.

Nearby are the Little Guernsey Lakes and the only one on the west side of Campground Road is the largest and most accessible for those with a hand-carried boat or canoe. Almost directly across from the campground entrance is an unmarked two-track that leads back to another Little Guernsey Lake.

Hiking: Sand Lakes Quiet Area is a 2,500-acre preserve that borders Guernsey Lake to the west with a trailhead in the campground. The foot trail within the quiet area is basically an 8-mile loop with most of the lakes clustered on the west side. It is a 2.6-mile trek to the backcountry campsite on Sand Lake No. 1 if you hike the north half of the loop and 4.4-mile walk along the southern half.

Season: On a July or August weekend this campground could be more than two-thirds full, but it is rare to arrive here and not find at least one open site.

77

Power Island

Grand Traverse County Park

Campground: Rustic
County: Grand Traverse
Nearest Community: Bowers Harbor
Sites: 5
Reservations: Yes
Fee: $31 for non-county residents
Information: Grand Traverse County Parks
☎ (231) 922-4818

One of the most unusual county parks in Michigan is Power Island, and located next to it is one of the most unusual campgrounds in the state, Bassett Island. The unique Grand Traverse County park sits in the heart of Grand Traverse Bay, 3 miles southwest of the public access site in Bowers Harbor.

The 212-acre Power Island was first called Marion Island after the daughter of a timber baron who bought it in the 1880s, and later served as the site of a commercial fishing camp, and then in the 1950s was owned by a oil company. In 1975 Eugene and Sadye Power of Traverse City gave the islands to Grand Traverse County to be preserved as a park.

Bassett Island is a two-acre islet just north of the much larger Power Island. When the lake level is high, there's a foot of water between them,

A pair of kayakers paddle past Power Island County Park.

but most of the time an isthmus connects the two islands and you can walk from one to the other without getting your feet wet. Most of the park's users arrive in a motor boat but not all. In recent years a growing number of kayakers have been paddling out to Bassett Island to spend the night and occasionally even a float plane arrives for the weekend.

Directions: If you don't have boat or kayak, check with the Traverse City Convention and Visitors Bureau (800-872-8377; www.traversecity.com) about transportation to the park. In the past there has been commercial ferry service to the islands.

Campground: There are five sites at Bassett Island, and they don't offer much in the way of amenities; only fire rings, tables, an outhouse, and raccoon poles to keep your provisions safe from masked raiders. For drinking water, you have to walk a quarter mile to a hand pump in the day-use area of Power Island. The setting is well worth the lack of amenities and the extra effort needed to camp here. Every site is along the shoreline and graced with views that include the Leelanau Peninsula to the west, Mission Peninsula to the east, and the length of the bay to the north. The sites that face the west allow you to enjoy the spectacular sunsets at night without leaving camp.

Day-use Facilities: The calmest water and nicest beaches are located on Power Island's leeward side where boaters are protected from the northern winds. This is the day-use area of the park and includes a dock, picnic tables, grills, and almost a mile of beach.

Hiking: Departing from near the Power Island dock is the park's trail system. More than five miles of footpaths either skirt the shoreline of Power Island or climb the forested ridge in the middle. The high point of the island is Eagle's Nest Lookout, which rises 142 feet above the bay. From this spot on the ridge, you can see all the way to Northport near the tip of the Leelanau Peninsula.

Season: The campground is open from Memorial Day through Labor Day. Because of its limited number of sites, it is filled most summer weekends. Some parties, in fact, reserved all five sites in advance. By Sunday night Power Island quiets down and in the middle of the week it's considerably easier to get a campsite. Sites can be reserved beginning the first business day after Jan. 1 for the following summer by calling the County Parks and Recreation Department ☎ 231-922-4818.

78

Whitewater

Whitewater Township Park

Campground: Modern and semi-modern
County: Antrim
Nearest Community: Williamsburg
Sites: 55
Reservations: Yes
Fee: $22–$27
Information: Park office
☎ (231) 267-5091
🌐 www.whitewatertownship.org

One of the most popular areas to boat in Northern Michigan is Antrim County's Chain of Lakes, a network of 12 lakes and handful of rivers that ends with Elk River flowing into the Grand Traverse Bay at Elk Rapids. What's missing from these lakes are campgrounds. As extensive as the chain is, there is only one public campground along its lakeshore, Whitewater Township Park on the southwest corner of Elk Lake. Thus, the nicest feature of this 117-acre park is its 2,500 feet of lakeshore and the rare opportunity to camp on a chain of lakes.

Directions: From M-72, turn north on Elk Lake Road, pass through the small town of Williamsburg, and continue north for three miles to Park Road. Whitewater Township Park is at the east end of Park Road.

Campground: Whitewater Township Park has 55 sites, including 42 with electrical hookups, along with a modern restroom with showers. Although much of the park is surrounded by cherry farms, the campground is in a rolling tract of red pine, providing a forested setting and a bit of privacy between sites not found in most modern facilities. The rustic sites include a handful along the edge of a shoreline bluff, featuring a view of the water through the trees. In fact, there may not be a better campsite in Antrim County than No. 13, well isolated and next to an observation deck, where in the evening you can watch the sunset over the shimmering waters of Elk Lake. Modern sites are $27 a night during the summer, $22 in May and October.

Day-use Facilities: Whitewater also includes a volleyball court, play equipment, bathhouse and swimming area, and a picnic grounds with a pavilion.

Hiking: Departing from the campsite is the park's nature trail, a 2-mile network of foot paths and benches that wind through the mostly open fields.

Fishing: Elk Lake is the second largest in the chain at 7,730 acres and a popular destination for smallmouth bass. Whitewater Park has an improved boat launch with a parking area for trailers. There is a $5 fee to launch a boat.

Season: The camping season at Whitewater Township Park is mid-May to mid-October. The campground is not nearly as popular as the state parks in the area but does fill-up on the weekends in July and early August. You can reserve sites beginning April 1 for that summer by calling the Whitewater Township office at ☎ 231-267-5141, ext. 24. There is an $8 reservation fee.

79

Barnes

Antrim County Park

Campground: Modern and semi-modern
County: Antrim
Nearest Community: Eastport
Sites: 86
Reservations: Yes
Fee: $21–$25
Information: Park office
☎ (231) 599-2712
🌐 www.antrimcounty.org

The highest speed bumps I've ever driven across are in Barnes County Park. They're so high they mark them on the park map, and if you go over one faster than 5 mph, you're likely to leave your trailer behind. But they're simply an indication of the quiet and family-oriented nature of this 120-acre county park.

Barnes Park, half hidden near Eastport, is an extremely clean and well maintained facility featuring both rustic and modern campgrounds. It lacks boating facilities and opportunities for anglers, but what a beach along scenic Grand Traverse Bay, the reason this campground is filled during the summer.

Directions: The park is 24 miles north of Traverse City along US-31. At the junction of US-31 and M-88, turn west and head a half mile towards the bay.

Campground: Barnes is a single loop of 86 sites and a mixed bag as far as campgrounds are concerned. Most of the sites are modern with electric and water hook-ups, but mixed in are rustic sites and even a handful of walk-in sites. There is a modern restroom with showers and a dumping station nearby on one half of the loop and vault toilets for the rustic sites on the other half. All sites have a table and either a pedestal grill or a fire ring.

Sites range from secluded spots in a hardwoods forest to a few near the open day-use area. None of them have a clear view of the bay. Nightly rates for non-residents of Antrim County are $25 for a modern site and $21 for a rustic one.

Day-use Facilities: Two shelters, picnic tables, and pedestal grills are located in a shady area as you enter the campground. The center of the loop is an open grassy area with play equipment and basketball and volleyball courts.

Next to site No. 66 and site No. 1 are parking areas for a handful of cars and next to site 57 is a changing shelter for swimmers. From either one you can access the bay. The beach is wide, sandy, and beautiful. To the north you can spot a few cottages, but to the south it's nothing but sand and surf as the park includes more than a quarter mile of lakeshore. The bay's sandy bottom makes for excellent swimming.

Hiking: Barnes has a paved handicap-accessible trail that extends from Barnes Road to a trailhead across from site No. 22 and is ideal for bicycles and in-line skating. East of the campground is a mile of foot trails that wind through a white pine and oak forest and along a wetland. The trails are well marked and feature interpretive displays along them.

Season: Barnes is open from mid-May through mid-October. In July through August it's often filled on the weekends even though there are some overfilled sites available. Within the campground, only 20 sites can be reserved in advance by calling the park office beginning April 1. All reservations require a $10 reservation fee and a minimum stay of 3 nights.

80

Fisherman's Island

State Park

Campground: Rustic
County: Charlevoix
Nearest Community: Charlevoix
Sites: 81
Reservations: Yes
Fee: $12 plus vehicle entry fee
Information: State park office
☎ (231) 547-6641

Half hidden from US-31 south of Charlevoix is Fisherman's Island State Park, and those who know about it often associate it with Petoskey stones. The 2,678-acre park is a haven during the summer for lapidaries and others looking for the state stone, a fossil with the honeycomb design.

The park also features some of the most beautiful stretches of beach in this crowded corner of Lake Michigan. And because of the beach, Fisherman's Island also has some of the nicest rustic sites in the state park system, spots where you can pitch your tent a few feet from the lapping waters of the Great Lake and be so secluded from the rest of the park you practically have a private beach of your own. They're hard to obtain during the summer but thanks to site-specific reservations you can now book them in advance.

Directions: From Charlevoix head five miles south on US-31 and then west on Bell Bay Road. The park is posted on US-31, and its entrance is 2.5 miles along Bell Bay Road.

Campground: The park has 81 rustic sites with tables and fire rings on three separate loops and along Lake Michigan. The loops are well forested in a mix of hardwoods, especially paper birch, and the sites are well secluded from each other—particularly the third loop, called South Campground, where there are even a few tent sites tucked up a hill and reached via a short stairway.

The most popular sites and some of the most scenic in the Lower Peninsula are those along the beach. Fisherman's Island has 11 sites (No. 9 and No. 26–35) right off the park drive where your tent or RV is on a sandy beach and within view of Lake Michigan. They are well spread and for the most part secluded from each other. Some are close to the road, but most are tucked away from the asphalt with a beach of their own.

Day-use Facilities: The picnic area is located at the south end of the park drive and includes parking, vault toilets, tables, pedestal grills, and access to a beach. A wooden foot bridge crosses Inwood Creek, and from here you can walk over a low dune to more beautiful stretches of sand and surf, totally undeveloped as far as you can see and crowned by Fisherman's Island just offshore. It's a beautiful setting for swimming or sunbathing.

Hiking: The park has a 4-mile network of trails which basically form a path from the contact station to the day-use area with a few spurs, including one to South Campground. There is a parking area near the contact station, and from the northern trailhead it's a walk of 3.2 miles to the day-use area and a trek of 2 miles to South Campground. The first portion of the trail is a foot path that remains in the woods as you cross McGeach Creek. But eventually it merges into an old farm road and passes through clearings and even an old apple orchard with the trees still bearing fruit. Here you can find some excellent berry patches.

Fishing: There is no boat launch within the park and fishing is limited to river angling for steelhead and salmon near the mouths of McGeach and Whiskey Creek with the best runs taking place in March and May.

Season: Despite being a rustic facility, the campground is full on weekends from the Fourth of July holiday to mid-August, and often daily if the weather is nice during that period. You can reserve a site in advance and the beach sites in particular with a site-specific reservations through Michigan State Park Central Reservations ☎ 800-447-2757 🌐 www.midnrreservations.com. Don't even plan on getting one when you show up.

81

Bill Wagner

Peaine Township Park

Campground: Rustic
County: Charlevoix
Nearest Community: St. James
Sites: 22
Reservations: No
Fee: $10
Information: Beaver Island Chamber of Commerce
☎ (231) 448-2505

Bill Wagner Memorial Campground, a Peaine Township facility along Lake Michigan, features a beautiful beach and is never crowded, not even on Fourth of July weekend. The catch? It's located on Beaver Island.

A two-hour ferry ride from Charlevoix, Beaver Island is spread over 37,385 acres and has 41 miles of shoreline, making it the third largest island in the Great Lakes. There are two public campgrounds on the island with Bill Wagner being the most pleasant one by far. Despite the cost of getting across, Beaver Island makes for a very unusual weekend camping trip. There are several interesting museums in St. James, lighthouses to view, and some scenic mountain biking along the island's two-track roads.

Directions: The round trip fare is $160 to take your car to the island, and that's above and beyond the fares for passengers. You also can rent a car in St. James for around $60 or bring a bicycle with you on the ferry to reach the campground. For more information call Beaver Island Boat Company (888-446-4095; www.beaverislandboatcompany.com), Beaver Island Chamber of Commerce (231-448-2505; www.beaverisland.org), or Gordan's Auto Rentals (248-448-2438).

Once in St. James, head south on the King's Highway, the only paved road outside the town, for 6 miles and then east on Hannigan's Road. Within 1.5 miles Hannigan's Road comes to an intersection with East Side Drive. The campground entrance is just south on East Side Drive.

Campground: Wagner has 22 rustic sites well scattered in a stand of red pine. None of the sites are directly on Lake Michigan, but all are only a short walk away. Facilities include tables, outhouses, and hand pump for water.

Day-use Facilities: The campground is on Big Sand Bay, a sweeping shoreline of sand where you can stroll for more than 3 miles. The lake here is shallow enough for swimming while the beach is ideal for falling asleep under the shade of a pine tree.

Hiking: Across from the campground entrance on East Side Drive is the Beaver Island Nature Trail, a state forest pathway that leads 2.5 miles to Oil Site No. 1 in the interior of the island. Keep in mind that the trails on Beaver Island are poorly marked and maintained.

Season: Bill Wagner Campground rarely fills up. Early October can be a particularly pleasant time to take a trip to Beaver Island. The fall colors can be stunning at this time of year yet most of the tourists have long since departed.

BIKING ON BEAVER ISLAND

In the summer Beaver Island is a place where you come to escape, slow down, lose track of time, and, if you bring your mountain bike, ride the island's 100-mile network of dirt roads and trails in search of isolated beaches. Don't even think about bringing your road bike. Except for St. James and 4 miles of the King's Highway, the roads are dirt and many of them little more than two-tracks. There is some technical mountain biking along state forest pathways in the southern half of the island, but most cyclists simply follow the roads that skirt the shoreline.

Unlike Mackinac Island, the other island haven for bikers, there are cars on Beaver Island but not many. Most of the traffic is encountered in the northern tip of the island where most of the summer cottages are located. Here the riding can get dusty at times. The cycling is much more pleasant in the rest of the island, especially along the forested two-tracks in the southern half.

The perimeter of the island is a long 35-mile day on a mountain bike. Many visitors do just a portion of it by arranging a drop-off by contacting the Beaver Island Chamber of Commerce (231-448-2505; www.beaverisland.org) about available transportation services on the island. Before you leave St. James, however, stock up on high-energy snacks, fill the water bottle, and purchase a map from the Chamber of Commerce office. There is no place to buy junk food outside of the small village and a road sign on Beaver Island is a rarity.

One of the best places to begin is Kelly's Point in the southeast corner. By following South End Road in a clockwise direction you immediately swing into view of the water and in two miles reach Old Beaver Head Lighthouse. The lighthouse is currently being renovated and is a natural spot to take a break. You can check out a few artifacts inside, climb the tower for a better view at the top, or walk to the lake.

Beyond the lighthouse, South End Road skirts Iron Ore Bay and turns to sand so soft it's easier to walk your bike than ride it. But you're well rewarded for the struggle through the open dunes. It's hard to imagine a more remote beach anywhere on Lake Michigan. For a half mile all that is there is you, your bicycle, and one picnic table.

From Iron Ore Bay you continue on West End Road, a forest road that ends in 10 miles at the Beaver Island Airport. The last leg of this 20-mile outing is the northern tip of the island, a 4-mile ride from McClauley's Point to St. James.

The Straits

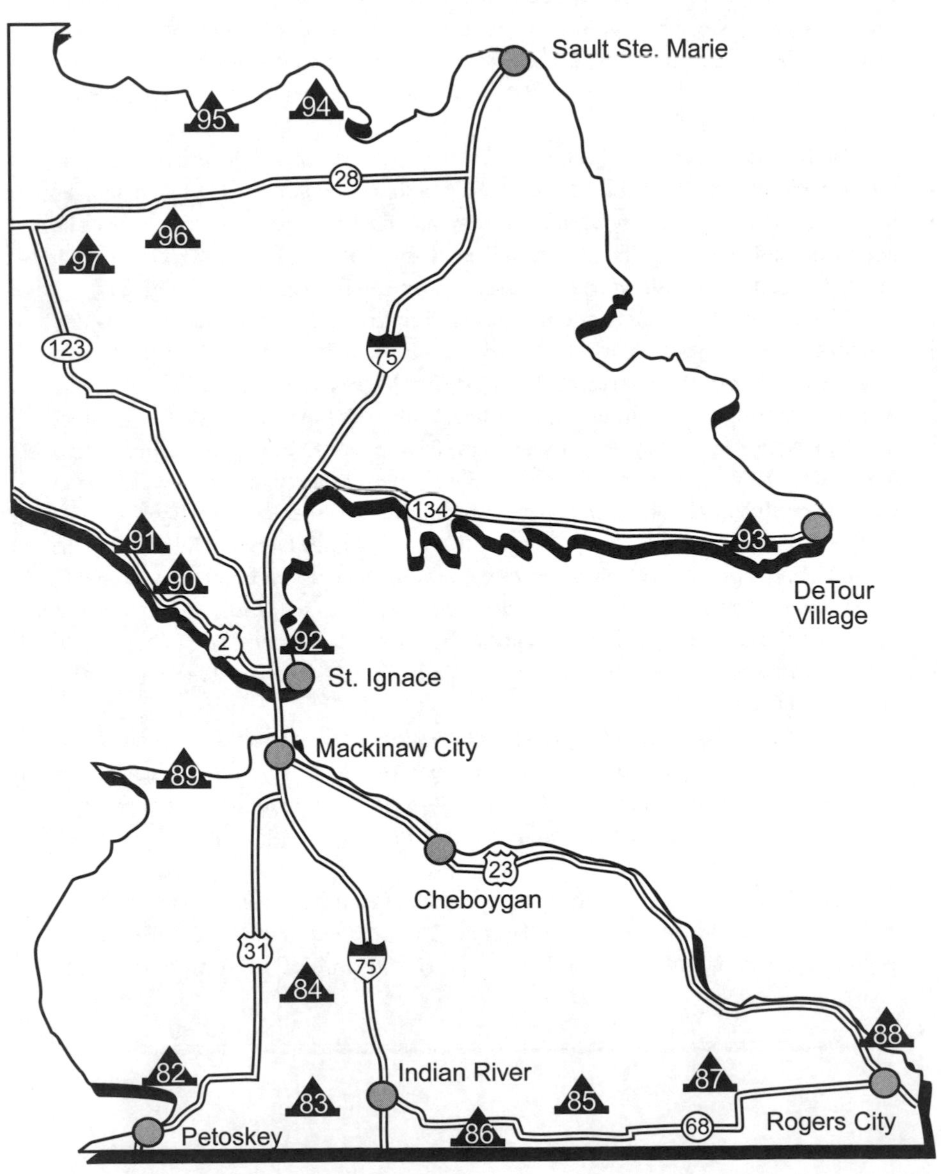

Sault Ste. Marie
95
94
28
96
97
123
75
134
93
DeTour Village
91
90
2
92
St. Ignace
Mackinaw City
89
Cheboygan
23
31
75
84
88
82
Indian River
87
85
83
86
68
Rogers City
Petoskey

#	PARK	MODERN	SEMI-MODERN	RUSTIC	SITES	DAY-USE FACILITIES	FISHING	HIKING	BIRDING	INTERPRETIVE CENTER	BIKING	CANOEING/ KAYAKING	BOATING
82	Petoskey	•			180	•		•			•		
83	Camp Pet-O-Se-Ga	•			90	•		•					
84	Maple Bay			•	36	•	•						•
85	Onaway	•			98	•	•						
86	Tomahawk Creek Flooding			•	39	•	•	•					
87	Ocqueoc Falls			•	14	•	•	•				•	
88	P.H. Hoeft	•			142	•	•	•			•		
89	Lakeshore	•			150	•	•	•					
90	Lake Michigan			•	35	•		•					
91	Brevoort Lake			•	70	•	•	•					
92	Foley Creek			•	54		•	•					
93	DeTour			•	21	•	•	•					
94	Monocle Lake			•	39	•	•	•					
95	Bay View			•	24	•				•			
96	Soldier Lake			•	44	•	•	•					
97	Three Lakes			•	28	•	•	•					

82

Petoskey

State Park

Campground: Modern
County: Emmet
Nearest Community: Petoskey
Sites: 180
Reservations: Yes
Fee: $27-$29 plus vehicle entry fee
Information: State park office
☎ (231) 347-2311

In that commercialized shoreline that is Little Traverse Bay, there is one haven from the strip of hotels, marinas, and condominiums that begins in Petoskey and doesn't quit until you leave Harbor Springs. That 303-acre sanctuary is Petoskey State Park that lies between the two tourist towns.

The state park may not be large, but it's amazing what it offers: some of the most secluded modern sites in the state, a beautiful beach, good hunting for Petoskey stones, even some short hiking trails. Needless to say, such a facility in a tourist area is going to be filled throughout much of the summer despite its two large campgrounds.

Directions: The park is 4.5 miles north of downtown Petoskey. Follow US-31 to M-119 and then north (left) for 1.5 miles to the posted entrance.

Campgrounds: The park has 180 sites divided between two campground loops. The Dunes Campground is the original facility and has 80 modern sites in a forested area of low dunes. For as close as they are to each other, these sites are as secluded as any modern campground you'll find in a state park. The area is heavily forested, and the terrain of rolling dunes allows most of the sites to occupy a little nook of their own. Along the backside of the loop, the foredunes are actually pouring into some of the campsites, and from here it's only a short walk to the beach. The loop is paved but not the spurs, and large RVs might have difficulty with some of the sites.

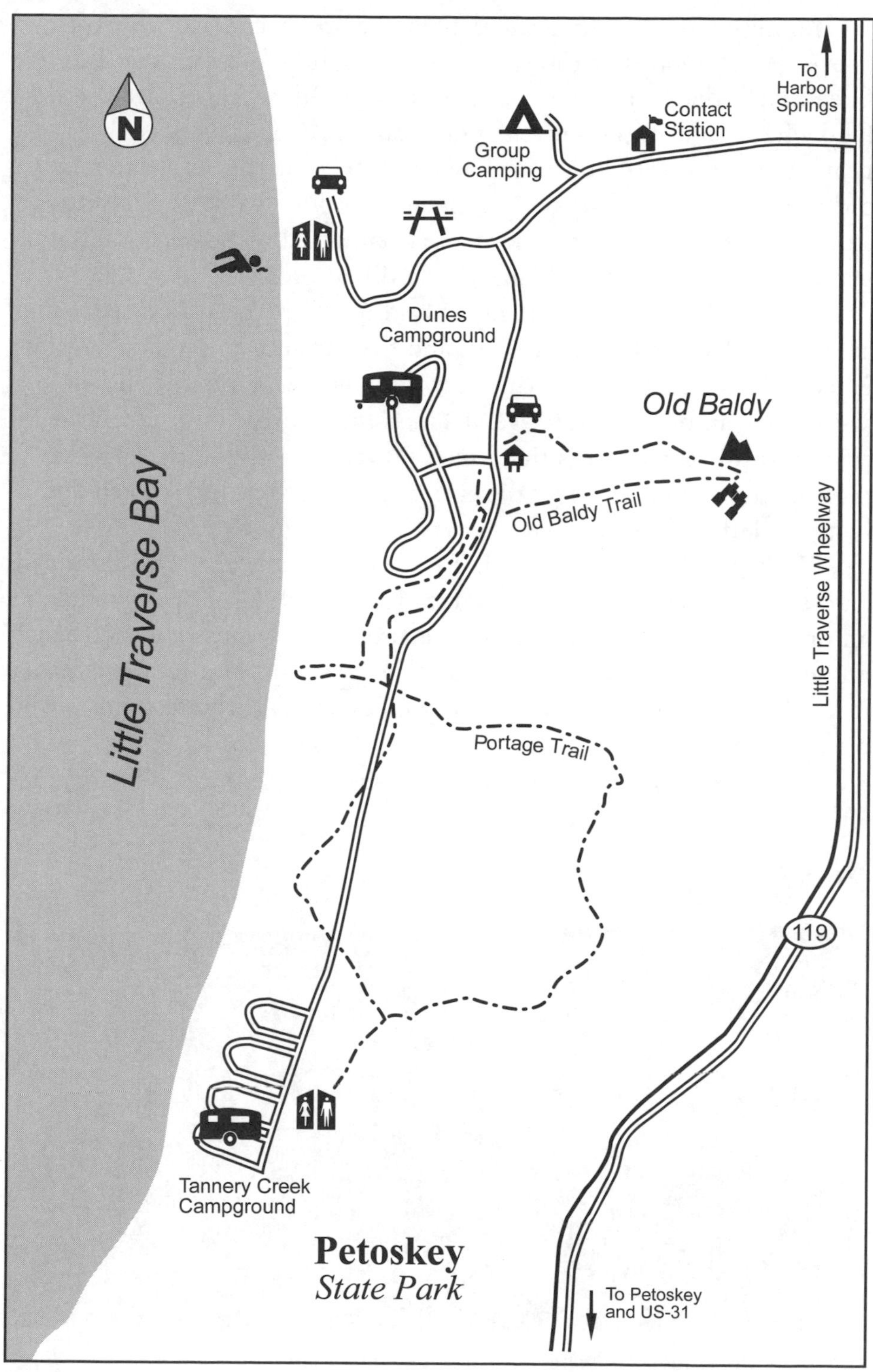
N
To
Harbor
Springs
Contact
Station
Group
Camping
Dunes
Campground
Old Baldy
Old Baldy Trail
Little Traverse Bay
Little Traverse Wheelway
Portage Trail
119
Tannery Creek
Campground
Petoskey
State Park
To Petoskey
and US-31

Tannery Creek Campground is at the south end of the park and consists of four loops of 100 sites in a level, lightly forested area. Tannery Creek lacks that charming seclusion of the Dunes, especially the final loop where many of the sites have no shade at all. Four wooden walkways provide access to Little Traverse Bay, and at this end the beach is a mixture of sand and pebbles, dismaying to swimmers but a paradise for Petoskey stone hunters. Both loops have restrooms with showers, sanitation stations, firewood bins, and tables and grills at each site.

Day-use Facilities: At the north end of the park is a shaded picnic area with tables and pedestal grills and the entrance to group campsites. Nearby is the beach and a marked swimming area. Here the shoreline is sandy, wide, and enclosed by several dunes. There is a bathhouse/concession store and two parking lots that hold 300 vehicles. The view of the bay is pleasant as you look out over the entire body of water that is often dotted by the colorful spinnakers of sailboats.

Hiking: Old Baldy Trail is a 0.75-mile loop that begins with a staircase across from the camper registration station near Dunes Campground. It's an uphill climb in the first half where at one point you come to a bench and a partial view of Little Traverse Bay at the top of a staircase. That's it for the view as there is none on top unless it's fall. The return is a wild romp down a soft sandy path.

A Petoskey stone hunter searches Lake Michigan for the state stone.

HUNTING FOR PETOSKEY STONES

The quintessential Michigan scene is somebody strolling the edge of a beach on a late summer day with a plastic bucket in hand, turning over pebbles with their toes, searching for that local gem, a small, roundish Petoskey stone with a perfect honeycomb pattern.

Good luck finding one then.

Diehard rock hounds and lapidaries will tell you that best time to search for a Petoskey is in the spring, the earlier the better. When the winter ice goes out on Lake Michigan, it's like a bulldozer turning everything over, leaving behind a new set of rocks and stones along the shore. Equip yourself with rubber boots, fingerless gloves, and a small rake and get out there for the prime pickings of Petoskeys.

Michigan's state stone, officially adopted in 1965, is actually petrified coral. Petoskeys are leftover fragments of the reefs that existed 350 million years ago during the Devonian Period when salty warm-water seas covered the northern half of the state. Eventually, layers of sediment covered the Hexagonaria coral and its distinctive six-sided pattern was preserved when the sediment was compacted into stratified rock.

There are Petoskey stones lying on beaches from Frankfort to Alpena, but when glaciers carved out Little Traverse Bay, they hit the motherlode, a strata outcropping that results in thousands of Petoskeys washing on shore every year.

Here's three great parks to hunt for a Petoskey, even in the middle of summer:

Fisherman's Island State Park: This 2,678-acre park just south Charlevoix features five miles of Lake Michigan shoreline, most of it cobbled beach, making it our best place to find the state stone. Hunting for a Petoskey is so popular here that the park has a handout on the stone and how to find them. The best spot in the park is its namesake island which, due to lower lake levels in recent years, is no longer an island and now can be easily reached on foot.

Barnes County Park: This 120-acre unit of Antrim County is also along US-31 and includes more than a quarter mile of beautiful beach sprinkled with patches of pebbles and stones. Hunting for a Petoskey is such a popular activity here that the park stages a Petoskey Stone Festival on Memorial Day weekend. Think you're a rock hound extraordinaire? Then enter the festival's Beach Hunt Contest when first, second, and third-place prizes are awarded for both the biggest and best quality stones.

Petoskey State Park: When a state park and the adjacent city are both named after our state stone, you just know the hunting is good there. The 303-acre state park has almost 2 miles of shoreline in the heart of Little Traverse Bay, ground zero for Petoskey stone hunters. If you find a trophy head over to Bailey's Place Petoskey Stones & Stuff ☎ 231-347-8043 on US-31 to have it rated.

Portage Trail has trailheads near the Tannery Creek restroom and the firewood bin at Dunes campground. Much of it runs parallel to the park drive and is a better ski trail in the winter than a hiker's path during the summer, but it does swing east of the road into a forested area of some surprisingly steep hills.

Cycling: Crossing the entrance of the park on M-119 is the Little Traverse Wheelway, a paved trail that stretches 26 miles from Charlevoix to Harbor Springs. This trail puts you so close to Little Traverse Bay at times that on a windy day you can feel the mist from the surf. Along with sweeping views of the water, Little Traverse Wheelway features numerous rest areas, a 50-foot-long tunnel, a half-mile-long boardwalk through a wetland, and a spur that leads to Petoskey's Gaslight Shopping District where you can easily fill your panniers. For a map or location of staging points contact the Top of Michigan Trails Council ☎ 231-348-8280 🌐 trailscouncil.org.

Season: The campgrounds fill daily from Fourth of July weekend to mid-August and are up to 85 percent filled through Labor Day and daily from July through mid-August. Reservations through Michigan State Park Central Reservations ☎ 800-447-2757 🌐 www.midnrreservations.com are a must here during the summer.

83

Camp Pet-O-Se-Ga

Emmet County Park

Campground: Modern
County: Emmet
Nearest Community: Alanson
Sites: 90
Reservations: Yes

Fee: \$16–\$18
Information: Park office
☎ (231) 347-6536
🌐 www.emmetcounty.org/petosega

If at Camp Pet-O-Se-Ga you feel like singing Kumbaya around the campfire, go ahead. You won't be the first.

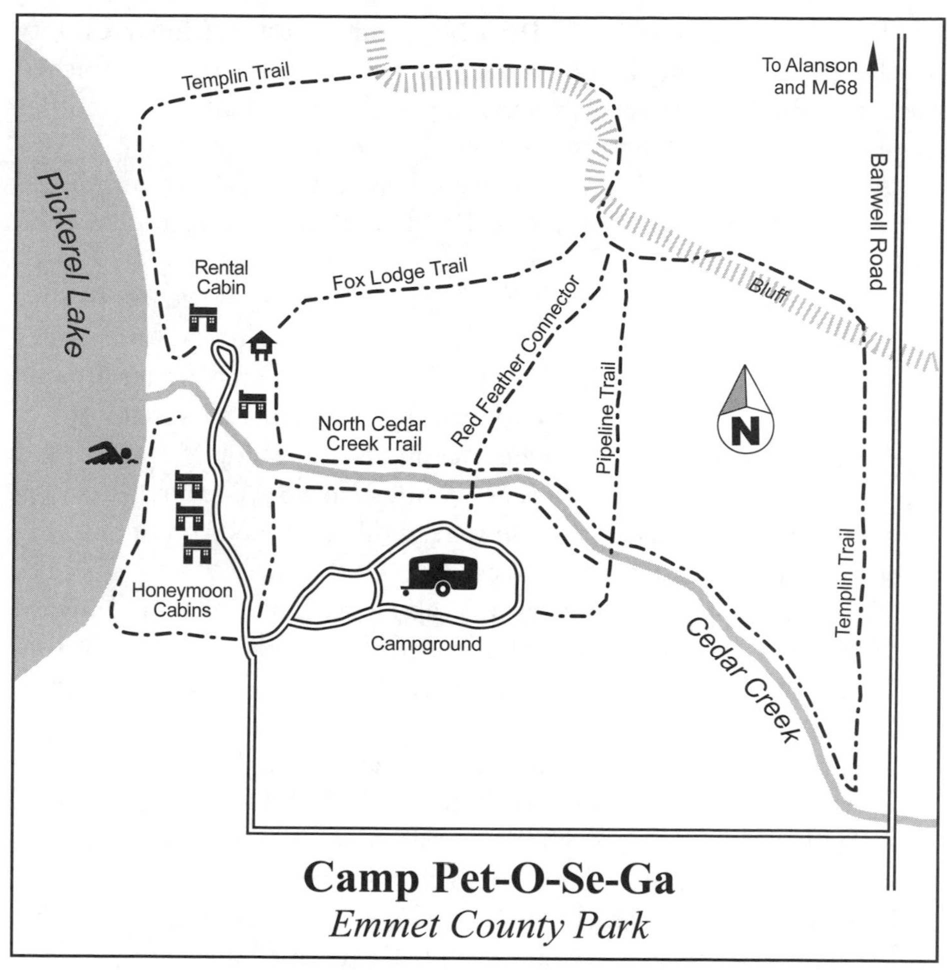

The Emmet County park at the west end of Pickerel Lake started out as a summer camp with boys sleeping in log cabins, eating in a mess hall, and spending their days learning archery, canoeing, hiking, and swimming. When the County Board of Commissioners purchased the land in 1992, they decided to create a new place to camp during the summer but preserve the history and ambiance of the old summer camp.

Camp Pet-O-Se-Ga dates back to 1934 when Jim Templin, a 23-year-old graduate of the University of Kentucky and former Eagle Scout, decided to postpone his business career and open a summer camp on 55 acres of abandoned property where Cedar Creek flows into Pickerel Lake. Templin eventually expanded his facility to 300 acres and 19 log buildings, creating a camp that hosted 100 boys.

Templin sold the camp in 1954 but returned after Emmet County purchased the property and organized an alumni group that refurbished the remaining cabins. Today, several are available for rent while another serves as a camp museum.

Directions: From US-31 in Alanson head east on M-68, and in less than a mile turn south on Banwell Road. The park entrance is reached within 6 miles on Banwell Road.

Campground: Camp Pet-O-Se-Ga has 90 sites spread across five loops that are well equipped to handle recreational vehicles. All the sites are wired for electricity, and almost half of them feature water as well. Despite being a modern campground, the sites are well spread out in a pine and hardwood forest, where campers can enjoy a wooded and private setting even on a busy weekend. Sites No. 86–90 are pull-through with full hook-ups that include sewage, while scattered throughout the campground are 10 barrier-free sites.

The county park also has several cabins available for rent. Three of them are small, four-bunk structures called the Honeymoon Cabins that date back to the 1920s when they were rented in Petoksey's Magnus Park.

The two most popular cabins, however, are classic log structures that Templin built for his camp and then refurbished for Emmet County. Both feature electric lights, kitchen areas with refrigerators and stoves, fieldstone fireplaces, and a front porch that lets you relax with a full view of Pickerel Lake. The largest one is a two-story cabin that sleeps nine with a bunkroom upstairs where seven beds are lined up side-by-side as if you were, well, at summer camp.

Campsites are $16 a night for county residents and $18 for non-residents. The Honeymoon Cabins are $40 a night for non-county residents, and the large log cabin is $70, the smaller one $60.

Day-use Facilities: The most unique part of the park, the area that makes you feel like you're back at summer camp, is Camp Pet-O-Se-Ga's waterfront. It's an open, grassy area bordered on one side by a sandy beach and Pickerel Lake and on the other by a string of cabins and the old mess hall. Flowing through the middle is Cedar Creek. In the back of one of the large cabins is a small museum with historic photos of the summer camp and display cases filled with uniforms, badges, and camp song books.

Hiking: The park also has several miles of nature trails. The longest is the Templin Trail that follows the lakeshore, climbs up and down a wooded ridge, and skirts the north side of Cedar Creek, a cedar-lined trout stream.

Season: Two of the cabins are rented year-round, and the rest, along with the campground, is open from early May to mid-October. The campground can be a popular place on weekends during the summer; it's best to reserve sites in advance, if possible, by calling the park office at ☎ 231-347-6536. Reservations are site specific from Memorial Day through Labor Day, and a campsite map and a reservation form are available on line at 🌐 www.emmetcounty.org/petosega.

84

Maple Bay

Mackinaw State Forest

Campground: Rustic
County: Cheboygan
Nearest Community: Brutus
Sites: 36
Reservations: No
Fee: $15
Information: Gaylord DNR office
☎ (989) 732-3541

Burt Lake is a busy and heavily developed lake as evident from the line of docks just outside this campground. Still the 17,120-acre lake is a beautiful body of water, especially on a calm morning when you can sit in the day-use area and enjoy that first cup of coffee while waiting for the sunrise over the east shore. And because of its immense size, there seems to be only minimum conflict between anglers and those zipping across the surface in motor boats or jet skis.

There are two state campgrounds on the lake, but my favorite has always been this state forest unit over the modern facility at Burt Lake State Park. Either one has an excellent beach and swimming area and both will be busy through the camping season.

Directions: From I-75, depart at exit 310 at Indian River and head west on M-68 as it curves around the southern end of Burt Lake and the entrance to the state park. In 11 miles you reach the junction with US-31 in the town of Alanson. Head north on US-31 and in 3 miles head east (right) on Brutus Road. In 3.5 miles you'll reached the posted entrance to Maple Bay.

Campground: Maple Bay is a three-lane loop with 36 sites and forested in hardwoods. Six sites on the outside overlook the day-use area and Maple Bay, receiving a nice breeze in the evening. The rest are in a forested area with heavy undergrowth. Though Maple Bay is not as secluded as most state forest campgrounds, it does offer far more privacy than the state park on the southeast corner.

Sites have tables and a fire ring, and many feature a pull-through spur, making them ideal for large RVs. Hand pumps and vault toilets are scattered throughout the loop. The two drawbacks in Maple Bay are that the low-lying areas between the sites can get buggy during a wet spell and the raccoons which have been a nuisance here in the past. Every bit of food should be locked in your car.

Day-use Facilities: Maple Bay features a sandy beach that, while not nearly as wide as the state park, still makes for a pleasant spot to spend a hot summer afternoon. There is a marked swimming area with a soft bottom that is knee-deep shallow for more than 50 yards, perfect for children to splash around. Bordering the beach in a shaded grassy strip are tables and pedestal grills but no playground equipment.

Boating: The campground has an improved boat launch with additional parking for a half dozen vehicles and trailers. Burt Lake is popular with boaters as it is part of the Inland Waterway, an historic 40-mile chain of four lakes and three rivers that was first used by the Indians as a safer and shorter alternative for paddling the Straits of Mackinac from Lake Michigan to Lake Huron. The route actually begins in Conway on Crooked Lake, 6 miles from Petoskey on Little Traverse Bay and ends with the Cheboygan River flowing into the Straits. Burt Lake is in the middle of the route.

Fishing: Burt Lake is one of the most heavily fished inland lakes in Michigan. It is regarded as an excellent walleye fishery and anglers are most productive with the gamefish from late May to mid-June and again in the fall. The lake, which is almost 10 miles long, also supports a good perch population as well as bass, rock bass, various panfish species, and to a lesser degree northern pike. There are bait and tackle shops in Alanson.

Season: Despite its size, Maple Bay fills up often on the weekends in July and August, and during mid-week still might have only a handful of sites open.

Onaway

State Park

Campground: Modern
County: Presque Isle
Nearest Community: Onaway
Sites: 98
Reservations: Yes
Fee: $20 plus vehicle entry fee
Information: State park office
☎ (989) 733-8279

The perception of state parks by many is a campground where the sites are close together and fill for much of the summer. That's true in some units but not Onaway State Park on the south end of Black Lake.

The rolling 158-acre unit is well forested in white pine, maple, and oak, attracts an army of morel mushroom hunters every spring, and contains almost a mile of shoreline. The park's most attractive features is the fact that it draws less than 60,000 visitors a year and that a "No Vacancy" sign is rarely seen here.

Directions: From I-75, depart east at exit 310 and follow M-68 to the town of Onaway. Turn north on M-211 and follow it 6 miles to the park entrance.

Campground: Onaway has 98 sites well scattered on a hillside loop that is lightly forested by towering red and white pine. Most of the sites lie uphill from Black Lake and have a view of the water, but sites No. 1–14 border the shoreline and feature a great watery view from your picnic table. Amenities include tables and fire rings while a restroom with showers and a sanitation station is located within the loop.

Day-use Facilities: There is a picnic area on the east side of the park that includes tables, grills, a shelter that can be rented, and parking for 75 cars. There is no beach and that's the major drawback of Onaway. The only sand is on the west side of the campground, and it's a very narrow strip at best. Limited play equipment is located here.

Fishing: Black Lake is the eighth largest in the state, measuring 6 miles long, 4 miles wide, and containing 10,130 surface acres. It's a beautiful body of water and regarded by many as one of the finest walleye fisheries in Michigan. The popularity of fishing on Black Lake prompted the Onaway staff to rebuild its boat launch west of the campground.

Black Lake also boasts self-sustaining populations of Great Lakes muskies, northern pike, and perch. The rocky shore and points, while not too attractive to swimmers and sunbathers, draws a number of shore anglers to try their luck with long casts.

Season: The campground is open from May through mid-October and generally only fills on Fourth of July and one or two other weekends during summer. Early and late in the season, before the water is turned on, sites are only $16 a night. To reserve a campsite contact Michigan State Park Central Reservations ☎ 800-447-2757 🌐 www.midnrreservations.com.

86

Tomahawk Creek Flooding

Mackinaw State Forest

Campground: Rustic
County: Presque Isle
Nearest Community: Onaway
Sites: 39
Reservations: No
Fee: $15
Information: Gaylord DNR office
☎ (989) 732-3541

There are three campgrounds in this section of the Mackinaw State Forest, and none of them more than a 10-minute drive from each other. Shoepac Lake offers the best hiking opportunities with the interesting

Sink Holes Pathway nearby and the High Country Pathway passing through the area. Tomahawk Lake by far has the best beach and swimming area as well as numerous sites that overlook the undeveloped lake.

A camper peers into a sinkhole from an observation deck reached from the Sinkhole Pathway near Tomahawk Creek Flooding Campground.

But Tomahawk Creek Flooding, at least the east side, has the most scenic views from the sites and the best fishery of the four bodies of water accessible here. Take your pick. I chose the Flooding, but this far north chances are you will find a site in any of them.

Directions: From Atlanta, head north on M-33 for 15 miles then turn east (right) on Tomahawk Lake Highway, which is not highway at all but rather a rough dirt road. The West Unit is posted within a mile; the East Unit follows. Both Tomahawk Lake and Shoepac Lake are posted farther east.

Campground: The newest campground in this noted karst (sinkhole) area, Tomahawk Creek Flooding is actually 39 sites split between two units with one on the east side of the lake and the other on the west. The campground was constructed in the early 1980s, and its East Unit is by far the most scenic. The three loops are lightly forested in hardwoods and on a bluff enclosed by a log fence and overlooking the water. A handful of sites have a spectacular view of not only the lake but the creek beyond and ridges in the distance. Most of the sites have tables and fire rings while vault toilets and a hand pump for water are located within each loop. Long stairways lead down from the edge of the bluff to the water below. The West Unit is closer to the shoreline but has no sites directly on it. These loops are heavily forested and the sites are more secluded but the view is not nearly as good.

Day-Use Facilities: Head to Tomahawk Lake where you will find a small but nice beach that is terraced with logs and located in the middle of the campground.

Fishing: Both units of Tomahawk Creek Flooding have an improved boat launch with a cement ramp and additional parking for a handful of vehicles and rigs. Of the four lakes in the area, the Flooding is by far the best with a strong bluegill fishery and other panfish as well as largemouth bass. There is also a pike fishery, but the northerns caught are generally under-sized. Like most floodings, there is a large number of deadheads, stumps, and timber still standing, especially at the south end of the lake. Fishing pressure appears moderate to light through most of the summer.

Hiking: Just beyond the entrance to Shoepac Lake Campground is a posted trailhead to Sinkholes Pathway. The 2.4-mile loop is an easy to moderate hike around five sinkholes, huge depressions in the ground formed when limestone caves collapsed. The first is the most impressive and is reached only 10 minutes from the trailhead. Also passing through here is the High Country Pathway, a 50-mile, five- to seven-day loop that many people begin at Clear Lake State Park to the south on M-33.

Season: All three campgrounds are large, and getting a site in any of them is easy mid-week or even on the weekend.

87

Ocqueoc Falls

Mackinaw State Forest

Campground: Rustic
County: Presque Isle
Nearest Community: Onaway
Sites: 14
Reservations: No

Fee: $15
Information: Gaylord DNR office
☎ (989) 732-3541

Although called Ocqueoc Falls State Forest Campground, the falls, the largest cascade and many say the only true one in the Lower Peninsula,

Ocqueoc Falls near Ocqueoc Falls State Forest Campground.

is actually across the street in a day-use area of its own. Even without a view of the small waterfalls, this rustic campground is worth pulling into and can provide you a secluded site among pines and hardwoods overlooking the scenic river.

Directions: The falls and campground are just off M-68 on Ocqueoc Falls Highway, 10 miles northeast of Onaway or 11.5 miles west of Rogers City.

Campground: Ocqueoc Falls is a single loop of 14 sites, all of them near the river and a half dozen on the edge of the low bluff that towers directly above water. The sites are well separated and secluded from each other in a forest of red pine, paper birch, and mixed hardwoods. There are tables and fire rings at most sites, but not all, and vault toilets and a hand pump for water in the campground.

Day-use Facilities: The posted entrance and paved parking area to Ocqueoc Falls Scenic Site are across the street from the campground and has a few tables, pedestal grills, and vault toilets. It's a short walk of 30 yards from the parking area to the river and falls. There is actually another set of falls off the Manistee River in the Lower Peninsula, but Ocqueoc is definitely the most impressive. It descends six feet in a series of levels with one drop a particular favorite for children to sit under on a hot summer day.

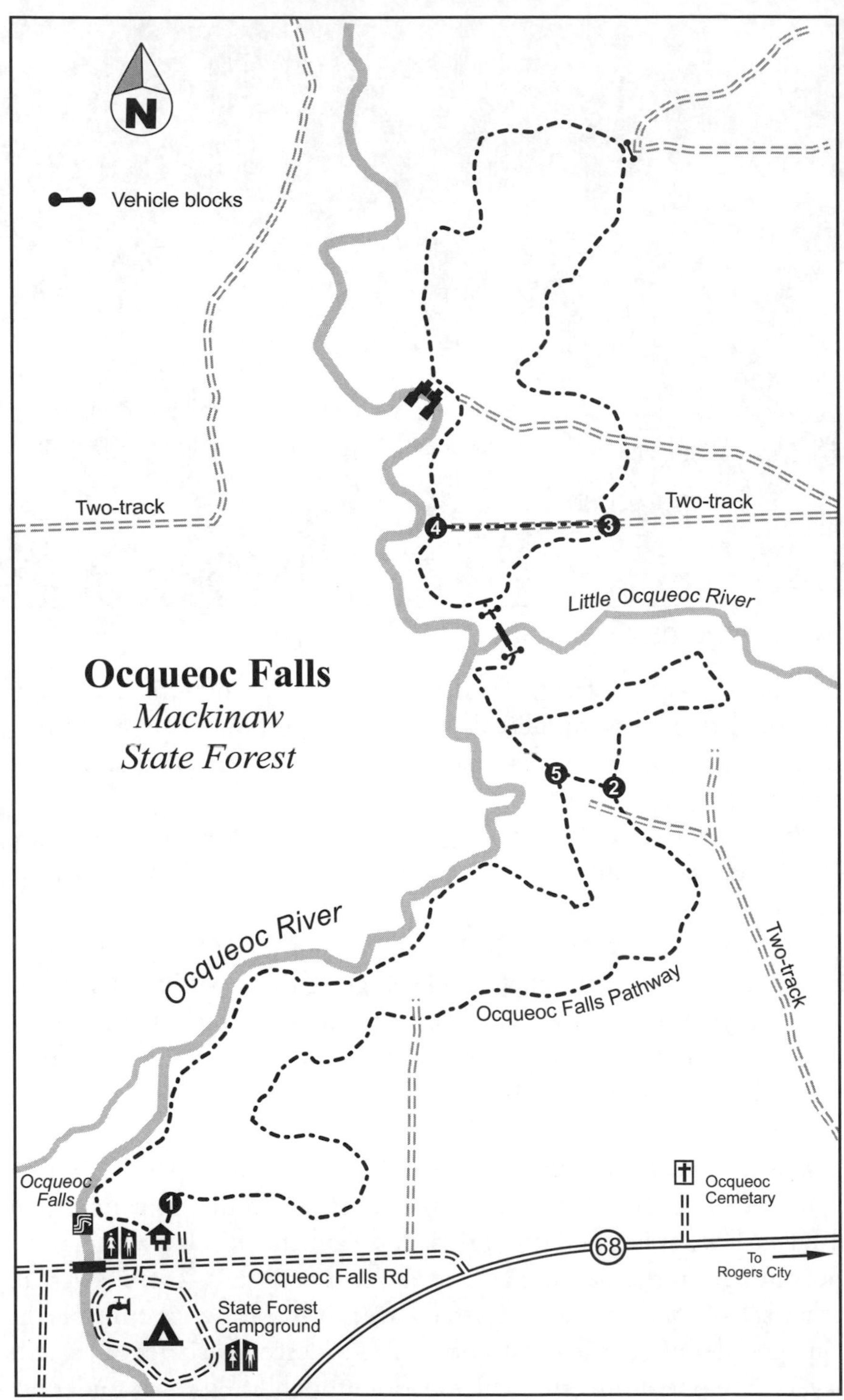

N
Vehicle blocks
Two-track
Two-track
Little Ocqueoc River
Ocqueoc Falls
Mackinaw
State Forest
Ocqueoc River
Two-track
Ocqueoc Falls Pathway
Ocqueoc Falls
Ocqueoc Cemetary
68
To Rogers City
Ocqueoc Falls Rd
State Forest Campground
1
2
3
4
5

Fishing: The Ocqueoc River offers a fishery that ranges from warmwater species of pike and smallmouth bass in its upper sections where it flows through Barnhart Lake to salmon, brown trout, and steelhead in its downstream stretches. Near the campground the river is 15–20 feet wide and can be easily waded in most places while just below the falls it is joined by the Little Ocqueoc River, one of two main tributaries and a noted brook trout stream. During the summer much of the Ocqueoc is not cold enough to hold trout, and its heaviest fishing pressure is from steelheaders who arrive in the spring and fall for the annual run.

Hiking: Ocqueoc Falls Pathway, built in 1976 as a Bicentennial project, begins with a posted trailhead in the parking lot of the day-use area. The trail is shared by hikers and mountain bikers during much of the year and consists of four loops: 2.85, 3.5, 4.6 and 6 miles. As far as hiking is concerned, the first loop is not only the shortest but the most scenic as it skirts the river for almost a mile at one point.

Canoeing: The Ocqueoc River makes for a 30-mile canoe route that begins at an access site on Lake Emma off of County Road 634 and ends at its mouth on Lake Huron's Hammond Bay. You have to portage around the falls, and other sections of this river can be challenging. Ocqueoc Falls is the only campground along the river.

Season: This is a lightly used facility that rarely fills up.

Campers at Ocqueoc Falls State Forest Campground.

88

P.H. Hoeft

State Park

Campground: Modern
County: Presque Isle
Nearest Community: Rogers City
Sites: 142
Reservations: Yes
Fee: $16–$22 plus vehicle entry fee
Information: Park office
☎ (989) 734-2543

In 1922, Paul H. Hoeft, who had spent most of his adult life chopping trees down in Michigan, gave the state 300 timbered acres along Lake Huron. The lumber baron's gift soon became a popular camping area and one of Michigan's original state parks.

Not much has changed since. With few exceptions, the original acreage and boundaries have remained intact. Despite drawing less than 70,000 visitors a year, most of them are campers who can easily fill the 142 sites on any weekend in July and August.

The popularity of Hoeft is easy to understand. The park has a beautiful beach, a series of low dunes for children to climb, a nice network of trails, and, if you're an early morning riser, some of the best sunrises in Michigan. Best of all, it rarely seems overrun like so many state parks along Lake Michigan.

Directions: The park is 5 miles northwest of Rogers City with an entrance on US-23.

Campground: The modern campground has 142 well spread out sites along several loops in a stand of hemlock and pine. There are 15 sites that border the low dunes and provide quick access to the Lake Huron beach. Site No. 35, though not along the dunes, might be the most secluded modern one in the Lower Peninsula while a few near the road are in a semi-open area.

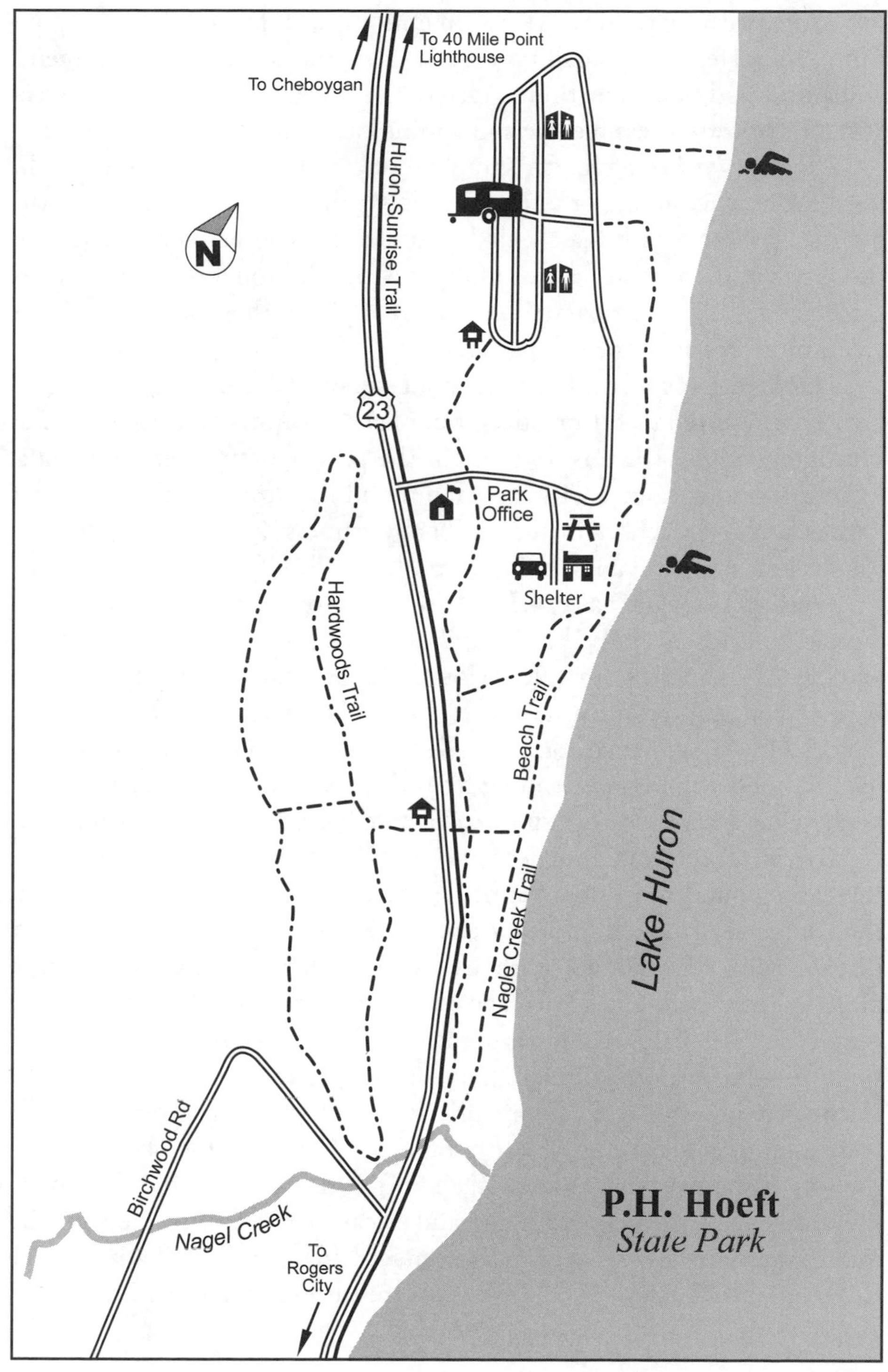
To 40 Mile Point Lighthouse
To Cheboygan
Huron-Sunrise Trail
N
23
Park Office
Shelter
Hardwoods Trail
Beach Trail
Nagle Creek Trail
Lake Huron
Birchwood Rd
Nagel Creek
To Rogers City
P.H. Hoeft
State Park

Along with two shower/restroom buildings, tables, and fire rings, the campground features a small store, horseshoe pits, limited play equipment, and a firewood bin where timber is sold daily during the summer. There is also a handicap-accessible site and a mini-cabin that can be rented.

Day-use Facility: Hoeft's shoreline is a mile of wide sandy beach, ideal for beachcombing or setting up a lawn chair to watch freighters sail by. The day-use area has a classic log and stone shelter, built in 1938 by the Civilian Conservation Corps along with additional play equipment, tables, and grills well separated in a stand of pines. There is also a marked swimming area near the campground.

Fishing: Annual plants of salmon, lake and brown trout off Rogers City have resulted in a strong deepwater fishery within a mile of the Lake Huron shoreline. There is no ramp in the park, but there are launching facilities in both Rogers City and Hammond Bay. The only fishing in the park is at Nagel Creek, which occasionally attracts river anglers in the fall for spawning salmon and steelhead trout.

Hiking: The park has a 4.5-mile network of foot paths that centers around the Beach Trail. This 1.2-mile loop begins between sites No. 21 and No. 23 and passes through the low dunes before returning through the park's wooded interior. At its east end, the Hardwood Trail heads south, crosses US-23, and then forms a 1.4-mile loop through a forest of oak, maple, and beech. Also extending from the east end of the Beach Trail is Nagel Creek Trail, which forms a 0.75-mile loop to the small creek.

Cycling: Departing from near site No. 129 is a paved spur that connects the campground to Huron-SunriseTrail. This beautiful paved trail skirts the shoreline of Lake Huron for eight miles from Rogers City north to historic Forty Mile Point Lighthouse, whose delightful park is the perfect place to linger before heading back. From the state park, the lighthouse is round trip ride of almost 5 miles to the north while Rogers City's Lakeside Park would be a outing of more than 10 miles to the south.

Season: Hoeft is open from April through October and offers an off-season semi-modern rate of $16 a night in April and October. During the rest of the season sites are $22 and often the campground fills up on the weekends in July and August and occasionally during the week in mid-August. To reserve a campsite contact Michigan State Park Central Reservations ☎ 800-447-2757 🌐 www.midnrreservations.com.

89

Lakeshore

Wilderness State Park

Campground: Modern
County: Emmet
Nearest Community: Mackinaw City
Sites: 150
Reservations: Yes
Fee: $27 plus vehicle entry fee
Information: State park office
☎ (231) 436-5381

There are two parks in Michigan where you can camp in view of the Mackinac Bridge. One is the Straits State Park in the Upper Peninsula and the other is Wilderness State Park west of Mackinaw City. Of the two... actually, there is no comparison between them. Wilderness makes for a far more enjoyable camping trip, offering some of the finest beaches at the Tip, an excellent trail network, and fishing opportunities for both children and diehard bass anglers.

The 10,512-acre park has two campgrounds. Pines offers 100 sites in a rolling terrain lightly forested in red pine and oaks. Then there is Lakeshore Campground, a loop of 150 sites with almost a third of them along Big Stone Bay. Quick access to the beach and the beauty of this historical waterway between the Lower and Upper Peninsula make Lakeshore one of the most popular state park facilities.

Directions: The park entrance is 8 miles west of Mackinaw City and is reached by following County Road 81 and continuing west on Wilderness Park Drive after crossing Carp Lake River.

Campground: Lakeshore has two loops of 150 sites in a lightly shaded area overlooking the Straits. Forty sites are along the shoreline, many right above the open beach, others are partly shaded and a short walk from the water. Site No. 38 is a gem, off by itself in a stand of pines. Throughout the loop there is a nice view of the Straits, the Mighty Mac, and the Upper Peninsula shoreline. The shoreline along Big Stone Bay is excellent for swimming or just strolling along its sandy beach. Lakeshore

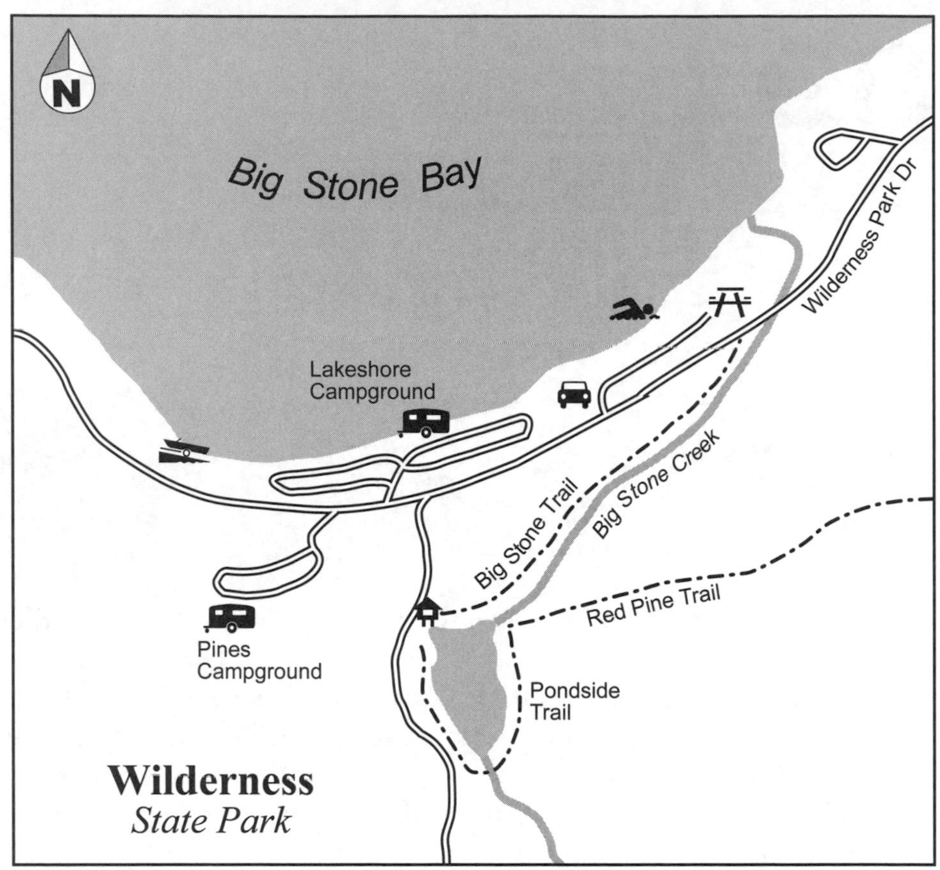

has tables, fire rings, two restrooms with showers, a sanitation station, and play equipment.

Day-use Facilities: The park's picnic area is also on Big Stone Bay, just east of the campground. Here you'll find tables overlooking the Straits, pedestal grills, vault toilets, and a marked swimming area bordered by a sandy beach.

Fishing: The park has an improved launch just west of Lakeshore Campground, but for Wilderness' most noted fishing opportunity, you don't even need a boat. The rocky inlets and pools along Waugoshance Point are a spawning area for smallmouth bass, and when the season opens in May, anglers don waders to stalk the beds along the north end of Sturgeon Bay. Drive to the end of the park road and from there it's a half mile walk to the first pools along the shoreline. Anglers rig up nightcrawlers or use small spinners such as Mepps or Panther Martins to entice the fish.

Children will find fishing opportunities for bluegill and other panfish in Goose Pond. The fish are stunted but plentiful, and the most popular spot to toss in bobbers and bait is off the bridge at the south end of the pond.

Hiking: Wilderness has 12 miles of designated foot trails, most of them resembling two-tracks roads that wander through the backside of the park. An excellent set of interpretive trails begins at a trailhead on Goose Pond. The Pondside Trail, a half-mile walk around the pond, begins here along with Red Pine Trail, a 1.25-mile walk east to Mt. Nebo Trail. At this point you can continue on the Hemlock Trail, a half-mile walk to the remains of an old lookout tower on Mt. Nebo where there is a partial view of the Straits after the leaves drop. Across from the day-use parking area is the posted trailhead for Big Stone Trail, which winds past some interesting beaver activity along the creek.

Season: The campgrounds are open from April to December and have electricity at all the sites at that time, but water and the restrooms are closed from November to May when vault toilets are installed and water is available from the headquarters. The off-season rate of $16 per night. During the summer both campgrounds are filled almost daily from July through mid-August, a time when it's best to arrive with reservations ☎ 800-447-2757 🌐 www.midnrreservations.com.

Lake Michigan

Hiawatha National Forest

Campground: Rustic
County: Mackinac
Nearest Community: St. Ignace
Sites: 35
Reservations: Yes
Fee: $16
Information: St. Ignace Ranger District
☎ (906) 643-7900
🌐 www.fs.usda.gov/hiawatha

Departing from I-75 at the Mackinac Bridge, US-2 heads west the length of the Upper Peninsula before entering Wisconsin and eventually ending at Everett, Washington. It's a beautiful drive, but the most scenic section of it might be right at the beginning when it skirts the northern end of Lake Michigan.

From Pointe Aux Chenes until you reach Little Brevort Lake, you enjoy an endless blue panorama of the Great Lake as US-2 is often within skipping stone distance of the water. Most of this shoreline lies in the Hiawatha National Forest, and in the middle of the 8-mile stretch is the Lake Michigan Campground. Talk about location. This is a beach lover's campground.

Two campers stroll the Lake Michigan beach from the Lake Michigan National Forest Campground, just a short drive from the Mackinac Bridge.

Directions: From the Mackinac Bridge head west on US-2. Within 11 miles, you cross Point Aux Chenes and from there the highway begins skirting the Lake Michigan shoreline. Lake Michigan Campground is reached in 7 miles.

Campground: Lake Michigan Campground is situated on a bluff above the lake with 35 rustic sites separated from each other by towering hardwoods and pines. Half the sites line the bluff above the lake, the other half are closer to US-2. The bad part about this campground is there is no view of Lake Michigan from any site—it's too heavily wooded—and you hear the traffic on US-2 when it's heavy. The good part is you're just footsteps from a beautiful beach. There are restrooms with flush toilets within the campground but not showers. Other amenities include tables, fire rings, and lantern posts.

Day-use Facilities: The campground has a picnic area with a separate parking lot for day visitors. Tables are on the edge of the bluff above the lake while a stairway leads down to a beach. The sunsets from this spot can be spectacular on a clear summer evening.

Hiking: There are no designated hiking trails at the campground, but you can follow the sandy Lake Michigan shoreline several miles in either direction.

Season: The campground is open from mid-May to mid-September. Being right on US-2 and the first facility passed heading west from the Mackinac Bridge, this campground is usually filled on the weekends during the summer and often in the middle of the week as well. If that's the case, keep in mind that nearby there is a large 70-site national forest campground on Brevoort Lake and a smaller state forest campground on Little Brevoort Lake. You can also reserve a site in advance though the National Recreation Reservation System ☎ 877-444-6777 🌐 www.recreation.gov.

91

Brevoort Lake

Hiawatha National Forest

Campground: Rustic
County: Mackinac
Nearest Community: Brevort
Sites: 70
Reservations: No
Fee: $16
Information: St. Ignace Ranger District
☎ (906) 643-7900
🌐 www.fs.usda.gov/hiawatha

Brevoort Lake is one of the most popular national forest campgrounds in the eastern half of the Upper Peninsula. It offers easy access to great fishing, interesting hiking, and the beautiful beaches along the northern shore of Lake Michigan. The sites are large, many are located on the lake, and there's even a sanitation station in the campground for recreational vehicles.

The drawback, of course, is that Brevoort Lake is so popular it's filled much of the summer. If there is an open site, grab it. If not, then luckily this is only one of many campgrounds along this stretch of Lake Michigan shoreline.

Directions: Brevoort Lake is located 20 miles west of St. Ignace and is posted along US-2, just past the Lake Michigan National Forest Campground. From US-2, turn north on Brevoort Camp Road and follow the signs into the campground.

Campground: Brevoort Lake is a large facility with 70 rustic sites located along the western end of the lake. The large sites are well separated from each other in a forested setting, and 39 of them overlook the lake to provide direct access to the water. Most of them are located along the small peninsula that divides Boedne Bay from the rest of Brevoort Lake. Facilities include fire rings, tables, lantern posts, and restrooms with flush toilets but not showers

Day-use Facilities: The eastern side of the campground peninsula features a sandy shoreline that is used as a beach and swimming area. Brevoort Lake is also only a five-minute drive from miles of golden beach and sand dunes along the Lake Michigan shoreline. It is a very common practice for people to park along US-2 to spend the day swimming or sunbathing. The sunsets here are spectacular on a clear evening.

Fishing: The campground features an improved boat launch on Boedne Bay with additional parking for trailers and cars. Brevoort is a relatively undeveloped lake that covers 4,233 acres. Its deepest spot is 30 feet, but most of the lake is in the 10- to 20-foot range. In thc mid-1980s, the U.S. Forest Service built a 2,100-foot-long walleye spawning reef near Black Point in the northeast corner of the lake. Since then walleye fishing has improved along with the lake's smallmouth bass fishery. Other species caught include perch, crappies, panfish, and northern pike. Located within the campground is a small store that sells bait and rents boats and canoes.

Hiking: Within the campground is the Ridge Trail, a half-mile interpretive loop that rises above Brevoort Lake. Ask the campground host for the accompanying guide to this nature trail. Crossing the entrance drive is the North Country Trail that heads north to cross the Carp River and east towards St. Ignace.

Season: The campground is open from mid-May to mid-September and filled almost daily in July and August. Brevoort Lake is a destination campground with families returning year after year, and the average stay is three to four days. You can reserve a site in advance though the National Recreation Reservation System ☎ 877-444-6777 🌐 www.recreation.gov.

92

Foley Creek

Hiawatha National Forest

Campground: Rustic
County: Mackinac
Nearest Community: St Ignace
Sites: 54
Reservations: Yes
Fee: $14
Information: St. Ignace Ranger District
☎ (906) 643-7900
🌐 www.fs.usda.gov/hiawatha

The closest campground to St. Ignace is Straits State Park, reached almost soon as you depart the Mackinac Bridge, but a nicer facility is just 3 miles north of the city: Foley Creek.

This national forest facility allows you to escape the summer crowds and the hustle and bustle that St. Ignace attracts as the gateway to the Upper Peninsula and especially Mackinac Island. At Foley Creek you're camping in the woods and are only a short hike away from a federally designated wilderness. Yet hop in your car and you're at Mystery Spot, Castle Rock, or any of the other tourist traps that have sprouted at the base of the Mackinac Bridge.

Directions: From I-75 depart at exit 348 and first east and then north on Old Mackinac Trail (H-63) to the entrance of the campground.

Campground: Foley Creek has 54 rustic sites that are well spread out on a single loop in a forest of large hardwoods. Only sites No. 2 and No. 4 are actually near Foley Creek. If you want to be near the trail to Horseshoe Bay select a site at the north end of the loop. Foley Creek has tables, fire rings, vault toilets, and four sites designated for handicapped campers. There is usually a camp host at the facility throughout the summer.

Hiking: The Horseshoe Bay Hiking Trail departs near site No. 42 and winds for 1.2 miles through to Horseshoe Bay on Lake Huron. This small, 3,790-acre federally designated wilderness was created in 1987 but has changed little since loggers passed through at the turn of the century.

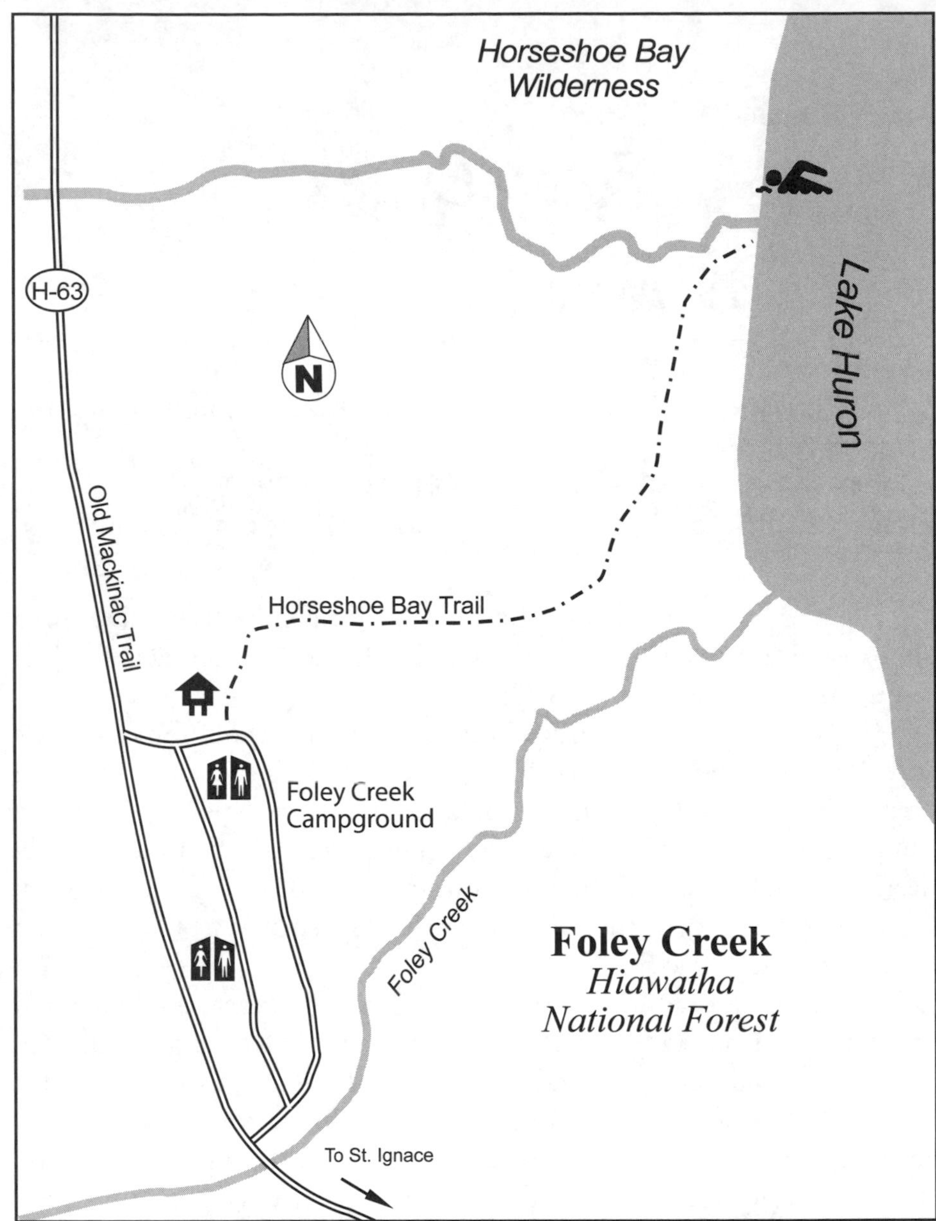

For the most part the tract is a series of low forested ridges separated by narrow, shallow swamps, whose dense cedar stands are especially attractive to deer.

The outstanding feature of this wilderness, however, is seven miles of undeveloped shoreline in Lake Huron's St. Martin Bay. The northern two-thirds of the shore includes Grosse Point and ranges from stretches of cobblestone to marsh. Horseshoe Bay itself is a beautiful beach, where the sand is smooth and the water is a tropical turquoise in color. Best of all, more times than not, there's nobody around.

Fishing: Seven miles north of Foley Creek is a public access site on the mouth of Carp River. The boat launch is reached via Old Mackinac Trail (H-63) and Forest Road 3127, and the river is fished for steelhead, salmon, brook trout, and brown trout depending the time of the year.

Season: Foley is open from early May to mid-October. Due to its close proximity to St. Ignace and Mackinac Island, Foley Creek is often full most weekends in July and August and often in the middle of the week as well. You can reserve a site in advance though the National Recreation Reservation System ☎ 877-444-6777 🌐 www.recreation.gov.

93

DeTour

Lake Superior State Forest

Campground: Rustic
County: Chippewa
Nearest Community: DeTour Village
Sites: 21
Reservations: No

Fee: $15
Information: Sault Ste Marie DNR office
☎ (906) 635-5281
🌐 www.fs.usda.gov/hiawatha

As small as it is, this rustic campground on St. Vital Point was at one time a state park. Today DeTour is part of the Lake Superior State Forest and is the only public campground along M-134, a beautiful road that skirts the northern end of Lake Huron.

Directions: DeTour is near the end of M-134, just five miles from the Village of DeTour or a 50-mile drive from the Mackinac Bridge.

Campground: DeTour has 21 sites that are well spread out on a single loop. Many of them are on St. Vital Bay or have a good view of the

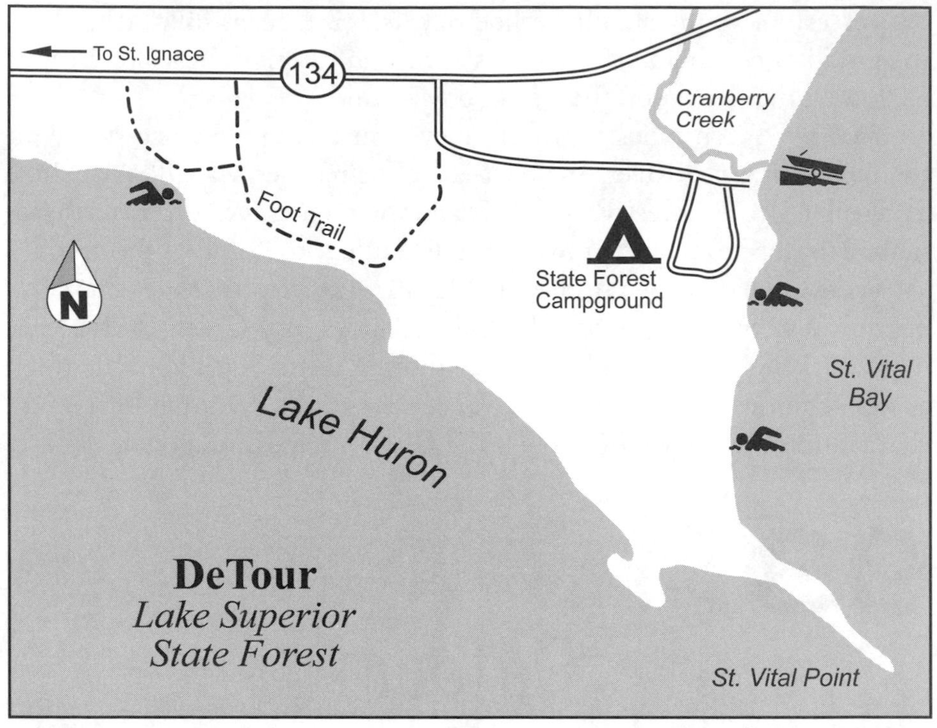

water, and three sites will accommodate 40-foot trailers or recreational vehicles. Facilities include hand pumps for water, tables, fire rings, and vault toilets.

Day-use Facilities: Past the Les Cheneaux Islands, M-134 skirts numerous Lake Huron beaches that are not as large as those along Lake Michigan and US-2 but not nearly as popular either. Here you can find a stretch of sand and surf you can call your own for an afternoon.

There are three beaches along St. Vital Point. One is at the end of the campground loop, and the largest is in the next cove to the south. Both these beaches face St. Vital Bay usually have calmer water. The third beach faces Lake Huron on the east side of the point.

Hiking: There is a half-mile foot trail that departs the campground road and swings back to M-134.

Fishing: DeTour also has a public access site where anglers can launch their boats for an afternoon of fishing in Lake Huron. The waters in the Les Cheneaux area are a popular destination for anglers to fish for perch.

Season: This is a lightly used facility that only fills up on an occasional weekend in the summer.

94

Monocle Lake

Hiawatha National Forest

Campground: Rustic
County: Chippewa
Nearest Community: Brimley
Sites: 39
Reservations: No
Fee: $13
Information: Sault Ste. Marie Ranger District
☎ (906) 635-5398
🌐 www.fs.usda.gov/hiawatha

Handicapped campers are still a rare sight at most public campgrounds but not at Monocle Lake, a Hiawatha National Forest facility that in 1994 became one of the first totally accessible rustic campgrounds in Michigan. Monocle Lake was built in the 1960s on the east shore of the 172-acre lake but had deteriorated to the point that in the early 1990s the U.S. Forest Service decided to renovate the entire facility. The Americans With Disabilities Act mandated that any improvement in the campground meet its guidelines, thus every site, every toilet, every pathway was made handicapped accessible.

Whether you're handicapped or not, this is a first class facility in a scenic area that can serve as a base while visiting many of the nearby sites, including Point Iroquois Lighthouse and Spectacle Lake Overlook.

Directions: Monocle Lake is 21 miles from Sault Ste. Marie. From Brimley head northwest on Lake Shore Drive, and in seven miles turn west on Forest Road 3699 to quickly reach the entrance of the campground.

Campground: Monocle Lake has 39 sites well spread out in a forest of northern hardwoods and white birch. None are directly on the water, but all are a short walk to the shoreline. There are 36 drive-in sites with a hard-packed surface and equipped with specially designed picnic tables, fire rings, and lantern posts that can be easily used by wheelchair-bound campers. The campground also includes three walk-in sites for tent campers, barrier-free flush bathrooms, and a pressurized water system that replaced hand pumps.

An angler casts off the fishing pier at Monocle Lake Campground.

Day-use Facilities: At the west end of the campground is a picnic area with a small swimming beach.

Fishing: The most impressive feature of the campground is a fishing pier that extends 20 yards out into a lake. At the end of the day the pier attracts not only anglers but also any camper who wants to watch the sun set behind the forested ridges that form the west shore.

With the exception of a few cottages at the north end, Monocle Lake is an undeveloped body of water that is spread over 172 acres and is 40- to 45-foot deep in places. The campground has a boat launch and anglers target smallmouth bass, perch, and bluegills. There is also a walleye fishery, the result of annual stocking, and a pair of man-made spawning reefs adjacent to the campground on the east shore.

Hiking: Departing from the day-use area is a nature trail that begins with a boardwalk across a beaver dam where at times it's possible to the see the resident engineer at work. From the pond the trail skirts Monocle Lake for a quarter mile and then begins climbing the high bluff on the west shore. Within 2 miles from the campground the trail reaches an overlook with benches that allows hikers to view St. Mary's River and the rugged hills on the Canadian side.

Season: Monocle Lake is open from mid-May to mid-October and features a campground host most of the summer. The campground is occasionally full on the weekends but usually has open sites from Sunday through Thursday.

Bay View

Hiawatha National Forest

Campground: Rustic
County: Chippewa
Nearest Community: Raco
Sites: 24
Reservations: Yes
Fee: $13
Information: Sault Ste. Marie Ranger District
☎ (906) 635-5398
🌐 www.fs.usda.gov/hiawatha

Bay View Campground is located on the shores of Lake Superior, only 6 miles north of M-28 at Raco and 24 miles from I-75. Its two dozen sites have the usual amenities found in most national forest campgrounds. What makes Bay View stand out is the fact that more than half of its sites face the Great Lake, where it's a short walk from your tent to one of the most beautiful beaches in the Upper Peninsula.

Okay, so maybe you can't swim except for those three days in August when the temperature actually breaks 90 degrees, but you can walk for miles in either direction and see where Michigan's most famous shipwreck, the Edmund Fitzgerald, still lies on the bottom of Lake Superior.

Directions: Depart I-75 at exit 386 (6 miles south of Sault Ste. Marie) and head west on M-28. Within 18 miles turn north on Ranger Road to Lake Shore Drive. Bay View Campground is two miles west on Lake Shore Drive.

Campground: Bay View Lake Campground has 24 rustic sites with 14 of them bordering Lake Superior. The facility is forested in white pine, oak, maple, and white birch, and the sites are well spread out. Each site is equipped with a picnic table, fire ring with a sliding grate, and lantern post.

Day-use Facilities: The campground borders a wide sandy beach, excellent for beachcombing. A mile east of the campground with a separate entrance and parking area is Big Pine Picnic Area with tables and grills. At either the campground or the picnic area, the sunsets are spectacular in the evening.

Interpretive Center: Six miles east of the campground on Lake Shore Drive is the Point Iroquois Lighthouse. Listed on the National Register of Historic Places, the lighthouse was built in 1870 and today contains a small museum dedicated to the lightkeepers who spent their lives saving ships. Even better is the sweeping view of Lake Superior from the top of the 65-foot tower. The lighthouse is open daily from Memorial Day through Labor Day.

Season: Bay View is open from mid-May to mid-October and is managed during the summer by a campground host. You can reserve a site in advance though the National Recreation Reservation System ☎ 877-444-6777 🌐 www.recreation.gov, but other than an occasional summer weekend, this campground is rarely filled.

Soldier Lake

Hiawatha National Forest

Campground: Rustic
County: Chippewa
Nearest Community: Strongs
Sites: 44
Reservations: No
Fee: $12
Information: Sault Ste. Marie Ranger District
☎ (906) 635-5398
🌐 www.fs.usda.gov/hiawatha

Soldier Lake Campground in the Hiawatha National Forest is just south of M-28 and only 23 miles west of I-75 in Chippewa County. Yet it retains a quiet, remote atmosphere, and in the middle of the week often less than a third of the 44 sites are occupied. Even on weekends you can usually count on getting a spot to pitch the tent.

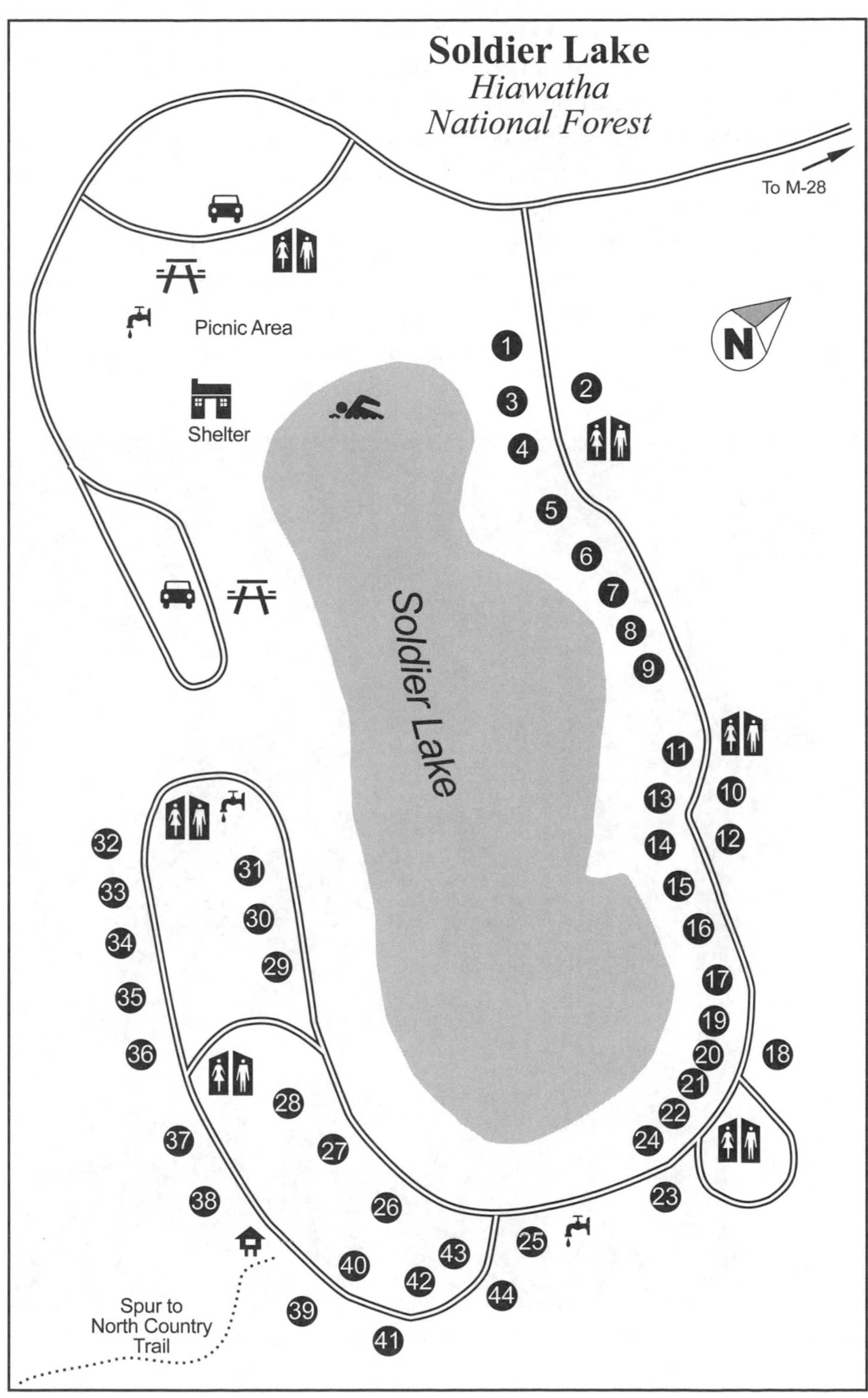
Soldier Lake
Hiawatha
National Forest
To M-28
Picnic Area
Shelter
Soldier Lake
N
1
2
3
4
5
6
7
8
9
10
11
12
13
14
15
16
17
18
19
20
21
22
23
24
25
26
27
28
29
30
31
32
33
34
35
36
37
38
39
40
41
42
43
44
Spur to
North Country
Trail

Directions: Six miles south of Sault Ste. Marie, depart I-75 at exit 386 and head west on M-28. The campground is posted along M-28, 4 miles before you pass through the village of Strongs.

Campground: The campground surrounds Soldier Lake, and 19 of the 44 sites line the lakeshore. All the sites are well spread out in a forest of jack pine, aspen, and maple.

Day-use Facilities: There are two large picnic areas at the northwest corner of the lake. The picnic areas are in an open grassy meadow and overlook an excellent beach and swimming area. Near the beach is a large log shelter with a stone fireplace built in the 1930s by the Civilian Conservation Corps.

A rustic campsite in a national forest campground in the Upper Peninsula.

Hiking: A short foot trail winds around the lake. For a longer hike, there is a trail that departs from site No. 38 as a two-track and within a quarter mile leads you to the North Country Trail.

Fishing: The 15-acre lake is non-motorized and fished for perch. There is no ramp in the campground, but boats can be easily hand launched from many sites and the picnic area.

Season: The campground is open from mid-May to mid-October. Usage is light and it is rarely filled.

97

Three Lakes

Hiawatha National Forest

Campground: Rustic
County: Chippewa
Nearest Community: Strongs Corner
Sites: 28
Reservations: No
Fee: $12
Information: Sault Ste. Marie Ranger District
☎ (906) 635-5398
🌐 www.fs.usda.gov/hiawatha

Nestled among three small lakes is Three Lakes Campground, a quiet and scenic spot to pitch a tent or park a trailer. The National Forest facility overlooks Walker Lake and is farther away from M-28 than Soldier Campground, making it not as busy and likely to have an open site even on the weekends. Two of the three lakes offer fishing opportunities while nearby bogs can be explored to view the abundance of insect-eating pitcher plants.

Directions: Three Lakes is 38 miles from Sault Ste. Marie. From Strongs Corner on M-28 head south on Strongs Road (Forest Road 3142) to the posted campground entrance.

Campground: Three Lakes is a single loop of 28 sites along the north shore of Walker Lake. Most of the sites are right off the lake but do not have a clear view of the water. The campground is situated in an impressive stand of white pines and mixed hardwoods, and the sites are well spread out and very secluded from each other. Facilities include tables, fire rings, vault toilets, and hand pumps.

Day-use Facilities: There is a picnic area on the east end of the lake that is separate from the campground. A trail connects the two areas.

Hiking: Walker Lake Trail, a 1.1-mile loop, winds around its namesake lake beginning in the picnic area and passing through the campground. The trail is easy and stays fairly close to the lake in the beginning. At one point you climb a ridge and descend to a view of the small, unnamed lake to the north.

Fishing: There are no boat ramps on the lakes but near the picnic area is a place to hand launch boats into Walker Lake. It is also easy to launch boats from many of the lakeside sites in the campground. A small pull-out on Strongs Road (FR 3142) allows you to do the same on Whitemarsh Lake. The lakes receive very light fishing pressure. Whitemarsh is reputed to be the best of the three with anglers targeting northern pike, bass, and crappie. Walker Lake is the largest at 19 acres and is fished for panfish and bass.

Season: The campground is open from late May to mid-October. Usage is light, even on most summer weekends.

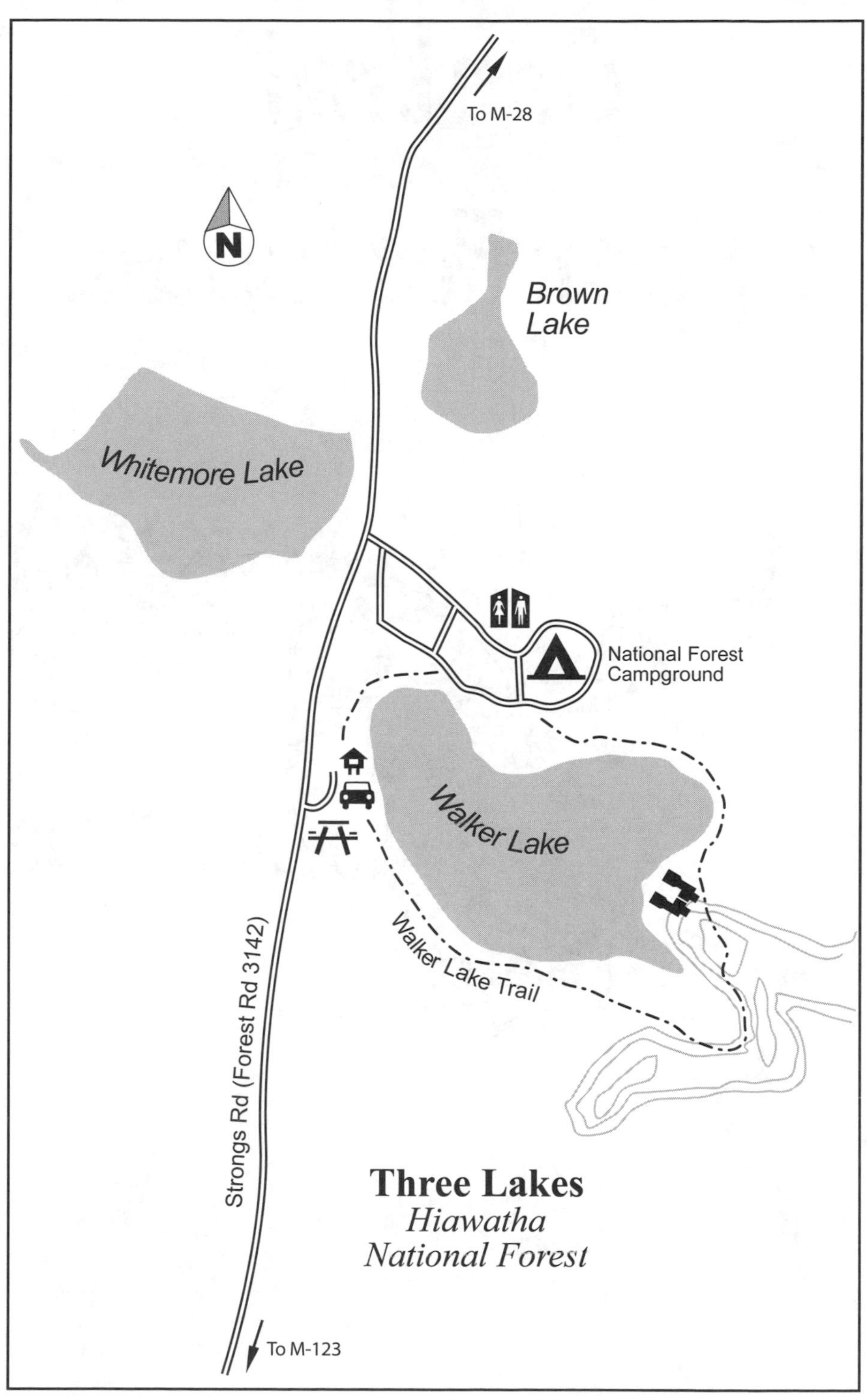
To M-28
N
Brown Lake
Whitemore Lake
National Forest Campground
Walker Lake
Walker Lake Trail
Strongs Rd (Forest Rd 3142)
Three Lakes
Hiawatha National Forest
To M-123

Central Upper Peninsula

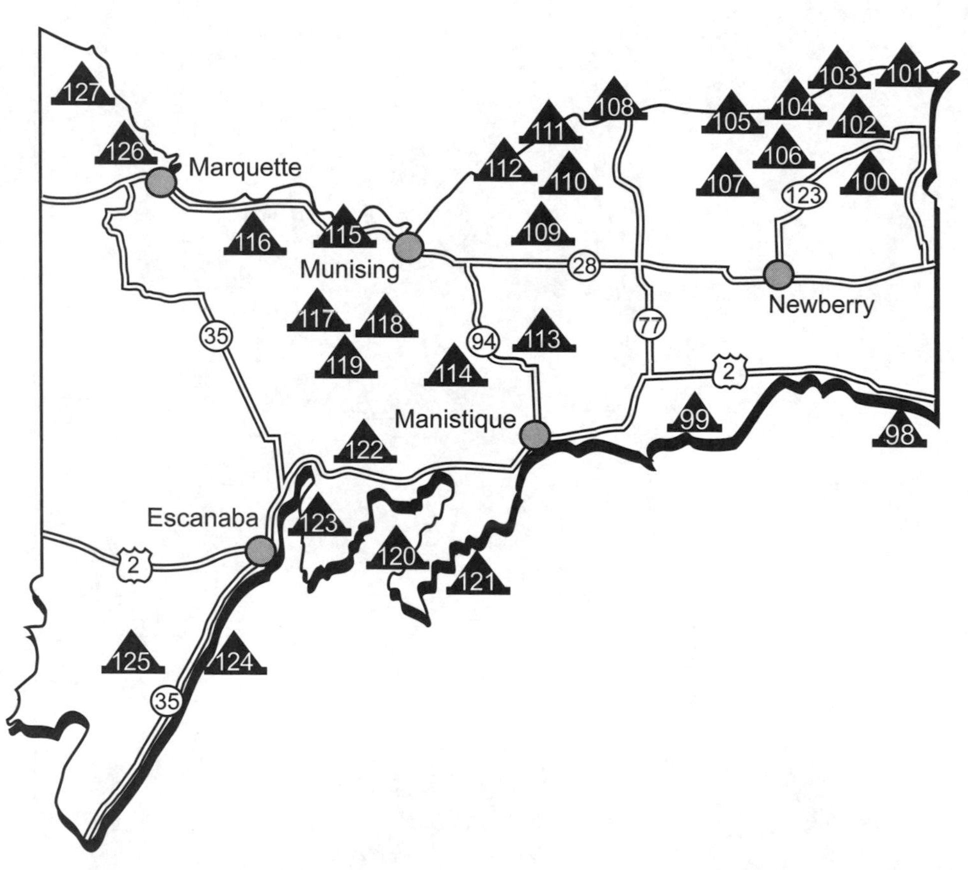

#	PARK	MODERN	SEMI-MODERN	RUSTIC	SITES	DAY-USE FACILITIES	FISHING	HIKING	BIRDING	INTERPRETIVE CENTER	BIKING	CANOEING/ KAYAKING	BOATING
98	Hog Island Point			•	50	•							
99	Big Knob			•	18	•		•					
100	Tahquamenon Falls	•	•		169	•	•	•					
101	Andrus Lake			•	25	•	•						
102	Bodi Lake			•	16		•	•					
103	Mouth of Two Hearted River			•	45	•		•				•	
104	Muskallonge Lake	•			159	•	•	•					
105	Lake Superior			•	18	•		•					
106	Perch Lake			•	35		•						
107	Bass Lake			•	18		•						
108	Woodland Park	•	•		110	•		•					
109	Cusino Lake			•	6	•	•						
110	Kingston Lake			•	16	•	•	•					
111	Hurricane River			•	12	•		•		•			
112	Twelvemile Beach			•	36	•		•					
113	Colwell Lake	•		•	35	•	•	•					
114	Little Bass Lake			•	12		•						
115	Bay Furnace			•	50	•		•					
116	Au Train Lake			•	37	•	•	•	•			•	
117	Council Lake			•	4	•	•	•				•	
118	Pete's Lake			•	41	•	•	•					
119	Widewaters			•	34		•	•					
120	Fayette		•		61	•	•	•		•			
121	Portage Bay			•	23	•		•					
122	Flowing Well			•	10	•	•					•	
123	Little Bay de Noc			•	38	•	•	•					
124	Fox Park			•	20	•							
125	Cedar River North			•	17		•	•					
126	Tourist Park	•	•		110	•	•	•			•		
127	Perkins	•	•		73	•	•						

98

Hog Island Point

Lake Superior State Forest

Campground: Rustic
County: Mackinac
Nearest Community: Naubinway
Sites: 50
Reservations: No
Fee: $15
Information: Sault Ste. Marie DNR office
☎ (906) 635-5281

Only a 30-minute drive west of the Mackinac Bridge, Hog Island Point is another in the series of Lake Michigan campgrounds along US-2. The state forest campground occupies a small peninsula 7 miles east of Naubinway, providing a scenic setting to spend a night or two.

The east side of the point is formed by a picturesque bay where rocky islets smooth out the surf rolling in from Lake Michigan. The west side is a stretch of shoreline that you can follow almost to Naubinway.

Directions: From the Mackinac Bridge head west to reach the posted entrance of the campgrounds in 35 miles.

Campground: There are 50 rustic sites in two loops on the point with most of them along the shoreline. The sites are well spread out in a moderately heavy forest for a bit of privacy, and 17 of them have an open view of Lake Michigan. Facilities include vault toilets, hand pumps for water, tables, and a handful of handicap-friendly sites.

Day-use Facilities: A small picnic area with a separate parking lot is on the east side of the point, where the best beach is located. Here the shoreline is sandy, and a rocky islet in the mouth of the bay protects it from the Lake Michigan surf. The water is shallow but swimmers need to be aware of the undertow. The shoreline on the west side is not nearly as sandy.

Season: Being right on US-2, this campground is often filled on the weekends and can be more than half filled during the week. If that is the case, try Big Knob State Forest Campground, which is more secluded from US-2 and thus more likely to have an open site. There is also Black River State Forest Campground, which is 7 miles northeast of Naubinway via US-2 and Black River Road, a relatively short drive. Overlooking the Black River, this campground has only 12 sites but is not filled nearly as often as Hog Island Point.

Big Knob

Lake Superior State Forest

Campground: Rustic	**Reservations:** No
County: Mackinac	**Fee:** $15
Nearest Community: Naubinway	**Information:** Sault Ste. Marie DNR office
Sites: 18	☎ (906) 635-5281

If for some reason Hog Island Point is full, continue west on US-2 for another 9 miles and then head south at the sign for Big Knob State Forest Campground. This dirt road winds and weaves its way through the woods until finally ending at one of the most remote beaches on Lake Michigan.

The campground is located in a mature pine forest just off a beautiful stretch of Lake Michigan. You can stroll the beach for more than a mile in either direction and not encounter a single hot dog stand or cottage. With three interesting trails nearby, this is a campground where you can stay put for a few days.

Directions: From the Mackinac Bridge head west on US-2 for 44 miles and then turn south on Big Knob Road and follow it for 6 miles to the campground at the end. Big Knob is posted along US-2, but it's easy to miss the sign.

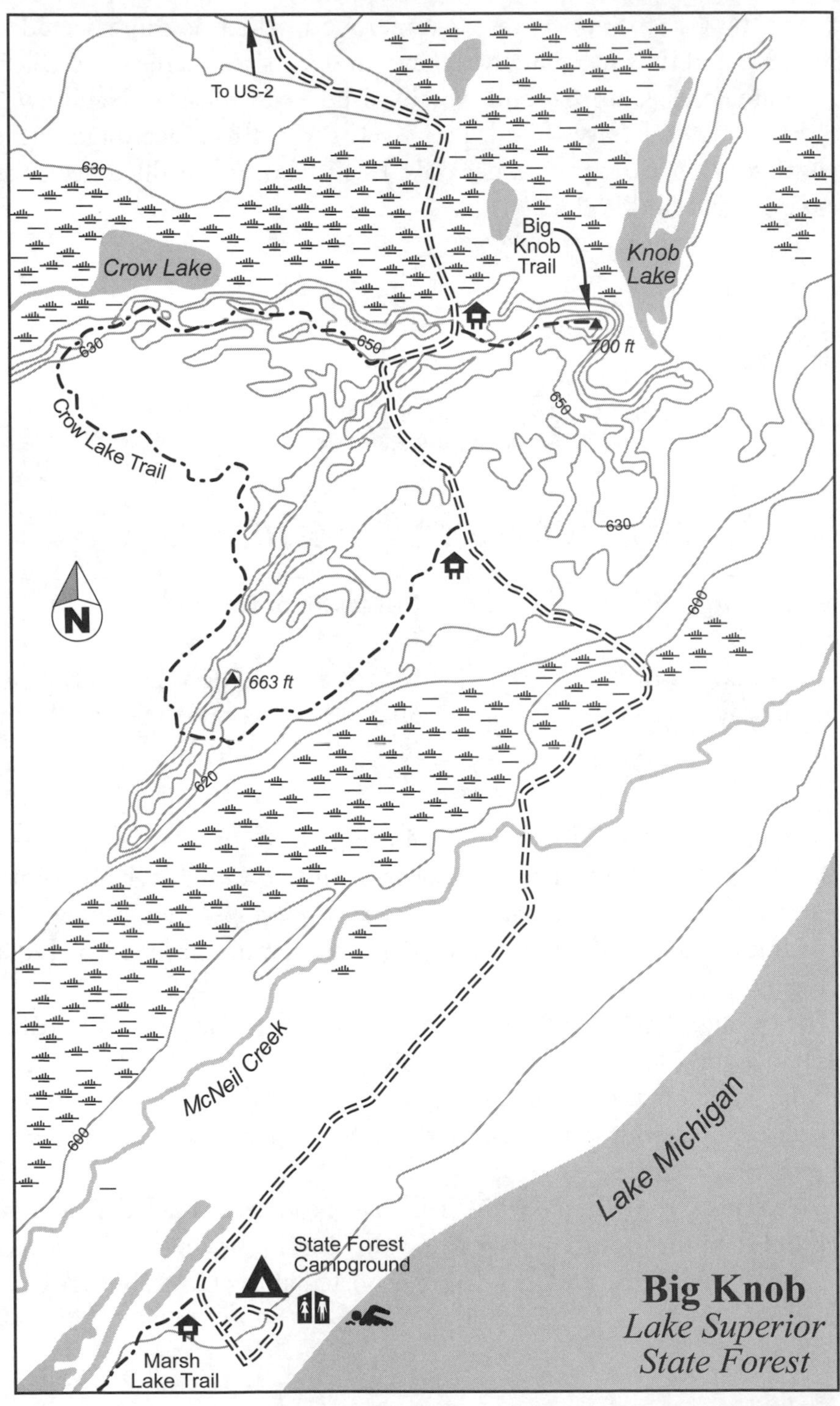
To US-2
630
Crow Lake
Big Knob Trail
Knob Lake
650
630
700 ft
650
Crow Lake Trail
630
600
N
663 ft
620
McNeil Creek
600
Lake Michigan
State Forest Campground
Marsh Lake Trail
Big Knob
Lake Superior State Forest

Campground: Big Knob is a single loop of 18 rustic sites that are well spread out in an older pine forest. Seven of the sites face Lake Michigan and have short paths leading through the trees right to the beach. Facilities include tables, fire rings, and vault toilets.

Day-use Facilities: The beach at Big Knob is stunning. It extends as far as the eye can see and is completely undeveloped. You can beachcomb for miles here, and the shallow water offshore makes for ideal swimming conditions. The campground has a small picnic area with a separate parking lot and a few tables.

A mother and her son enjoy a morning walk on the Lake Michigan shoreline at Big Knob State Forest Campground. Great beaches are a special feature of several campgrounds in this region of the state including Hog Island Point State Forest Campground and Fox Park.

Hiking: Near the campground are three short trails. Departing from the day-use parking area is the Marsh Lake Trail, a 1.5-mile loop that begins in the forest but within a half mile begins to skirt several bogs and marshes. Eventually you come to a viewing area of Marsh Lake, a great place to spot wildlife in the early evenings.

The other two trails have trailheads across from each other on Big Knob Road 2.5 miles from the campground. On the west side of the road is Crow Lake Pathway, a 2.5-mile hike that swings past views of Crow Lake. On the east side is Big Knob Trail, a delightful quarter-mile walk to an overview of Knob Lake. All three trails pass through extensive blueberry patches.

Season: Because of its distance from US-2, Big Knob is not filled as often during the summer as other campgrounds right on the highway. You can usually count on getting a site on the weekends and almost always in the middle of the week.

100 Tahquamenon Falls State Park

Campground: Modern and semi-modern
County: Chippewa
Nearest Community: Paradise
Sites: 169
Reservations: Yes
Fee: $16–$23 plus vehicle entry fee
Information: State park office
☎ (906) 492-3415

The Upper Falls at Tahquamenon Falls State Park is the most impressive cascade in the Upper Peninsula and very possibly the most beloved natural attraction in the state. The falls, nearly 200 feet across with a 50-foot drop, are often cited as the third largest east of the Mississippi River as only Niagara Falls in New York and Cumberland Falls in Kentucky have longer drops. So spectacular are the falls and the wooded setting, especially during autumn colors, that it easily makes this unit the most popular park in the Upper Peninsula with more than 500,000 visitors annually.

The park contains 46,179 acres and stretches 13 miles from Whitefish Bay in Chippewa County into Luce County. There are three developed areas, and two of them contain four campgrounds with a total of 319 sites. The most popular campground in the park is Riverbend Campground near the Lower Falls. There are no camping facilities anywhere near the Upper Falls. The other developed area with camping is the Rivermouth Unit on Whitefish Bay

Directions: The Rivermouth Unit is 4 miles south of Paradise on M-123, while the Lower Falls Unit is 12 miles from the small town where the state highway swings to the west. The Upper Falls unit is 21 miles from Newberry on M-123 or 2 miles west of the Lower Falls

Visitors stand at the observation deck above the Upper Falls at Tahquamenon Falls State Park, the most impressive cascade in Michigan and the third largest east of the Mississippi River.

Campground: The park has four separate campgrounds with two in each of its Lower Falls and Rivermouth units. At the Lower Falls there are 169 modern sites with 81 of them in the Riverbend Campground, including eight along the river itself. The rest are located in the Overlook Campground, and both areas are well wooded. Scattered throughout both campgrounds are 15 pull-through sites and 24 sites with 50 amp service. In Riverbend there are also eight handicap-accessible sites.

At the Rivermouth Unit there is a modern campground of 72 sites that includes 18 with 50 amp service and 59 pull-trough sites. The Rivermouth Pines Campground is a rustic facility with 36 sites and vault toilets but only a short walk away from the restrooms and showers in the modern campground.

Modern sites at Tahquamenon Falls are $21 to $23 per night; rustic sites at the Rivermouth Campground are $12 to $16 per night. Tahquamenon Falls is one of ten state parks open year-round, and during the off-season sites feature electric hook-ups and vault toilets and are $16 per night.

Day-use Facilities: The Upper Falls is a day-use area, and from its huge parking lot there is a paved path that winds a quarter mile through a stately beech-maple forest to an impressive overview of the cascades. In contrast, the Lower Falls lack the overwhelming power of those upstream, but they possess a charm of their own. The Lower Falls are actually a series of seven cascades on both sides of a 25-acre island with a total drop of 30 feet. Access to the falls from the parking area is via a barrier-free, half-mile path. The best way to view the Lower Falls, however, is to rent a rowboat or canoe from a park concessionaire to cross the river to the island. Skirting the island is a mile-long foot trail that provides a close view of the falls or even an opportunity to cool off by stepping into the smaller ones.

Other facilities at the Lower Falls include a picnic area along the banks of the Tahquamenon and a concessionaire that rents rowboats and canoes daily during the summer.

Hiking: The park has 40 miles of hiking trails including several interconnecting loops in the Tahquamenon Natural Area north of M-123 that provide an escape from the crowds around the falls. Among those on the north side is the Giant Pines Loop, a 3.7-mile hike that begins and ends at the Upper Falls parking area and includes a stand of giant hemlocks.

The most interesting hike south of M-123 and the most popular one in the park is the Tahquemenon River Trail, a one-way hike of 4 miles from the Upper Falls to the Lower Falls. This moderately difficult trail skirts the river most of the way, allowing hikers to pass through old growth forests of beech, maple, and hemlock or view stretches of rapids. Beginning at the east loop of the Overlook Campground is the Overlook Nature Trail, a two-mile walk with interpretive displays that skirts a 90-foot ridge to the Lower Falls and then loops back a long a small tributary of the Tahquamenon River. The North Country Trail also passes through the park.

Fishing: The best fishing in the park is found in the Tahquamenon River. Anglers in canoes or waders cast below the Lower Falls for northern pike, muskies, and walleye that measure up to 28 inches in length. Walleyes and brown trout are caught in the river between the two falls, while farther up, above the Upper Falls, there are good populations of perch. There is also a run of steelhead in the Tahquamenon up to the

Lower Falls after ice-out in spring and late October. Most anglers fish for the trout either from boats in the lower portions of the river or by surf casting spoons and spawn near the mouth in Whitefish Bay. The park maintains a boat access site at the Rivermouth Unit, while canoes can be launched in the Lower Falls Unit.

Season: Because the park is a vacation destination, the modern sites are occasionally filled Monday through Wednesday from July through mid-August but available on the weekends. Often there are open rustic sites throughout the summer in the Rivermouth section of the park. To reserve a campsite contact Michigan State Park Central Reservations ☎ 800-447-2757 🌐 www.midnrreservations.com.

A visitor admires the Upper Falls at Tahquamenon Falls State Park.

LOOKING FOR CRISP POINT LIGHTHOUSE

The first time we visited Crisp Point Lighthouse our drive turned into an unexpected hike. We were trying to reach the remote Lake Superior light from Paradise when the rutted two-track we were bumping along at 10 mph became a quagmire of loose sand and large rocks.

Crisp Point Lighthouse along Lake Superior

The washout forced us to abandoned the vehicle, lace up the hiking boots and grab the county map. Two miles later we emerged at the Great Lake and there, a half mile down the beach, was the light.

The 58-foot-tall, rounded brick tower was picturesque, the setting was stunning. Like a beacon in the wilderness, the light was the only structure along a sweeping shoreline where we were the only souls.

The washout, we decided, was necessary. The best way to appreciate the desolation and loneliness that most lighthouse keepers faced at the turn of the century is to reach one of the historical structures today on foot.

Today Crisp Point Lighthouse is much easier to reach along a route that is much better marked, but the lighthouse is still Michigan's most remote lighthouse. From M-123, 5 miles west of the Upper Falls of Tahquamenon Falls State Park, head north on County Road 500 for 8 miles after it passes Little Lake and continue east on County Road 412 for 6 miles following signs to the lighthouse.

Keep in mind that these are mostly dirt roads beyond M-123 that curve and wind through the woods with few posted road signs. Keep alert! Once at the lighthouse you'll find a boardwalk around the structure and interpretive displays erected by the Crisp Point Light Historical Society that was formed to try and save it.

For a map to the lighthouse contact the Newberry Area Tourism Association ☎ 906-293-5562 🌐 www.newberrytourism.com or the Crisp Point Light Historical Society 🌐 www.crisppointlighthouse.org.

101

Andrus Lake

Lake Superior State Forest

Campground: Rustic
County: Chippewa
Nearest Community: Paradise
Sites: 25
Reservations: No
Fee: $15
Information: Newberry DNR office
☎ (906) 293-3293

North of the town of Paradise in an isolated section of the Upper Peninsula, seemingly on the edge of the world, is Andrus Lake State Forest Campground. This rustic campground is a pleasant place spend a night or two thanks to shoreline campsites, a good swimming beach, and fishing opportunities.

It also has an ideal location, especially if you can't get a site at Tahquamenon Falls State Park. The famous cascades are only a 20-minute drive away while a short drive to the north is the very intriguing Great Lakes Shipwreck Museum ☎ 906-635-1742; 🌐 www.shipwreckmuseum.com. For a very unusual outing, spend an afternoon driving out to Crisp Point Lighthouse on the shores of Lake Superior.

Directions: From Paradise head north on Whitefish Point Road for 5 miles and then turn left on Vermillion road. Within a quarter mile Vermillion Road passes the campground entrance.

Campground: Andrus Lake has 25 sites on two loops. The sites are well spread out in a stand of red pine, and 10 of them are right along the shoreline of the scenic lake. The campground has tables, fire rings, vault toilets, hand pumps for water, and handicap-accessible sites. The only drawback is the vast clear cut just north of the campground.

Day-use Facilities: The campground also has a picnic area that leads to a sandy beach and a nice swimming area on the lake. The swimming is excellent in the clear-water of this spring fed lake.

Fishing: Andrus is a 33-acre lake with an undeveloped shoreline. It reaches depths of up to 30 feet almost due west of the campground and is fished for bass, northern pike, and bluegill. The campground has an unimproved boat launch and a fishing pier. Shore anglers can also follow trails to fish much of the east shoreline.

Season: Like many state forest campgrounds in this region of the Upper Peninsula, this is a lightly used facility.

102

Bodi Lake

Lake Superior State Forest

Campground: Rustic
County: Luce
Nearest Community: Newberry
Sites: 16
Reservations: No
Fee: $15
Information: Newberry DNR office
☎ (906) 293-3293

There aren't many places to park a trailer farther north in Michigan than the area many refer to as Superior Country. Nor is there any place in the state with a greater concentration of campsites than in the northern half of Luce County.

Lake Superior State Forest stretches from Munising to the east tip of Drummond Island to comprise 1,026,058 acres, by far the largest of any of the six state forests. Clustered around the Two-Hearted River, along the Lake Superior shoreline and on many of the hundreds of inland lakes north of Newberry, are almost half of its 43 rustic campgrounds. All of them are traditional camping spots, frequented by families and fishermen almost as soon as the first Model Ts began to appear in the U.P. in the 1920s. Today in Superior County you have a camper's paradise: great scenery, lots of water to fish, and always an open site.

One of the many campgrounds on inland lakes is Bodi Lake. This state forest facility combines scenic sites on the water, good fishing opportunities, and even a short pathway into the surrounding the woods.

Directions: From Newberry head northeast on M-123 and in 17 miles turn north on County Road 500. Follow the dirt road for 13 miles and after the entrance of Culhane Lake State Forest Campground head east on County Road 437. The posted entrance to Bodi Lake is reached in 1.5 miles on CR-437. The nearest food, supplies, and gas is at Pike Lake, seven miles away on County Road 414.

Campground: Bodi Lake has 16 sites on a single loop with 10 of them overlooking the lake. All the sites are well spread out in a forest of hardwoods and large red pines for a very scenic setting. Facilities include vault toilet and tables.

Fishing: Bodi Lake can be a productive fishery for anglers. The 200-acre lake reaches depths of 40 feet in several spots and is targeted mostly for walleyes, perch, and northern pike. Next to the campground is an improved boat launch. The nearest bait shop is at Pike Lake.

Hiking: Within the campground is the trailhead for the Bodi Lake Pathway, a 1.25-mile long trail into the pine and hardwood uplands that surround the lake.

Season: This is a lightly used facility.

103
Mouth of Two Hearted River

Lake Superior State Forest

Campground: Rustic
County: Luce
Nearest Community: Newberry
Sites: 45
Reservations: No
Fee: $10
Information: Newberry DNR office
☎ (906) 293-3293

The Mouth of Two Hearted River is the third largest campground in Lake Superior State Forest, the most remote, and, in my mind, the most scenic. It's hard to imagine a campground with a more scenic location than this rustic facility located at the end of the river that Ernest Hemingway immortalized.

An impressive swingbridge crosses the Two-Hearted River and provides access to the Lake Superior shoreline at the Mouth of the Two Hearted River State Forest Campground.

The campground is perched on the spot where the Two-Hearted River empties into the Great Lake. From the first loop, a large swing bridge crosses the river to the low dunes along Lake Superior which give way to the shoreline itself. This is a rare stretch of undeveloped Great Lake shoreline where to the west you can beachcomb for miles while the sunsets are spectacular anywhere along the dunes.

Directions: Driving to this campground is an adventure. The facility is 35 miles northeast of Newberry and is best reached from M-123 where it is posted at County Road 500. Head north and then follow the signs to the Rainbow Lodge. From CR-500 you turn northwest on CR-414, continue on CR-412 and finally CR-423 which ends at Rainbow Lodge, a small store and gas station at the entrance to the campground.

Campground: There are two loops at the Mouth of the Two-Hearted River with 25 sites on the first one. These sites are in an area of birch, aspen, and other woods with a few of them along the river. The second loop has 20 sites including four walk-in sites a short stairway above the campground. Most of this loop is situated in a stand of red pine with moderate undergrowth. Sites at the second loop are more spread out and thus a little more private than the first loop.

Rainbow Lodge ☎ 906-658-3357 just outside the campground has a café and motel rooms and sells gas, limited groceries, bait, and camping supplies.

Day-use Facilities: From the first loop you can cross an impressive swing bridge to Lake Superior and hike the shoreline for miles. The scenery here is spectacular as you can stand on the low dunes and gaze at a watery horizon. Also located on this sandy spit is a state historical marker detailing the lifesaving station that was here in 1876. The stone foundations of the lighthouse can still be seen. Even more interesting to many campers are the pebbles at the waterline. The shoreline attracts agate hunters and others interested in taking home a Lake Superior gem.

Hiking: The North Country Trail passes right through the campground and is posted in the second loop near site No. 19. Also in the second loop is a trail that winds 50 yards uphill to a bench and a scenic overlook.

Canoeing: The Big Two Hearted River is designated wilderness upstream from the weir, and motors are not allowed. A parking area with a cement boat launch is provided near the first loop for entry into the river. Rainbow Lodge rents canoes and will provide drop-off and pick-up service along the river.

Season: Despite its remote location, or maybe because of it, the campground is often half to three-quarters filled from July through mid-August. Not finding any open sites on a weekend, however, would be rare.

104

Muskallonge Lake

State Park

Campground: Modern	**Fee:** $16-$18 plus vehicle entry fee
County: Luce	
Nearest Community: Newberry	**Information:** State park office
Sites: 159	☎ (906) 658-3338
Reservations: Yes	

The narrow, quarter-mile wide strip of land between Lake Superior and Muskallonge Lake was the site of the original village of Deer Park, a lumbering town in the 1800s that included a hotel, store, doctor's office, and, of course, the sawmill. Other than a few of the original dock pilings on Lake Superior, it's hard to imagine Muskallonge Lake State Park as a bustling lumbering town.

Located in northern Luce County, the 217-acre park is split by County Road H-37 (also labeled County Road 497). To the south you can set up at a lakeshore camp, go fishing, or take a dip in the warm waters of Muskallonge Lake. Cross the gravel road and you can descend the shoreline bluffs to a sandy and pebbled beach along Lake Superior where rockhounds search for colorful agates. The two lakes combine to give the park an exceptionally moderate climate year-round, rarely hot in the summer, not as cold as the rest of the Upper Peninsula during the winter.

Directions: Muskallonge Lake is 28 miles from Newberry and 18 miles east of Grand Marais. From Newberry head north on M-123 for four miles then turn west on H-37 and follow it 14 miles to the park entrance.

Campground: The park has 159 modern sites on seven loops along the shores of Muskallonge Lake. The area is well shaded and a number of sites overlook the lake, while others are near a small beach for the campers. Site No. 155 is a gem, secluded in a heavy-forested corner of the loop with a picnic table overlooking the water. Facilities include modern restrooms with showers, a sanitation station for RVers, and horseshoe courts. In the evening a concessionaire sells firewood in the campground.

Day-use Facilities: The park has a day-use area on a small bay of Muskallonge Lake east of the campground. The lake is shallow enough so that the water warms up quickly during summer for swimmers. There is parking for 20 vehicles and an adjacent picnic area.

Located right off County Road H-37 is a parking and picnic area for Lake Superior. From here visitors can descend a wooden staircase to reach the beautiful lakeshore and views of the Great Lake. The lake is generally too cold to swim but is a popular destination for agate hunters. The best time to search is after a storm or a heavy north wind, which will push a layer of new rocks onto the beach. The most sought-after rock is the Lake Superior agate and can be seen in both its rough and polished state at the two stores located near the park.

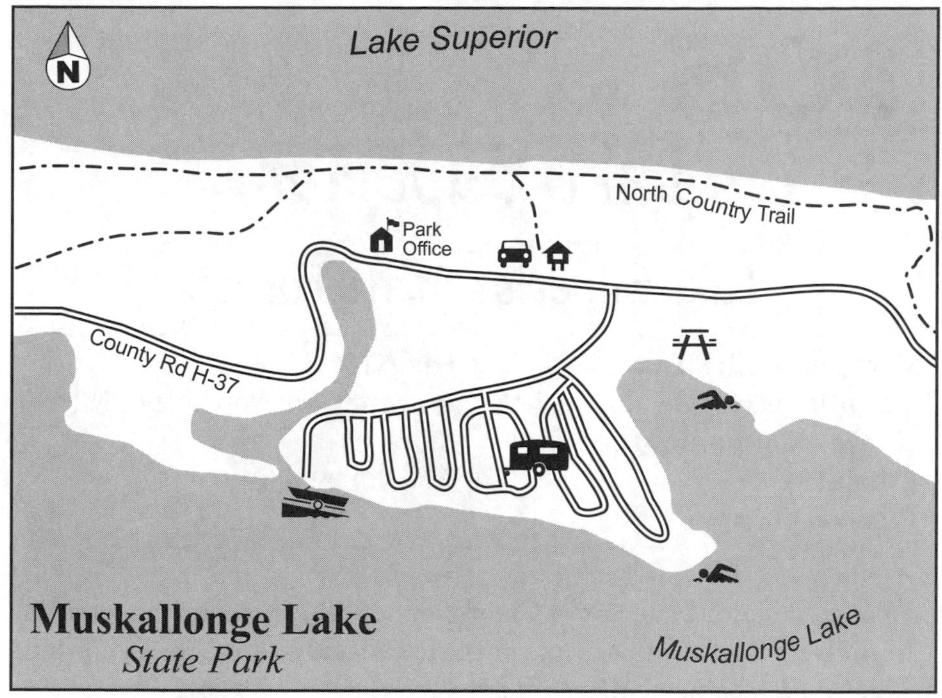

Hiking: Following the Lake Superior shoreline within the state park is the North Country Trail. To the west the national trail leads 5 miles to Lake Superior State Forest Campground and eventually to Lakeshore Trail in Pictured Rocks National Lakeshore. To the east the NCT reaches the Mouth of Two Hearted River State Forest Campground in 10 miles. A spur turns a portion of the North Country Trail into a 1.5-mile loop beginning at the Lake Superior parking area and then continuing to the west end of the state park.

Fishing: The 780-acre Muskallonge Lake is known best by anglers for northern pike, perch, and smallmouth bass. The lake has also been stocked with walleye. An improved boat launch with a cement ramp and a dock is located at the west end of the campground. There are no launching facilities on Lake Superior. Three resorts, located just outside the park, rent boats and motors and allow campers to tie them up at the park.

Season: Most of the summer a site is easily obtained, but from July Fourth to mid-August, the facility is vulnerable to filling up on weekends. To reserve a campsite contact Michigan State Park Central Reservations ☎ 800-447-2757 🌐 www.midnrreservations.com.

105

Lake Superior

Lake Superior State Forest

Campground: Rustic
County: Luce
Nearest Community: Newberry
Sites: 18
Reservations: No
Fee: $15
Information: Newberry DNR office
☎ (906) 293-3293

Lake Superior State Forest Campground is another remote and scenic gem in Luce County. This is one of the few places in the Upper Peninsula where you can camp along the Lake Superior shoreline.

When the Great Lake is kicking up, the surf here is an awesome sight with the rollers crashing onto the beach and the roar of the waves filling the air. On such evenings, the power of Lake Superior stays with you long after you have fallen asleep at your campsite.

Directions: The campground is on County Road H-58, west of Muskallonge Lake State Park or 15 miles east of Grand Marais.

Campground: Lake Superior is a single loop of 18 sites that lies between CR-H58 and Lake Superior. All but one site is located just inside the treeline on a low bluff overlooking the Great Lake, and many have a partial view of the water. Sites are well spread out in the predominately hardwood-birch forest, and the moderate undergrowth provides a bit of seclusion from your neighbors. Facilities include tables, fire rings, vault toilets, and a hand pump for water.

Day-use Facilities: From the campground, a low sandy bluff with patches of dune grass descends to a pebbled shoreline that is well known for its agates. Usually there is a rockhound at the campground who will be searching the beach for the colorful and waxy stones. A few times in August after a high-pressure system settles in, temperatures soar above 80 degrees and hardy swimmers take a dip in the lake, but most of the time Lake Superior is too cold for most people to handle.

Hiking: Passing through the campground is a portion of the North Country Trail. To the east the NCT winds along the edge of the trees in the campground and is marked by faded blue blazes. After it passes the vault toilets at the east end, it dips down to the open beach and follows it for quarter mile until you arrive at a large trailside map for Blind Sucker. To the west the NCT skirts the edge of the shoreline bluff for some nice views as it rises steadily above the beach below.

Blind Sucker Pathway is a 6-mile loop that passes the large impoundment to the south before circling back. Within 0.7 miles of the campground you arrive at the stream and in another half mile you arrive at Blind Sucker No. 1 State Forest Campground. Here a path goes over the dam to Blind Sucker No. 2 Campground while another trail, clearly marked with a trailside map, heads west back to Lake Superior. This is great blueberry country, especially where Blind Sucker Pathway passes through open areas that have been logged.

Season: Lake Superior is very popular, and despite its remote location will often fill up on the weekends and mid-week as well. This campground tends to be a destination spot and sometimes you may have to wait a day or two get in. Nearest state forest campground is Blind Sucker No. 2 Unit.

106

Perch Lake

Lake Superior State Forest

Campground: Rustic
County: Luce
Nearest Community: Newberry
Sites: 35
Reservations: No
Fee: $15
Information: Newberry DNR office
☎ (906) 293-3293

Perch Lake Campground is 20 minutes north of Newberry and right off paved County Road H-37, making it considerably easier to reach than many of the state forest facilities to the east and west. Yet on the Sunday

I was there setting up a tent, only three other sites were occupied. The state forest campground provides access to good fishing opportunities while its location makes it ideal as a base camp to explore this unique region of the Upper Peninsula.

A campsite at the rustic Perch Lake State Forest Campground.

Directions: Perch Lake is 25 miles north of Newberry via M-123 and CR-H-57. The entrance is at the corner of CR-H37 and County Road 410.

Campground: Perch Lake has two loops of 35 sites with most of them situated in a stand of red pines. There is little to no undergrowth here but the sites are well spread out for some privacy. More than a dozen sites are situated along the edge of a bluff overlooking the lake. They make for an especially nice spot to pitch a tent as you can sit at your table and view the entire lake. Facilities include tables, fire rings, vault toilets, and hand pumps for water.

Fishing: An improved boat launch with a cement ramp is located just outside the campground. Parking for a dozen cars and rigs is provided, indicating the popularity of the lake among anglers. Fishing pressure is moderate on the large and mostly undeveloped lake that is known more for bass than it is perch.

Season: Perch Lake receives moderate use.

107

Bass Lake

Lake Superior State Forest

Campground: Rustic
County: Luce
Nearest Community: Newberry
Sites: 18
Reservations: No
Fee: $15
Information: Newberry DNR office
☎ (906) 293-3293

Bass Lake is for those who like the drive to a campground to be as adventurous as the camping. A miles-from-civilization feeling is the reward when you finally arrive with mud on the head lights, bugs on windshield, and branches clinging to the roof.

The Superior State Forest facility is 15 miles northwest of Newberry in the remote heart of Luce County and reached via County Road 455. The dirt road plunges into a thick hardwood forest and for 7 miles there are usually more deer along the side of road than signs indicating where you could possibly be. If you don't get lost, you'll end up at a scenic and very isolated campground where you never have to worry about getting a site.

Directions: From Newberry head north on M-123 but veer off on CR H37 within 4 miles. In another 4 miles head west onto CR 455. The campground is reached in 7 miles.

Campground: The 18-site campground is a typical state forest facility, small and rustic with lots of space between you and your neighbors. Half of the sites are in a grassy clearing that in the early 1900s was the site of a logging camp. The rest of them are scattered in that thick hardwood forest. None of the sites are directly on Bass Lake.

Fishing: On the other side of CR 455 from the campground is an improved boat launch with a small parking area. Bass Lake is a good sized body of water, 143 acres on the surface and reaching a depth of 74 feet at one point. Its shoreline is totally uncluttered with cottages and littered with downed trees and half-submerged deadheads, making it a perfect habitat for smallmouth bass. The lake also supports a trout fishery.

Season: Bass Lake is a lightly used state forest facility. Being so remote, it's hard to imagine this campground ever filling up.

108

Woodland Park

Grand Marais Township

Campground: Modern and semi-modern
County: Alger
Nearest Community: Grand Marais
Sites: 110
Reservations: No
Fee: $18–$25
Information: Park office
☎ (906) 494-2613
🌐 www.grandmaraismichigan.com/WoodlandPark

Located at the eastern end of Pictured Rocks National Lakeshore is Grand Marais, a sleepy little town with one of the most scenic ports along Lake Superior, a well-protected harbor with a sandy beach, a lighthouse, and usually a sailboat or two anchored in the middle.

Just three blocks from the harbor and downtown area is Woodland Park. The park dates back to 1902 when the land was donated to the town by a group of lumbermen and today is a municipally-operated campground that puts you within easy walking distance of the Grand Marais' museums and restaurants. Here you can park the trailer and stroll over to the Lake Superior Brewing Company for a cold beer or a whitefish sandwich.

Directions: From Seney on M-28, head north on M-77 for 25 miles. The state highway leads you right into the heart of Grand Marais. From the downtown area head west on Brazel Street to reach the campground.

Campground: Woodland Park is a pleasant, modern campground with a 110 sites on a semi-open bluff overlooking the blue horizon of Lake Superior. There are 38 sites that near the edge of the bluff with a partial view of the lake and a higher nightly rate. The park began

SABLE FALLS: A WALK IN THE DUNES

Within minutes of lacing up our boots, we arrived at a fork in the trail and were faced with our first decision of the hike, dunes or waterfalls? To the right, the trail sign said, is Sable Falls. To the left is Grand Sable Dunes.

There are dozens of trails in the Lower Peninsula that will lead you to sand dunes and there are probably an equal number in the Upper Peninsula that wind past waterfalls, but the Dunes and Falls Trails in Pictured Rocks National Lakeshore is the only one we know of that gives you the option to view falling water or climb steep sandy slopes.

We decided to do both and use a stretch of Lake Superior beach, known for its abundance of agates, to turn this hike into a 2.6-mile loop.

We headed left for the dunes, descended to a bridge across Sable Creek and on the other side began the long climb to the top of the dunes. The transition was amazing. We began climbing in a shady, serene jack pine forest and then suddenly, in three steps or less, were in the hot, sandy, and unsettled world of the Grand Sable Dunes. We crossed the open dunes to a highpoint where stretched out before us was Lake Superior, blue and endless.

We descended to the shoreline, headed east, and within a mile were at the mouth of the Sable Creek. On its east bank was Sable Falls Trail that entered a narrow canyon the creek has carved and within 0.3 mile arrived at Sable Falls. Sable Creek descends 140 feet on its way to Lake Superior, with a good bit of it occurring as a series of drops that is Sable Falls. The waterfall makes for a quiet, shady spot where you can sit for a spell and listen to the water splash pass you. And you should. The final leg of this loop is a stairway of a 125 steps.

To reach the Sable Falls trailhead from Grand Marais, head a mile west on County Road H-58. Just beyond the trail is the Grand Sable Visitor Center ☎ 906-494-2660 for Pictured Rocks National Lakeshore.

upgrading modern sites in 2007 and now most have electric hook-ups, water, and even cable TV service. There is also a secluded primitive area with 20 walk-in sites, mostly designed for backpackers who plan to hike the Lakeshore Trail from Grand Marais to Munising.

The campground also has two bathhouses with coin-operated showers, a dump station for RVers, and fire rings at most sites. Lakefront sites with electricity and water are $25 per night (cable TV is an additional charge); all other modern sites are $24 and walk-in sites $18.

Day-use Facilities: Three stairways descend the bluff from the campground to a wide sandy beach along Lake Superior. The shore is great for beachcombing or to look for agates, but the swimming can be chilly for much of the summer. Other facilities include a picnic area, two play areas for children, horseshoe pits, tennis courts, basketball court, and a softball diamond.

Hiking: By heading west for 2 miles along the Lake Superior Shoreline you will enter Pictured Rocks National Lakeshore and reach the Sable Falls Trail. The trail heads inland along Sable Creek to this beautiful cascade. An entire afternoon can be spent hiking to the falls and nearby Grand Sable Dunes.

Season: Arrive early at Woodland Park. The campground does not accept reservations and can be occasionally filled from July through mid-August.

109

Cusino Lake

Lake Superior State Forest

Campground: Rustic	**Reservations:** No
County: Schoolcraft	**Fee:** $15
Nearest Community: Seney	**Information:** Shingleton DNR
Sites: 6	☎ (906) 452-6227

M-28 between Seney and Shingleton is a road so straight that if your wheels are properly aligned you may never have to turn the steering wheel. The scenery is so blasé, at least for the U.P., that many people never stop between the two towns. Better to skip M-28 and traveled from Seney to Munising via Forest Road 450. What is usually a 40-minute drive can be turned into a three-day adventure.

That's because FR-450 heads north into Lake Superior State Forest where it skirts the Fox River and provides access to both this noted trout stream and the Fox River Pathway. Then it swings west and stays in the state forest until it emerges at H-52 on the underside of Pictured Rocks National Lakeshore.

What you will find along the way are eight state forest campgrounds, small facilities where there might be only four or five sites, not 40 or

50. The Forest Management Division calls it "small campsites in wild settings." That pretty much describes Cusino Lake Campground, one of the facilities in this area.

Directions: From M-28 in Seney, follow FR-450 for 22 miles to Cusino Lake Campground signs. From Munising head east along H-58 to the hamlet of Melstrand. Cusino Lake is 11 miles from Melstrand via HR-52 and FR-450.

Campground: Cusino Lake has six sites, all of them along the shoreline in a stand of impressive hemlock pines on the east side of the lake. Facilities, like any state forest campground, are basic: fire pit, picnic table, and a pair of outhouses that may or may not be stocked with toilet paper, but you don't come to this campground for the facilities; you're here for the remoteness.

Day-use Facilities: Cusino Lake has a small beach and swimming area.

Fishing: The 160-acre lake is totally undeveloped and fished for northern pike, panfish, and bass. There is no boat launch in the campground, but it is easy to hand launch canoes and small boats from most of the campsites.

Season: Usage of Cusino Lake is light, and you can usually secure a spot. With only six sites, the campground can be unexpectedly filled anytime during the summer.

110

Kingston Lake

Lake Superior State Forest

Campground: Rustic
County: Alger
Nearest Community: Grand Marias
Sites: 16

Reservations: No
Fee: $15
Information: Shingleton DNR office
☎ (906) 452-6227

Kingston Lake is a spectacular place to pitch the tent because of both its location and setting. The state forest facility was already established when in 1966 Pictured Rocks National Lakeshore was created. The

A camper sets up her tent at Kingston Lake State Forest Campground located south of Pictured Rocks National Lakeshore.

campground is still managed by the state, but now it's surrounded by the crown jewels of a national park.

A 10-minute drive from your site is the sweeping Lake Superior shoreline at Twelvemile Beach. Within 15 minutes you can be checking out shipwrecks near Hurricane River or hiking to the restored Au Sable Light Station. In 30 minutes you're frolicking in the Grand Sable Dunes.

As good as the location is, the campground's setting is even better as almost every site overlooks Kingston Lake. The lake lies on the northern edge of the Kingston Plains, the result of loggers clearing thousands of acres of pines in the 1880s and the slash fires that followed. The plains are now a mix of second growth forest and open meadows which provide ample opportunities to pick wild berries as well as observe wildlife, the reason for the "Beware of Bears" warning in the campground.

Directions: From M-28 in Seney head north 25 miles on M-77 to Grand Marais and then west on County Road H-58. Kingston Lake is posted along H-58 and is a 22-mile drive from Grand Marais.

Campground: The campground's 16 sites are on a peninsula that stretches into the middle of the 123-acre lake and all but two face the water. Site No. 3 is the charmer, a private spot isolated on a small knob and surrounded on three sides by the lake.

Day-use Facilities: Before entering the campground you pass a small picnic area with a handful of tables near the shoreline. It's possible to go swimming in this section of the lake.

Fishing: A boat launch in the picnic area allows anglers to spend their days fishing Kingston Lake for muskellunge, smallmouth bass, walleye, and panfish.

Hiking: Passing through the campground is the Fox River Pathway, the 27.5-mile trail that stretches from Pictured Rocks to the town of Seney. Head south and within a couple of miles you'll be hiking through an area of Kingston Plains dubbed the "stump museum" due to the sea of giant white pine stumps that surround you.

Head north from the campground on the pathway and within four miles you'll be standing on a remote stretch of Lake Superior shoreline. Even if your party is not up for a long hike to the Great Lake, the first half mile north is interesting. The trail skirts the shore of Kingston Lake and then breaks out into an open, sandy area so thick with blueberries you could pick a quart in 10 minutes or less.

Season: Due to its close proximity to Pictured Rocks, Kingston Lake can be filled on the weekends in July and August or even in the middle of the week.

111

Hurricane River

Pictured Rocks National Lake

Campground: Rustic
County: Alger
Nearest Community: Grand Marias
Sites: 12
Reservations: No

Fee: $14
Information: Munising Interagency Visitor Center
☎ (906) 387-3700
🌐 www.nps.gov/piro

There are three drive-in campgrounds within Pictured Rocks National Lakeshore. Twelvemile Beach is the largest with 37 sites, Little

Beaver Lake (8 sites) is the farthest from Lake Superior, and—in my opinion—Hurricane River is by far the most scenic.

This National Park Service facility is located where the Hurricane River rushes into the Great Lake under a natural archway of cedars. None of the sites are directly on the lake, but all are close enough so at night you can hear the waves pounding the shoreline. Passing through the campground is the Lakeshore Trail where you can spend hours or even the entire day exploring.

Directions: From Grand Marias head west on County Road H-58, past Grand Sable Lake to reach the entrance of the campground in 9 miles. Three miles farther east along H-58 is Twelvemile Campground.

Campground: Hurricane River has 21 sites with 11 on a lower loop and 10 on an upper loop near the mouth of the river. None of the sites are directly on the water, but all are only a short walk from the Lake Superior shoreline. Because of tight turning radii and limited site sizes, the campground is not recommended for recreational vehicles more than 36 feet long or car-and-trailer combinations more than 42 feet in length.

Facilities include tables, fire grate, and a tent pad while nearby are hand pumps for water and vault toilets. Volunteer campground hosts usually staff the lakeshore campgrounds in Pictured Rocks.

Day-use Facilities: The shoreline here is a sandy beach, but Lake Superior is usually too cold for most people to do anything but stick a toe into it.

Hiking: Passing through the campground is the park's Lakeshore Trail, a popular backpacking route that stretches almost 43 miles from Grand Marias to Munising. Even if you're not up for hauling a pack around, the Lakeshore Trail makes for a very interesting day hike. Just 1.5 miles east of the campground is the Au Sable Lightstation, reached along a stretch commonly known as the Shipwreck Trail. A gate in the campground's lower loop marks the Lakeshore Trail, but a "Shipwreck" sign next to it has most people scrambling immediately to the beach. The first wreck, the Mary Jareck, lies 20 yards off the beach and can be hard to see clearly when there is a chop on the water. The wooden bulk freighter was carrying iron ore and grounded on the Au Sable Reef in July 1883. After being pulled off the reef, the ship was left to be battered by Lake Superior.

A hiker studies the shipwreck ruins near Hurricane River Campground in Pictured Rocks National Lakeshore.

The Lakeshore Trail departs from the campground as an old two-track and skirts the shoreline from above. Within a mile you arrive at the second shipwreck sign. After descending to the beach, head east (right) 1,500 feet to the first remains. These lie on the beach, and the timbers and ironwork indicate it's the ships' hulls that are half buried in the sand. The first wreck is the Sitka, a wooden freighter that grounded Oct. 4, 1904, and the next day broke in half. The second is the Gale Staples, another wooden freighter built in 1881 and was loaded with coal when she beached herself on the sandy reef Oct. 1. From these shipwrecks it is only a short walk to the Au Sable Lighthouse.

Interpretive Center: From late June through Labor Day NPS rangers offer tours of the Au Sable Light Station from 11 AM to 5 PM Wednesday through Sunday. The 40 minute tour begins at the lighthouse front porch and includes climbing to the top of the lighthouse for a view of the shoreline. There is a small per-person fee for the tours.

Season: Pictured Rocks campgrounds are popular during the summer and often filled both weekend and weekdays from July through mid-August. Sites are handed out on a first-come-first-served basis, so it is wise to plan a mid-morning arrival and have a backup campground in mind in case there are no openings.

112
Twelvemile Beach

Pictured Rocks National Lake

Campground: Rustic
County: Alger
Nearest Community: Grand Marias
Sites: 36
Reservations: No
Fee: $14–$16
Information: Munising Interagency Visitor Center
☎ (906) 387-3700
www.nps.gov/piro

In case Hurricane Campground is filled, head 3 miles west along County Road H-58 to Twelvemile Beach Campground, the other National Park Service facility along Lake Superior. This is the park's largest campground but is also very popular during the summer and often filled in July and August.

Directions: From Grand Marias head west on County Road H-58 past Grand Sable Lake to reach the entrance of the campground in 12 miles.

Campground: Twelvemile Beach has 36 sites along two loops with many of the sites on a sandy bluff above its namesake Lake Superior beach. Both the entrance road and many of the sites lie in a picturesque stand of white birch. Facilities include tables, fire grate, and a tent pad while nearby are hand pumps for water, a pavilion, and vault toilets. There are two handicap-accessible campsites. Lakeshore sites are $16 a night, all others $14.

Day-use Facilities: Near the campground is a small picnic area while three stairways lead to shoreline below. Lake Superior is too cold for most people to swim in, but Twelvemile Beach is a great place to beachcomb or to take in a sunset on a clear evening.

Hiking: Passing through the campground is the park's Lakeshore Trail, a popular backpacking route that stretches almost 43 miles from Grand Marias to Munising. It is roughly a 5-mile hike from the campground

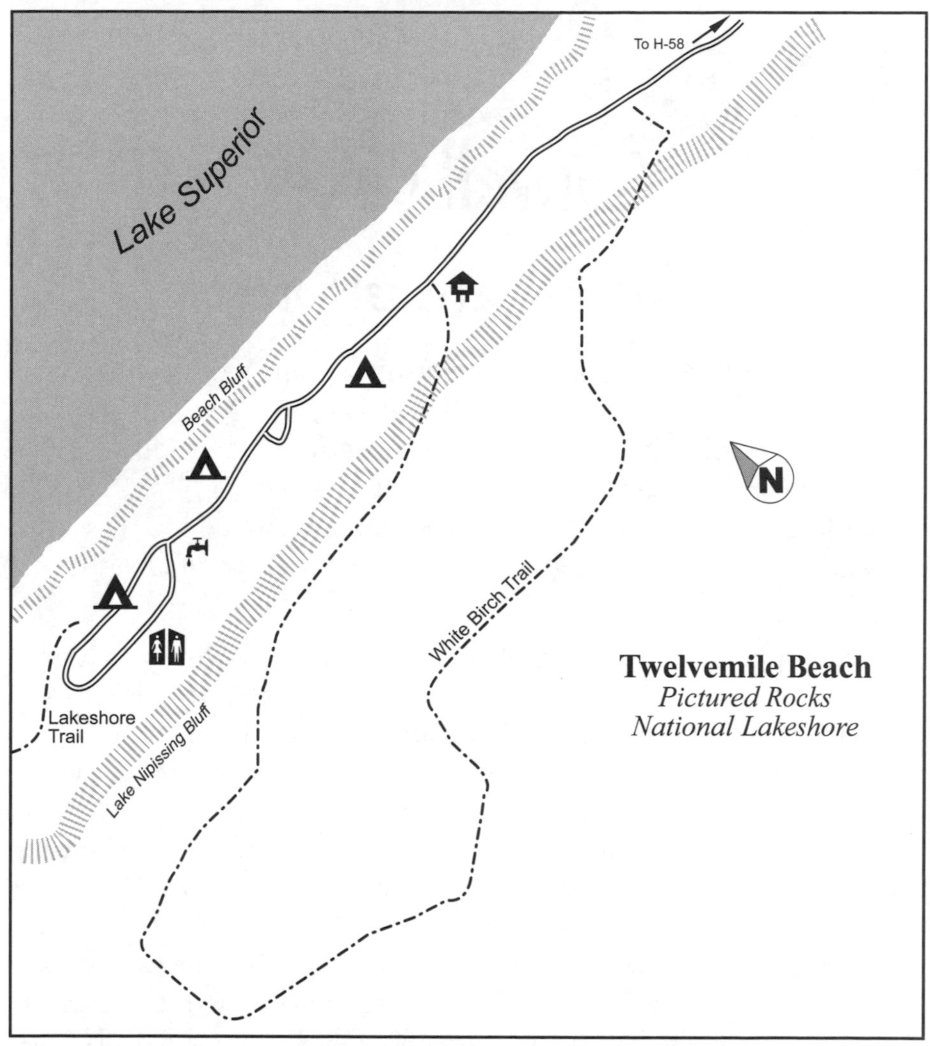

east to the Au Sable Lightstation. To the west the backcountry campsites at Seven Mile Creek are reached in 3 miles.

Also at the campground is the White Birch Trail. This 2-mile loop is an interpretive trail that explores the ancient Lake Nipissing beach and the upland plants and trees. There is usually a supply of trail brochures at the trailhead.

Season: Like Hurricane River, Twelvemile Beach can also be filled both weekend and weekdays from July through mid-August. Sites are only handed out on a first-come-first-served basis so it is wise to plan a mid-morning arrival and have a backup campground in mind in case there are no openings.

113

Colwell Lake

Hiawatha National Forest

Campground: Modern and rustic
County: Schoolcraft
Nearest Community: Shingleton
Sites: 35
Reservations: Yes
Fee: $12–$16
Information: Manistique Ranger District
☎ (906) 341-5666
🌐 www.fs.usda.gov/hiawatha

Located just off M-94 is Colwell Lake, a large facility with a great beach, a nature trail, and access to a diverse fishery in the lake. Most unusual, Colwell is one of the few national forest campgrounds with electric hook-ups. There are not many, but such a site can be reserved in advance through the National Recreation Reservation Service.

Directions: From Shingleton, a small town 10 miles east of Munising, head south on M-94 to reach the campground in 10 miles. From Manistique, Colwell is 25 miles north on M-94.

Campground: Colwell has 35 sites on a single loop. The sites are well secluded and spread out in a maple and beech forest, and more than half of them are along the lake with a partial view of the water. Sites No. 1–5 feature electric hook-ups for RVs while No. 33 and 34 are walk-in campsites. Amenities include tables, fire rings, hand pumps for water, vault toilets, and a dump station. Sites are $12 a night or $16 if you use the hook-up.

Day-use Facilities: Between Sites No. 4 and 6 is a sandy beach surrounded by an open grassy area and parking for a few additional vehicles. Colwell is an excellent lake for swimming. The campground maintains a marked swimming area that features a sandy and gently sloping bottom.

Fishing: At the north end of the loop is an improved boat launch with cement ramp, pier, and a parking area for vehicles and trailers. At 145 acres, Colwell is a large lake but reaches depths of only 20 feet. The lake is totally undeveloped and attracts moderate fishing pressure from anglers casting for largemouth bass, black crappies, bluegills and other panfish, and northern pike.

Hiking: Near the boat launch is the trailhead for the Stutts Creek Nature Trail, a 2-mile walk through the forest along the east side of the lake.

Season: Colwell is open from mid-May through early October and receives a moderate number of campers though it rarely fills up even on the weekends. Some of the sites, including two with electric hook-ups, can be reserved in advance through the National Recreation Reservation Service ☎ 877-444-6777 🌐 www.recreation.gov.

114

Little Bass Lake

Hiawatha National Forest

Campground: Rustic
County: Schoolcraft
Nearest Community: Steuben
Sites: 12
Reservations: No

Fee: $12
Information: Manistique Ranger District
☎ (906) 341-5666
🌐 www.fs.usda.gov/hiawatha

Little Bass Lake is a scenic facility located in an isolated area of the Hiawatha National Forest near Steuben. There are only 10 sites at Little Bass Lake, but it is rare for this campground to be filled even though a small campground on a totally undeveloped lake makes for a quiet evening in a wilderness-like setting.

Directions: Little Bass Lake is 23 miles northwest of Manistique and 25 miles southwest of Munising. From Shingleton, a small town 10 miles east of Munising, head south on M-94 for 12 miles to Forest Road 437. The forest road is posted along M-24 by a "Steuben" sign. Turn west on FR 437, head 2 miles into the hamlet of Steuben, and then turn south on Bass Lake Road. The campground is reached 2 miles south on Bass Lake Road.

Campground: Little Bass Lake is a single paved loop of 12 sites. Situated in a predominately maple-beech forest, four of the sites are on a high bank with a partial view of the lake. The entire facility is well wooded with moderate undergrowth, but the sites are not totally secluded from each other. Amenities include tables, fire rings with sliding grills, lantern posts, and vault toilets.

Fishing: The campground has an unimproved boat launch for hand carried boats only, as a post blocks you from driving a trailer into the water. There is parking here for four vehicles and rigs. Bait and limited fishing supplies are available in Steuben, 2 miles away.

At 84 acres, Little Bass Lake is small enough to be easily covered in a canoe or small rowboat with electric motor. It is a horseshoe-shaped body of water with the northern end reached from a path next to the boat launch, obviously a favorite stretch for shore anglers. The lake is undeveloped, only 18 feet deep, and features a shoreline of many small bays with pencil weeds and lily pad patches, which attract the attention of anglers. Perch is the main species caught, but anglers also land largemouth bass, northern pike, bluegill, and black crappies.

Season: Little Bass Lake is a lightly used facility that is open from mid-May through October.

115

Bay Furnace

Hiawatha National Forest

Campground: Rustic
County: Alger
Nearest Community: Christmas
Sites: 50
Reservations: Yes

Fee: $16
Information: Munising Interagency Visitor Center
☎ (906) 387-3700
🌐 www.fs.usda.gov/hiawatha

Situated on Lake Superior and near the bizarre little town of Christmas, Bay Furnace has the distinction of being the most popular campground in the Hiawatha National Forest. Part of its popularity is due to its location. It's a funnel during the summer for campers traveling from Pictured Rocks to their next stop, often in the Keweenaw Peninsula.

And part of it is its setting. In the 19th century, this was the site of the town of Onoto, a prosperous little iron-smelting town of 500 people until it burnt down in 1877. Today, all that remains of the past is an iron kiln in the picnic area. The rest of the rustic campground is a pleasant mix of open and secluded wooded sites, many with a view of Lake Superior and Grand Island only two miles away.

Directions: From Munising, head west on M-28 for 5 miles to reach the campground in the town of Christmas.

Campground: Bay Furnace Campground has 50 sites along two loops. A few of the sites overlook Lake Superior, and a row of them are near Furnace Creek, which is crossed when entering. The sites are well spread out in the trees and feature fire pits, tables, and lantern posts. There is also a sanitation station for trailers and recreational vehicles.

Day-use Facilities: An open picnic area with tables and grills overlooks Lake Superior. The shoreline here is sandy, and occasionally in August the water warms up enough that people go swimming.

Hiking: From the picnic area, a short 200-yard interpretive trail winds around the ruins of the remaining blast furnace and features interpretive displays re-telling the story of Onoto.

Season: The campground is open mid-May to October. Bay Furnace has an occupation rate of more than 75 percent from June through September, and in July and August it's filled nearly every night. Sites can be reserved in advance through the National Recreation Reservation Service ☎ 877-444-6777 🌐 www.recreation.gov.

116

Au Train Lake

Hiawatha National Forest

Campground: Rustic
County: Alger
Nearest Community: Au Train
Sites: 37
Reservations: Yes
Fee: $16
Information: Munising Interagency Visitor Center
☎ (906) 387-3700
🌐 www.fs.usda.gov/hiawatha

The national forest campground at the southeast corner of Au Train Lake in Alger County is called a "recreation area" because it offers more than just fire rings and pit toilets. And by far the most interesting aspect of the Au Train Recreation Area is its Songbird Trail. On this nature trail hikers first rent a tape recorder then listen to a narrative tape while walking to learn about the more than 40 species of songbirds that commonly frequent the area.

The recreation area also boosts a wildlife observation deck, a sandy beach, a large campground, good fishing on the lake, and a popular canoe route that ends in Lake Superior. Being only 10 miles from Munising, this is a delightful place to set up camp for a few days while you're exploring Pictured Rocks National Lakeshore.

Directions: From Munising head west on M-28 for 10 miles and then at the town of Au Train turn south on County Road H-03 for 4 miles. Turn east on Forest Road 2276 for a mile and then north on Forest Road 2596 for 2 miles to reach the campground.

Campground: Au Train has 37 rustic sites that are well spread out in a hardwood forest of maple and beech. Ten of them overlook the lake's Buck Bay, and these are always the first to be selected. Facilities include tables, fire pits, vault toilets, and hand pumps for water.

Day-use Facilities: The campground has a picnic area that includes a bathhouse and a sandy beach. The swimming in Au Train Lake is only fair. More spectacular is Au Train Beach on Lake Superior near the M-28 and CR H-03 intersection. Lake Superior, however, can be a cold place to swim throughout most of the summer. Au Train also has a wildlife-viewing platform on the lake where birders have sighted bald eagles, ospreys, wood ducks, and shorebirds.

Fishing: Within the campground is an improved boat launch with parking for vehicles and trailers. Au Train is the largest inland lake in Alger County at 830 acres. It has a depth of up to 30 feet and an average depth of 12 feet. Fishing is considered good for walleye, northern pike, and yellow perch. There are several bait shops and boat liveries along CR H-03 on the west shore of the lake.

Hiking: The Au Train Songbird Trail begins next to site number 12 and is a 2-mile loop. Before the hike rent a songbird kit for a small fee from the campground host or AuTrain Grocery or A & L Grocery on County Road H-03. Each kit contains a tape recorder, binoculars, and a bird identification guide. The 28-minute tape is keyed to 20 color plaques posted along the trail, each one devoted to a different songbird. Biologists estimate that the area around Buck Bay Creek attracts more than 40 species of songbirds. From the campground, the trail swings past Grass

Pink Bog and then Buck Bay Creek and a posted junction with the North Country Trail. Plan on at least 90 minutes to walk the trail and stop at each interpretive plaque to listen to the tape. To spot the most birds, hike either at dawn or dusk.

For a longer day of hiking, there is the North Country Trail, the 3,200-mile national pathway that swings near the recreation area.

Canoeing: Au Train Lake is the beginning of an easy but scenic canoe route that ends 10 miles to the north on the shores of Lake Superior. The route includes the Au Train River, a slow-moving and meandering waterway due to the heavy logging activity that took place in 1800s. The result is an absence of rapids and portages, the perfect conditions for a relaxing five-hour paddle that usually includes a number of encounters with waterfowl, great blue herons, turtles, and other wildlife. Canoes are available for rent from many of the resorts along Au Train Lake and can be put in at the recreation area or at one of two bridges where County Road H-03 crosses Au Train River.

Season: Au Train is open from mid-May to October and can be a popular campground at times. Sites are usually available except on holidays and an occasional weekend during the summer or can be reserved in advance through the National Recreation Reservation Service ☎ 877-444-6777 🌐 www.recreation.gov.

The wildlife observation tower that overlooks Au Train Lake at Au Train Lake National Forest Campground.

CALLING THE SONGBIRDS AT AU TRAIN

From the little boombox we were instructed to carry down the trail, a taped narrator discussed the life of a common yellow throat warbler and gave a sample of the bird's call.

"Witchery-witchery-witchery."

My children and I were just casually hiking along when we suddenly stopped dead in our tracks. From out of the trees, high above us, came a resounding "Witchery! Witchery! Witchery!" Was it real or was it Memorex?

Well, we had the tape so it had to be a real. A common yellow throat was calling back to our boombox, rather angrily I thought, making the Au Train Songbird Trail as realistic a nature trail as we've ever hiked.

It was Lon Emerick, a retired Northern Michigan University professor, who realized that the woods, wetlands, and water around Buck Bay Creek were the perfect habitat for songbirds. In 1989 he convinced the U.S. Forest Service to build the unusual nature trail that includes renting a songbird kit with a cassette tape. The 28-minute tape is keyed to 20 color plaques posted along the two-mile trail, each one devoted to a different songbird.

You learn that the black-throated green warbler actually has a yellow face and is often seen in conifers, that the white-breasted nuthatch descends trees head first and the ovenbird, unlike most other warblers, walks on the ground rather than hops. In the forested areas, you may see chickadees and cedar waxwings.

Then there are the calls at every stop, often prompting the birds to call back and once so infuriating a red-eyed vireo that it flew down and attacked Emerick's tape recorder.

The songbird kit for the Au Train Songbird Trail.

117
Council Lake

Hiawatha National Forest

Campground: Rustic
County: Alger
Nearest Community: Munising
Sites: 4
Reservations: Yes
Fee: $8
Information: Munising Interagency Visitor Center
☎ (906) 387-3700
🌐 www.fs.usda.gov/hiawatha

County Road H-13 that heads south of Munising is an avenue to seven national forest campgrounds and several chains of lakes. The most obscure chain, so obscured there isn't even a name for this collection of small lakes, is located just north of Widewaters. Anchoring the chain are Council Lake and Halfmoon Lake while lying between them are five smaller ones, all connected by a series of channels and unmarked portages.

Council Lake Dispersed Camping Area is the main access point to the chain and makes for a great place to set-up for a weekend of camping, fishing, and paddling, but you need to plan ahead as camping is by reservation only.

Directions: From M-28, just east of Munising, you head south on H-13 for 10 miles and then turn west on Forest Road 2661. It's a dirt road that is poorly marked but within 1.5 miles ends at Council Lake.

Campground: Council Lake has four sites in a mixed stand of hardwood and beech trees with two of them along the shoreline. There are pit toilets and fire rings but no source of safe drinking water—bring a filter or boil water from the lake—and, more importantly, no toilet paper. Bring your own.

Just before you reach Council Lake, Forest Road 2216A is marked and veers off to northwest and in a quarter mile reaches Red Jack Lake, the other access point. Red Jack Lake is connected to Council Lake by a small channel and has a single dispersed camping site and a dirt launch that can handle trailers.

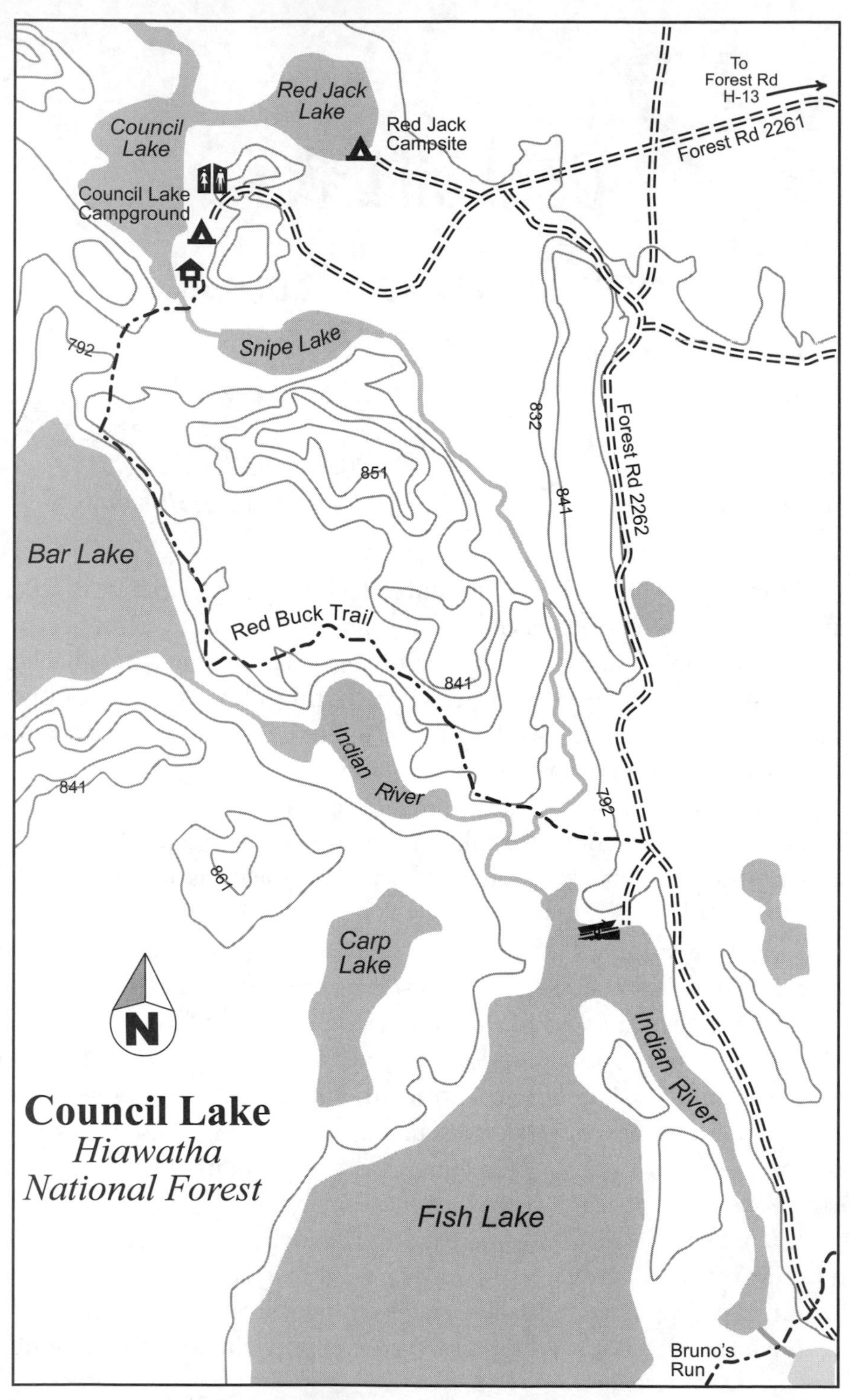
Red Jack Lake
Council Lake
Red Jack Campsite
To Forest Rd H-13
Forest Rd 2261
Council Lake Campground
Snipe Lake
792
832
851
841
Forest Rd 2262
Bar Lake
Red Buck Trail
841
Indian River
841
792
861
Carp Lake
N
Indian River
Fish Lake
Bruno's Run
Council Lake
Hiawatha National Forest

Children swim in Council Lake at the Hiawatha National Forest campground.

Day-use Facilities: At Council Lake there is a stretch of sandy beach that is used by the campers as a swimming beach.

Fishing: You can launch hand-carried boats at Council Lake and trailer boats at Red Jack Lake. Council Lake is 14 acres in size, has a depth of 20 feet, and produces bluegill, perch, black crappie, northern pike, and largemouth bass. At the north end of the lake a channel leads east to Red Jack Lake, 12 acres in size, while another leads north to even smaller Scout Lake. It's an easy paddle north from Scout Lake into Lion Lake, which is as far as anybody can go who trailered their boat in.

Paddling: Lion Lake is boarded on the west side by a 60-foot-high forested bluff. Climb that with a canoe or kayak and you can reach two more lakes, Rock and Hike Lake. There are no marked trails, but it's hard to miss them. The portage to either is less than 100 feet long. Hike Lake is the most interesting. It's only 11 acres in size but more than 34 feet deep in places, enabling it to support a brook trout fishery.

At the north end of Lion Lake is another small channel, the smallest one of all, that leads into Halfmoon Lake, the largest of the chain at 31 acres. A single kayaker or a canoer in an empty boat can squeeze through the marsh area that separates the two lakes without getting their feet wet. Halfmoon is a quiet lake free of any cabins and famed by hardwoods that are beautiful in the fall.

Hiking: Departing from the Council Lakes campsites is Red Buck Trail that winds 2 miles south to end at Bruno's Run Trail (see Pete's Lake Campground) near Fish Lake. Along the way you pass three walk-in campsites.

Season: Council Lake is lightly used, but with only four sites it can easily be filled on any weekend in the summer. You must reserve a site in advance through the National Recreation Reservation Service ☎ 877-444-6777 🌐 www.recreation.gov. Non-reservation camping is not allowed.

118

Pete's Lake

Hiawatha National Forest

Campground: Rustic
County: Alger
Nearest Community: Munising
Sites: 41
Reservations: Yes

Fee: $16–$21
Information: Munising Interagency Visitor Center
☎ (906) 387-3700
🌐 www.fs.usda.gov/hiawatha

More than any other Forest Service campground along County Road H-13, Pete's Lake Recreation Area is a destination rather than just a place to park the trailer or pitch a tent. This rustic campground offers so much to do it's best to plan on staying for a few days.

There's a day-use area with a bathhouse and a swimmer's beach bordered by an open grassy area where you can lie out in the sun if it isn't black fly season in the Upper Peninsula. Passing through the campground is Bruno's Run Trail for hikers and mountain bikers while the 190-acre lake offers anglers a mixed warm water fishery.

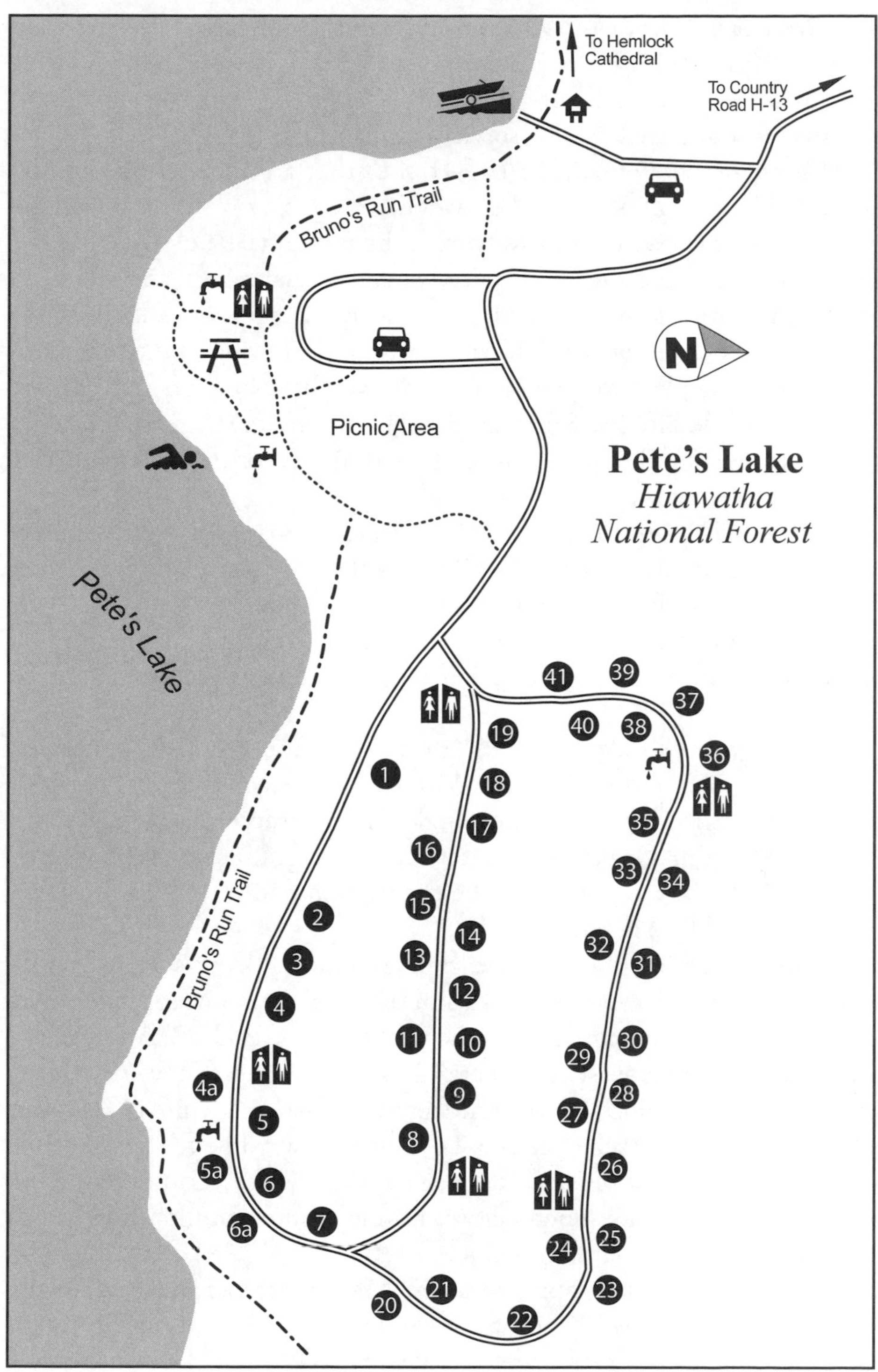
To Hemlock Cathedral
To Country Road H-13
Bruno's Run Trail
Picnic Area
N
Pete's Lake
Hiawatha National Forest
Pete's Lake
Bruno's Run Trail
41
39
37
40
38
36
19
1
18
35
17
16
33
34
15
2
14
32
13
31
3
12
4
11
10
29
30
4a
9
28
27
5
8
26
5a
6
7
25
6a
24
21
23
20
22

Directions: From M-24/94, 3 miles east of Munising, head south on County Road H-13. Pete's Lake is posted 12 miles south and is 0.3 mile east of H-13 on Forest Road 2173. It is best to stock up on supplies in Munising. There are very few services available along CR H-13.

Campground: Pete's Lake has 41 sites that are well spread out and secluded in a stand of mixed hardwoods. A couple of the sites overlook the lake, but the rest are well away from the shoreline. Pete's Lake has five handicap-accessible sites with paved spurs, special tables, and stand-up grills. There are also two walk-in sites, reached after a short walk from the east end of the campground. If you don't mind carrying in the tent, both are a charming place to spend a night or two. Site No. 7A is right on the lakeshore while Site No. 8A is another quarter mile to the east and set in an impressive stand of pines. Both are within view of the water and, like all sites, have fire rings and picnic tables.

Day-use Facilities: Pete's Lake has a large day-use area with a separate parking area. Picnic tables and grills are set under large hardwood trees with a view of the lake. A grassy area surrounds the beach, and the swimming area features clear water with a sandy bottom. Also nearby are changing rooms for day visitors. A paved path connects the beach area to the campground.

Fishing: Pete's Lake has an improved boat ramp with a large parking area for vehicles and trailers. The 190-acre lake reaches depths of up to 40 feet and is mainly targeted by anglers for northern pike, smallmouth bass, and bluegill. Other warm water species caught include yellow perch and black crappie. Just south of the campground on CR H-13 is a small store with tackle and bait.

Hiking: Passing through the campground is Bruno's Run Trail, a 9.7-mile loop that winds around eight other lakes and near Widewaters National Forest Campground on the west side of CR H-13. An excellent day hike is to head west from Pete's Lake to a stand of towering pines known as the Hemlock Cathedral. These 300-year-old white pines tower above you and are reached after a 2.6-mile one-way hike. A quarter mile beyond the stand of old-growth pines is Widewaters Campground, an excellent place to have lunch before turning around. Bruno's Run is also a popular trail for mountain biking.

Season: Pete's Lake is open from mid-May to October and occasionally is filled on summer weekends. Sites can be reserved in advance through the National Recreation Reservation Service ☎ 877-444-6777 🌐 www.recreation.gov.

119

Widewaters

Hiawatha National Forest

Campground: Rustic	**Fee:** $16
County: Alger	**Information:** Munising
Nearest Community: Munising	Interagency Visitor Center
Sites: 34	☎ (906) 387-3700
Reservations: Yes	🌐 www.fs.usda.gov/hiawatha

On the west side of Country Road H-13 and within a mile of Pete's Lake is Widewaters Campground, a scenic spot that lies between Irwin Lake and the Indian River. Widewaters not only offers you a secluded setting in the woods but also access to some quiet lakes for fishing or wildlife viewing.

A canoe would be an excellent item to pack along while camping at Widewaters. From the campground you can paddle the Indian River into a chain of six small lakes and ponds for a wilderness-like fishing adventure.

Directions: From M-24/M-94, 3 miles east of Munising, head south on County Road H-13. Widewaters is posted 13 miles south and is a half mile west of H-13 on Forest Road 2262.

Campground: Widewaters has 34 sites well spaced out on a single loop. On the west side of the loop the sites are near the Indian River where there are benches along the banks. On the east side, Forest Road 2262 lies between the sites and Irwin Lake. Sites are well secluded from each other and have fire pits with sliding grills and tables. There is a small store just north of the campground on CR H-13, but it is best to stock up on supplies either in Munising or Manistique.

Fishing: Within the campground is an improved boat launch on the Indian River. Widewaters picks up its name from this stretch of the Indian River, which heads north into a series of three wide ponds. From there it is easy to continue into Fish Lake or even farther into Bar Lake. In all, the campground provides access to six ponds and lakes that

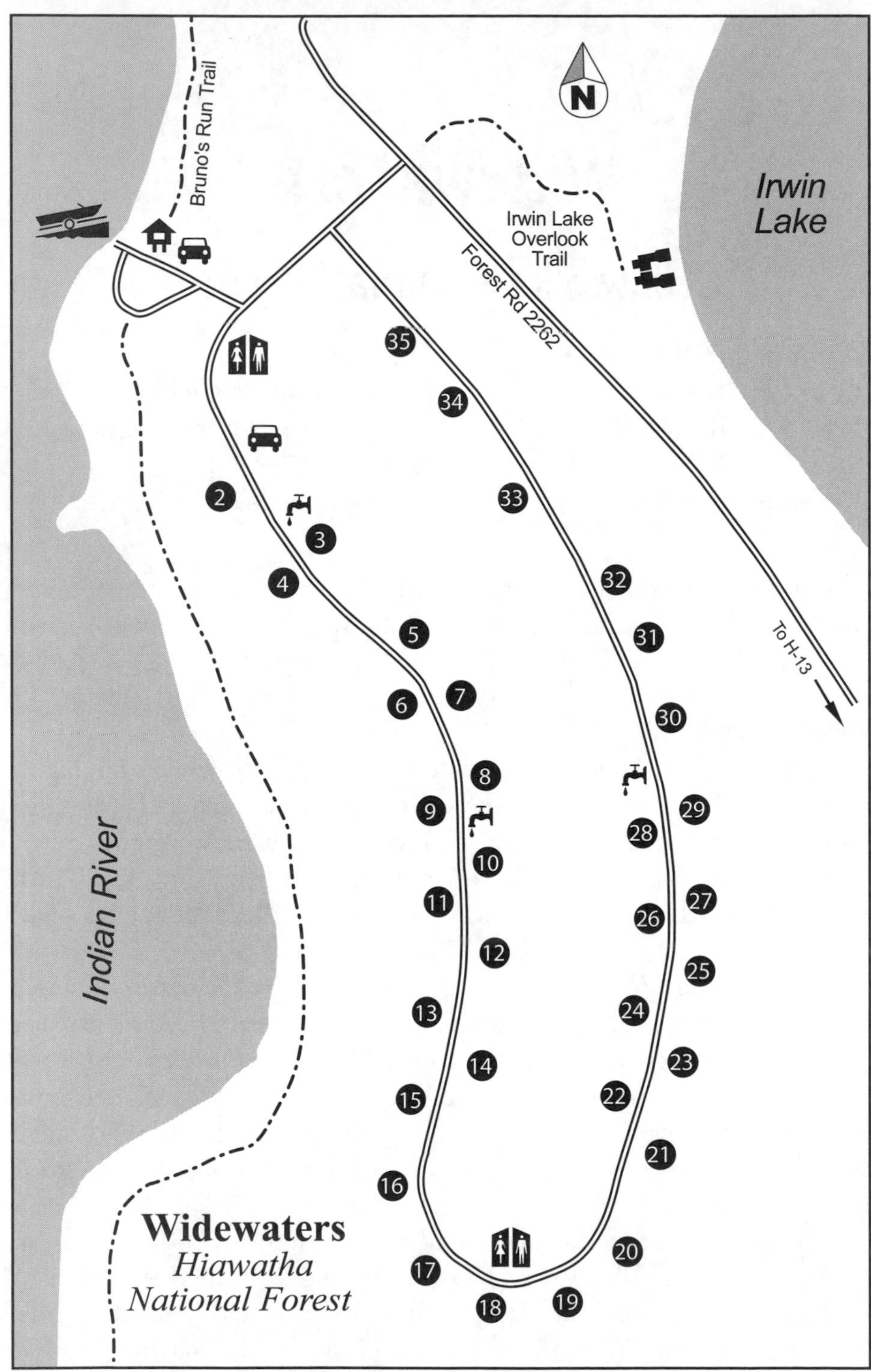
Bruno's Run Trail
Irwin Lake
Irwin Lake Overlook Trail
Forest Rd 2262
To H-13
Indian River
35
34
33
32
31
30
29
28
27
26
25
24
23
22
21
20
19
18
17
16
15
14
13
12
11
10
9
8
7
6
5
4
3
2
Widewaters
Hiawatha National Forest

can be reached without portaging your canoe. There is also a boat access site to Irwin Lake passed on Forest Road 2262 just before reaching the campground entrance.

Fish Lake is the largest at 60 acres and reaches depths of 40 feet. Anglers fish it for bluegill, largemouth bass, and northern pike. Occasionally somebody even catches a walleye. Bar Lake is smaller but slightly deeper in spots at 50 feet. It is also fished for panfish, largemouth bass, and northern pike but not walleyes. Both 10-acre Irwin Lake and the Indian River are fished for brook trout.

Hiking: Like Pete's Lake, Bruno's Run Trail also passes through Widewaters Campground. This 9.7-mile loop winds around eight other lakes and crosses CR H-13 twice. Just a quarter mile north of Widewaters Bruno's Run passes through an impressive stand of towering pines known as the Hemlock Cathedral.

Season: Widewaters is open from mid-May to October and occasionally is filled on summer weekends. Sites can be reserved in advance through the National Recreation Reservation Service ☎ 877-444-6777 🌐 www.recreation.gov.

120

Fayette

State Park

Campground: Semi-modern
County: Delta
Nearest Community: Garden
Sites: 61
Reservations: Yes
Fee: $16-$18 plus vehicle entry fee
Information: State park office ☎ (906) 644-2603

In the mid-1800s, raw iron ore was being shipped from the Upper Peninsula to the foundries in the lower Great Lakes at a tremendous cost. Fayette Brown, general manager of the Jackson Iron Company, studied the problem and decided the solution was a company-owned furnace not far from the mine where the ore could be smelted into pig iron before it was shipped to the steel-making centers. In 1866 Brown chose a spot on the Garden Peninsula overlooking Big Bay De Noc because it possessed a natural harbor for shipping and the limestone and hardwood forests needed to smelt the ore. He then oversaw the construction of a company town, gave it his first name when it was finished, and Fayette was born.

In 1891 Jackson Iron closed down the furnaces, and within a few years Fayette was a ghost town of more than 20 buildings and structures. Today the area is preserved as Fayette State Park, a 711-acre unit in Delta County. The state park contains not only a fascinating interpretive area but also a scenic campground, a swimming beach, and an interesting trail system. Fayette requires a little out-of-the-way driving to reach, but this state park is worth it. Plan on spending at least two nights here if not three.

Directions: From US-2, head south on Country Road 483 for 15 miles on the Garden Peninsula. The park entrance is 8 miles beyond the town of Garden.

Campground: Fayette has a semi-modern campground that lacks modern restrooms and showers but provides electricity at all 61 sites, including some with 50-amp service. There are also 11 pull-through sites.

The sites are located on three loops in a wooded area near Lake Michigan but not directly on it. Foot trails provide access to both the historic town to the north and the park's swimming beach to the south.

Day-use Facilities: Fayette features a beautiful beach on Sand Bay at the south. The facility includes parking, tables, and a bathhouse and has a separate entrance just south of the park's main entrance on County Road 483.

Interpretive Center: At its height some 500 people lived, worked, and enjoyed a good life in Fayette. The town featured not only a furnace complex and numerous charcoal kilns but also baseball fields, a hotel, even an opera house. A walking tour of the area begins in the Visitor Center. The centerpiece of the museum is a scale model of Fayette as it was in the late 1880s. The tour continues in the ghost town, where there are 22 buildings and structures, including the kilns and furnaces needed to produce pig iron. Many have been renovated and feature displays inside including the Company Office, Opera House, and Machine Shop. Although you can visit the town anytime of the year, the museum and buildings are open from 9 AM to 5 PM daily from mid-May to mid-June

A kayaker paddles past the old townsite of Fayette, now an interpretive area of Fayette State Park.

and after Labor Day to mid-October. During rest of the summer the townsite is open from 9 AM to dusk daily when visitors can join a guided tour staged from mid-June through Labor Day.

Hiking: Fayette has 7 miles of hiking trails with the longest loop being a 2-mile path that begins in the campground and swings through the wooded interior south of the park road before returning. Of the four loops, however, the most scenic is the 1.5-mile Overlook Trail. This path begins just up a hill from the townsite parking lot and then passes three viewing points from the edge of the limestone bluffs above Snail Shell Harbor.

Fishing: Big Bay De Noc is a well-known fishery for perch, smallmouth bass, and northern pike as well as walleye which are planted annually. The park maintains an improved boat launch located in its day-use area. Often during July and August, schools of perch move into Snail Shell Harbor and attract the interest of anglers who fish for them from anchored boats or off a dock located in the small bay.

Season: Fayette rarely fills up during the summer with the exception of Fourth of July weekend. To reserve a campsite contact Michigan State Park Central Reservations ☎ 800-447-2757 🌐 www.midnrreservations.com.

121

Portage Bay

Lake Superior State Forest

Campground: Rustic
County: Delta
Nearest Community: Garden
Sites: 23
Reservations: No
Fee: $15
Information: Escanaba DNR office
☎ (906) 786-2351

One of Michigan's most secluded shoreline campgrounds accessible by car is located on the east side of Garden Peninsula, not far from Fayette State Park. Portage Bay State Forest Campground features 23 sites that are well hidden among the towering red pines and border its namesake bay. No matter where you camp, you're only three steps from a beautiful sandy beach and the clear waters of Lake Michigan

For campers who take the time to find this charming little bay, it often turns out to be a personal paradise. For only $15 a night they enjoy a beach they can call their own in a setting that is almost tropical in the middle of the summer.

Directions: Just reaching this campground is an adventure. From the town of Garden, head south on County Road 483 for 2 miles to the junction known as Devil's Corner. Curve to the west and you'll head for Fayette State Park. To reach Portage Bay continue straight on the gravel road posted with a State Forest Campground sign. Turn left on Lane 12.75 and then hang on. The rugged dirt road bumps for 5 miles on its way to the east shore and the campground entrance.

Campground: Portage Bay has 23 sites that line this quiet bay on the east side of Garden Peninsula. Sites face Lake Michigan and are well separated from each other. You end up with not only a place to pitch the tent but you own private stretch of beach. The rustic facilities include vault toilets, a hand pump for water, fire rings, and picnic tables.

Day-use Facilities: Portage Bay is a crescent moon beach, lined by pines and enclosed by a pair of rocky points at each end. The water in this part of Lake Michigan warms up nicely by mid-July and the swimming here is excellent.

Hiking: Departing from the campground is the Ninga Aki Pathway, a 2.2-mile interpretive trail of several loops, including the 1.5-mile Lake Michigan Loop marked by a display sign at the north end of the campground. Ninga Aki is an Objiway word that means "Mother Earth," and posts along the trail point out the staples of Indian life here when they lived off the land. Though many of the posts are missing, trail guides can still be obtained by stopping at the DNR Escanaba Field Office ☎ 906-786-2351 at the corner of US-2 and M-41/M-35 in Gladstone.

Season: Portage Bay is a lightly used facility though people tend to spend a longer time camping here due to its incredible setting. Subsequently the campground can be filled occasionally during the summer.

122

Flowing Well

Hiawatha National Forest

Campground: Rustic
County: Delta
Nearest Community: Rapid River
Sites: 10
Reservations: Yes

Fee: $12
Information: Rapid River Ranger District
☎ (906) 474-6442
www.fs.usda.gov/hiawatha

Flowing Well is only 3 miles north of US-2, a road that is beset with travelers during the summer, but the campground might as well be a hundred miles from anywhere. Tucked away on the banks of the Sturgeon River, this small facility provides a quiet and serene setting, unlike most campgrounds along US-2.

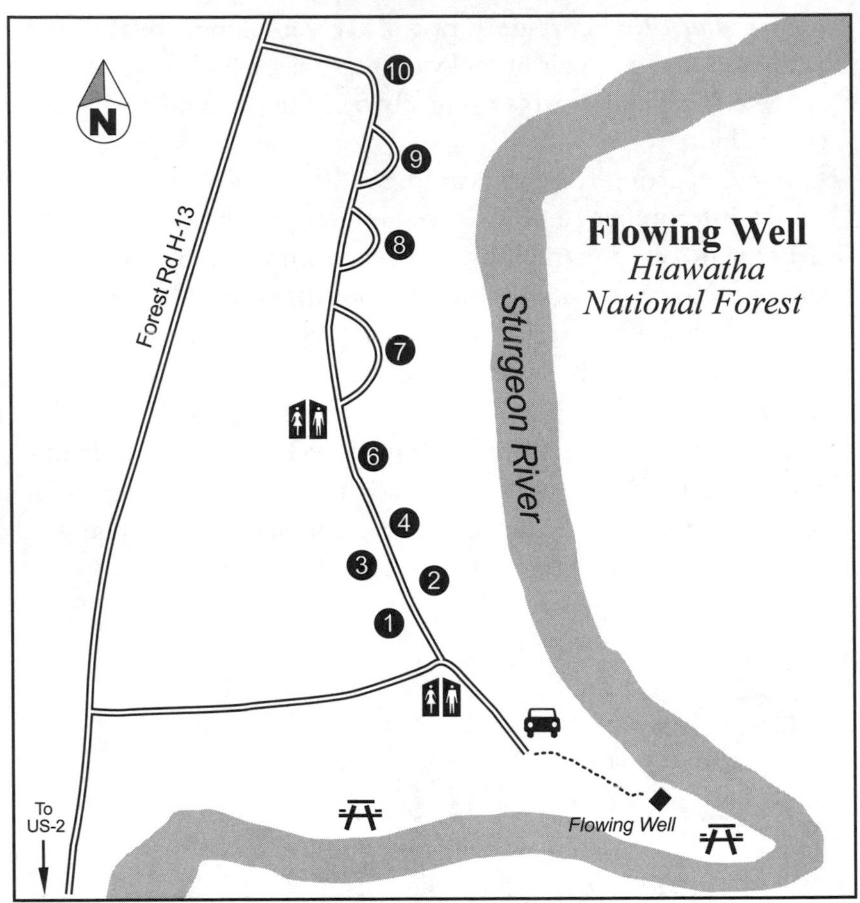

The campground's name is from the well in the picnic area that was the result of oil exploration in 1929. They drilled 1,160 feet into the ground only to watch water, not crude, bubble up. They abandoned the test drill but left the well flowing, and today it produces 100 gallons a minute from the same strata of sandstone which forms the Pictured Rocks 30 miles due north on Lake Superior.

Directions: Flowing Well is right off H-13, three miles north of US-2 and 25 miles west of Manistique.

Campground: Flowing Well has 10 sites that are well spread out and isolated from each other. Six of the sites are on the edge of the Sturgeon River with a view of this scenic waterway. Each site is equipped with tables and fire rings. The only source of water in the campground is the flowing well in the picnic area, which is safe to drink, but has a heavy iron and sulfur content. To many people it tastes like somebody's been boiling eggs all morning.

Day-use Facilities: The campground also has a small picnic area with tables and grills on a grassy point that is surrounded by the Sturgeon River on three sides. The flowing well is located here.

Fishing: The Sturgeon River is fished for brook trout during the summer and steelhead and salmon in the spring and fall. There are bait and tackle shops in Rapid River, 14 miles to the west on US-2.

Canoeing: Short paddling trips are possible both north and south of the campground on the Sturgeon River. You can put in at the campground and then paddle south for an easy 3-mile trip down the gentle flowing Sturgeon before pulling out at County Road 497, just beyond US-2.

For something more thrilling there's Tenmile Rapids. Driving 2 miles north on H-13 and put in at 14 Mile Bridge. It is a 4-mile paddle back to the campground.

Season: Flowing Well is open from mid-May through October and is a lightly used facility. You can reserve a site in advance through the National Recreation Reservation Service ☎ 877-444-6777 🌐 www.recreation.gov.

123

Little Bay de Noc

Hiawatha National Forest

Campground: Rustic
County: Delta
Nearest Community: Rapid River
Sites: 38
Reservations: Yes

Fee: $12–$13
Information: Rapid River Ranger District
☎ (906) 474-6442
🌐 www.fs.usda.gov/hiawatha

The Hemlock Cathedral in the Little Bay de Noc Recreation Area is a stand of hemlocks that somehow survived the logging era Michigan experienced at the turn of the century. In Escanaba, residents could see the giant trees on the other side of Little Bay de Noc, and by the late 1800s the spot was a popular weekend retreat known as Maywood. When a small resort hotel was built there in 1904, this pocket of old growth was preserved from the loggers advancing down the Stonington Peninsula.

Today the Hemlock Cathedral is as quiet and impressive as it was a century ago and is where you go to see what a 300-year-old tree looks like. These giant pines are just one reason why Little Bay de Noc is a popular stop for campers and nature lovers crossing the Upper Peninsula.

Directions: Little Bay de Noc is on the west shore of the Stonington Peninsula. From US-2, east of Rapid River, head south on County Road 513, to reach the campground in 7 miles.

Campground: Little Bay de Noc has 38 individual sites along three loops. The sites in the North Maywood (sites No. 1–14) and Oaks Loop (sites No. 17–29) are scattered in a hemlock/hardwood forest and offer a bit privacy from your neighbors. Twin Springs Loop (sites No. 30–38) is an open grassy area, and the sites here provide the best views of the bay and Gladstone on the other side. All sites face Little Bay de Noc, allowing campers to enjoy a cooling breeze during the summer, but other than Two Springs Loop, most sites do not have a clear view of the water. Facilities include fire rings, tables, vault toilets, and drinking water.

Day-use Facilities: A picnic area is located between the campground and Hunter's Point Boat Launch. Picnic tables and grills are scattered in a large grassy area that overlooks a sandy beach and designated swimming area on the bay. From the picnic area or anywhere along the shoreline, the sunsets on a clear evening are spectacular.

Fishing: Hunter's Point is an improved boat launch with a separate entrance a half mile north of the campground entrance on County Road 513. Little Bay de Noc is generally regarded as one of the finest walleyes fisheries in Michigan as well as a place to go for yellow perch and smallmouth bass. There are bait and tackle shops in Rapid River and Gladstone.

Hiking: The recreation area has four trails that total 3.5 miles. To view the Hemlock Cathedral, hike the half-mile Maywood History Trail, a paved, interpretive path that departs from near the Maywood Groups sites. The Bayshore Trail is 1.2 miles long and skirts the shoreline from the boat launch to Twin Springs Loop. The Big Hemlocks Trail is a 0.8-mile loop that also wanders through the Hemlock Cathedral, and the White Pine Trail is 1.3 miles long. It departs from the Bayshore Trail and crosses to the east side of the park road.

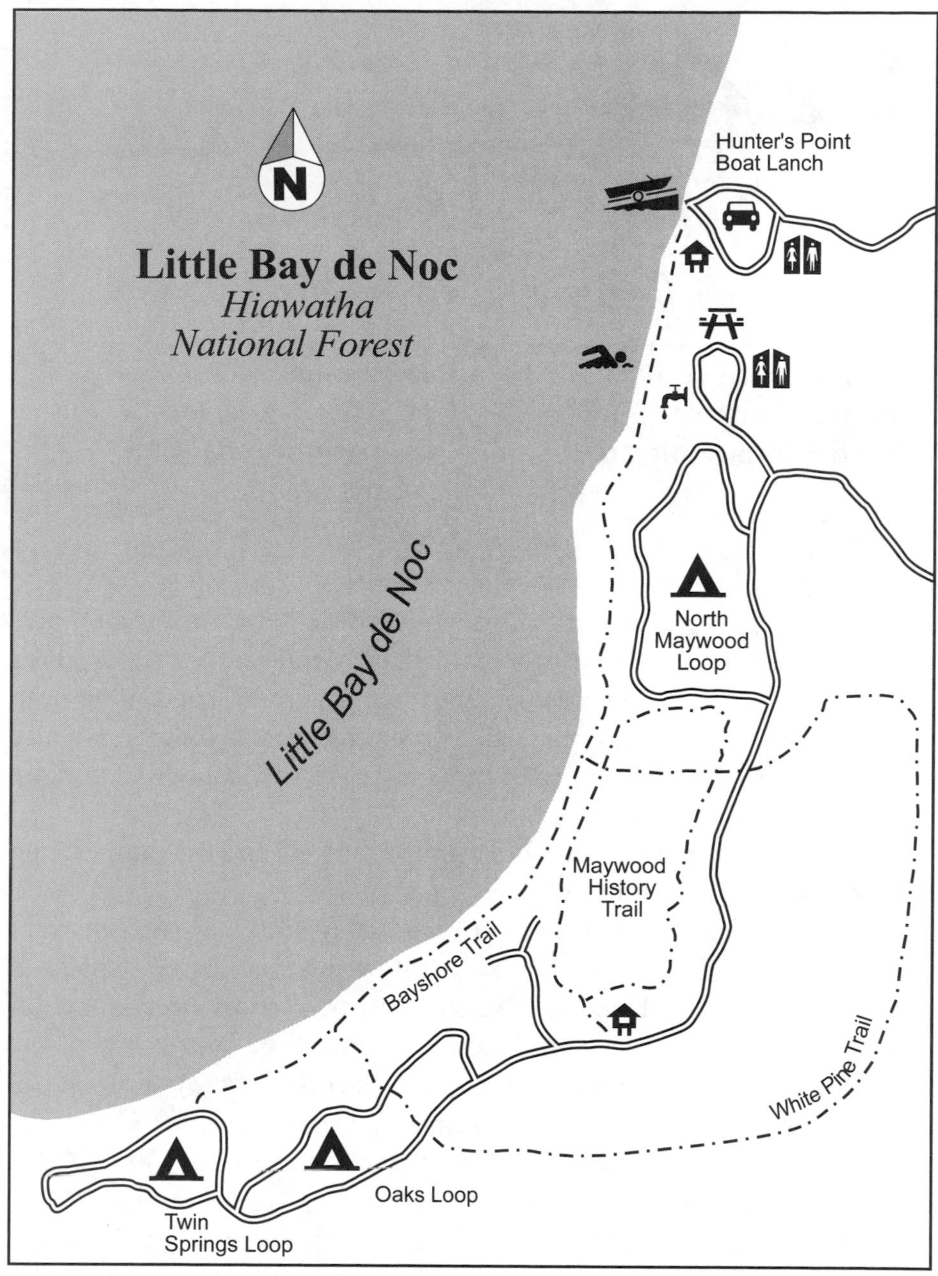

Season: Little Bay de Noc is a popular facility in the Hiawatha National Forest but large enough that it is usually not a problem securing a site other than holiday weekends. The campground is open mid-May to early October, and sites can be reserved through the National Recreation Reservation Service ☎ 877-444-6777 🌐 www.recreation.gov.

124

Fox Park

Cedarville Township

Campground: Rustic
County: Menominee
Nearest Community: Cedar River
Sites: 20
Reservations: No
Fee: $10
Information: Cedarville Township Hall
☎ (906) 863-4721

Only 30 miles north of the Wisconsin border, Fox Park is a 60-acre Cedarville Township park with more than a mile of shoreline along Green Bay. It also includes a rustic beach campground, and, if you can stand all the Cheddarheads that will be camping around you, this is a nice and very affordable place to spend the night. The fee, only $10 a night, hasn't been raised in years.

Directions: From Escanaba, head south on M-35 and the campground will be reached in 25 miles.

Campground: The park has 20 rustic sites with 11 of them right along Lake Michigan. Sand and surf will be less than three steps from your trailer. Site No. 12 on the beach is surrounded by brush for a bit of privacy. In all the rest you'll know your neighbor by the end of the weekend. If you're not camping along the beach, then you're near M-35, and the traffic noise might get tiresome on a busy weekend. Otherwise there is a campground host that enforces quiet hours from 11 PM to 6 AM. Facilities include tables, fire pits, and vault toilets.

Day-use Facilities: The park has a nice picnic area with tables, grills, and playground equipment. The beach here is beautiful, wide, and sandy. There are no lifeguards.

Season: The campground is open from Memorial Day to Labor Day. The beach sites fill up fast, but there is usually an opening in this small county park for another tent or trailer.

125 Cedar River North

Escanaba State Forest

Campground: Rustic	**Reservations:** No
County: Menominee	**Fee:** $15
Nearest Community: Cedar River	**Information:** Escanaba DNR office
Sites: 17	☎ (906) 786-2351

The water from the well at the Cedar River North State Forest Campground is not to be missed. It's so cold, pure, and sweet that locals come to the remote campground from miles around to fill up large bottles and take it home with them.

It tastes best, however, on a warm summer evening just after you finish pitching your tent or setting up the trailer in this state forest campground. This is a pleasant place to set up camp. There always seems to be a site open, and you can spend a day or two hiking, mountain biking, trout fishing, or relaxing without leaving the campground.

Directions: From M-35, just north of the town of Cedar River, turn west onto River Road where there is a state forest campground sign. Follow River Road in a northwest direction for 6 miles to the posted campground entrance.

Campground: Cedar River North has 17 rustic sites in a wooded setting. Four of the sites are right on the banks of the river where you can pitch your tent in the shade of towering pines and spend the evening watching trout rise. The rest of the sites are away from the river. Unfortunately, many of the sites are missing a table or fire ring.

Fishing: The Big Cedar River flows 80 miles from northern Menominee County to Lake Michigan. It is stocked with brook, rainbow, and brown trout and also hosts a steelhead run in the spring.

Hiking: Near the campground is the Cedar River Pathway. This state forest pathway totals 8.5 miles and has three crossover spurs that form four different loops. Loop 1 (2 miles in length), Loop 2 (3.5 miles), and Loop 3 (5 miles) are predominantly in mature stands of hardwoods and pines and twice break out at the Cedar River. Loop 4 is the longest at seven miles and crosses over River Road to wind through an area that was actively logged in 1994. The main trailhead is in a parking lot, reached before you enter the campground itself.

Season: Cedar River North is a lightly used facility. There are usually few problems getting a site even on the weekends.

126

Tourist Park

City of Marquette

Campground: Modern and semi-modern
County: Marquette
Nearest Community: Marquette
Sites: 110
Reservations: Yes
Fee: $18–$32
Information: Park office
☎ (906) 228-0465

A half century ago, the trend in northern Michigan was for communities to build "tourist parks," public campgrounds located in town. The idea was to attract more tourists to the area by offering them an inexpensive place to stay near all the sights they wanted to see.

The tradition lingers on in the Upper Peninsula where a handful of towns still maintain tourist parks with the best one located in Marquette. Built in 1951, Marquette Tourist Park is a campground on 40 acres along the Dead River minutes from the Northern Michigan University campus. Its location allows you to spend the day exploring the museums and sights surrounding the largest city in the Upper Peninsula while enjoying a campfire at night.

Directions: From US-41/M-28, on the west side of the city near the Wal-Mart store, turn north on County Road 492. Continue on CR-492 as it swings east and becomes Wright Street and then turn north on Sugarloaf Avenue. The campground entrance will be a half mile on the left.

Campground: Tourist Park has 110 campsites, including 61 with electric hook-ups and 38 with full hook-ups—electricity, water, and sewer. All hook-ups are 30-amp service. Some sites are open, but most are shaded by towering red pines, birch, and hardwoods.

The most interesting sites are 11 designated for tents. The rustic sites have a view of the water, and three of them are on the edge of the shoreline where the Dead River is less than 15 feet from your picnic table.

Tent sites are $18 a night, electric sites are $27, and full hook-ups are $32. There is also a dump station and restrooms with showers.

A short drive north of Tourist Park on County Road 550 is Little Presque Isle State Forest Recreation Area that offers some of the most scenic hiking in Marquette, including sweeping vistas from Hogback Mountain.

Day-use Facilities: Other park amenities include three picnic areas with tables and grills, a children's play area, a softball field, and a sandy beach that is split in the middle by a grayish rock so flat and large three people could sunbathe on top of it. The water of the Dead River is much more suitable for swimming than the nearby Lake Superior beaches.

Fishing: A small dam has turned this stretch of the Dead River into a reservoir, an undeveloped body of water with only the campground at its east end. In the summer the Dead River Basin attracts paddlers in canoes and kayaks and anglers casting for northern pike and panfish. Near its entrance on County Road 550, just below the power dam, is a handicap-accessible fishing pier on the Dead River where salmon and trout are caught. There is no boat ramp at the park, but hand-carried boats can be launched.

Cycling: At the park's entrance on Sugar Loaf Road is Marquette Bike Path, 6 miles of paved trail that loops around the city. Cycling is such a popular way for campers to reach Marquette's museums and other attractions that bicycles are rented at Tourist Park.

Next to the fishing pier is a trailhead for the Noquemanon Ski Trail that heads west towards Ishpeming and in the summer is used by mountain bikers.

Hiking: A five-minute drive north on CR-550 is Little Presque Isle State Forest Recreation Area, a 3,040-acre tract offering some of the finest hiking in the area. Sugar Loaf Trail is a 1.2-mile climb to the top of the granite knob for a panoramic view of the Lake Superior shoreline. Wetmore Pond is an interpretive trail with an extensive boardwalk through bogs and wetlands. Hogback Mountain Trail is a 3.2-mile trek with a steep climb to its rocky peak for an even more lofty view than Sugarloaf.

Season: Tourist Park campground is open from mid-May to mid-October. You can reserve sites after Jan. 1 by calling the Parks and Recreation Department ☎ 906-228-0460 or online at 🌐 www.mqtcty.org.

127

Perkins

Marquette County Park

Campground: Modern and semi-modern
County: Marquette
Nearest Community: Big Bay
Sites: 73
Reservations: Yes
Fee: $15–$17
Information: Park office
☎ (906) 345-9353
🌐 www.co.marquette.mi.us

County Road 550 heads north from Marquette and in 26 miles ends at Big Bay, a delightful village overlooking Lake Independence and nestled in the foothills of the Huron Mountains.

Established in 1904, Big Bay was a bustling lumber town and the site of one of Henry Ford's many factories in the Upper Peninsula. It's best known as the place where scenes from the 1959 film *Anatomy of a Murder*, starring Jimmy Stewart and Lee Remick, were shot. The story is true and today you can still belly up to the bar for a beer at the Lumberjack Tavern where the famous murder occurred.

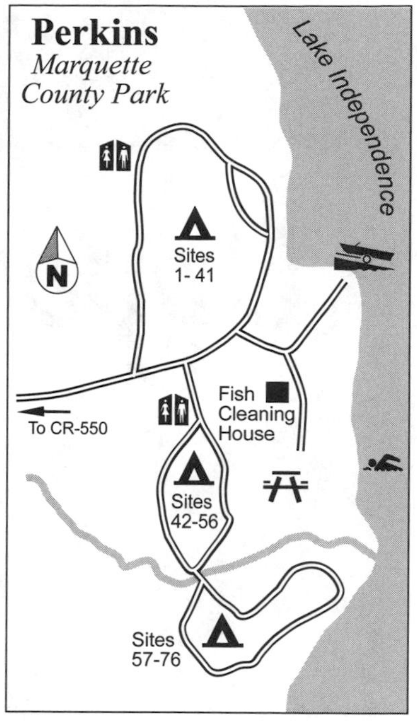

On the edge of town is Perkins Park, a Marquette County campground with 72 campsites on the west shore of Lake Independence. Perkins Park is a pleasant campground that is an easy walk to "downtown Big Bay" and well worth spending a couple of nights at to explore the area.

Directions: From Marquette head north on County Road 550 and in 25 miles, just before entering Big Bay, is the entrance to Perkins Park.

Campground: Perkins Park has 73 sites, 29 with full hook-ups including 6 that are pull-through sites with 50-amp service, 21 electric-only, and 23 rustic. The park also maintains a rental-tent at one site. The sites are scattered along three loops in a well-shaded area and almost a dozen of them have a good view of the lake.

Perkins Park has undergone a series of upgrades over the years that included new restroom and shower buildings, utility upgrades, additional play equipment, and a dump station for recreational vehicles. Full hook-ups are $25 a night, pull-through sites $27, electric-only $20, tent sites $15 a night, and the rental platform tent is $20 a night. There are discounts for stays five nights or longer.

Day-use Facilities: The campground has a small sandy beach and marked swimming area on Lake Independence along with a bathhouse. Nearby is play equipment for children, a picnic area with a pavilion, and a basketball court.

Fishing: Lake Independence is spread across 1,860 acres and reaches depths of 30 feet in places. It is regarded as a good fishery for northern pike, walleye, and smallmouth bass. Many anglers also fish it for yellow perch. Perkins Park features a boat ramp, a fish cleaning house, and a wonderful barrier-free fishing pier for boatless campers. Within Big Bay is a sports and bait shop that sells tackle, minnows, and crawlers.

Season: Perkins Park is open Memorial Day to mid-October and occasionally fills on weekends. You can reserve sites in advance by calling the park office ☎ 906-345-9353 after Jan. 1 for the following summer. Reservations require the first night's camping fee plus a $2 booking fee.

Western Upper Peninsula

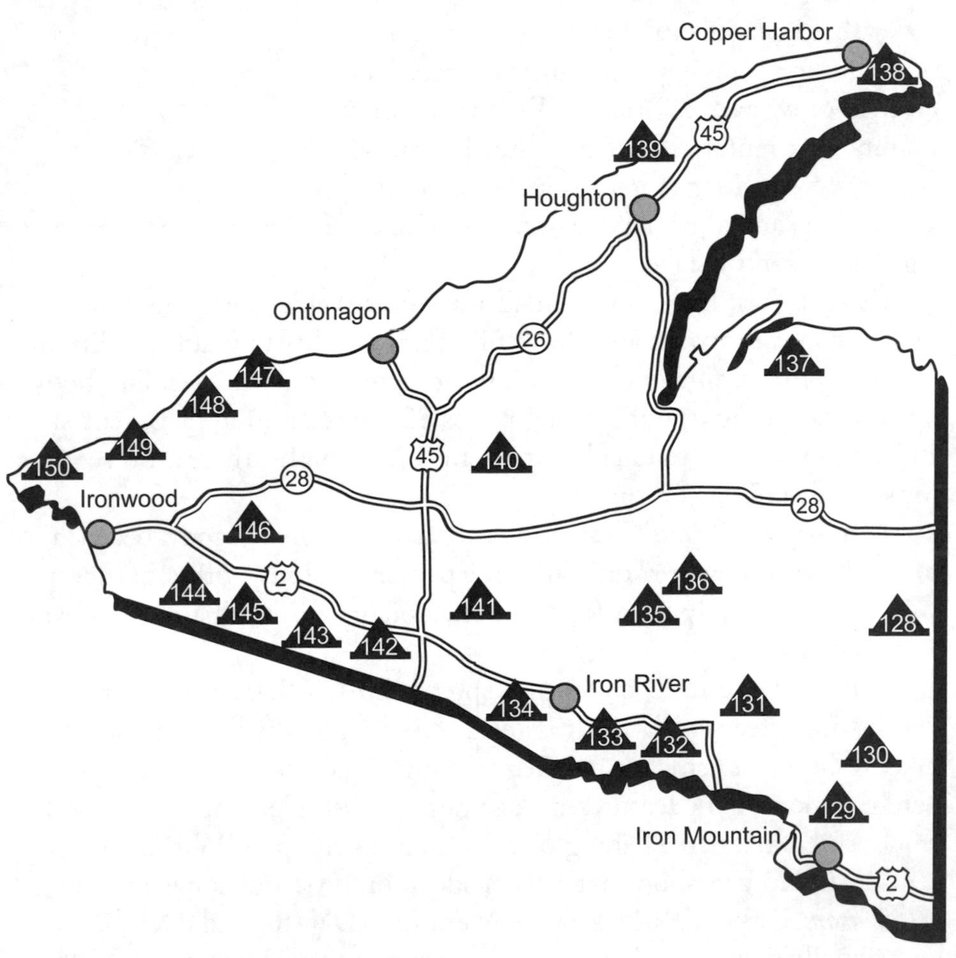

#	PARK	MODERN	SEMI-MODERN	RUSTIC	SITES	DAY-USE FACILITIES	FISHING	HIKING	BIRDING	INTERPRETIVE CENTER	BIKING	CANOEING/ KAYAKING	BOATING
128	Squaw Lake			•	15		•						
129	Carney Lake			•	16	•	•						
130	Gene's Pond			•	14		•	•					
131	Glidden Lake			•	23	•	•	•					
132	Bewabic	•	•		137	•	•	•				•	
133	Pentoga	•			100	•	•	•					
134	Lake Ottawa			•	32	•	•	•					
135	Lake Ste. Kathryn			•	24	•	•	•					
136	Norway Lake			•	27	•	•	•					
137	Big Eric's Bridge			•	20								
138	Fort Wilkins	•			160	•	•	•		•			
139	F.J. McLain	•			98	•	•	•					
140	Bob Lake			•	17	•	•	•					
141	Burned Dam			•	5		•					•	
142	Clark Lake		•		48	•	•	•					
143	Moosehead Lake			•	13		•						
144	Henry Lake			•	11		•				•		
145	Pomeroy Lake			•	17		•				•		
146	Lake Gogebic	•	•		127	•	•	•					
147	Union Bay	•			99	•	•	•		•			
148	Presque Isle			•	50	•	•	•					
149	Black River Harbor			•	40	•	•	•					
150	Little Girl's Point	•	•		32	•	•						

128
Squaw Lake
Escanaba River State Forest

Campground: Rustic
County: Marquette
Nearest Community: Witch Lake
Sites: 15
Reservations: No
Fee: $15
Information: Gwinn DNR office
☎ (906) 346-9201

Squaw Lake is a small state forest campground in the remote southwest corner of Marquette County. It takes a little effort to drive to it, but in doing so you are ensuring yourself a quiet evening in the middle of the Upper Peninsula in a campground that is rarely filled.

What price is solitude these days?

There are more scenic state forest campgrounds in the Upper Peninsula than Squaw Lake, but for those who camp here that's unimportant. Squaw Lake's trophy fishing is the reason they seek out this obscured campground.

Directions: In Marquette, stock up on your favorite lures and bait—there is little in Witch Lake—and then head west on US-41/M-28 for 27 miles and south on M-95 for 18 miles. At Witch Lake turn west on Fence River Road and follow it past the posted entrance road to Horseshoe Lake. In another 2 miles head north on Squaw Lake Road, a narrow winding road through the woods which will lead to the campground in 2 miles.

Campground: Squaw Lake has 15 rustic sites on two loops on the west side of the lake. None of them are directly on the water or even in view of it, but all are well spread in very private settings. Three sites are large enough to handle 40-foot recreational vehicles. One pleasant aspect of the campground is that Squaw Lake is home to nesting loons and often the birds can be heard and seen in the evenings.

Anglers launch their boat at Squaw Lake State Forest Campground southwest of Marquette.

Fishing: The boat launch is separate from the campground and features a cement ramp and parking for seven vehicles and trailers. The lake covers 247 acres and reaches depths of 80 feet, the reason for its long history of being stocked with rainbow trout and splake. Most anglers do better fishing for bluegill and smallmouth bass. Since 1995 Squaw Lake has produced seven Master Angler fishing awards. Five of them were for bluegills that ranged from 10.5 to 12 inches in length. Another was for a 21-inch long smallmouth bass. One of the best spots to fish for bluegills is near the campground at the south end of the lake where there are some remnants of fish shelters in 10 to 20 feet of water.

Season: This is a very lightly used campground.

129

Carney Lake

Copper Country State Forest

Campground: Rustic
County: Dickinson
Nearest Community: Iron Mountain
Sites: 16
Reservations: No
Fee: $15
Information: Crystal Falls DNR office
☎ (906) 875-6622

The road to Carney Lake is a rough ride of flying gravel and rising dust, but if its washboard surface doesn't slow you down, the scenery will. Along the way you pass towering rock outcroppings, rolling wooded ridges on the horizon, and possibly even some wildlife ranging from flocks of wild turkeys to whitetail deer.

By the time you arrive at in this isolated spot in Dickinson County, you'll be ready to kick back and relax for a few days. This is an excellent place to do it. Often called one of the most scenic state forest campgrounds in the Upper Peninsula, Carney Lake offers not only a spectacular setting but also good fishing.

Directions: Carney Lake is 16 miles northeast of Iron Mountain. Just before US-2 swings west to cross the Michigan/Wisconsin border, continue north on M-95 for four miles to Merriman, the site of a small store and restaurant. Turn east on Merriman Truck Trail. The first 2 miles are paved and then the road becomes gravel. At an intersection posted with a State Forest Campground sign, you turn south and follow the dirt road for 5 miles to Carney Lake. Along the way you pass the public access site for Rock Lake.

Campground: Carney Lake has 16 sites that are well spread out on single loop in an area forested in primarily birch. Eight sites are right on the lake with a good view of the shoreline. The rest are only a short walk away from the water. Facilities include vault toilets, tables, fire rings, and a hand pump for water.

Day-use Facilities: The campground has a picnic table in an open grassy area along the lake. There is no beach here, but the sandy bottom of the lake provides some opportunities for swimming.

Fishing: Carney Lake is a beautiful body of water. There are a few cabins on the lake, but for the most part they are set away from the water and hidden in the large birches that ring the shoreline. The campground has an improved boat launch with a separate parking area large enough to handle a half dozen vehicles and trailers. The lake is primarily fished for walleye and smallmouth bass. Pick up tackle and bait in Iron Mountain before arriving at the campground.

Season: This is another lightly used campground in the Western Upper Peninsula.

Carney Lake and many state forest campgrounds in the Western U.P. offer outstanding fishing for walleye as well as smallmouth bass and bluegills.

130

Gene's Pond

Copper Country State Forest

Campground: Rustic
County: Dickinson
Nearest Community: Felch Mountain
Sites: 14
Reservations: No
Fee: $15
Information: Crystal Falls DNR office
☎ (906) 875-6622

We were in the land of misnomers. We couldn't find any mountains in Felch Mountain; Gene's Pond, where we camped that evening, is no pond; and Labor Day, one of the busiest holidays for campgrounds, was a quiet weekend in northern Dickinson County. You've gotta love the Upper Peninsula, where a hill is a mountain, a lake is a pond, and a crowded campground is when there is another family two sites away.

Part of the Copper Country State Forest, this rustic campground is what we expect to find in the U.P., small, out-of-the-way, wooded sites that are well spread out. This is a quiet place where you can spend an evening observing wildlife.

Directions: Gene's Pond is 6.5 miles northwest of Felch Mountain. From M-69 turn north onto Country Road G-67 and then west on Country Road 422 where the campground is posted.

Campground: Gene's Pond has 14 sites well spread out in a mature hardwood forest on two loops. None of the sites are directly on the water, but all are a short walk away from this undeveloped lake. Facilities include fire rings, vault toilets, tables, and a hand pump for water.

Hiking: Technically a flooded portion of the Sturgeon River's East Branch, Gene's Pond is surrounded on its south side by marshes. The wetlands and the open water make this a crossroads for wildlife, the reason the campground is designated as a Wildlife Viewing Area by the Department of Natural Resources. Best ways to spot wildlife are to be on the lake at dusk or hiking Gene's Pond Pathway.

This trail is a 2.3-mile loop that departs from near the boat launch and heads east through the rolling woods. It begins on an old two-track, switches to an overgrown trail, and within a half mile leads to the top of a rocky bluff where you can view most of Gene's Pond and the scenic wetlands that surround it. The other interesting stop along the pathway is Old Hans Mine. In the 19th century it was a small iron mining operation; today all that remains is a large pit, a few rotting timbers, and a small hill of tailings that have long since been covered by moss and ferns.

Fishing: There is an unimproved boat launch at the campground. Gene's Pond is reputed to be a good fishing hole with catches of smallmouth bass, crappie, bluegill, and perch possible.

Season: This is a lightly used facility.

131

Glidden Lake

Copper Country State Forest

Campground: Rustic
County: Iron
Nearest Community: Crystal Falls
Sites: 23

Reservations: No
Fee: $15
Information: Crystal Falls DNR office
☎ (906) 875-6622

Located southwest of Crystal Falls in the corner of Iron County is Glidden Lake, a pleasant state forest campground on a small, remote body of water. Demand for spots in this campground is not heavy during most of the summer, and its lakeshore sites are often available. Departing from the campground is the Lake Mary Plains Pathway, a trail system providing hiking opportunities for those who want to walk for an hour or all day.

Directions: From Crystal Falls, head east on M-69 for 4 miles and then south on Lake Mary Plains Road to Glidden Lake Campground.

Campground: Glidden Lake has 23 sites that are well spread out on two loops in a heavily forested area. Ten sites are close enough to the shoreline for a view of the lake through the trees. The campground has vault toilets, hand pump for water, and tables and fire rings at every site.

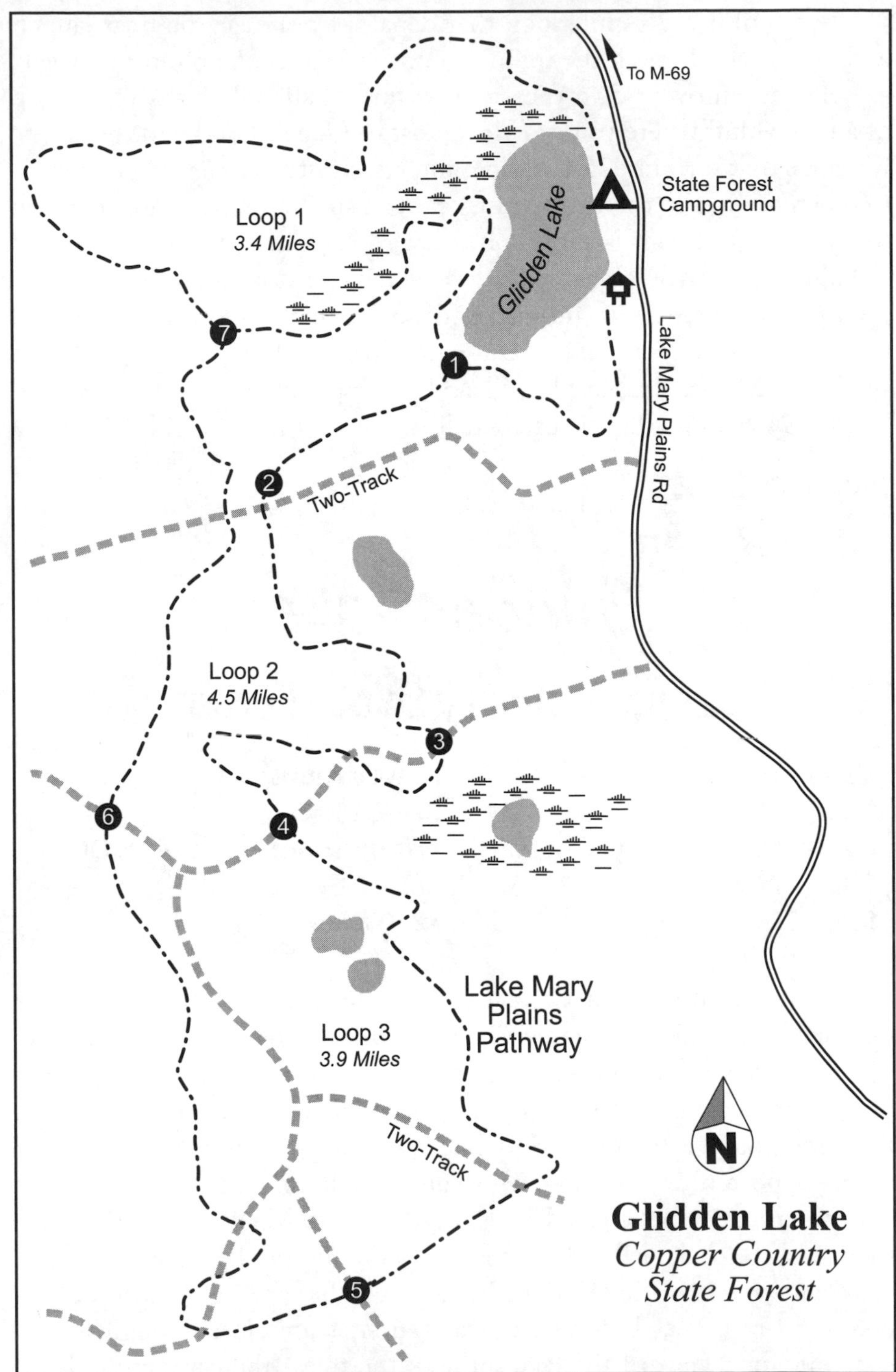
To M-69
State Forest Campground
Glidden Lake
Loop 1
3.4 Miles
7
1
2
Two-Track
Lake Mary Plains Rd
Loop 2
4.5 Miles
3
6
4
Lake Mary Plains Pathway
Loop 3
3.9 Miles
Two-Track
5
N
Glidden Lake
Copper Country State Forest

Day-use Facilities: The campground has a picnic area with a small sandy beach where you can quickly cool down on a hot summer afternoon.

Hiking: Since being partially destroyed by a forest fire in 1983, Lake Mary Plains Pathway has been restored as one of the finest trail systems in Iron County. A portion of its first loop has also been upgraded into a handicap-accessible nature trail that includes a long boardwalk through the swamp at the north end of Glidden Lake.

The pathway is comprised of three loops that total more than 9 miles, with the perimeter being a 7.3-mile walk. Designed primarily as a cross country ski trail, Loop 3 has a tendency to be wet and sandy in spots and, having been recently logged, is not nearly as interesting. The first two loops can be combined into a 4.5-mile hike that is hilly in stretches and very scenic at the end. The entire system is extremely well marked with trail maps at almost every junction and is accessed through trailheads in the campground and the parking area for the beach.

Fishing: There is an unimproved boat launch in the day-use area of the campground. Glidden Lake is an undeveloped body of water that is fished for walleye and perch.

Season: This is a light to moderately used facility.

132

Bewabic

State Park

Campground: Modern and semi-modern	**Reservations:** Yes
County: Iron	**Fee:** $16–$20 plus a vehicle entry fee
Nearest Community: Crystal Falls	**Information:** State park office
Sites: 137	☎ (906) 875-3324

Bewabic State Park is located on the corner of the first Fortune Lake. Head south in a canoe or boat and you'll enter the Second Lake, the Third Lake, and finally the Fourth Lake. This chain of small lakes extends south of US-2 and is the most attractive feature of the 315-acre park in Iron County.

Thanks to its Civilian Conservation Corps (CCC) past, Bewabic is also blessed with several classic log-and-stone structures that are still in use. Even more unique, Bewabic is the only state park in Michigan to offer tennis courts.

Directions: The park is located 4 miles west of Crystal Falls on US-2.

Campground: Bewabic has 133 modern sites and four semi-modern ones (no electric hook-ups) in a campground located on a hill above the lake. The sites are located along three loops and range from many in an open grassy setting to No. 84–119, which are in a wooded area. More than a third of the modern sites have 50-amp service while the semi-modern ones are walk-in sites. All the sites are well spread out and, thanks to buffer strips between them, offer a surprising amount of privacy for a modern campground.

Modern sites are $20 a night and walk-in are $16. During the off-season, when the restrooms are closed, the rate drops to $16 and $10.

Day-use Facilities: Bewabic's beach on Fortune Lake is limited, but the rest of the day-use facility is a lightly shaded, grassy area that features tables, play equipment and a shelter. Most unusual are the tennis courts. Built in the 1940s when the area was a county park, the courts remained when the state acquired the land in 1966, and now Bewabic is only state park where visitors arrive packing their racket along with their fishing pole.

Fishing: A small boat and motor can reach all four Fortune Lakes in a day, and anglers often do in their search for perch, largemouth and smallmouth bass, walleye, and bluegill. Most anglers concentrate in First Lake, the largest one at 192 acres with a depth of 72 feet. Bewabic maintains an improved boat launch near the day-use area with parking for 12 vehicles and rigs. Additional parking is allowed along the park drive. Shore fishermen can also wet a line, and perhaps the best spot is off the island at the north end of the park. There is a steep drop off on the far side of it where it's possible to catch perch and bluegill.

Hiking: The Bewabic Nature Trail is 2-mile path that begins at site No. 121 in the campground and drops through the wooded section in the south end of the park before circling back to the day-use area. There is also a very short trail that follows the shoreline of the island just off the day-use area. Visitors use a footbridge to reach the trail.

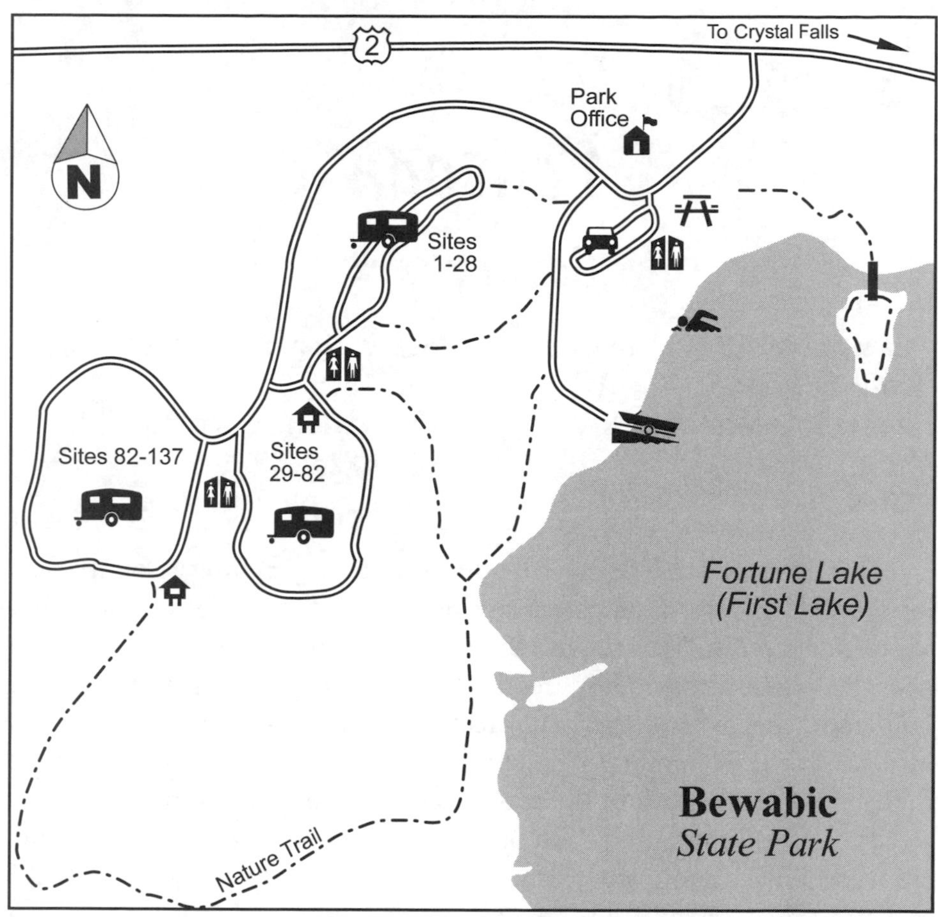

Canoeing: The chain of lakes makes for an ideal day trip, departing from the state park and returning through the four lakes, connected by small channels. Keep in mind that there are many cabins on the first two and no public land, other than the state park, on any of the lakes where paddlers could camp overnight.

Season: The campground fills up only for Fourth of July weekend during the summer. To reserve a campsite contact Michigan State Park Central Reservations ☎ 800-447-2757 🌐 www.midnrreservations.com.

133

Pentoga

County Park

Campground: Modern
County: Iron
Nearest Community: Crystal Falls
Sites: 100
Reservations: No
Fee: $18–$20
Information: Park office
☎ (906) 265-3979
🌐 www.pentogapark.net

There is usually a difference of opinion as to why Pentoga County Park is such a great place to camp. Ask any kid there and it's the water slides that make this place so special. Located on the south end of Chicagon Lake near the Wisconsin border in Iron County, Pentoga features slides that can only be reached after getting your feet wet. You splash your way 20 yards into the lake's swimming area, climb up either slide, and swish! You're flying down the ramp into the cool, clear waters of Chicagon Lake.

That's good old fashion fun on a hot day in August, but many adults enjoy Pentoga County Park for another reason. This place is loaded with Indian history, legend, and lore. Where else in Michigan can you camp next to Ojibway burial grounds complete with spirit houses?

Several interpretive displays cover the significance of this spot, including a huge stone monument that was erected in 1934 denoting the park as the last home of the Ojibway Indians in Iron County and honoring their chief, Mush-Quo-No-Na-Bi, and his wife, Pen-To-ga, whom the park is named after.

The area was discovered in 1851 when Guy H. Carleton, a government surveyor, stumbled onto a little known Indian village. The lake and its trout fishery was such a favorite gathering spot for the tribes that the small trees along the shore today are due to, not loggers, but Indians clearing the area for their tepees.

The tribe dwindled in numbers until 1891 when the chief and his wife sold the land and moved away. By 1903 only a few burial houses and a brush fence remained from the ancient village. Then along came Iron County engineer Herbert Larson who convinced local officials to preserve the area and restore the grounds for its historical significance, and in 1922 Pentoga became one of the first county parks in the state.

Indian spirit houses are one of the historic features of Pentoga County Park in Iron County.

Directions: From Iron Mountain, follow US-2 through Wisconsin and back into Michigan. Three miles south of Crystal Falls turn west onto County Road 424 through the town of Alpha and past Indian Lake to the posted entrance of the park.

Campground: Pentoga Park has 100 sites with electric and water hook-ups on two loops. Sites are close together with little privacy but well shaded by large maples and oaks. Also within the campground are showers, a fish cleaning station, and a wood shed where firewood is sold nightly.

The rates are $18 a night for Iron County residents and $20 for non-residents. There is also a $3 registration fee.

Day-use Facilities: Pentoga's picnic grounds are a grassy area that leads down to the lakeshore. There is no beach here, but the lake has a sandy bottom that makes it ideal for wading and splashing around. Within day-use area is a stone bathhouse, picnic shelter, playground equipment, horseshoe pits, volleyball courts, and tennis courts.

Fishing: Pentoga does not have a boat launch, but there is an access site nearby on the south end of the lake. Chicagon Lake is a large body of water at 1,075 surface acres and a length of three miles. It's also a deep lake with one spot 115 feet deep. The spring-fed lake is best known for its northern muskellunge and often yields muskies more than 20 pounds. Most anglers, however, focus on walleye and smallmouth bass.

Hiking: The south end of the Pentoga Trail is located in the campground, and from here the foot path winds through paper birches until it reaches its northern trailhead on US-2, a walk of 2 miles.

Season: From July through mid-August this campground is often filled on the weekends and occasionally Wednesdays and Thursdays as well. In mid-August nightly rates drop to $17 for county residents and $18 for non-residents and the campground closes at the end of September.

134

Lake Ottawa

Ottawa National Forest

Campground: Rustic
County: Iron
Nearest Community: Iron River
Sites: 32
Reservations: No
Fee: $14
Information: Iron River Ranger District
☎ (906) 265-5139
🌐 www.fs.usda.gov/ottawa

The most popular campground in Ottawa National Forest is Lake Ottawa, located west of Iron River. Despite also being one of the largest with 32 sites, this facility is filled almost daily during July. Its popularity comes from the great swimming and scenic beauty of Lake Ottawa, a large body of water that is crystal clear and practically free of cottages, cabins, or any other development.

The Civilian Conservation Corps (CCC), whose work during the Great Depression is seen in parks and campgrounds across the Upper Peninsula, is evident at Lake Ottawa as well. Within the day-use area, the log picnic tables and lodge were built in the late 1930s by the CCC and are still being used today.

Directions: From Iron River head west on US-2 and in 2 miles turn south on M-73. Within a mile turn west on Lake Ottawa Road (also known as Forest Road 101) and follow the signs to the entrance of the park.

Campground: Lake Ottawa has 32 sites that are well spread out and isolated from each other in a maple forest. None of the sites are directly on the lake, but a short trail leads from the campground to the day-use beach area. Facilities include paved access roads and sites, pressurized water systems, and restrooms with flush toilets. There are no showers.

Day-use Facilities: Next to the campground is a grassy picnic area that leads to a sandy beach on Lake Ottawa. The swimming is excellent here.

Fishing: There is a fishing pier in the day-use area and an improved boat launch reached from a separate entrance next to the campground. Lake Ottawa covers 550 acres and reaches depths of 90 feet. The main species targeted is walleye, but anglers also catch northern pike, bass, and yellow perch.

Hiking: The Ge-Che Trail is an 11-mile system that extends between Lake Ottawa, Hagerman Lake to the south, and Brennan Lake to the east. You can pick-up the trail in the boat launch and then head east on the Breenan Lake Loop, a 3-mile hike, or south on the Ge-Che Loop, a 5-mile outing.

Season: Lake Ottawa is open mid-May to mid-September. This is a popular facility and often filled five out of seven days in July and most weekends in August. Best days to obtain a site are Sunday through Tuesday.

135

Lake Ste. Kathryn

Ottawa National Forest

Campground: Rustic
County: Iron
Nearest Community: Sidnaw
Sites: 24
Reservations: No
Fee: $12
Information: Kenton Ranger District
☎ (906) 852-3501
🌐 www.fs.usda.gov/ottawa

Lake Sainte Kathryn is located in the Kenton Ranger District of the Ottawa National Forest and features opportunities for both fishing and hiking. It is also a fairly large campground by national forest standards in a semi-remote location. Chances are good that a site will be available no matter when you arrive.

Directions: From Sidnaw on M-28, head south on South Sidnaw Road. Within 7 miles is the intersection with Marten Lake Road (Forest Road 2125) where the northern trailhead of Deer Marsh Trail is located. Continue another mile south on South Sidnaw Road to reach Lake Sainte Kathryn.

Campground: Lake Sainte Kathryn has 24 sites that are well spread out in a forested setting. Six sites are on the water with a nice view of the entire lake. The rest have a partial view of the water or are a short walk away. The campground includes tables, fire rings, hand pumps for water, and vault toilets.

Day-use Facilities: The campground has a picnic area with tables and grills along with a small beach adjacent to the boat launch.

Fishing: Sainte Kathryn is a 151-acre lake that reaches depths of up to 20 feet. It has been planted with fish cribs and today anglers target northern pike, walleye, and smallmouth bass. Along with a boat launch and parking for trailers and vehicles, the campground is equipped with a fishing cleaning area.

Hiking: The Deer Marsh Interpretive Trail is a 2.5-mile loop that includes a series of interpretive displays. The trail winds around a large marsh but for the most part offers dry footing. Early in the morning and at dusk the marsh is an excellent place to spot deer, beavers, and other wildlife. The main trailhead is a mile north of campground at the corner of South Sidnaw Road and Marten Lake Road, but a spur extends from the boat launch to the west side of the loop.

Season: Lake Sainte Kathryn is open from May through the firearm deer season in November. In the summer this is a lightly to moderately used campground where obtaining a site is rarely a problem.

136

Norway Lake

Ottawa National Forest

Campground: Rustic
County: Iron
Nearest Community: Sidnaw
Sites: 27
Reservations: No
Fee: $12
Information: Kenton District Office
☎ (906) 852-3501
🌐 www.fs.usda.gov/ottawa

Norway Lake is a delightful campground in a remote section of the Ottawa National Forest. In case you want to put even more distance between yourself and civilization, there is also a pair of walk-in campsites reached from Norway Lake Trail. Haul a tent and sleeping bag a half mile to the first one, and you are guaranteed a quiet evening alone on your own corner of the lake.

Directions: From M-28 in Sidnaw, head south on Sidnaw Road for 6 miles and then west on Forest Road 2400 where Norway Lake Campground is posted on the corner. You reach the campground in 2 miles.

Campground: Norway Lake has 27 drive-in sites on two loops on a bluff above the water. The first loop has 18 sites with half of them featuring an incredible view of the lake. Site No. 4 is the best of them all, a secluded spot in the pines with a panorama of this undeveloped lake. There are eight more sites on the second loop, but most are not within view of the lake. Campground facilities include a log shelter that makes for a nice place if it's raining. There is also a payphone in the picnic area.

Day-use Facilities: There is a pleasant picnic area in the campground with tables overlooking the lake from the bluff. Norway Lake also has a small sandy beach, a designated swimming area, and a bathhouse. A better beach is nearby in the day-use area of Nesbit Lake.

Fishing: There is an improved boat launch in the campground. Norway Lake has depths up to 20 feet and was planted with five fish cribs in 1988 and a few more in 1995 to provide more structure and

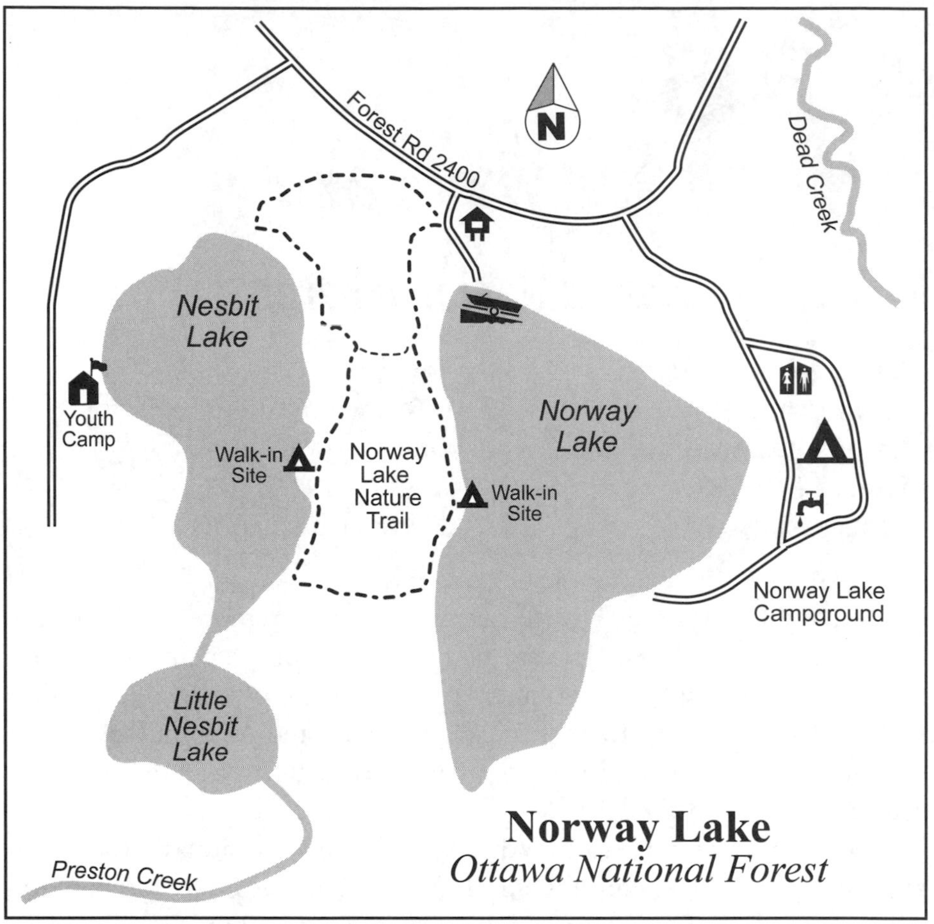

improve the fishing. Still, the action is reportedly slow for walleye and bass, the main species most anglers target.

Hiking: Norway Lake Trail is a 1.2-mile loop that departs the boat launch and winds along the narrow strip of land that separates its namesake lake from Nesbit Lake to the west. It features 15 interpretive posts that examine everything from deer tails to where you can look for pitcher plants. The charming aspect of this short trail is its pair of walk-in campsites, one on each lake.

The first is less than half mile from the trailhead. There are absolutely no facilities here, but the site is a level spot in a stand of red pine. At this point the trail swings away from Norway Lake and cuts over to Nesbit Lake. Heading north you reach the second campsite 0.7 mile from the boat launch trailhead. This one is delightful. It's situated on a small peninsula on the east side of the lake and usually catches enough wind to keep the bugs at bay. The spot is not very big nor very level, but there is more than enough room for a small tent that can be pitched only a few feet from the water. If there is no group at the youth camp, you'll virtually have the lake to yourself.

Season: Norway Lake is a lightly to moderately used campground.

137

Big Eric's Bridge

Copper Country State Forest

Campground: Rustic
County: Iron
Nearest Community: Skanee
Sites: 20
Reservations: No
Fee: $15
Information: Bargara DNR office
☎ (906) 353-6651

There are popular campgrounds that are usually overrun with trailers and families. There are rustic, hidden-in-the-woods campgrounds where only a handful of people spend the night. Then there is Big Eric's Bridge Campground. When we arrived one weekend in July, nobody was there.

This remote facility, located on the edge of the Huron Mountains in the Upper Peninsula, does attract a crowd in April and May when anglers line the banks of the Huron River in an effort to catch a steelhead or two. For much of the summer, however, Big Eric's Bridge Campground is a very lightly used facility. Sometimes it's just plain empty.

The state forest campground is located off by itself in upper Baraga County in a spot that's not on the way to anywhere. In an area of the state that is blessed with many scenic places to pitch a tent, this is one of the best in the U.P.

Directions: From L'Anse on US-41, head north out of town on Skanee Road. In 18 miles you'll pass through the town of Skanee and then reach the posted entrance of the campground in another 6 miles.

A camper enjoys Big Eric's Falls just below Big Eric's Bridge State Forest Campground northeast of L'Anse.

Campground: Big Eric's Bridge is a single loop of 20 rustic sites, well spread out and secluded in a hardwood forest with moderate undergrowth. Most of them are on the edge of a bluff above the Huron River. It is tough to see the river from your campsite. The gorge is so steep and the foliage so thick you barely get a glimpse of the water through the trees, but you can clearly hear what lies below. The cascading rumble of Big Eric Falls is the most charming aspect of the campground.

Waterfalls: Big Eric Falls begins just downstream from the Huron River bridge and is actually a series of small cascades, drops, and swirls that form a stretch of whitewater the length of the campground. There are three main cascades, the largest a five-foot drop over an embankment of smooth stone. In between the patches of whitewater are deep pools, the attention of anglers in the spring and overheated campers in the summer. All around are slabs of bronze-colored boulders.

You can spend a spare day searching and exploring three other nearby waterfalls along the Huron River that are accessed from Black Creek Road, passed just before reaching the campground. They include West Branch Falls, Eric's Falls, and Big Falls, and all are upstream from the bridge. Pick up the Baraga County Guide to Waterfalls brochure at the Baraga County Tourist Center in L'Anse on US-41 for directions and descriptions of all the cascades in the area.

Season: The campground is open year-round, but roads are not plowed beyond Skanee during the winter. Other than during the spring and fall steelhead runs, this is a lightly used facility.

138

Fort Wilkins

State Park

Campground: Modern
County: Keweenaw
Nearest Community: Copper Harbor
Sites: 160
Reservations: Yes
Fee: $23–$25 plus vehicle entry fee
Information: State park office
☎ (906) 289-4215

Sometimes you have to learn your history. Sometimes a lesson is inevitable. At Fort Wilkins State Park, a history lesson is inevitable but enjoyable even to children on summer vacation. This 698-acre park, which includes the narrow band of land between Lake Fanny Hooe and Lake Superior, is where the U.S. Army chose to build a military post in 1844 during the height of the Keweenaw Peninsula copper stampede.

The copper rush began in 1843, and Copper Harbor quickly became the center of exploration parties, newly formed mining companies, and "a rough population" of enterprising prospectors, miners, and speculators. Due to the seedy nature of the miners and the constant threat of Chippewa tribes wanting to reclaim their lost land, Secretary of War William Wilkins dispatched two companies of infantry to the remote region of Michigan. They arrived in late May of 1844, and by November Fort Wilkins was built.

The appearance of the fort has changed little since that boom-and-bust period and today is the main reason why the state park attracts almost 200,000 visitors a year. The vast majority of them arrive in the summer when this far north the area is so scenic and pleasant you're ready to enlist at the fort.

Directions: Fort Wilkins is 49 miles northeast of Houghton near the tip of the Keweenaw Peninsula. The main entrance to the park, including the fort, East Campground, and the day-use area, is a mile east of Copper Harbor on US-41.

Campground: Fort Wilkins has 160 modern sites and a Mini-cabin divided between the East Campground and the West Campground. Both are in wooded areas with a row of sites near the shoreline of Lake Fanny Hooe and a trail to the historic fort. Each has its own entrance off US-41 and the West Campground features nine pull-through sites with 50-amp service. All sites are equipped with tables, fire rings, and electric hook-ups. Within the campgrounds are restrooms with flush toilets and showers, sanitation stations, and pressurized water systems.

Nightly fees are $23 for a modern campsite, $25 for a site with 50-amp service, and $16 during the off-season when the restrooms are closed.

Day-use Facilities: Just east of the fort, there is a pleasant wooded picnic area that includes a shelter. Also in the area is a park store but no beach or designated swimming area on Lake Fanny Hooe.

Interpretive Centers: The centerpiece of the state park is the restored Fort Wilkins. When it was built, the stockade was the northernmost post in a chain of forts that stretched from Gulf of Mexico to the tip of the Keweenaw Peninsula in forming a western perimeter of national defense. In reality, however, the fort was of little military importance as the threat of Indian hostilities never materialized and the troops quickly discovered the Upper Peninsula winters were long and cold. In 1846, less than two years after it was built, Fort Wilkins was abandoned.

Although insignificant militarily, the fort is an outstanding example of a mid-nineteenth-century frontier outpost as 12 of its 19 buildings are from the original structure. The individual buildings are open daily from mid-May through mid-October from 8:30 AM to dusk. The historic buildings range from a kitchen and mess room to the bakery, company barracks, and hospital, and most contain restored furnishings and artifacts depicting the rough life troops endured here. From mid-June to Labor Day, interpreters in period dress give tours daily and add a touch of realism to the fort.

Also part of the state park is the Copper Harbor Lighthouse. The structure was built in 1866 and was occupied until 1919. Today the interior is restored as a lighthouse museum and can be visited through a boat tour operator that leaves the Copper City Harbor hourly from 10 AM to 6 PM Memorial Day to Labor Day. There is a fee for the boat tour to the lighthouse but none for viewing the fort other than a vehicle entry permit.

Fort Wilkins State Park includes a modern campground and a military fort that dates back to 1844.

Hiking: The park has almost 2 miles of trails, much of it connecting the fort with the campgrounds and day-use area. The Lake Superior Nature Trail begins in the picnic area and forms a circuit that runs along Lake Fanny Hooe, Copper Harbor, and Fanny Hooe Creek before passing the fort.

Fishing: Lake Fanny Hooe is stocked annually with rainbow trout and splake and in the past with walleye. Anglers also catch smallmouth bass. The park maintains a boat launch on Lake Fanny Hooe near the West Campground. There is no ramp on the Lake Superior side of the state park, but the DNR Waterways Division maintains a large public marina in Copper Harbor.

Season: Fort Wilkins is a popular tourist attraction so the campgrounds tend to fill a handful of weekends in July and early August. To reserve a campsite contact Michigan State Park Central Reservations ☎ 800-447-2757 🌐 www.midnrreservations.com.

139

F.J. McLain

State Park

Campground: Modern
County: Houghton
Nearest Community: Hancock
Sites: 98
Reservations: Yes
Fee: $26 plus vehicle entry fee
Information: State park office
☎ (906) 482-0278

One of only four state parks overlooking Lake Superior, F.J. McLain State Park is a 443-acre unit located northwest of the Houghton-Hancock area in the heart of Michigan's Copper Country.

Its best feature is 2 miles of Lake Superior shoreline and the bluff that rises above it. The sun melting into the shimmering horizon of Lake Superior on a clear evening in the summer makes for a spectacular sunset.

Directions: The park entrance is on M-203, 8 miles north of Hancock.

Campground: At one time McLain featured more than 20 sites on the edge of the shoreline bluff with great views of the Great Lake, but most have since been removed due to erosion. The park now has 98 modern sites on a single loop in an area lightly forested in red pine and oaks.

McLain also features some of the finest mini-cabins in the state park system. The six mini-cabins, perfect for a family of four, are along the park road that skirts the Lake Superior bluff, well away from the bustling campground. Three of the cabins are tucked back into the trees, and three of them are just off the road with a clear view of the water. Mini-cabins are $45 a night.

Day-use Facilities: The park has a small, sandy beach and a bathhouse located where Portage Lake Ship Canal flows into Lake Superior. The sand is protected from the ravages of the Great Lake by a long breakwall and the walk out to the Keweenaw Upper Entry Light makes for an interesting stroll. The park also has a picnic area with a shelter.

A surf angler, in the warm glow of a sunset, fishes Lake Superior at McLain State Park.

Hiking: Bear Lake Trail is a 3-mile loop that crosses M-203 and then follows the shoreline of Bear Lake to an old fishing pier before returning. The trail is a pleasant hike anytime of the year and spectacular in the late September when autumn colors are peaking.

Fishing: There is little fishing activity in Bear Lake. Shore anglers, however, gather along the breakwall where in the spring and fall they cast spoons and spawn for steelhead and coho salmon and in the summer fish for whitefish.

Season: McLain is a popular destination for campers and from mid-July to mid-August can be filled any day of the week but particularly on weekends. It is usually also filled on Labor Day weekend. To reserve a campsite contact Michigan State Park Central Reservations ☎ 800-447-2757 🌐 www.midnrreservations.com.

140

Bob Lake

Ottawa National Forest

Campground: Rustic
County: Houghton
Nearest Community: Mass City
Sites: 17
Reservations: No
Fee: $17
Information: Ontonagon District Office
☎ (906) 884-2085
🌐 www.fs.usda.gov/ottawa

Bob Lake is one of those wonderfully remote campgrounds in the Ottawa National Forest that is hard to find and even harder to leave. It features lakeshore sites, an interesting nature trail, a small sandy beach, and even the opportunity to see some wildlife. If you love secluded, rustic campgrounds seemingly in the middle of nowhere, you'll love Bob Lake and should plan on spending at least a couple of nights here.

Directions: From M-38, 30 miles west of L'Anse, turn south on Forest Highway 16 for 5 miles and then west on Pori Road for two miles. Turn south on Forest Highway 1470 to reach the campground in 2 miles.

Campground: Bob Lake has 17 rustic sites well spread out in a heavily forested area. Six of them are right on the shoreline where at night you can sit at your picnic table and watch a pair of loons.

Day-use Facilities: Next to the campground is a day-use area with a small sandy beach, changing rooms, and a few picnic tables.

Fishing: Bob Lake is a totally undeveloped lake that is accessed via a boat launch in the campground. The lake is spread over 133 acres and is a shallow body of water with depths averaging 3 to 10 feet and the deepest hole only at 17 feet. Most anglers fish it for walleye, smallmouth bass, and perch.

Hiking: Originally built in the late 1960s, Beaver Lodge Nature Trail was renovated in the early 1990s which included installing walkways, bridges, and 24 interpretive plaques. In 1995, the loop was designated a Watchable Wildlife Trail by the U.S. Forest Service.

The trailhead for 1.2-mile loop trailhead is near the day-use area with the trail beginning and ending on a former railroad bed that still features a few of the original ties. In between you skirt a small pothole lake, pass a spur that leads to the North Country Trail, and in a half mile from the trailhead arrive at a beaver pond with an active lodge and a huge dam. A second pond is just down the trail, and at either you can sit quietly and often spot a variety of wildlife ranging from waterfowl and bald eagles to whitetail deer, fox, a fisher, and, of course, beavers.

Season: Bob Lake is open from mid-May to mid-November and is a lightly used campground.

141

Burned Dam

Ottawa National Forest

Campground: Rustic
County: Iron
Nearest Community: Watersmeet
Sites: 5
Reservations: No
Fee: None
Information: Watersmeet Ranger District
☎ (906) 358-4551
🌐 www.fs.usda.gov/ottawa

I didn't know much about Burned Dam Campground the first time I was headed there except for the one thing that always tugs at the heartstrings of the budget camper that I am.

It was free.

Burned Dam is a no charge "dispersed campground" in the Ottawa National Forest, making it something of a rarity in Michigan these days. It's also located on the Middle Branch of the Ontonagon River, renown for its trout fishing, and not far from Mex-i-min-e Falls. In short, it's a free campground where you can catch a fish and view a waterfall.

Priceless.

One of the main attractions for campers in the Western Upper Peninsula are the many waterfalls located near the campgrounds.

The campground picks up its unusual name from a dam that was built here in 1892 to impound water for log drives on the Ontonagon River. During the spring floods, logs were floated to the impoundment and then held by chains anchored to rock cribs. One of the rock cribs is still visible today above the falls.

When the drive was ready to start, the chains were dropped, the dam was opened, and the logs and water rushed out in what must have been an incredible scene to witness. The timber was floated six miles downriver to the town of Interior where there was a three-band sawmill. By 1896 the trees were gone and the lumberjacks had moved on, and four years later slash fires destroyed both the town and the dam, thus the campground's name, Burned Dam.

Directions: From US-45 in Watersmeet, turn east on Old US-2 (also known as County Road 208), and in 6 miles turn north on Forest Road 4500. The campground is reached within a mile on FR-4500.

Campground: The rustic facility is small, five sites spread out in a stand of red and white pine, second growth trees that in the century since the logging era have reached lofty heights. Amenities are limited: a few picnic tables, fire rings, and a vault toilet but no source of drinking water. Either bring your own or filter water from the river.

Fishing: The Middle Branch is one of Michigan's designated Blue Ribbon trout streams and is almost legendary among anglers for its wild brook trout. This stretch near the campground also harbors rainbow and brown trout, allowing skilled anglers to achieve a "triple double," three species of trout greater than 10 inches in length. The Middle Branch here can be floated or waded, and its popularity is evident by a special disposal can in the campground for anglers cleaning their catch.

Waterfalls: The real attraction at Burned Dam is Mex-i-min-e Falls. Almost 40 feet wide, Mex-i-min-e is where the Middle Branch descends 15 feet by leaping through a series of small drops and sliding across huge slaps of black rock. The cascade is reached by a 200-yard trail from the campground but heard the minute you arrive. Even by Upper Peninsula standards, Mex-i-min-e is a scenic and loud waterfall. You'll hear the cascade while cooking dinner in your site, even over the roar of a campstove, then at night you'll fall asleep to the never-ending rush of water, the sweetest lullaby in the woods.

Canoeing: The Middle Branch of Ontonagon River offers 23 miles of floatable river from Forest Road 6110 3 miles west of Watersmeet to Bond Falls Flowage. There are no major rapids and only one portage, making the river suitable for intermediate canoers.

Canoe access and parking is available at a Forest Service wayside in the town of Watersmeet where US-45 crosses the river. Burned Dam Campground is 10 miles downstream where Mex-i-min-e Falls represents the only hazard that must be portaged around. At Bond Falls Flowage, there is a boat landing, a small store, a picnic area, and a campground.

Season: This is a lightly used national forest campground but can easily be filled by anglers due to the limited number of sites.

142

Clark Lake

Sylvania Recreation Area

Campground: Semi-modern
County: Gogebic
Nearest Community: Watersmeet
Sites: 48
Reservations: No
Fee: $14 plus vehicle entry fee
Information: Sylvania Entrance Station
☎ (906-358-4404)
🌐 www.fs.usda.gov/ottawa

Sylvania Wilderness is an 18,327-acre tract that includes 36 named lakes connected to one another by portages and footpaths. This non-motorized area is renowned among paddlers looking for a wilderness adventure, good fishing, and the possibility of spotting a variety of wildlife from black bears to bald eagles.

At the north end of the wilderness, overlooking Clark Lake, is Sylvania Recreation Area. Even if you have no desire to haul a canoe between lakes, you can enjoy this pristine slice of the Ottawa National Forest by staying at this drive-in campground within the recreation area. But bring a canoe if you can. The only way to enjoy the beauty or outstanding fishing in Clark Lake is by paddling.

Directions: Near the corner of US-2 and US-45, just south of Watersmeet, is the Watersmeet Visitor Center that has maps, books, and displays about the area and the Ottawa National Forest. From the center head west on US-2 for four miles and then south on County Road 535, which passes the posted entrance to the Clark Lake Campground.

Campground: Clark Lake has 48 sites on four loops spread out between Clark Lake and Katherine Lake. The campground lies just beyond the wilderness area but is well wooded by old growth hemlocks and other towering trees. None of the sites are within view of the lakes but are well isolated from each other for a good bit of privacy. The campground has

Clark Lake is part of the Sylvania Wilderness, an 18,327-acre tract that includes 36 named lakes connected to one another by portages. The lakes are non-motorized, making a canoe the best form of transportation for campers.

flush toilets, tables, fire rings, and a pressurized water system. Showers are available in the day-use area.

A site at Clark Lake is $14 a night, but because the campground is part of the Sylvania Wilderness management, a $5 daily vehicle permit or a $20 annual pass is also required.

Day-use Facilities: A developed beach and picnic area is at the north end of Clark Lake, a mile west of the campground. The swimming is excellent and facilities include a bathhouse with hot showers.

Fishing: Within Sylvania are 36 named lakes with six lakes larger than 250 acres in size. Clark Lake is one of the largest at 820 acres and depths up to 75 feet. From the south end of Clark Lake, portages extend to three more: Hay Lake, Loon Lake, and Crooked Lake.

What makes these lakes so precious is their clarity. They sit on the divide between the Lake Superior and the Mississippi River drainages but have no surface outlet to either one. Neither do they have any rivers or streams pouring nutrient matter into them. They are landlocked lakes fed by springs, bogs, and rain. They are, for all practical purposes, rain barrels with water so clear that you can lean over the side of your canoe and see the bottom... 30 or 40 feet down.

A trophy fishery, especially for smallmouth bass, has developed over the years due to inaccessibility of the lakes, and there are special regulations to protect it. Only artificial lures are allowed, no worms or other live bait can be used to entice the fish. You can't fish before the last Saturday in April or after October, and you couldn't keep a bass regardless of its size.

Clark Lake is non-motorized, and there is a boat launch near the day-use area with additional parking for vehicles and trailers. The lake is fished primarily for smallmouth bass and trout. Other lakes can be fished for northern pike and panfish as well.

Hiking: Within the wilderness are 30 miles of foot trails for those who want nothing to do with canoeing. These paths traverse the old growth forests and pass the shores of many lakes. One of the best hikes is the eight-mile loop that departs the day-use area and skirts Clark Lake. For much of the way, the trail skirts the shoreline and at times passes through stands of old growth hemlocks.

Season: Clark Lake is open from the last week of May through November. It's not unusual for the campground to be filled anytime in July and the first half of August.

143

Moosehead Lake

Ottawa National Forest

Campground: Rustic
County: Gogebic
Nearest Community: Marenisco
Sites: 13
Reservations: No
Fee: $10
Information: Bessemer Ranger District
☎ (906) 932-1330
🌐 www.fs.usda.gov/ottawa

Even if you have been to Wisconsin before, the attraction of camping on Moosehead Lake is being able to paddle to Wisconsin, several times a day if you want to. Moosehead is a pleasant, rustic campground on the state border that is connected to Little Presque Isle Lake, just to the south and outside of Ottawa National Forest. In fact, it's even out of Michigan. Here you can camp, visit, and fish two states and never get in your car once.

Directions: From US-2, east of Marenisco, head south on Forest Road 7300 for 8 miles. Turn right on County Road 530 (also called Pomeroy Lake Road), and in a mile veer left onto Forest Road 6860. Within 1.5 miles veer left at Forest Road 6862 and the campground is 2 miles at the end of the road.

Campground: Moosehead Lake has 13 sites on the edge of a shoreline bluff forested in red pine. The sites are well spread out and from half of them you have a view of the lake, which on a topographical map really does look like the head of a moose. The campground has the usual U.S. Forest Service amenities: tables, fire rings, lantern posts, a hand pump for water, and pit toilets.

Fishing: Moosehead is a 43-acre lake with a depth up to 35 feet and a shoreline that is undeveloped. There is a boat launch in the campground, and anglers fish the lake for northern pike, largemouth bass, and even a muskie. It's is also possible to catch bluegills and perch.

Even better, Moosehead is surrounded by other lakes. This is canoe country. Just north of the campground are seven lakes, all small bodies of water where you can drop in a canoe in and spend a morning casting a lure. The most interesting one is Little Presque Isle Lake, reached from the campground's boat ramp by heading south. At the south end of Moosehead Lake is a small marshy channel and somewhere in this channel you enter Wisconsin and become a cheddarhead.

Presque Isle Lake is a body of water that was almost twice as big as Moosehead. There are a few cottages on the lake, but most of them are along the south end and set so far back in the trees that it's easy to miss them.

Season: The lightly used campground is open from mid-May to mid-October.

144

Henry Lake

Ottawa National Forest

Campground: Rustic
County: Gogebic
Nearest Community: Marenisco
Sites: 11
Reservations: No
Fee: $10
Information: Bessemer Ranger District
☎ (906) 932-1330
🌐 www.fs.usda.gov/ottawa

Henry Lake is a small campground in the Ottawa National Forest that makes for an ideal stop during a family camping adventure in the western Upper Peninsula. The lake is small enough where you can easily explore it in a canoe. There's a pier where children can cast for bluegills and have a good opportunity to catch them, and its remote location evokes a wilderness sense of adventure when camping here.

Is that a bear on the other side of the lake?

If you do plan on camping at Henry Lake, pack along the mountain bikes. The campground lies in the middle of the Henry Lake & Pomeroy Lake Mountain Bike Complex where riders follow a posted route along gravel roads for easy outings.

Directions: The nearest town to Henry Lake is Marenisco, which is 26 miles west of Watersmeet along US-2. From Marenisco head west on US-2, and then turn onto Old US-2 and follow it west four miles to Forest Road-8100. Turn south on FR-8100 to reach the campground in 5 miles.

Campground: Henry Lake is a small and pleasant campground with 11 sites well spread out in a heavily forested area. Five sites are located on a low rise above the lake and have a nice view of the water. Sites have tables and fire rings while within the campground are vault toilets and a hand pump for water.

Fishing: Henry Lake is only 43 acres in size but reaches depths of up to 30 feet. It supports a good fishery of largemouth bass, perch, bluegill, and other panfish. The campground has an improved boat launch with additional parking for vehicles and trailers. Nearby is a large, T-shaped fishing pier where a 20-foot drop-off is within easy casting distance, even for children. Fish cribs have been placed both around the pier and elsewhere in the lake to improve the fishing. The nearest bait and tackle shops are in Marenisco.

Mountain Biking: The Henry and Pomeroy Lake Mountain Bike Complex is a vast system of forest roads in the lake-studded region of the Ottawa National Forest along the Michigan/Wisconsin border. The U.S. Forest Service posted the 86-mile network in 1994 in response to the increasing number of "where can we ride" inquires it was receiving from mountain bikers.

Part of the Mines and Pines Mountain Bike Trail System that spreads across western U.P. and into Wisconsin's Iron County, Henry and Pomeroy Lake complex was purposely set up for novice off-road cyclists and families. There are no twisty single tracks here or beaver dams to tiptoe across. All the routes are laid out on either gravel forest roads or the State Line Rail-Trail, which resembles a two-track. You could ride most of the system on a road bike but it would be laborious at best. A hybrid is better choice and a true mountain bike would provide the easiest trip of all.

The system is located south of the town of Marenisco and split by M-65. On the west half is the 22.8-mile Henry Lake portion; on the east is the 63-mile network around Pomeroy Lake. The State Line Rail-Trail crosses M-64 to connect the two halves. The routes are well posted by a blue mountain biker symbol and are easy to follow. The number of different loops you can ride in this complex is almost limitless. If passing through Watersmeet stop at the Ottawa National Forest Visitor Center ☎ 906-358-4404 for the Ottawa National Forest on US-2 and pick up a trail map.

Season: Henry Lake is open from mid-May to mid-October and is a lightly used facility.

145

Pomeroy Lake

Ottawa National Forest

Campground: Rustic
County: Gogebic
Nearest Community: Marenisco
Sites: 17
Reservations: No
Fee: $10
Information: Bessemer Ranger District
☎ (906) 932-1330
🌐 www.fs.usda.gov/ottawa

This is the other campground in the Henry & Pomeroy Lake Mountain Bike Complex, a lake-studded region of the Ottawa National Forest. Pomeroy Lake is not as heavily forested as its counterpart, Henry Lake, nor does it have a pier for shore anglers. Both the campground and especially the lake are larger, and overall the fishing is better. Once again, bring a mountain bike to enjoy some scenic and interesting rides.

Directions: From Marenisco head east on US-2 and in four miles south on Forest Road 7300. FR-7300 reaches the national forest campground in 10 miles.

Campground: Pomeroy Lake has 17 sites that are spread out in a wooded area at the north end of the lake. Twelve sites are right on the lakeshore, the others a short walk away. Facilities include tables, fire rings, and vault toilets.

Fishing: The campground has an improved boat launch with additional parking for vehicles and trailers that is reached from a separate entrance from FR-7300. Pomeroy is a 303-acre lake with its deepest point being only 15 feet. Most of the lake is less than 10 feet in depth. Pomeroy has a mixed bag for a fishery and includes walleye, northern pike, Black crappie, largemouth bass, bluegill, and yellow perch. At its southeast corner is a portage trail to Little Pomeroy Lake, a much smaller body of water that is fished for bass and bluegill.

Mountain Biking: The Henry & Pomeroy Mountain Bike Complex is split by M-65. The eastern half around Pomeroy Lake is a 63-mile network of marked gravel roads along with a section of the State Line Rail-Trail that in the summer resembles a two-track. The rail-trail makes for an interesting ride. From the campground it is a 4.5-mile ride north on FR-7300 to where the rail trail crosses the forest road. Head east on State Line and in the next 5 miles you pass two isolated lakes and cross several creeks. State Line eventually skirts US-2, which you follow to Langford Lake Road that heads southwest back to Pomeroy Lake. Such a loop would be a 17-mile ride.

Season: Pomeroy Lake is a lightly used facility.

A kayak along the shoreline at the Pomeroy Lake National Forest Campground.

146

Lake Gogebic

State Park

Campground: Modern and semi-modern	**Reservations:** Yes
County: Gogebic	**Fee:** $16–$18 plus vehicle entry fee
Nearest Community: Marenisco	**Information:** State park office
Sites: 127	☎ (906) 842-3341

Lake Gogebic State Park borders the largest inland lake in the Upper Peninsula and perhaps the most beautiful body of water anywhere in the state. The 361-acre state park also lies on the edge of the rugged highlands that extend west into the heart of the Ottawa National Forest. These ridges and hills include a highpoint of 1,545 feet and are penetrated only by a 2-mile trail.

M-64 conveniently separates the park's split personality. On the east side of the state highway is the 0.75 mile of Lake Gogebic shoreline and a well developed area catering to campers, swimmers, boaters, and anglers. To the west is the park's rugged interior that intrigues hikers wanting to view an impressive stand of old growth timber.

Directions: The state park is 25 miles east of Wakefield. Follow US-2 16 miles and then turn north (left) on M-64 for 9 miles to the posted entrance. From M-28 turn south of M-64 for 8 miles.

Campground: Lake Gogebic has 105 modern sites in its campground with 33 of them situated right along the shoreline. The rest have a good view of the water, and all are in a semi-open area that is lightly shaded. There are also 22 semi-modern sites without electricity while sites No. 58, 60, and 62 are pull-throughs ideal for large recreational vehicles. Facilities include tables, fire rings, heated restrooms with flush toilets, and showers.

Modern sites are $18 a night, semi-modern $16, and during the off-season when the restrooms are closed the rate drops to $16 and $12.

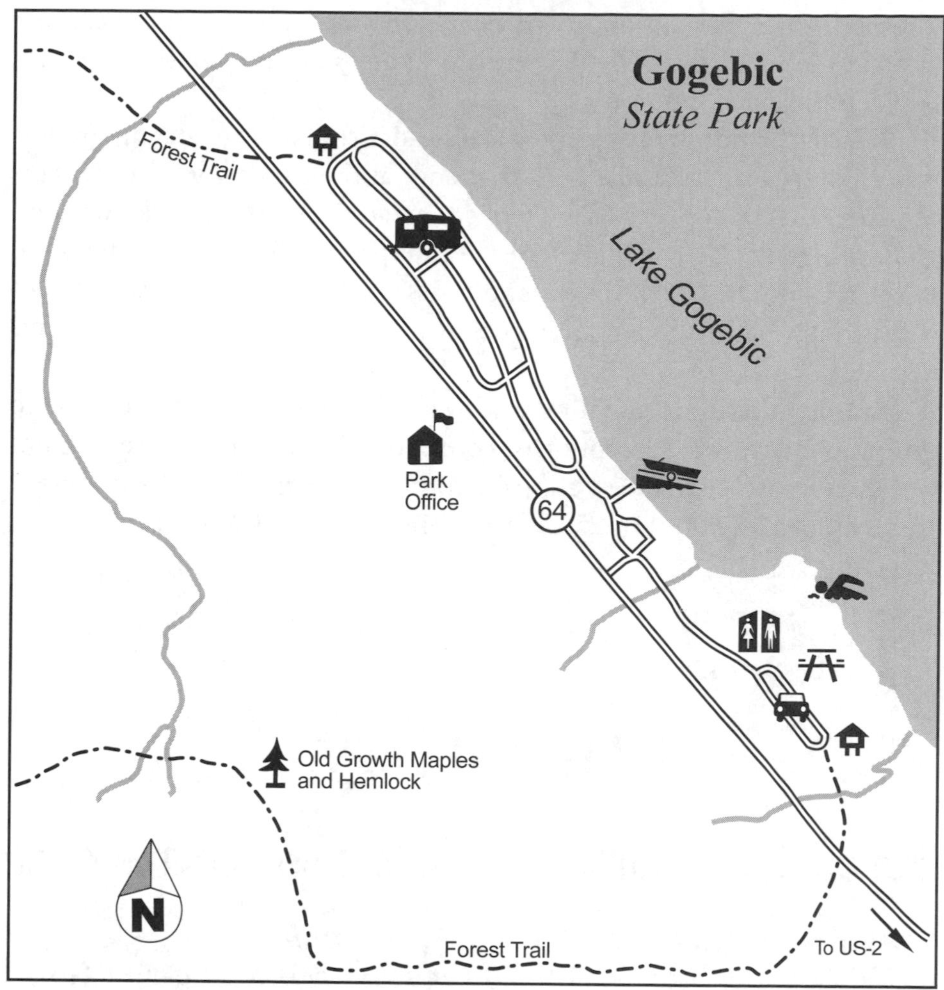

Day-use Facilities: Lake Gogebic has a small, sandy beach bordered by a large grassy bank in its day-use area. Other facilities include a bathhouse, play area, parking for a 100 vehicles, and an exceptionally pleasant picnic area situated on a small point with a nice view of the lakeshore to the north.

Fishing: The largest lake in the Upper Peninsula is also a noted one for walleye fishing. The 14-mile Lake Gogebic covers more than 20 square miles and is stocked annually with walleye. Although there are a variety of ways to fish for walleyes, many anglers prefer drifting or slowly trolling inflated night crawlers or leeches. Working rocky points and drop-offs with lead jigs tipped with minnows is another productive method. Lake Gogebic is also highly rated for its population of northern pike and perch.

The park maintains an improved boat ramp near the day-use area. Just outside the park along M-65 there are numerous bait shops and resorts that rent boats and motors.

Hiking: Beginning at a marked trailhead in the back of the campground is the Forest Trail, a 2-mile walk that ends at the parking lot for the day-use area. The trail crosses M-64 twice to wind through the park's wooded and rolling interior, passing a series of interpretive displays. The first mile of the trail can be wet at times as you pass a cedar swamp, but the second half is a dry path through an impressive stand of old growth maple and hemlock.

Season: There are usually sites available in Lake Gogebic's scenic campground with the exception of Fourth of July weekend and the second week in August. To reserve a campsite contact Michigan State Park Central Reservations ☎ 800-447-2757 🌐 www.midnrreservations.com.

147

Union Bay

Porcupine Mountains Wilderness State Park

Campground: Modern
County: Ontonagon
Nearest Community: Silver City
Sites: 99
Reservations: Yes
Fee: $25 plus vehicle entry fee
Information: State park office
☎ (906) 885-5275

The Porcupine Mountains Wilderness is the largest state park in Michigan, stretching 59,020 acres across Ontonagon and Gogebic counties. The park is 25 miles long and 10 miles at its widest point. It contains 26 miles of Lake Superior shoreline, four lakes—including the impressive Lake of the Clouds—and numerous rivers, trout streams, and waterfalls. This is impressive country to say the least.

Porcupine Mountains has five campgrounds accessible by road. At the west end is Presque Isle (see page 356). At the east end is Union Bay,

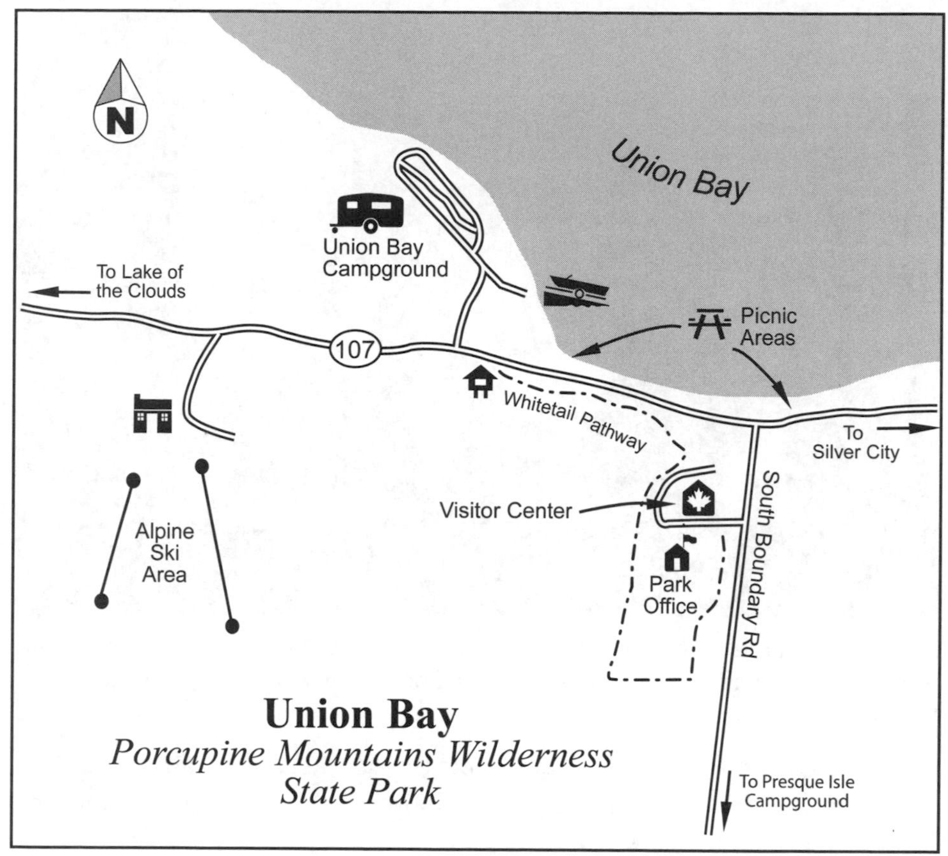

the largest and most modern facility. In between these two campgrounds are three rustic facilities called outposts that offer a degree of privacy. A mile south of the visitor center on South Boundary Road is Union River Outpost with three sites. Another 6 miles to the west is Lost Creek Outpost with three sites, and 3 miles farther still, White Pine Extension Outpost with seven drive-in sites.

At any of these campgrounds, plan to set up and stay put for at least three days to enjoy the stunning scenery this park has to offer. Day hiking in the Porkies is excellent with destinations such as waterfalls, isolated lakes, or sweeping views from the top of high points.

Directions: Union Bay Campground is near the park's east entrance. From M-64 in Ontonagon, head west on M-107 to reach the campground in 18 miles.

One of the most beautiful trails in Michigan if not the Midwest is the Escarpment Trail, not far from Union Bay Campground. The trail skirts a high rocky ridge above Lake of the Clouds.

Campground: With 99 sites Union Bay is the largest campground in the park. The sites are situated along a loop on a grassy shelf overlooking Lake Superior, and 20 of them have an unobstructed view of the water. There are a few large trees in the campground but otherwise little shade. Facilities include tables, fire rings, electric hook-ups, modern restrooms with flush toilets and showers, and a sanitation station for recreational vehicles. Nearby Whitetail Path departs M-107 and leads to the park's visitor's center, a mile walk through the woods.

Day-use Facilities: There is a day-use area on each side of the park. On the east side of the park, a picnic area is adjacent to the Union Bay Campground and features tables and grills overlooking Lake Superior.

Interpretive Center: Porcupine Mountains has an impressive visitor center, located a half mile south of M-107 on South Boundary Road. Inside there are exhibits explaining the geological history of the mountains plus a three-dimensional relief map that every hiker should study before striking out. There is also a room devoted to the diverse wildlife in the park and a small theater where multi-slide presentations are repeated throughout the day. The center is the best source of maps and trail information for hikers and backpackers and is open daily from late May to mid-October from 10 AM to 6 PM.

Scenic Viewpoints: From the end of M-107, it's a short walk to perhaps Michigan's most famous panorama, Lake of the Clouds Overlook. The viewing point is set on the side of a vertical cliff, and from the high point of almost 1,300 feet, it's possible to see the picturesque lake set among forested ridges and much of the Porkies' rugged interior. Another spectacular viewing area is Summit Observation Tower. The deck and observation tower is constructed on Summit Peak, 1,958 feet, and reached with a half-mile walk from the end of Summit Peak Road. The view includes the center of the Porkies and a portion of Mirror Lake.

Hiking: The Porkies is best known as a destination for backpackers, but not all hiking adventures in the park have to be overnight trips. On the perimeter, there are a number of short loops that make for scenic day hikes. Along M-107, west of Union Bay Campground, is the trailhead for the Overlook Trail, which is combined with a short portion of the Government Peak Trail to form a 3.5-mile loop to a number of scenic viewpoints above 1,200 feet.

The same trailhead is also the east end of the Escarpment Trail, a 4-mile hike along a ridge that includes Cuyahoga and Cloud peaks and ends at the Lake of the Clouds Overlook on M-107. The views of Lake of the Clouds and the park's interior from this rocky ridge make this trail one of the most scenic in Michigan. Along South Boundary Road, 2 miles south of M-107, is Union Mine Trail. This mile-long loop features the ruins of the old Union Copper Mine that are explained in an interpretive brochure available at the Visitor Center.

Fishing: The park also has an improved boat launch at Union Pier Campground for anglers who want to troll Lake Superior for lake trout in June and July as well as steelhead, salmon, and brown trout other times of the year.

Season: The restrooms and other facilities in Union Bay are open from mid-May to the third week in October. The campground fills daily for two weeks from late July through mid-August and is full five out of seven nights during the rest of the summer. Sites are easy to obtain before mid-June and beginning in September. To reserve a campsite contact Michigan State Park Central Reservations ☎ 800-447-2757 🌐 www.midnrreservations.com.

148

Presque Isle

Porcupine Mountains Wilderness State Park

Campground: Rustic
County: Gogebic
Nearest Community: Wakefield
Sites: 50
Reservations: Yes
Fee: $14 plus vehicle entry fee
Information: State park office
☎ (906) 885-5275

The Presque Isle River in the Porcupine Mountains Wilderness State Park is one of the most spectacular spots in Michigan. In its final mile before emptying into Lake Superior, the Presque Isle descends more than 100 feet and in doing so has carved a rugged and steep-sided gorge that is filled with impressive waterfalls and wild whitewater.

On the bluffs above this scenic waterway is the park's Presque Isle Campground. The rustic facility provides access to both the scenic end of this river and Lake Superior. It also allows you to hike the trails in the west end of the park without having to carry a backpack.

Directions: Porcupine Mountains Wilderness State Park is 17 miles west of Ontonagon via M-64 and M-107. Once in the park, head south on South Boundary Road and follow it until ends at County Road 519. Head north on CR-519 to reach the campground. Presque Isle can also be reached from US-2, where the campground is 16 miles from Wakefield at end of County Road 519.

Campground: Due to budget problems in 2003, Presque Isle was reduced in size by 33 sites and changed from a semi-modern campground with restrooms and showers to a rustic facility with vault toilets. Presque Isle now features 55 large, well spaced-out sites that are scattered around two loops with a dozen of them along the bluff overlooking Lake Superior. The rest are in a large grassy area, shaded by a scattering of large maples while the campground itself is surrounded by woods. Within the woods are six walk-in sites.

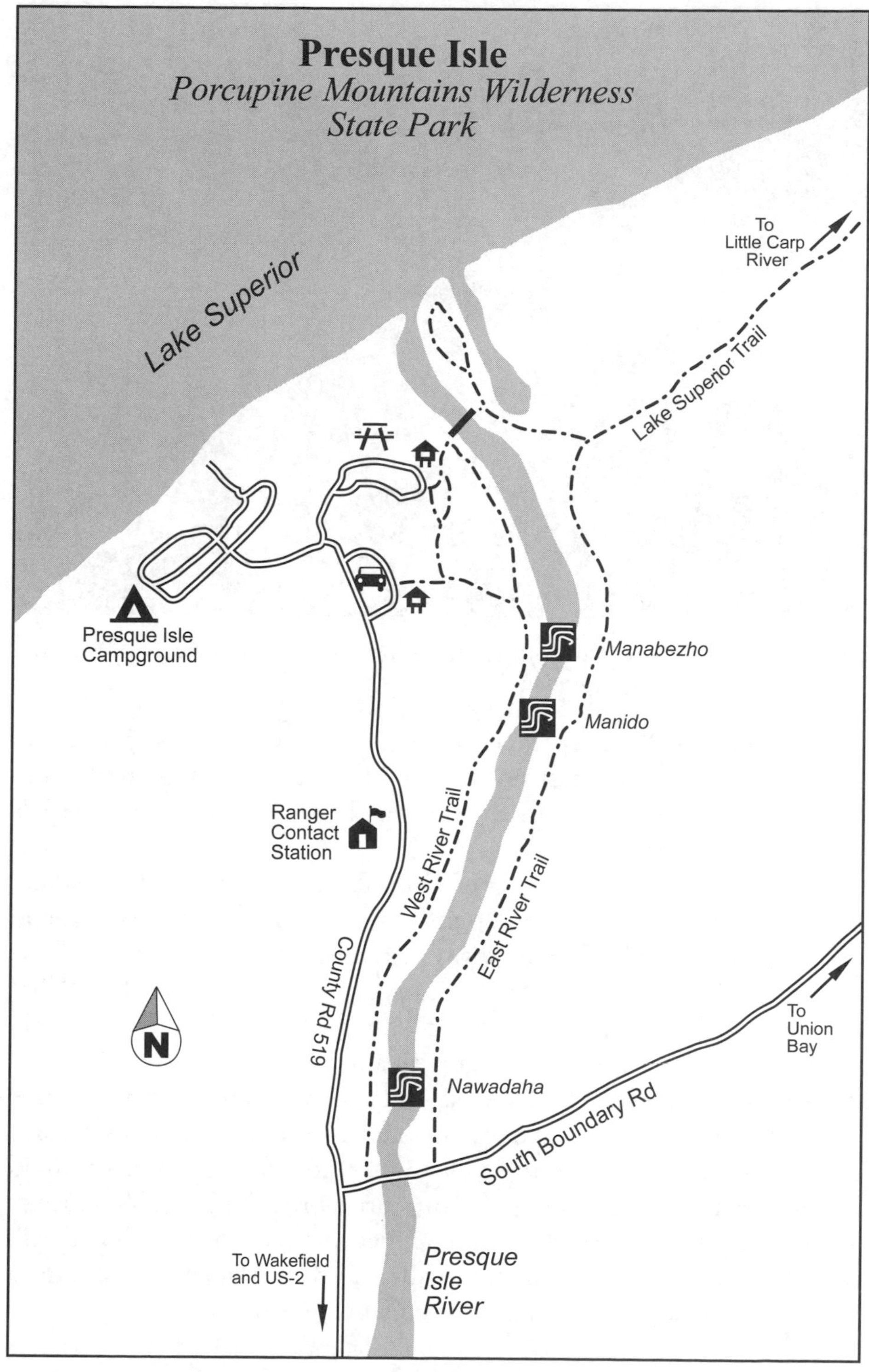
Presque Isle
Porcupine Mountains Wilderness State Park
Lake Superior
To Little Carp River
Lake Superior Trail
Presque Isle Campground
Manabezho
Manido
Ranger Contact Station
West River Trail
East River Trail
County Rd 519
N
To Union Bay
Nawadaha
South Boundary Rd
To Wakefield and US-2
Presque Isle River

The roaring whitewater of the Presque Isle River in the spring as seen from the West River Trail near Presque Isle Campground.

Day-use Facilities: There is a picnic area with tables, grills, and separate parking on the east side of CR-519 near the campground. From the picnic area you can access the stairs and boardwalks to the waterfalls in the Presque Isle Gorge.

Hiking: The Presque Isle River Trail, also referred to as the East and West River Trails, is a 2-mile loop that climbs in and out of the gorge and passes three waterfalls. Pick up the trail in the Presque Isle Day-use Area, where you immediately descend to an impressive swing bridge. What appears on maps as a peninsula on the other side of the bridge is actually an island in the mouth of the river with a dry channel on one side.

You can follow a spur on the island to the view the rugged shoreline of Lake Superior or cross the waterless channel to the east bank to pick up East River Trail. This trail heads south to the South Boundary Road Bridge where you can cross over to return north along the West River Trail. Along the way West River Trail becomes an extensive boardwalk that puts you right above Manido Falls and then Manabezho. You're so close you can feel their cooling mist on a hot afternoon.

THE CROWNING JEWEL OF MICHIGAN TRAILS

The Escarpment is the crowning jewel of trails not only in the Porkies but possibly in all of Michigan. The trail combines a high rocky bluff and alpine-like vistas with views of the park's rugged interior, Big Carp River Valley, and, of course, the center piece of the park, Lake of Clouds. Unlike the tourists who simply drive to the overlook and look down, the Escarpment Trail provides you with views of the famous lake from several different angles, and if the day is clear, you can easily fill half your camera's memory card by the time you return to M-107.

The only drawback is that the Escarpment is a point-to-point trail. You begin here, you end up over there 4 miles from your vehicle. There is a spur reached halfway along the trail that can be used to access M-107 after 2 miles and, of course, you can always turn around and simply retrace your steps. However, it would be a shame to go that far to hike one of the most awe-inspiring trails in the Midwest and not finish it.

The easiest direction to follow the route is beginning from the Lake of the Clouds Overlook. Before departing remember to fill the water bottles. There is no drinking water at the overlook, and on a clear summer day the route across the Escarpment can be a hot one. You actually begin at the posted North Mirror Lake Trailhead. Within a half mile at a posted junction, North Mirror Lake Trail plummets towards Lake of the Clouds while the Escarpment officially begins with a climb through a mixed forest.

Quickly you arrive at the first overlook, staring down at the middle of the lake. The trail resumes with a sharper climb and in half a mile you break out at a second vista. This one is spectacular, as good or better than overlook at the end of M-107 because you're at a much higher elevation (1,480 feet). Below you, 400 feet straight down, is Lake of the Clouds in royal blue. To the west you can see visitors who have just stepped out of their cars and to the east is the rest of the Escarpment and the Upper Carp River winding its way into the lake.

The trail continues along the open cliff where you enjoy the scenery almost every step of the way. You also pass the posted site of Carp Lake Mine. Carp Lake was the name for Lake of the Clouds when the mine was established in 1858. The operation lingered into the 1920s but reached its peak in 1865 when a company of more than 50 men used a small stamping mill to produce 13,000 pounds of copper from several shafts into the Escarpment. Near the trail is a fenced-off cistern where a spur leads down the slope to the twin boilers of the stamping mill that can still be seen today.

You depart the mine site by immediately ascending towards Cuyahoga Peak, climbing more than 200 feet to the highpoint of the day of 1,600 feet. In less than half a mile from the junction, you break out to another panoramic scene of the Upper Carp River where the trail skirts the edge of the Escarpment.

The East River Trail also passes a junction to Lake Superior Trail, at a length of 17 miles the longest foot route in the park. Lake Superior Trail departs from the Presque Isle River and follows the shoreline before emerging at M-107.

Fishing: Porcupine Mountains State Park is best known for its steelhead and salmon runs in the spring and fall. Presque Isle River attracts the most attention with wading anglers either surf fishing or working the mouth of the river, as Manabezho Falls blocks farther runs upstream.

Season: Demand on the campground varies from year to year, but the lack of electricity for RVers and modern restrooms are the reasons, no doubt, why Presque Isle rarely fills to capacity even after it was reduced in size. To reserve a campsite contact Michigan State Park Central Reservations ☎ 800-447-2757 🌐 www.midnrreservations.com.

149
Black River Harbor

Ottawa National Forest

Campground: Rustic
County: Gogebic
Nearest Community: Bessemer
Sites: 40
Reservations: No
Fee: $14
Information: Bessemer Ranger District
☎ (906) 932-1330
🌐 www.fs.usda.gov/ottawa

County Road 513 is a trip in itself. Also known as Black River Road, it heads north from Bessemer and passes the towering Copper Peak Ski Flying Hill and the trailheads to five stunning waterfalls. The road finally ends at Black River Harbor, an Ottawa National Forest recreation area on Lake Superior where you could easily spend the rest of the week camping.

One of only two harbors located in a national forest, Black River Harbor offers recreational opportunities to not only boaters and campers but also hikers, agate hunters, anglers, and people who simply like to spend an afternoon listening to the roar of a waterfall. This is a popular place to camp during the summer, a breathtakingly beautiful one in late September when the surrounding hardwood forests ignite in fall colors.

The Potawatomi Falls, one of five spectacular waterfalls accessed from Black River Road on its way to Black River Harbor Campground on the shores of Lake Superior.

Directions: From Bessemer, head west on US-2 and then turn north on Powderhorn Road, marked by the Big Powderhorn Mountain skier statue. Powderhorn Road merges into CR 513 (Black River Road). From US-2 it is a 15-mile drive to the harbor at the north end of CR 513.

Campground: Black River Harbor has 40 well secluded sites in an area forested in hardwoods and pines. Although there are no hook-ups for recreational vehicles, both the campground road and the sites are paved, and there are flush toilets, a pressurized water system, and a sanitation station. Seven campsites provide an overlook to Lake Superior while nearby short trails lead to sweeping views of the Great Lake or descend to the beach. Other facilities include tables and fire rings but not showers.

Day-use Facilities: Also on the west side of the river next to the campground is a picnic area surrounded by impressive pines and hemlocks and featuring tables, grills, play equipment for children, and a unique stone pavilion. The Lake Superior shoreline on either side of the river's mouth is a broad sandy beach. The west side beach is reached from a trail in the campground while a suspension bridge over the Black River provides access to the beach east of the river. The water is usually too cold for most people to swim in, but the beaches are excellent for beachcombing or agate hunting.

Fishing: The recreation area has a improved boat launch on the Black River with additional parking for vehicles and rigs as well as docks inside the breakwalls on Lake Superior. A concessionaire sells fuel, sewage pumping services, and limited supplies. On the Great Lake, anglers troll for lake trout in June and July as well as brown trout, salmon, and steelhead in the spring and fall. Shore fishermen will also cast off the docks and breakwalls to catch brown trout and coho salmon at various times of the year.

Hiking: The North Country Trail passes through the recreation area and can be picked up at the day-use area parking lot. To the south the NCT is a stunning stretch of trail that skirts the Black River to pass five waterfalls before arriving at Copper Peak Ski Flying Hill. It's a one-way hike of five miles from Black River Harbor to Copper Peak. To the east the NCT crosses the suspension bridge over the Black River and heads south to Rainbow Falls before swinging east for the Porcupine Mountains.

Waterfalls: Five waterfalls can be accessed from CR-513 (Black River Road). The closest to the campground is Rainbow Falls, a 40-foot long cascade that—when the sunlight is right—creates a rainbow with its mist. You can follow the North Country Trail from the day-use area parking lot and reach the falls after a 0.75-mile hike.

Most people reach the other falls by driving to posted trailheads along CR-513 and then descending a half mile of trails and stairways into Black River Canyon to the cascades. Not far from the Copper Peak, you pass the parking lot of the first waterfall, Great Conglomerate Falls, and the others quickly follow one by one along the road: Potawatomi, Gorge, Sandstone, and finally Rainbow Falls. All are well worth the extra effort spent but especially Potawatomi and Gorge, which are practically next to each other. Potawatomi is a thin, 130-foot wide veil flowing over a rock embankment while just down river is Gorge Falls, a narrow, 24-foot drop of water between two granite walls of the canyon.

Season: Black River Harbor is open from mid-May to mid-October and will occasionally fill in July and August.

THE VIEW FROM COPPER PEAK

From Bessemer, Black River Drive heads north past steep rocky bluffs, ski hills waiting for winter's first snow, and, finally, the highest point of all, Cooper Hill Peak, 10 miles north of town. It's impossible to miss the peak; there's a ski ramp at the top, so you might as well pull in.

Built by the Gogebic Range Ski Association in 1970, the 469-foot slide towers 241 feet above the summit of Copper Peak. The structure is so immense they needed 300 tons of steel grids to support the ramp. Call it the Eiffel Tower of the U.P., the ramp is only one of six ski flying peaks in the world and the only one in the Western Hemisphere.

For all that steel, the hill is used by a lot more by leaf peepers in the fall, who have no intention of leaving the ramp, than by skiers looking for a world record in the winter.

A small fee puts you in the chairlift for a ride 810 feet to the summit where you step inside an elevator and continue your journey up another 188 feet. Once you step out of the elevator, you can still walk up a little higher, and you'll want to. The view on a clear autumn day is spectacular. You can see parts of three states—Michigan, Wisconsin and Minnesota—as well as Canada and the endless blue horizon of Lake Superior.

Colors traditionally peak from the last week of September to early October. Copper Peak is open for non-skiers from 10 AM to 4:30 PM Wednesday through Sunday from mid-June through Labor Day and then Saturday and Sunday through mid-October. The fee to the top for adults is $12. For a fall color check contact Copper Peak ☎ 906-932-3500; 🌐 www.copperpeak.org.

150 Little Girl's Point

Gogebic County Park

Campground: Modern and semi-modern
County: Gogebic
Nearest Community: Ironwood
Sites: 32
Reservations: Yes
Fee: $20
Information: Park office
☎ (906) 932-1913

This campground may be as far west as a person can drive in Michigan, but the Gogebic County Park is well worth all the hours you have to spend in the car to reach it. There are few campgrounds like Little Girl's Point anywhere in the state. The views from this point are spectacular, and the park's picnic pavilions, caretaker's house, and trim stone bathhouse are from another era.

Perched on bluffs above Lake Superior, Little Girl's Point is a well-maintained county park with an edge-of-the-world view. To the northeast you gaze on the rolling silhouettes of the Porcupine Mountains and to the southwest the Apostle Islands. At night the suns melts into the endless blue horizon of Lake Superior.

Directions: Little Girl's Point is located 17 miles north of Ironwood on County Road 505. From US-2 in Ironwood head north out on Hemlock and then Vanderhagen Road which becomes CR-505.

Campground: Little Girl's Point has 32 sites in a grassy and semi-wooded area with 16 of them overlooking Lake Superior. The rest are set back from the bluff. Most have electricity on site but three, sites No. 6, 10, and 29, lack hook-ups. The campground has vault toilets, but in the day-use area of the park there are flush toilets in the bathhouse but not showers. Camping fees are $20 for non-county residents for a site with an electric hook-up or a tent site. Either one is a bargain. County residents pay $15 a night.

Day-use Facilities: The park has a picnic area with tables, grills, pavilions, a classic stone bathhouse, and that million-dollar view. A trail also leads from the picnic area down the steep bluff to Lake Superior. The shoreline here is a sandy beach, and during the summer brave souls can be seen swimming in the frigid Great Lake.

Campers stroll along the Lake Superior shoreline at Little Girl's Point Campground, a Gogebic County park that is almost as far west as you can drive in Michigan.

Fishing: West of the campground, a road leads down to an improved boat launch on Lake Superior. Anglers arrive at the park to troll for lake trout June and July and steelhead, salmon, and brown trout in the spring and fall.

Season: The campground is open from May through September and often this facility will be filled on a near daily basis in July and August. You can reserve sites in advance by calling The Gogebic County Forest and Parks Division ☎ 906-663-4687 during the winter or the park office ☎ 906-932-1913 beginning in May.

Alphabetical Facilities Index

#	PARKS	MODERN	SEMI-MODERN	RUSTIC	SITES	DAY-USE FACILITIES	FISHING	HIKING	BIRDING	INTERPRETIVE CENTER	BIKING	CANOEING/ KAYAKING	BOATING
5	Addison Oaks County Park	•			174	•	•	•			•		•
101	Andrus Lake			•	25	•	•						
74	Arbutus Lake			•	40	•	•						•
116	Au Train Lake			•	37	•	•	•	•			•	
79	Barnes	•	•		86	•		•					
107	Bass Lake			•	18		•						
115	Bay Furnace			•	50	•		•					
95	Bay View			•	24	•				•			
48	Benton Lake			•	24	•	•	•					
21	Bertha Brock			•	23	•		•					
132	Bewabic	•	•		137	•	•	•				•	
64	Big Bear Lake			•	44	•	•	•					
137	Big Eric's Bridge			•	20								
99	Big Knob			•	18	•		•					
81	Bill Wagner			•	22	•		•					
149	Black River Harbor			•	40	•	•	•					
140	Bob Lake			•	17	•	•	•					
102	Bodi Lake			•	16		•	•					
52	Bowman Bridge			•	20		•	•				•	
91	Brevoort Lake			•	70	•	•	•					
141	Burned Dam			•	5		•					•	
46	Buttersville	•			44	•							

#	PARKS	MODERN	SEMI-MODERN	RUSTIC	SITES	DAY-USE FACILITIES	FISHING	HIKING	BIRDING	INTERPRETIVE CENTER	BIKING	CANOEING/ KAYAKING	BOATING
83	Camp Pet-O-Se-Ga	•			90	•		•					
129	Carney Lake			•	16	•	•						
125	Cedar River North			•	17		•	•					
45	Charles Mears	•			175	•	•	•					
142	Clark Lake		•		48	•	•	•					
19	Cold Brook	•	•		44	•	•	•					
113	Colwell Lake	•		•	35	•	•	•					
117	Council Lake			•	4	•	•	•				•	
3	Crooked Lake			•	25	•	•	•			•		
109	Cusino Lake			•	6	•	•						
69	D.H. Day			•	88	•		•					
20	Deep Lake			•	120	•	•	•			•		
93	DeTour			•	21	•	•	•					
16	Ess Lake			•	28	•	•						
139	F.J. McLain	•			98	•	•	•					
120	Fayette		•		61	•	•	•		•			
80	Fisherman's Island			•	81	•	•	•					
122	Flowing Well			•	10	•	•					•	
92	Foley Creek			•	54		•	•					
138	Fort Wilkins	•			160	•	•	•		•			
124	Fox Park			•	20	•							
130	Gene's Pond			•	14		•	•					
31	Gladwin City Park	•			61	•	•	•					
131	Glidden Lake			•	23	•	•	•					
37	Goose Lake			•	54	•	•						
40	Grand Haven	•			174	•	•						
73	Green Lake			•	60	•	•	•					

#	PARKS	MODERN	SEMI-MODERN	RUSTIC	SITES	DAY-USE FACILITIES	FISHING	HIKING	BIRDING	INTERPRETIVE CENTER	BIKING	CANOEING/ KAYAKING	BOATING
76	Guernsey Lake			•	30	•	•	•					
15	Harrisville State Park	•			195	•	•	•					
62	Hartwick Pines	•			100	•	•	•		•	•		
36	Hemlock			•	19	•	•						
22	Henning	•	•		68	•	•	•				•	
144	Henry Lake			•	11		•				•		
30	Herrick Recreation Area	•			73	•	•						
51	Highbank Lake			•	9	•	•	•					
98	Hog Island Point			•	50	•							
13	Horseshoe Lake			•	9		•	•					
111	Hurricane River			•	12	•		•		•			
32	Island Lake			•	17	•	•	•					
14	Jewell Lake			•	32	•	•	•					
58	Keystone Landing			•	18		•					•	
110	Kingston Lake			•	16	•	•	•					
59	Kneff Lake			•	26	•	•	•					
72	Lake Dubonnet			•	50		•	•					
146	Lake Gogebic	•	•		127	•	•	•					
60	Lake Margrethe			•	40	•	•						
90	Lake Michigan			•	35	•		•					
56	Lake Michigan Recreation Area			•	99	•		•					
134	Lake Ottawa			•	32	•	•	•					
135	Lake Ste. Kathryn			•	24	•	•	•					
105	Lake Superior			•	18	•		•					
89	Lakeshore	•			150	•	•	•					
70	Leelanau			•	51	•		•		•			

#	PARKS	MODERN	SEMI-MODERN	RUSTIC	SITES	DAY-USE FACILITIES	FISHING	HIKING	BIRDING	INTERPRETIVE CENTER	BIKING	CANOEING/ KAYAKING	BOATING
34	Leverentz Lakes			•	17		•	•					
114	Little Bass Lake			•	12		•						
123	Little Bay de Noc			•	38	•	•	•					
150	Little Girl's Point	•	•		32	•	•						
18	Long Lake	•	•		124	•	•						
38	Long Lake			•	16		•						
47	Ludington	•	•		355	•	•	•					
84	Maple Bay			•	36	•	•						•
29	Merrill Lake	•	•		146	•	•						
6	Metamora-Hadley	•			214	•	•	•					
94	Monocle Lake			•	39	•	•	•					
11	Monument			•	19	•		•				•	
143	Moosehead Lake			•	13		•						
103	Mouth of Two Hearted River			•	45	•		•				•	
104	Muskallonge Lake	•			159	•	•	•					
42	Muskegon	•			106	•	•	•					
24	Newaygo			•	99		•						
49	Nichols Lake			•	28	•	•	•					
136	Norway Lake			•	27	•	•	•					
87	Ocqueoc Falls			•	14	•	•	•				•	
53	Old Grade			•	20		•	•					
85	Onaway	•			98	•	•						
17	Ossineke			•	42	•		•					
88	P.H. Hoeft	•			142	•	•	•			•		
41	P.J. Hoffmaster	•			293	•		•					
28	Paris	•			68	•	•	•				•	

#	PARKS	MODERN	SEMI-MODERN	RUSTIC	SITES	DAY-USE FACILITIES	FISHING	HIKING	BIRDING	INTERPRETIVE CENTER	BIKING	CANOEING/ KAYAKING	BOATING
133	Pentoga	•			100	•	•	•					
106	Perch Lake			•	35		•						
127	Perkins	•	•		73	•	•						
118	Pete's Lake			•	41	•	•	•					
54	Peterson Bridge			•	30	•	•					•	
82	Petoskey	•			180	•		•			•		
67	Pickerel Lake			•	39	•	•	•					
65	Pigeon River			•	19	•	•	•					
9	Pinconning	•	•		42	•	•	•					
44	Pines Point			•	33	•	•	•				•	
43	Pioneer	•			235	•							
68	Platte River	•	•		174	•	•	•				•	
71	Platte River			•	26		•	•				•	
145	Pomeroy Lake			•	17		•				•		
8	Port Crescent	•			137	•	•	•					
121	Portage Bay			•	23	•		•					
2	Portage Lake	•			136	•	•	•		•			
77	Power Island			•	5	•		•					
148	Presque Isle			•	50	•	•	•					
4	Proud Lake	•			130	•	•	•				•	
12	Rollways			•	19	•	•					•	
55	Sand Lake			•	45	•	•	•					
23	Sandy Beach	•	•		200	•	•						
75	Scheck's Place			•	30		•	•				•	
26	School Section Lake Veteran's Park	•			167	•	•						
57	Seaton Creek			•	17	•	•	•				•	

#	PARKS	MODERN	SEMI-MODERN	RUSTIC	SITES	DAY-USE FACILITIES	FISHING	HIKING	BIRDING	INTERPRETIVE CENTER	BIKING	CANOEING/ KAYAKING	BOATING
50	Shelley Lake			•	8		•						
63	Shupac Lake			•	30	•	•						
35	Silver Creek			•	26		•	•				•	
96	Soldier Lake			•	44	•	•	•					
128	Squaw Lake			•	15		•						
100	Tahquamenon Falls	•	•		169	•	•	•					
10	Tawas Point	•			193	•		•	•				
97	Three Lakes			•	28	•	•	•					
86	Tomahawk Creek Flooding			•	39	•	•	•					
126	Tourist Park	•	•		110	•	•	•			•		
66	Town Corner Lake			•	12		•	•					
27	Tubbs Island			•	12		•						
112	Twelvemile Beach			•	36	•		•					
147	Union Bay	•			99	•	•	•		•			
61	Upper Manistee River			•	40		•					•	
7	Wagener County Park	•			96	•	•	•					
33	Wagner Lake			•	12	•	•						
39	Warren Dunes	•	•		221	•		•					
25	White Cloud	•	•		103	•		•					
78	Whitewater	•	•		55	•	•	•					
119	Widewaters			•	34		•	•					
1	William C. Sterling	•			256	•	•	•	•				
108	Woodland Park	•	•		110	•		•					

About The Author

Jim DuFresne has a deep rooted passion for two things, sunsets and shoreline, no doubt the result of living his entire life in the two states that have more coastline than any other, Alaska and Michigan.

Within a year of graduating from Michigan State University with a journalism degree, Jim moved to Juneau, Alaska, as the outdoors and sports editor of the Juneau Empire and became the first Alaskan sportswriter to win a national award from the Associated Press. More significant than the writing award, he discovered his passion for the mountains and wilderness travel while living in Alaska's capital city.

In 1981, Jim spent a winter in New Zealand to backpack and write his first book, *Tramping in New Zealand* for Lonely Planet. He followed up with the first edition of *Lonely Planet's Alaska* and later *Hiking in Alaska* and then returned to Michigan to write *Isle Royale National Park: Foot Trails & Water Routes*. The guide to the wilderness areas of Isle Royale has been in publication in various editions for almost 30 years and today is known as the "backpacker's bible" to the Lake Superior island.

Today Jim lives in Michigan where he's never more than an hour's drive from the shoreline of the Great Lakes. He is the main contributor to www.MichiganTrailMaps.com, a resource web site devoted to trail users and the promotion of trails in his home state. Among his other tiles are *Backpacking In Michigan* and *12 Classic Trout Streams in Michigan: A Handbook for Fly Anglers* (University of Michigan Press), *Michigan: Off the Beaten Path* (Globe Pequot Publications), *50 Hikes In Michigan* (Backcountry Publications) and *Porcupine Mountains Wilderness State Park* (Thunder Bay Press).